Music is my Mistress

Music is my Mistress

by

Edward Kennedy Ellington

A DA CAPO PAPERBACK

S

Library of Congress Cataloging in Publication Data

Ellington, Duke, 1899-1974
  Music is my mistress.

  (A Da Capo paperback)
  Reprint of the 1973 ed. published by Doubleday,
Garden City, N.Y.
    Discography: p.
    1. Ellington, Duke, 1899-1974.   2. Jazz musicians—
Correspondence, reminiscences, etc.   I. Title
[ML410.E44A3 1976]   785.4'2'0924 [B]   75-31665
ISBN 0-306-80033-0

This Da Capo Press paperback edition of MUSIC IS MY MISTRESS is an
unabridged republication of the first edition published in New York in 1973.
The discography for this edition has been revised and updated by Stanley Dance.
It is reprinted with the permission of Doubleday & Company, Inc.

Published by Da Capo Press, Inc.
A Subsidiary of Plenum Publishing Corporation
233 Spring Street
New York, N.Y. 10013

To my mother and father,
Daisy Kennedy Ellington
and
James Edward Ellington

Grateful acknowledgment is made to the following for permission to reprint their material:

Lyrics from "New York City," originally appeared in slightly different form under the title "A Son of My Town." Copyright © 1968 by American Heritage Publishing Co., Inc. Reprinted by permission from *New York, N.Y.*, an American Heritage Extra.

"History of Jazz for Young People" by Duke Ellington. Copyright © 1972 by The Boy Scouts of America. Reprinted by permission of *Boy's Life* Magazine.

Excerpts from *Music on My Mind* by Willie "The Lion" Smith with George Hoefer. Copyright © 1964 by Willie Smith and George Hoefer. Reprinted by permission of Doubleday & Company, Inc. Published in England by MacGibbon & Kee Ltd.

"City of Jazz" from the book *Just Jazz 3* by Gerald Lascelles and Sinclair Traill. Published by Four Square Books, 1959.

Review of Duke Ellington's concert. Reprinted by permission of The Indian Express, Madras.

Lyrics from "Uncle Tom's Cabin Is a Drive-In Now." Lyrics: Paul Francis Webster; Music: Hal Borne. Copyright 1941; Renewed 1968 Robbins Music Corporation. Used by permission.

Lyrics from "We're the Sun-Tanned Tenth of the Nation." Lyrics: Paul Francis Webster; Music: Hal Borne and Otis Rene. Copyright 1941; Renewed 1968 Robbins Music Corporation. Used by permission.

Lyrics from "You Make That Hat Look Pretty" by Duke Ellington. Copyright © 1968 by Tempo Music Inc., New York, N.Y. Reprinted by permission of the Copyright owner.

"James P. Johnson" from notes to album entitled *Father of the Stride Piano*. Reprinted by permission of Columbia Records.

ACKNOWLEDGMENTS

For their careful research and power of recall, I am variously indebted to many people, especially beautiful friends and relatives like Harry Carney, Polly Winchester, Bernice Williams, Louis Brown, Mrs. Doc Perry, Betty McGettigan, Sonny Greer, and Tom Whaley. And one, Stanley Dance, I hail as Monarch Miracolissimo for extrasensory perception revealed in his amazing ability to decipher my handwriting.

PHOTO CREDITS

Courtesy Ruth Ellington Stamiatou frontispiece, page 55; Courtesy Louis Brown, 25; Courtesy Sonny Greer 31, 74, 120; By permission of International Book Corporation, photo from the International Library of Negro Life and History 96; Photo by Otto F. Hess 105; Photo by Richard H. Tucker, Jr. 107; Photo by Richard Veit 117; Photo by Henry Delorval Green 123; Photo by Leonard Halpern 142; Photo by Ian Yeomans 144; Courtesy of Carlyle Productions 157; Photo by Hervé Derrien 160; Photography by Siegfried H. Mohr 163; By permission of Universal City Studios, Inc. 165; Photo by David Redfern 197; Photos by Jack Bradley 83, 235; Photo by C. Stam 250; Courtesy of Impulse Records, Photo by Joe Alper 253; Photo by Bettencourt's 254; Courtesy of Studio Bernateau 264, 265; Courtesy of W. Fontaine Jones Advisory Committee 267; By permission of United Press International 268; By permission of New York Public Library Performing Arts Collection at Lincoln Center 48, 91, 101, 168, 237, 245; Courtesy of New Britain *Herald*, photo by Roger Gaudio 281; Photo by Mary Campbell 289; Photos by Takashi Arihara 332; Photos by Katsuji Abe 96, 333; Courtesy of *Pops* magazine, photo by Masami Hotta 335; By permission of Time-Life, Inc., photo by Pierre Boulat 365; Photos by Victor Berezsky 371, 373; Courtesy of the White House Archives 425, 426, 427, 429; Courtesy of Robert L. Knudsen 431; By permission of Columbia Broadcasting System, photo by Murray Neitlich 439; Photo by Jimmy Hamilton 448; Courtesy of Mrs. Vi Lomoe 477; Courtesy of *Washington University Magazine*, photo by Herb Weitman 479; and Courtesy of Daniel Fitz Randolph 480

Prologue

The Road

Once upon a time a beautiful young lady and a very handsome young man fell in love and got married. They were a wonderful, compatible couple, and God blessed their marriage with a fine baby boy (eight pounds, eight ounces). They loved their little boy very much. They raised him, nurtured him, coddled him, and spoiled him. They raised him in the palm of the hand and gave him everything they thought he wanted. Finally, when he was about seven or eight, they let his feet touch the ground.

The first thing I did was to run out into the front yard, and then through the front gate, where I found someone who said, "Go ahead, Edward! Right over there." Once on the other side of the street, I ran into someone else who gave me the Go sign for a left-hand turn to the corner. When I got there, a voice said, "Turn right, and straight ahead. You can't miss it!" And that's the way it has always been. Every time I reached a point where I needed direction, I ran into a friendly advisor who told me what and which way to go to get what or where I wanted to get or go or do.

So there are many names here, some you may have heard of, and some you may not. I owe so much to so many, all the way. Every intersection in the road of life is an opportunity to make a decision, and at some I had only to listen.

My road runs from Ward's Place to my grandmother's at Twentieth and R, to Seatan Street, around to Eighth Street, back up to T Street, through Ledroit Park to Sherman Avenue. (Many people thought that I bought J.E.'s house at 1212 T Street N.W., but that is not true. J.E. bought his own house and car, and D.E. bought his little old place at 2728 Sherman Avenue, a little old fun place.) I'll always remember the night they entertained the new hero of that particular football season—Paul Robeson. And then there was the Virginia society party, the all-time highlight of Warrenton, Virginia, when the Prince of Wales made his visit.

The road leads on to New York City, to Leroy Jeffries' mother's flat on 142nd Street, to Forny Brooks's flat on 129th Street. Forny and his wife said, "We like the way you kids play. You can stay here as long as you want. Don't worry about the rent. You can pay when you get it, because we think you kids are really going somewhere." Next is Leonard Harper's flat on Seventh Avenue between 123rd and 124th Street—I was rehearsal pianist for Leonard at Connie's Inn while we were working at both Barron's and the Kentucky Club.

Then I am in my own place at 381 Edgecombe Avenue, from where the road takes us all over the U.S.A., to the dominion of Canada, to Great Britain and to France. From 935 St. Nicholas Avenue, my next home, the peregrinations continue, to Belgium, the Netherlands, Germany, Denmark, Sweden, Norway, Italy, Switzerland, Luxemburg, and Finland. Coming more up to date, to 400 Central Park West as a base, the road takes us to Syria, Jordan, Afghanistan, India, Ceylon, Pakistan, Iran, Iraq, Lebanon, Cyprus, Turkey, Kuwait, Japan, Spain, Senegal, Brazil, Argentina, Uruguay, Chile, Peru, Costa Rica, Panama, Venezuela, Nicaragua, Mexico, Bermuda, the Bahamas, the Virgin Isles, Jamaica, Czechoslovakia, Poland, Hungary, Romania, Jugoslavia, Okinawa, the Philippines, Taiwan, Hong Kong, Thailand, Malaya, Laos, Burma, Indonesia, Australia, Fiji, New Zealand, U.S.S.R. . . .

Where do I call home? I pay rent in New York City.

"Duke" is not the only nickname I've had or enjoyed. Because I was such a good second-baseman, I was nicknamed "Otto" after the great Otto Williams. That was just the first of a long string of sobriquets—"Cutey," "Stinkpot," "Duke," "the Phoney Duke" . . . Doc Perry called me "Wucker," and Sonny Greer, who brought me to New York and told me not to look at the high buildings, called me "The Kid." Juan Tizol's wife called me "Apple Dumpling." Cootie Williams' wife called me "Dumplin'." Johnny Hodges' wife called me "Dumpy," and Cootie still calls me "Dump." It was Louis Bellson who started calling me "Maestro." Cress Courtney called me "Pops," and my son, Mercer, calls me "Pop" and "Fathoo." Sam Woodyard called me "Big Red," Chuck Connors called me "Piano Red," and Ben Webster used to tell people to "See the 'Head Knocker.'" Haywood Jones, of the dance team of Ford, Marshall, and Jones, calls me "Puddin'." Richard Bowden Jones, my man, my real man, called me "Governor" at the beginning of the Cotton Club days. Herb Jeffries cut it short to "Govey." And a lot of friends and relations in Washington, D.C., still call me "Elnm't'n"!

Contents

Act One

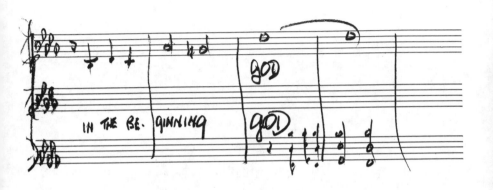

Rollin'

The house lights dim . . . there is a fanfare . . . a voice comes over the loud-speaker . . .

"Ladies and gentlemen, may I present today's most honored musician—Duke Ellington!"

Harry Carney stamps his foot and the band begins to play "Take the 'A' Train."

A grinning fellow enters. He bounces along, almost swaggering, apparently casual, but trying to hide the stage fright he expects any minute. When he gets to the microphone, no matter what position it's in, he has to readjust it, or fidget with it, or fondle it. Finally, over the microphone, he speaks:

"Thank you, ladies and gentlemen, for such a wonderful warm reception. All the kids in the band want you to know that we do love you madly. Now I would like to have you meet one of my favorite people, our new, young apprentice piano player!"

He gestures expectantly to the wings, but no one enters, so he goes immediately to the piano stool and sits down. The stool is almost always in the wrong position, but he doesn't change it, and he starts plunking the piano. The rhythm section of bass and drums joins him in the prologue strains of "Rockin' in Rhythm." At a certain—or uncertain—point, this goes into the eight bars that precede the five saxes getting up from their seats, walking downstage to the microphone, and all together playing down from the top of "Rockin' in Rhythm." Harry Carney's clarinet solo is followed by Booty Wood's plunger-muted trombone, and Cootie Williams and Money Johnson join the latter in a wa-wa fete. Back to their seats they all go, and the ensemble screeches to a climax, doing chords up and out, to the end of "Rockin' in Rhythm."

Duke Ellington gets up from the piano, waves to the band and enjoins the musicians to "look handsome." They all rise, some quick and military, and

3

some so slowly we wonder whether or not they will make it, but they all do, eventually.

"Thank you," says Duke Ellington at the microphone. "That was 'Rockin' in Rhythm,' 1929. And now, 'Creole Love Call,' 1927. I shall never forget 1927. I was three weeks old that year."

The audience acknowledges the mathematical miscalculation with smiles, and sometimes laughs at the fun in his fantasy.

There is a four-bar piano introduction, and then the three clarinets are at the microphone for "Creole Love Call." As it ends, Duke Ellington gestures to and announces Russell Procope as the clarinet soloist. Russell, holding the clarinet delicately, at magic wand angle, takes a distinguished bow.

Having established his obvious era, Duke Ellington pauses and says, "At the Monterey Jazz Festival, we introduced a new suite called *The Afro-Eurasian Eclipse*. It was inspired by a statement made by Mr. Marshall McLuhan of the University of Toronto. He says the whole world is going oriental, and that nobody will be able to retain his or her identity—not even the orientals. Now, we travel around the world quite a bit and during the last seven or eight years we have noticed this coming about. We have written this suite and would like to play a piece of it for you now. In this particular segment, ladies and gentlemen, we have adjusted our perspective to that of the kangaroo and the dijiridoo, which automatically puts us Down Under or Out Back. From this viewpoint, it is most improbable that anyone can tell who is enjoying the shadow of whom. Harold Ashby has been inducted into the responsibility and obligation of scraping off a tiny chip of the charisma of his chinoiserie, almost immediately after the piano player completes his riki-tiki . . ."

The audience seems to enjoy this variegated performance as Ash takes them from Down Under to Down Home in between oriental motifs.

"At the New Orleans Jazz Festival," Duke Ellington resumes, "we premiered another new work called *The New Orleans Suite,* and we would like to have Norris Turney come up for the solo spot. He, ladies and gentlemen, will attempt to give a tone parallel to the excruciating ecstasy one finds oneself suspended in when one is in the throes of the tingling, rhythmic jollies of Bourbon Street."

This introduction doesn't quite prepare the audience for what follows: Norris' lyrical portrayal of the overall pastel enchantment of New Orleans on his *flute.*

4

And so the program rolls on until it is time to bid farewell, and Duke Ellington is saying "Love you madly," not only in English, but in the languages of all the many countries he has visited since the band first went to Europe in 1933.

Washington

Because of the fact that no one else but my sister Ruth had a mother as great and as beautiful as mine, it is difficult to put into understandable words an accurate description of my mother, Daisy. My cousins called her Aunt Daisy, and that became the name by which everyone knew her. She called my father, Edd, although he was really James Edward Ellington. The kids in the family called him Uncle Ed, but to his closest friends and cronies he was always J.E.

When my parents were first married, they lived with my mother's mother, Mrs. Kennedy. She was the wife of a District of Columbia policeman, a captain. I only remember him by his pictures, but Mamma, which is what we called my mother's mother, and my grandfather had ten children, five boys and five girls. Grandma was always surrounded by this flock of young girls, who, even after they were married, still came back to visit as though they lived there. It was a wonderfully warm family, and whatever one owned, they all felt they too owned a part of it—and that included me.

So I was pampered and pampered, and spoiled rotten by all the women in the family, aunts and cousins, but my mother never took her eyes off precious little me, her jewel, until I was four years old, when I proceeded to the front lawn with some authority to examine the rosebushes, stumbled over the lawn-mower, fell on a piece of broken milk bottle, and cut the fourth finger of my left hand. This, of course, was a major emergency that called for the whole family to decide what should be done. The mark is still there, and I think I got pneumonia in the same year. My first awareness of how serious that was was when they called *two* doctors. There may have been more, because I know my mother wanted every doctor in Washington to come and work the miracle of saving her little child. She stayed at my bedside night and day until the fever broke. I couldn't speak, but I can still see her, kneeling, sitting,

To my dear little Henry
From
Aunt Daisy

My mother

standing to lean over the bed, praying, and crying, "My own child doesn't even recognize me!" Obviously, her prayers brought me through, and back I raced to my grandmother's backyard, to the grape arbor that surrounded four pear trees, to play with her two dogs and my five little girl cousins. Since I had been sick, they allowed me to take complete charge of all situations and

Four years old

discussions. We used to climb the trees and have all kinds of adventures, imaginary and otherwise. Everybody called me Edward then.

When I was five years old, my mother put my age up to six so that I could get into first grade at school. She dressed me, and sent me off to school just a few blocks away. She didn't think I saw her, but I did, and every day she followed me, all the way to that school. After school, she was waiting for me at the front door of our home, if she wasn't waiting in front of the school door.

School went all right, I suppose, because I made my grades in spite of my enthusiasm for baseball. One day, a boy was demonstrating his skill at batting, and I turned around for some reason or other, and got hit with that bat— bam!—right in the back of the head. My mother saw it happen. She rushed into the street and rushed me off to the doctor's. It hurt at the moment, and I suppose the mark is still there, but I soon got over it. With this, however, my mother decided I should take piano lessons.

My piano teacher, Mrs. Clinkscales (that was really her name), got paid several times a week for many weeks for these lessons, but I missed more than I took, because of my enthusiasm for playing ball, and running and racing through the street. That I remember very well, because when she had her piano recital with all her pupils in the church, I was the only one who could not play his part. So Mrs. Clinkscales had to play the treble and I just played the umpy-dump bottom! The umpy-dump bottom was, of course, the foundation and understanding of that part of piano-playing I later learned to like. I would like to have learned it, too, because of its strong relationship with what the really outstanding pianists of that day were doing with their left hands. So later for that!

At this point, piano was not my recognized talent. Why, I thought, take it so seriously? After all, baseball, football, track, and athletics were what the real he-men were identified with, and so they were naturally the most important to me. Washington was in the American League and every day I had to see the game. The only way for me to do that was to get a job at the baseball park. I succeeded in getting one and had my first experience of stage fright. I had to walk around, in and out and in front of all those people, yelling, "Peanuts, popcorn, chewing gum, candy, cigars, cigarettes, and score cards!" I soon got over my nervousness, although the first day I missed a lot of the game hiding behind the stands. By the end of the season, I had been promoted to yelling, "Cold drinks, gents! Get 'em ice cold!" I was so crazy about baseball, it's a wonder I ever sold anything. The opportunity to walk around there, looking at all those baseball heroes, whose pictures were a premium in the cigarette packages, meant a lot to me.

There were many open lots around Washington then, and we used to play baseball at an old tennis court on Sixteenth Street. President Roosevelt would come by on his horse sometimes, and stop and watch us play. When he got ready to go, he would wave and we would wave at him. That was Teddy Roosevelt—just him and his horse, nobody guarding him.

My father had a job working as a butler for Dr. Cuthbert at 1462 on the south side of Rhode Island Avenue. I believe the house is still there. The cook and the maid were under him, and he was the fellow who made the decisions around the house. The doctor was rather prominent socially, and he probably recommended my father for social functions, because my father also belonged to what you might call a circle of caterers. When he or one of his cronies got a gig, all the others would act as waiters. They hired good cooks and gave impeccable service. They even had a page, I remember, because one day something happened to the page and I had to stand in for him.

My father kept our house loaded with the best food obtainable, and because he was a caterer we had the primest steaks and the finest terrapin. But he insisted on baked chicken, macaroni and cheese on Sunday; baked beans and greens and cornbread on Wednesday; and on the other days there were special dishes that I've forgotten.

During World War I, he quit the butler job and rented a big house on K Street, in the fashionable area where all the suffragettes were. He rented out rooms, and continued as a caterer until he went to work on blueprints in the Navy Yard. He kept at that till he had trouble with arthritis in his knee.

J.E. always acted as though he had money, whether he had it or not. He spent and lived like a man who had money, and he raised his family as though he were a millionaire. The best had to be carefully examined to make sure it was good enough for my mother. Maybe he was richer than a millionaire? I'm not sure that he wasn't.

My mother came to New York first. She came to see me at the Ziegfeld Theatre in 1929, and came back to live in 1930, We finally got J.E. to come the following year. All the standing he had to do while making blueprints was not good for his arthritis, but he kept insisting he had to work. "What am I going to do?" he kept asking. "There's nothing up there for me to do."

Left to right: Freddy Guy, James E. Ellington, and Duke Ellington, 1925

So when he finally arrived, I told him I had a job for him. I handed him a fountain pen, and said, "You're my social secretary."

My mother, as I said before, was beautiful, but my father was only handsome. While my mother had graduated from high school, I don't think my father even finished eighth grade. Yet his vocabulary was what I always hoped mine would be. In fact, I have always wanted to be able to be and talk like my pappy. He was a party man, a great dancer (ballroom, that is), a connoisseur of vintages, and unsurpassed in creating an aura of conviviality. When I first went to Europe on the *Olympic* in 1933, I felt so *au fait* with all that silverware on the table. He had told me a gentleman never had any problem selecting the proper fork, spoon, or knife, and he had made sure I knew which to use.

He was also a wonderful wit, and he knew exactly what to say to a lady—high-toned or honey-homey. I wrote a song later with a title suggested by one of those sayings he would address to a lady worth telling she was pretty. "Gee, you make that hat look pretty," he would say. He was very sensitive to beauty, and he respected it with proper gentility, never overdoing or underdoing it. He would never scratch a lady's charisma or injure her image. "Pretty," he used to say, "can only get prettier, but beauty compounds itself."

Whatever place he was in, he had appropriate lines. "The millions of beautiful snowflakes are a celebration in honor of your beauty," he declared in Canada. Complexions were compared to the soft and glorious sunsets in California. In the Midwest, he saw the Mississippi as a swift messenger rushing to the sea to announce the existence of a wave of unbelievably compelling force caused by the rebirth of Venus. In New York and on the East Coast, he spoke about "pretty being pretty, but not that pretty." Sometimes he would attempt to sing a song of praise, and then apologize for the emotion that destroyed the control of his voice.

My mother started telling me about God when I was very young. There was never any talk about red people, brown people, black people, or yellow people, or about the differences that existed between them. I don't remember exactly when, but I was quite grown when I first heard about all that. I am sure my mother felt that God took some rich black soil, some red clay, and some white sand, and mixed them all together to make the first man, so that forever after no man would feel he was better than another.

She was mainly interested in knowing and understanding about God, and she painted the most wonderful word pictures of God. Every Sunday, she

My mother's father,
James William Kennedy

Grandmother Alice Kennedy

Aunt Maud Kennedy

Uncle Johnny Kennedy

took me to at least two churches, usually to the Nineteenth Street Baptist, the church of her family, and to John Wesley A.M.E. Zion, my father's family church. It was never made clear to me that they were of different denominations, and to her, I'm sure, it did not matter. They both preached God, Jesus Christ, and that was the most important thing.

When I was old enough, I was sent off to Sunday School as well. I didn't understand it so much then in spite of the fact that it gave me a wonderful feeling of security. Believing gave me that. As though I were some very, very special child, my mother would say, "Edward, you are blessed. You don't have anything to worry about. Edward, you are blessed!"

Do I believe that I am blessed? Of course, I do! In the first place, my mother told me so, many, many times, and when she did it was always quietly, confidently. She was very soft-spoken, and I knew that anything she told me was true. No matter where I was, or what the conditions, my subconscious seemed very much aware of it. So until this day I really don't have any fears, beyond what I might do to hurt or offend someone else. There have been so many extraordinary and inexplicable circumstances in my life. I have always seemed to encounter the right people in the right places at the right time, and doing the right thing to give me the kind of instruction and guidance I needed.

My mother eventually began to trust me out of her sight with Sonny Ellington as my protector. His real name was William, and he was the son of my father's brother, John. Several years older than I, he was cousin, companion, advisor, bodyguard, and confidant. When we were kids, he used to give me a complete account of everything that was happening according to the sports magazines and *Police Gazette*. Sonny was a very good athlete. His baseball and track prowess were acknowledged by all the guys in the neighborhood, and the way things were going, I should have turned out to be a very good athlete too. Walking is, of course, very good training for athletes, and after church every Sunday he would take me for a little tour that meant walking to all extremes of the District of Columbia, to visit our relatives (like twenty-four aunts and uncles), who just happened to be the greatest bakers of cakes and freezers of ice cream. Aunt Laura was at Fifteenth and H, N.E., Aunt Ella in S.W., Aunt Emma in Georgetown, and so on.

I have never figured how far we walked, but as I look back on it now the distances were actually impossible. One day, out at the Chesapeake and the District line, I got carried away with enthusiasm or desire for some sort of con-

Uncle Jim Kennedy, center, and friends

fection, and spent the money that was to be for my carfare home. So we had to walk all the way back to Twelfth and T Streets, N.W. Several times he took me to Rock Creek Park to teach me to swim, but I never got around to taking off my clothes, and I never learned to swim. I just chased rabbits and squirrels, and expected to be a good athlete.

Sonny used to buy all the Western pulp magazines he could find. Uncle John and Aunt Hannah, his father and mother, forbade his reading them, but he'd take them into the bathroom and lock the door, or go into the woodshed, or into the park—anywhere where he could have isolation with the good and bad guys of those mighty Westerns, out of sight of all the objectors. When he finished reading them, he would hand them down to me, and I would go through the same procedure.

By the time I was eleven or twelve years old, I had read Sherlock Holmes, Cleek of Scotland Yard, and Arsène Lupin, and I knew all the literary burglar's theories as well as the murder devices. I knew how to mark cards, deal seconds, and recognize the proper hand position and decoy of pickpockets. Someone once said I'd have made a very good criminal lawyer, but I worry more about how well I would *not* have done as a criminal. What kind of music would I have written while locked up in those dingy old prison cells?

All through grade school, I had a genuine interest in drawing and painting, and I realized I had a sort of talent for them. My mother and father both encouraged me, and the piano was allowed to fade into the background. Our studies became a bit more serious in the eighth grade. In addition to arithmetic, algebra, history, and English, which were taught as the most vital things in the world, my teacher—Miss Boston, the principal of the school— would explain the importance of proper speech. It would be most important in our lives to come. When we went out into the world, we would have the grave responsibility of being practically always on stage, for every time people saw a Negro they would go into a reappraisal of the race. She taught us that proper speech and good manners were our first obligations, because as representatives of the Negro race we were to command respect for our people. This being an all-colored school, Negro history was crammed into the curriculum, so that we would know our people all the way back. They had pride there, the greatest race pride, and at that time there was some sort of movement to desegregate the schools in Washington, D.C. Who do you think were the first to object? Nobody but the proud Negroes of Washington, who felt that the kind of white kids we would be thrown in with were not good enough. I don't know how many castes of Negroes there were in the city at that time, but I do know that if you decided to mix carelessly with another you would be told that one just did not do that sort of thing. It might be wonderful for somebody, but not for me and my cousins. There was a demonstration of how all levels could and should mix at Frank Holliday's poolroom, about which I'll have more to say later.

Every summer, my father would send my mother and me on our vacation, to visit his sister Carrie in Atlantic City, or my mother's brother, John Kennedy, in Philadelphia. We 'd travel by Pullman parlor car, and they were wonderful times, but one year she decided to go to Asbury Park. I was about ready for high school then and, although it was a vacation for her, I went out looking for a job.

There was the big Atlantic Ocean and all those big hotels, but it was a rainy season and bellhop jobs were hard to get. A lot of us kids were all crowded around a hotel one day, hoping something would turn up, when

My parents and sister, Ruth, in Cincinnati, 1932

the man came out and said, "Well, we don't have any need of a bellhop, because business is so bad, but over on First Avenue they need a dishwasher." So then there was a race of all the kids to First Avenue to get the dishwashing job, and I got there first.

"I hear you have a dishwashing job open," I said, when the housekeeper came to the door.

"Yes, we need a dishwasher," she said, "but you don't look like no dishwasher to me. You ain't nothin' but a child." Then she took another look at me and said, "But come on in!"

She sat me down at the kitchen table and put a great heap of biscuits, cornbread, muffins, pancakes, butter, jam, and milk in front of me.

"I'll go see the madam," she said, "and see what she says."

She left me there with that food, and when she came back with the madam the plates were all empty.

"Here he is," she said. "He says he's a dishwasher and he looks like a child, but he eats like a man."

I got the job and entered another world. There was a guy there by the name of Bowser, who had been the dishwasher the year before and was now the headwaiter.

"Boy, I can tell you don't know nothin' 'bout dishwashin'," he said, the very first day. "Let me see what you do."

So I started to wash the dishes.

"No, not like that," he said. "What you do, you take all the dishes, stack them up in this big tank, sprinkle the powder on them, and fill it up with scalding hot water."

He did it, went through the whole thing, and showed me how to dip down to the bottom and pull out a plate.

"That's easy," I said, and I stuck my arm down, but that water nearly burned it off, and I came up *so* quick, with nothing.

"Uh-huh," he said. "I knew you weren't nothin' but a child."

He was a nice guy though, and he did nearly all my dishwashing the whole season, although he had become headwaiter. We used to talk together, and I told him I had been listening to the piano players around Washington.

"Man, in Philadelphia they've got a young piano player called Harvey Brooks," he said. "He's just about your age. You ought to hear him play. He's terrific."

We stayed in Asbury Park the whole summer, but my mother went home before me. On the way back to Washington, Bowser and I stopped off in Philadelphia, where I heard this young kid, Harvey Brooks. He was swinging, and he had a tremendous left hand, and when I got home I had a real yearning to play. I hadn't been able to get off the ground before, but after hearing him I said to myself, "Man, you're just going to *have* to do it." I went around to a couple of piano players, but I couldn't learn anything they were trying to teach me.

My mother used to play piano, pretty things like "Meditation," so pretty they'd make me cry. My father used to play too, but by ear, and all operatic stuff. When I was confined to the house for a couple of weeks with a cold, I started fiddling around on the piano, using what was left over from my piano lessons—mostly the fingering—and I came up with a piece I called "Soda Fountain Rag," because I had been working as a soda jerk at the Poodle Dog Cafe. I started playing this around, and it attracted quite a lot of attention.

About this time, too, just before I went to high school, and before my voice broke, I got my nickname, Duke. I had a chum, Edgar McEntree (he preferred the accent on the "en"), a rather fancy guy who liked to dress well. He was socially uphill and a pretty good, popular fellow around, with parties and that sort of thing. I think he felt that in order for me to be eligible for his constant companionship I should have a title. So he named me Duke.

One day, soon after I went to high school, the seniors had a party in the gym. Edgar McEntree, my friend, crony, and buddy, pushed into the party, pulling me with him. His friend "The Duke," he announced, was a pianist who wouldn't object if asked to play. With this, I was invited, and I played. It was probably "What You Gonna Do When the Bed Breaks Down?" my second composition, and a pretty good "hug-and-rubbin'" crawl. "Encore, encore!" they cried when I finished. Then the senior boys came over and took me to the grocery store, where they told me they were going to make me a senior right away. They ordered some gin and blackberry wine, mixed them together, passed it on to me and told me it was "Top and Bottom."

The next morning, three of the prettiest little girls you ever saw in your life stood out in front of my house looking up at the second story. "Mrs. Ellington, is Edward ready?" one of them called. "Yes, honey," she answered, "he'll be right down." When I came down, we turned the corner in the direction of the school, but in the middle of the block the girls told me, "We're not going to school today. We are going over to Ina Fowler's house and have a hop.

Gertie Wells

Gertie Wells is going to be there. So are Roscoe Lee, Earl Hyman, Shrimp Brauner, and Claude Hopkins. They're all cutting school." (Gertie Wells was a great piano player, but she never did anything professionally outside Washington.)

Well, that's what we did, and it was quite a success. From then on, I was invited to many parties, where I learned that when you were playing piano there was always a pretty girl standing down at the bass clef end of the piano. I ain't been no athlete since. But if at that time I had ever thought I was learning to play piano to make a living, I would never have made it!

During World War I, I worked at the Navy Department as a messenger. Then they switched me over to the State Department. This was pre-Pentagon, and the State, War, and Navy departments were all in one building to the west of the White House; the Treasury was to the east. I found myself in a newly created section called the State, War, and Navy Transportation Division, and what we did was to make reservations for the brass. My boss welcomed me to my little messenger's desk. Guys in his position were rich, dollar-a-year men, and he, of course, sat at the big desk.

"Now, Edward," he said on the very first morning, "I'm going out to lunch, and I'd like you to watch the telephone."

When he came back, he said I had done very well, and a little later in the afternoon he had to leave again.

"I'm going over to the club for cocktails, and I'm going to ask you to watch the phone again. If anyone calls up and wants a reservation, call up the Pullman Company and have the tickets sent here. Then you personally deliver them wherever they are required."

I did that, and when he came back in the evening he said I had done a splendid job. From that day on, I moved over to the big desk, and I remained there until the war was over. I think I knew the schedule of every big train in the country, and that came in useful later.

My man got to like me, and one day he told me how to get rich.

"All you have to do is get the first thousand dollars. When you get that, you will want another thousand. When you get to ten thousand, you will want another ten. And when you get to a hundred thousand, it's just on and on to the million."

So I know exactly what to tell any budding young man who wants to get rich, but putting the plan into operation is something else again. As Django Reinhardt used to say, "Tomorrow, maybe." Of course, I was born rich.

Some of my other extracurricular activities also deserve mention here. Boys under sixteen were not allowed to go to burlesque shows, but at twelve our high-school crowd decided it was time for us either to be or to act like sixteen. So down we went to the Gaiety Theatre, and bought tickets, and got away with it. We found it very interesting, and went back many other times. There were a lot of jokes, and if you had a tendency toward instruction as well as entertainment, as I had, you could begin to understand the foundation, and how these things were built. The shows were very good and I made a lot of observations, on show business techniques, on the great craftsmanship involved, and on the rather gorgeous girls, who looked good in anything they wore. They also looked good, I should say, in *everything* they took off! And then, at about fourteen, I started going to the poolroom, and boys, of course, were not allowed in there either until they were sixteen.

There was one great poolroom on T Street, between Sixth and Seventh N.W., Frank Holliday's poolroom, next to the Howard Theatre. It was not a normal, neighborhood-type poolroom. It was the highspot of billiard parlors, where all the kids from all neighborhoods came, and the great pool sharks from all over town. Some would come from out of town, too, and there would be championship matches. Guys from all walks of life seemed to converge there: school kids over and under sixteen; college students and graduates, some starting out in law and medicine and science; and lots of Pullman porters and dining-car waiters. These last had much to say about the places they'd been. The names of the cities would be very impressive. You would hear them say, "I just left Chicago," or "Last night I was in Cleveland." You do a lot of listening in a poolroom, and all this sounded very big.

Then there were the professional *and* amateur gamblers. One whose name, I think, was Strappy Manning, was regarded as a champ. Freddy Woods was a man who could run the scale on the dice, on the regular straight dice, on an ordinary pool table, and run it from two up to twelve and back to two. He used to do all sorts of demonstrations. Cats would come in there, too, who would take a deck of cards and demonstrate dealing seconds and all other kinds of cheats. When a dealer is dealing with marked cards at Black Jack, and he sees you need five or seven to make twenty-one, and the top card is the card you need, he has to be able to put it back and pull the second one out.

Interns used to come in, who could cure colds. And handwriting experts who would enjoy copying somebody's signature on a check, go out and *cash* it, and bring back the money to show the cats in the poolroom what *artists* they were. They didn't need the money. They did it for the kicks. There were also a couple of pickpockets around, so smooth that when they went to New York they were not allowed in the subway. At heart, they were all great artists.

Lester Dishman

Among the professional men was Dr. Charles Drew, who was the first to make blood plasma work. Then there were the Curtis brothers. One eventually became an eye specialist, the other a heart specialist. Bub Boller and George Hayes were lawyers. Frank Holliday's very tight buddy was Clarence Cabiness, whose nickname was "Snake." He was the ideal picture of cool—Mr. Cool. His family was rather social, but then he got mixed up and became involved with race horses and that sort of thing.

Of course, all the piano players used to hang out there, too. There was Ralph Green, who never really became a professional piano player. Claude Hopkins was there. Shrimp Bronner was another. Phil Word, who used to play piano at the Howard Theatre, was a good song writer, too. Roscoe Lee, who became a dentist, would be there. He and Claude Hopkins were reader piano players, like Doc Perry, Louis Brown, and Louis Thomas, who came by from time to time. Les Dishman was the *great* left hand. Then there were Clarence Bowser, Sticky Mack, and Blind Johnny. These cats couldn't read, but there was a wonderful thing, an exchange, which went on between them and the guys who did. And I mustn't forget the great drummers who later

Louis Brown

on used to drive me. Men like Bill Jones and Bill Beasley would go into three-four and five-four, and that kind of thing, and try to throw me.

I used to spend nights listening to Doc Perry, Louis Brown, and Louis Thomas. They were schooled musicians who had been to the conservatory. But I listened to the unschooled, too. There was a fusion, a borrowing of ideas, and they helped one another right in front of where I was standing, leaning over the piano, listening. Oh, I was a great listener!

Louis Brown had unbelievable technique. He played chromatic thirds faster than most of the greats of that time could play chromatic singles (his left hand could play an eleventh in any key). The others could only marvel at this, but not with envy, for they enjoyed another piano player's sterling performance. They applauded with wonder and appreciation, laughed and slapped each other on the back when he finished, and then each would take his turn and display his own unique devices. Doc Perry and Louis were the Conservatory Boys but they had also a profound respect for the cats who played by ear, and in spite of the fact that their techniques were as foreign to each other as Chinese, they lauded them, praised them, and there was the most wonderful exchange. Everybody seemed to get something out of the other's playing—the ear cats loved what the schooled guys did, and the schooled guys, with fascination, would try what the ear cats were doing. It was a wonderful, healthy climate for everybody. Even the listeners were enchanted and never had enough. When Doc Perry first heard me play, he obviously heard some talent and I was invited to his home for refreshments, and one by one he showed me things, some of which I still use as guidance out of a cramp. For all he taught me, he never asked a fee: he just somehow liked me, I guess. I was rather a nice kid, of course, but I respected him more than he could ever know.

Doc Perry wore glasses and looked very much like the kids try to look today. He was intelligent, had beautiful posture at all times—sitting, walking, in a poolroom, or playing the piano—and talked with a sort of semi-continental finesse. He was extremely dignified, clean, neat, and had impeccably manicured nails and hands. When playing the piano he had that form athletes have. He was respected by musicians, show people, and the laymen as well. Doc was an impressive sight no matter what he was doing, and in spite of his own masterly digital dexterity, he respected any musician, school or ear. It was all a matter of taste. He felt that if the composer wrote it that way, then that's the way the composer would like it played.

Oliver "Doc" Perry

I met him like all the other kids who went to dances, and when he heard me play, I think he saw possibilities for me in piano playing. As my drawing and painting teacher at high school, Mr. Dodson, used to say, "You have the ability, now all you have to do is apply yourself." What they meant was, "Apply yourself and learn everything you can about music." I used to go up to Doc

Perry's house almost every day, sit there in a glow of enchantment, until he'd pause and explain some passage. Being an educated man of intelligence and tolerance, he had the patience to share with me his theories and observations. He also could switch from his own precise, clean style to that of any other piano player he heard. He was absolutely the most perfect combination of assets I could have encountered at that time. He first taught me what I called a system of reading the lead and recognizing the chords, so that I could have a choice in the development of my ornamentation. He was my piano parent and nothing was too good for me to try. Even if I didn't learn to play it, I knew how it was done. Doc Perry was probably the first in the parade where I found the right person in the right frame of mind to do all that he could for me and my advancement.

He never charged me five cents, and he served food and drink throughout the whole thing. How does one pay off this type of indebtedness? Back in those days, if you were a constant listener and hanger-on like I was, any piano player in D.C. was wide open and approachable. If you were to ask any one of them something like, "How did you do that, that you just played?", they would stop doing whatever they were doing and play it again, while I watched and listened to it and its explanation. Great people like Lester Dishman, top ear-man Clarence Bowser, Sticky Mack, Louis Brown, Louis Thomas, Caroline Thornton, Roscoe Lee, Gertie Wells, The Man with a Million Fingers, all of whom had their own individual style. Like Joe Rochester from Baltimore, but he was not so easily accessible. In his case, I could ask any one of the D.C. guys, mainly Doc Perry, and he would show me, and he knew what he was doing. Everyone else there too. I absorbed everybody and when I found that something I wanted to do was a little too difficult for the yearling that I was then, I would cop-out with something appropriate to my limitations. Naturally and eventually, sooner than I expected, I found my own musical self breaking through with fitting substitutions, some of which were good enough to attract the attention of my superiors. They all encouraged me, and soon it got around that I was a pretty good piano player, and by that time Henry Grant, who taught music in our high school, heard about me and invited me to come to his house to study harmony. It ended up a hidden course in harmony that lighted the direction to more highly developed composition. It was a music foundation, and I jumped at the opportunity because most of the advanced musicians had taken harmony from Henry Grant. All of my teachers, with the excep-

Henry Grant

tion of Mrs. Clinkscales, had given me instructions orally. There was no question of writing music, but just talk, and I suppose that was the birth of my primitive system of memorizing, which is more or less what I still depend upon.

The main thing about the poolroom, too, besides all the extraordinary talent, was the *talk*. Frank Holliday's poolroom sounded as though the prime authorities on *every* subject had been assembled there. Baseball, football, basketball, boxing, wrestling, racing, medicine, law, politics—everything was discussed with authority. Frank Holliday's poolroom was a great place.

One of my first professional jobs as a musician was playing for a man who traveled and did an act that was half magic and half fortunetelling. I can remember now only his first name, which was Joe. To begin with, I was completely at a loss as to what I was to play on the piano. He told me to ad lib and try to match the mood of what he was doing. I did that, and was rather amazed at my ability to fall into the spirit of the very serious and sometimes mystic moods. I wish it had been recorded, because I think it would have revealed another facet of my character. What happened to Joe afterwards, I never did hear. But I hope that he is still alive and telling of the heavenly future paradise through the grace of God.

I became not only the relief piano player to Doc Perry, Louis Brown, Lester Dishman, and Sticky Mack, but I also worked in about the Number Five band for people like Louis Thomas and Russell Wooding, who had the class work. We moved out into the society world, and I remember playing at Mrs. Dyer's, a dance hall where all the nice young society kids used to go. Louis Thomas furnished the music for it all the time, and I was lucky to go in there. That was where I started throwing my hands up in the air, trying to look like Luckey Roberts, whom I had seen at the Howard Theatre, and they all said, "Oh, yes, Duke's a great pianist. Send him back again!" This, although I still knew only about four numbers. One was "The Siren Song." I never forgot that. Louis Thomas' musicians were all good readers, and the first time I went in there they had been stuck for a piano player. "The big number this week," they told me, "Is 'The Siren Song,' and you're going to have to learn it." I took the music home and wrestled with it all afternoon. That night, I took the music to work, put it up on the piano, and everybody thought I was really reading with the music sitting up there!

After I had been playing for him a couple of years, Louis Thomas sent me on another job I can never forget. It was out at the Ashland Country Club—nothing but millionaires—and there was nobody to play but me. I

In Louis Thomas's cabaret, Ninth and R Street, Washington, D.C. Left to right: Sonny Greer, Bertha Ricks, Duke Ellington, Mrs. Conaway, Sterling Conaway

sat there and played the whole length of the gig without a drummer or even a banjo player. "You're playing by yourself tonight," Thomas had told me. "It'll be mostly atmosphere, just under-conversation music. Collect a hundred dollars and bring me ninety." He was paying me ten dollars a night at that time, but I thought to myself, "What, a *hundred* dollars a night!"

I gave him his ninety dollars, but the very next day I went down to the telephone office and arranged for a Music-for-All-Occasions ad in the telephone book. It was during the war, and there were a lot of people from out of town, war workers, who didn't know Meyer Davis and Louis Thomas from Duke Ellington. My ad looked just like theirs, and I began to get work. And give it. It got so that I would sometimes send out four or five bands a night, and work in them, too. I had real good business sense then. I bought a car and a house, and lived up on Sherman Avenue at 2728. In partnership with

Ewell Conway, I was also operating a sign-painting business on T Street between Sixth and Seventh, N.W. When customers came for posters to advertise a dance, I would ask them what they were doing about their music. When they wanted to hire a band, I would ask them who's painting their signs.

Before I left high school, I had won an art scholarship to Pratt Institute. I had talent as an artist and was supposed to make use of it. What I was getting out of music then seemed like a gift or a bonus, and I didn't realize that that was where my future lay. But I never took up the scholarship to Pratt, because by playing piano, and by booking bands for dances, I was making a lot of money.

One of the unique things about being in the band business was that you never knew what would be required when the telephone rang. One time a fellow called from Orange, Virginia.

"We're going to give a barn dance, Duke," he said. "But I want to make sure that *you* will be coming your*self*. I want the Number One band."

"Why, certainly," I said. It was very important, you see, to have me there. This was a special barn dance! But about the night before it was due to take place, he called me again.

"Oh, my goodness . . ." he began.

"What's wrong?" I asked.

"Well, you know, we put a hardwood floor upstairs in the barn," he said, "and we forgot to leave a hole, or a window, big enough to take the piano in!"

"Don't worry about that," I said. "I also play guitar."

So that night I sat up there and played guitar with Bill Miller, and Bill played so loud, of course, that it didn't make any difference whether I was right or not. I had a good personality, but that night I could have been a statue.

Those were the days when I was a champion drinker. I was eighteen, nineteen, or twenty, and it was customary then to put a gallon of corn whiskey on the piano when the musicians began to play. There were four of us in the group, and one hour later the jug was empty. At the end of every hour the butler would replace the empty jug with another full gallon of twenty-one-year-old corn.

The personnel changed from day to day, because sometimes we'd have to split up and put a strong man in another group that was going out. Usually, it was the three Miller brothers with me. Bill played guitar, banjo, and banjorine; Felix played drums; and Brother played saxophone. That was before Toby Hardwick was old enough to go out and play, and before Sonny Greer came to town.

Chauncey Brown was originally a drummer with good contacts in Virginia society. He worked with us, and sometimes we worked with him—a case of one hand washing the other. Since those days he has married, raised a family, and found enough time to play guitar and sing. He is *the* society musician right there in the middle of that society swirl in Warrenton, Virginia. I wonder if I would have been that lucky if I had stayed in Washington?

We used to play the dances that followed horse shows quite often, but one day somebody heard us and decided he wanted us to play the horse show itself. We were getting to have such a good reputation. Normally, they would have a thirty-piece brass band, but I think with only four pieces we went out and played louder than they did.

In Washington there were always a lot of dances, some given by clubs on special occasions, and others on a regular weekly basis. There was an afternoon dance every Wednesday run by a kid named Shrimp Collins. That was a popular affair, and Doc Perry always used to play it. I would take over the last set when Doc had to go to the Ebbett House, where he played dinner. I would play "What You Gonna Do When the Bed Breaks Down?" there, too, and it got to the point where it was a pretty fair song. Nothing happened with it, but sometimes now I think I should sing it with a rock 'n' roll group.

I was beginning to catch on around Washington, and I finally built up so much of a reputation that I had to study music seriously to protect it. Doc Perry had really taught me to read, and he showed me a lot of things on the piano. Then when I wanted to study some harmony, I went to Henry Grant. We moved along real quickly, until I was learning the difference between a G-flat and an F-sharp. The whole thing suddenly became very clear to me, just like that. I went on studying, of course, but I could also hear people whistling, and I got all the Negro music that way. You can't learn that in any school. And there were things I wanted to do that were not in books, and I had to ask a lot of questions. I was always lucky enough to run into people who had the answers.

Percy Johnson was a drummer and a buddy of mine. His nickname was "Brushes." One day he invited me over to his house just across from that sign shop on T Street.

33

"You've got to listen to this," he said when we got there.

He had a player-piano and he put on a roll by James P. Johnson. This was, of course, an entirely new avenue of adventure for me, and I went back there every day and listened. Percy slowed the mechanism down so that I could see which keys on the piano were going down as I digested Johnson's wonderful sounds. I played with it until I had his "Carolina Shout" down pat, and then Percy would go out on the town with me and show me off. I really had it perfect, so that when James P. Johnson himself came to Washington to play at Convention Hall my cheering section and pals waited until he played "Carolina Shout" and then insisted that I get up on the stand and cut him!

I was scared stiff, but James P. was not only a master, he was also a great man for encouraging youngsters. He went along with the whole scene, and when I finished "Carolina Shout" he applauded too. I didn't play any more that night but just leaned over the piano and listened to the one and only. What I absorbed on that occasion might, I think, have constituted a whole semester in a conservatory. Afterwards, he elected me his guide for a tour of all the Washington joints, and I stayed up until 10 A.M. The friendship that began then was important to me later when we got to New York. And all of that was thanks to my good buddy Percy Johnson, to whom I shall always be indebted. God bless him.

The nucleus of the early band was the Miller brothers. Then Otto Hardwick, who later became "Toby," joined us. He was playing bass fiddle, and he was so small his father used to carry the instrument to work for him. When he got a C-melody saxophone, I began to send him out on other jobs, and he was soon known as one of the best saxophone players in town. Artie Whetsol, the trumpet player, used to work with us too, and for years he was one of the band's most indispensable members. Elmer Snowden came in with his banjo, and around this time I met Juan Tizol, the trombonist who came to the Howard Theatre with a band from Puerto Rico led by Marie Lucas. This group impressed us very much, because all the musicians doubled on different instruments, something that was extraordinary in those days. Tizol enters the story again a few years later, but the year before, in 1919, Sonny Greer had come to Washington after playing drums in a trio with Fats Waller at Asbury Park.

He was in the poolroom next door to the Howard when there was an urgent need for a drummer in the pit band. The show was due to go on in half an hour and Sonny didn't hesitate to volunteer. That was how he got the job at the Howard. He struck up an acquaintance with Toby Hardwick, who introduced him to me.

Although Sonny was from Long Branch, New Jersey, he had been to New York, and anybody who had been to New York had the edge on us. We watched him in the pit, and he used a lot of flash tricks. We decided to find out what kind of guy he was, so we stood on the street corner, waited for him, and greeted him. He answered our questions with a line of jive that laid us low. Not long after that, he quit the Howard and joined us.

A place musicians used to gather in after work was the Industrial Cafe, and there every guy used to try to tell a taller tale than anybody else. That's where Sonny showed what he was made of, because he always carried off the honors. He was also a major help to me in band contests, when we needed to employ psychology. One I remember was between Elmer Snowden with eight pieces, and Sonny, Sterling Conway (on banjorine), and myself. We worked out a lot of tricks on piano and drums, and walked away with the cup. The next time, when we were up against Blind Johnny's band—and Johnny played a lot of piano—we were not so lucky. So Sonny organized a cheering section for me, and he soon became the nearest thing I ever had to a brother.

When Leroy Smith's band came to Washington and played at the Belasco Theatre, it made a big impression on me. It was well dressed and well rehearsed, and all the musicians doubled on different instruments. This desire to explore the further reaches of music's possibilities. Later on, I heard created an effect of legerdemain or magic that caused an explosion in my Leroy Smith at Connie's Inn in New York.

There was a period when we were all crazy about automobiles. Claude Hopkins had a Hudson limousine, and I had a Chandler. Toby Hardwick bought a Pullman from a dealer we knew only as Dear-Me. Toby's car was named the "Dupadilly," and it used to stall at the most awkward places. In fact, it was so refractory that one day they all got out and just left it standing on the street.

While we were still in Washington, we were fascinated by the descriptions of players and singers in other cities that visiting musicians gave us. We heard about Joe Rochester, Pike Davis, Reggie Haymer, Cliff Dorsey, and Ike Dixon in Baltimore, but it was New York that filled our imagination. We were awed by the never-ending roll of great talents there, talents in so many fields, in society music and blues, in vaudeville and songwriting, in jazz and theatre, in dancing and comedy.

We heard of Florence Mills, Edith Wilson, Gladys Bentley, Ethel Waters, Gertrude Saunders, Bessie Smith, Monette Moore, Lucille Hegamin, Mamie Smith, Andy Razaf, Spencer Williams, Alberta Hunter, Garvin Bushell, Barron's, Joe Smith, Johnny Dunn, Charlie Johnson, June Clark, Clara Smith, Clarence Williams, Connor's, Ford Dabney, George Tynes (Boston), Jim Europe, Cricket Smith, Leroy's, Bert Williams, J. Rosamond Johnson, Allie Ross, W. C. Handy, Vernon and Irene Castle, Gold Grabben's, Flo Ziegfeld, Sissle and Blake, Smalls' Bob Cole, Jerry Preston, Porter Grainger, Miller and Lyles, Bill Robinson, Bob Gillette, Johnny Powell, Casper Holstein, Madame Walker (Indianapolis), Addington Major, The Beetle, Mattie Hite, Lizzie Miles, Tommy Morris, Broadway Jones, Mal Frazier, Johnny Cobb, Tim Brymm, Rudolf Brown, and many, many more.

Harlem, to our minds, did indeed have the world's most glamorous atmosphere. We had to go there.

Then Sonny Greer came up with the opportunity to work for Wilbur Sweatman, who was playing three clarinets at once in a vaudeville show. He had been making records for a long time, and I think he was famous for "The Barnyard Blues." We joined him in New York and played some split weeks in theatres. It was another world to us, and we'd sit on the stage and keep a straight face. I began to realize that all cities had different personalities, which were modified by the people you met in them. I also learned a lot about show business from Sweatman. He was a good musician, and he was in vaudeville because that was where the money was then, but I think things were beginning to cool off for him, and soon we were not doing so well.

Fortunately, Sonny Greer had a lot of face. He would walk in any place, see someone he knew, and go over to him. "Hey, So-and-so, remember me?" he'd say. "Sonny Greer. Jersey kid. Remember?" And we'd be in. He and I hustled around playing pool. We might start with a quarter. The minute we got two dollars, we'd quit, go home, dress up, order two steak dinners, give the girl a quarter, and have a quarter left for tomorrow. We'd be pretty, clean, and neat, and we'd go cabareting, visit Willie "The Lion" Smith, or James P. Johnson, or Fats Waller. You could never want for anything around them, and The Lion was always very encouraging. "I like you kids, you're nice, clean kids," he would say, "and I want you to do well." One day he came up to me and said, "Gee, you need a haircut! Here's fifty cents. Go get one." A beautiful man.

We would never send home for any money, because we knew that would scare our people to death, and stories about our splitting a hot dog five ways were more of a gag than anything else. We were getting more bored with our situation than desperate, until one day I had the luck to find fifteen dollars on the street. Then we had a square meal, got on the train, and went back to Washington to get ourselves together before we tried it again.

Categories

The category is a Grand Canyon of echoes. Somebody utters an obscenity and you hear it keep bouncing back a million times. Categories are sometimes used by a person who feels that the one he's talking to doesn't know enough about the language in which he speaks. So he uses lines, boxes, circles, and pigeonholes to help the less literate one to a better understanding.

On the other hand, categories are sometimes used as a crutch for a weak artistic ability to lean on. The category gives the artistic cripple's work an attractive gloss.

An agreeable smell is in the nose of the one who smells it.

Sometimes bad taste is resorted to for its shock effect, to attract attention. A magnificent feast is to be served, but when the guests sit down and start eating, the host changes the lighting effects to make the food look sickening.

A categorist must be loyal to his category, and when he is experiencing cacophony he must wear an ecstatic expression on his face to prove that he digs the vibrations, man! And some really *do* dig distortion. Abstraction can reach a point where it represents or says anything the artist claims. Since no one else speaks his language, or the language the *pièce de résistance* is written or painted in, he—the artist—is the only one to understand it. But if you want to be *in,* just make believe you dig it, man! Can you really blame people, with social requirements so demanding? Almost everybody wants to be somebody socially.

Music

Music is a beautiful woman in her prime,
Music is a scrubwoman, clearing away the dirt and grime,
Music is a girl child
Simple, sweet and beaming,
A thousand years old,
Cold as sleet, and scheming.

Wise and patient,
Unfathomably kind,
Music is the woman you always wanted to find.

As fragile as a flower,
A single petal of a rose,
And what you think you think,
She already knows she knows.

A system of ribbons,
A multiplicity of ramifications,
Sparkling from her brain down through her core,
A million facets of gossamer sensations.

And you could be
A most inadequate bore.

Music is a gorgeous bitch, . . .
A volcano of desire
Makes your blood to boil
As you get higher and higher.

Music is like the woman
Who is like mathematics:
Music is a woman who's true.

No matter how well you know her,
There's always more to learn;
An endless adventure, every day she's brand-new.
Music is that woman, who
You'll hope will say,
"There's very few who do a new-do like you do."
But, alas, you're the victim of her coup,
'Cause *she* can always satisfy you.

Music is the woman
You follow day after day;
Music is the woman
Who always has her way.

The topless chick—
You like to see shake it—
No matter how hard you try,
You never quite make it.

When you don't hear her,
You desperately miss her,
And when you embrace her,
You wish you could kiss her.

Dramatis Felidae

MERCER ELLINGTON

My son, Mercer Ellington, is dedicated to maintaining the luster of his father's image. By this I mean that in his position as band manager he seeks out the best, and only the best, musicians and associates to bolster the formidable foundation established over many working years. He is proud of the name, and also proud of the fact that this organization is unique, besides having a splendid record in terms of performances, conquests, and recordings. Its most unique point is that it is the only band in the world that works fifty-two weeks a year. It is probably the only organization of any kind doing anything fifty-two weeks a year, with no holidays and no weekends off. Mercer says, "The Old Man loves what he's doing and has no desire to do anything that is not related to music. To him, those fifty-two weeks in a year are his holidays."

Mercer is always up straight and standing tall in defense of Duke Ellington. He accepts the responsibility on any occasion he thinks might prove uncomfortable or lead to unhappiness for the Old Man, and sees to it that he gets all the respect that is ever due him. Refurbishment, such as Wild Bill Davis' engagement provided, is a luxury selected and arranged for Duke Ellington's personal kicks. If Mercer hears a singer he thinks will enhance the program, she's hired immediately and given a chance to impress me. Since he became manager, he has brought in such fine musicians as Norris Turney, Harold Ashby, Rufus Jones, Money Johnson, Joe Benjamin, and Harold "Geezil" Minerve. Regardless of cost, the Duke Ellington image must remain glistening.

I talked Mercer into quitting his disc-jockey job on WLIB in New York, where he was doing well and becoming more and more popular every day. It was a great radio show and it had a great listening audience. "I know that

With Mercer Ellington

you've been off your horn for a long time and that you ain't got no chops," I said, "but I've decided that if any more band managers steal any more money, then I want the manager to be—you!"

Before Mercer became a disc jockey, he was musical director for Della Reese, who was just about the hottest thing around at that time, her records selling in millions.

Originally, Mercer had been educated at the Evander Childs High School. Then he studied at Juilliard and, while working at Republic Aircraft, took composition and orchestration at New York University, which he graduated from with an instructor's degree. During the war, he was in the U. S. Army, and when he came out he organized his own band. They played at the Savoy as house band, and swung like crazy. The band was loaded with nothing but the greatest young talent, such as Kenny Dorham, Ray Copeland, Alva McCain, Luther Henderson, Joe Benjamin, and Carmen McRae.

By now, we had acquired a big commercial name and were getting big bookings. I had not been down South or deep in the provinces for several years, so I suggested and pleaded with him to print his first name small and let us book him on some of our very lucrative dates. With that good old-school-tie spirit, he refused, said he didn't think it was fair, and wanted to make it on his own. Maternal honesty was making itself felt. He and his great band never got sufficient publicity, and having to follow in the footsteps and buck his Old Man proved insurmountable obstacles. So after they had played the Golden Gate Ballroom in New York, he broke up the band and got swallowed up in the bureaucracy of Duke Ellington, Inc., and its executive activities. He branched out with some very good singers and formed Mercer Records, which soon had—and still has—a wonderful catalog. Then along came a fellow with a lot of money who persuaded him to become a representative for J. W. Dant whiskey. He did well at that, too, but the job did not take care of his appetite for music. At different times he formed other big bands for special engagements when he employed men like Clark Terry, Dizzy Gillespie, Harold Ashby, Cat Anderson, and Chico Hamilton.

Before he went to Juilliard, he was a sort of helper with the stagehands, and bandboy with us. He was strong and ready for this job because his most recent interests had kept him playing football. Later, he played for Columbia University and as a semipro. When he was a kid, he played all the athletic games, from stickball in the street on up.

In his childhood, he had to go from one household to the other, his mother's and mine alternatively, so he had absorbed the full range of *love* and disci-pline. I always used to take him up to Salem in Massachusetts when our band was based there in the summertime for Charlie Shribman's New England dates. The Salem Fire Department were kind of crazy about him, and they spoiled him by letting him ride the fire truck. It was a ball for him, and he got to think he was an apprentice fireman.

Mercer has a beautiful wife, like all of his forefathers. All their wives were beautiful. He has two beautiful daughters, too. Mercedes studied ballet at Juilliard, became captain of the June Taylor dancers on the Jackie Gleason Show, and as this is written is dancing in *No, No, Nanette*. Gaye went to the Oakwood School for Girls and studied art at Howard University. She has a very good position in the art department of a publishing firm in New York. Mercer's son, Edward Kennedy Ellington II, went to Morris Brown School and Howard University. He played basketball and was in the rowing crew at college, and was a sound technician at National Recording studios in New York. He's now at Berklee School of Music in Boston. They are all wonderful kids, and I love them.

Just to think I remember Mercer even from the day he was born . . .

RUTH DOROTHEA ELLINGTON

I was just about a grown man when Ruth, my sister, was born. She naturally became our little doll. I remember teaching her to walk holding her by a long braid of hair, which horrified my mother, although Ruth seemed to enjoy it. We all had something to say about everything she did or wore, just as kids do with their dolls. So she too was spoiled from birth, all through school and up until she and my mother came to live in New York. While I had been living there, my father had continued to spoil her, to ensure nothing but the best for her, and to lecture her on the dos and don'ts appropriate to a young lady.

In New York she went to New College at Columbia University, where they had a very special, avant-garde course. (I believe it is no longer a part of the curriculum there.) She majored in biology, and her friend, Fran Hunter, tells me Ruth gave her the privilege of handling the worms. A provision of the course was that the students had to go to Europe for part of it, so in 1938 Ruth went to Europe with a personal chaperone, Mrs. Walter Singleton.

44

To a very sweet cousin, Henry

Ruth D. Ellington

My sister, Ruth, age sixteen

Minnie Green Singleton was the epitome of the genteel Southern lady. Her gracious manner, erect carriage, and well-modulated voice always gave her listeners the impression of undivided attention, which produced an immediate communication with old and young alike. She was, to her older friends, a staunch pillar of the community, and, at the same time, to her younger friends a confidante of romantic secrets. The most wonderful thing about her was that at the age of sixty-five she still blushed!

Raised with love by her father and mother, Ruth's upbringing and education equipped her as a gentlewoman and were not designed to develop aggressive or businesslike qualities. So to this day she lives in New York and operates Tempo Music as though it were a publishing house of classical music rather than of jazz (or Top Forty pop!), and she is more concerned with its prestige than its profitability. In the same way, she is more interested in such honors as I may receive than in any large sums of money.

Besides the business ventures in which I have involved her, she not only entertains our friends sumptuously and endlessly, but she watched over my Aunt Flossie, who was confined to bed for years, and constantly brought her words of cheer.

Ruth has two sons by her first husband, Danny James. Michael, the older, possesses a prime intellect, but he always seemed to have a resistance to curricularized education, and always seemed to be a little ahead of what they were trying to teach him. Clark Terry thought he would make a good trumpet player and started teaching him, but somebody talked him out of it. I don't remember who, but maybe me. Mike has made several trips with the band at home and abroad, and found them rewarding. I find that I can rely on his ear and good taste. He has also done some recording and disc-jockeying with Stanley Dance, but they were glad to put the disc-jockeying down, because, as Stanley said, they began to feel like "recusants" among all the "with-it" kids.

Mike's brother, Stephen, also has a great interest in music, and he has made Europe a second home. His light-and-sound sculptures impressed a lot of people in New York. This is the telegram I sent him on the occasion of his first exhibition on September 12, 1970:

I am so proud to be the close relative of one whose mind and imagination have gotten him into a position to have a show at this distinguished gallery. When I first saw your work, I suspected something good would come to you, and the Lee

Nordness Gallery is to be congratulated for making such a pure and unbiased decision.

Don't stop now. As Billy Strayhorn used to say, "Ever onward and upward!" Create, and be true to yourself, and depend only on your own good taste. Tomorrow is in the wings waiting for you to sound her entrance fanfare.

Good Luck. God bless.

D.E.

SIDNEY BECHET

Sidney Bechet was one of the truly great originals. I shall never forget the first time I heard him play, at the Howard Theatre in Washington around 1921. I had never heard anything like it. It was a completely new sound and conception to me.

He joined us in 1926 during the summertime, when we were working around New England for Charlie Shribman. We lived in Salem, and it was there that he and Otto Hardwick developed a very close friendship. Those two cats would go out on a forty-mile drive nearly every night, and when I asked them where they were going, or what they were doing, all they would say was, "Just visiting!"

Bubber Miley and Bechet used to have a cutting contest nightly, and that was a kick. They would play five or six choruses at a time, and while one was playing the other would be backstage taking a nip. They were two very colorful gladiators. Often, when Bechet was blowing, he would say, "I'm going to call Goola this time!" Goola was his dog, a big German shepherd. Goola wasn't always there, but he was calling him anyway with a kind of throaty growl.

Call was very important in that kind of music. Today, the music has grown up and become quite scholastic, but this was *au naturel,* close to the primitive, where people send messages in what they play, calling somebody, or making facts and emotions known. Painting a picture, or having a story to go with what you were going to play, was of vital importance in those days. The audience didn't know anything about it, but the cats in the band did.

Most of the time, Bechet played soprano saxophone, but now and then he would take out his clarinet. Although it wasn't really his thing, he had the

Sidney Bechet

world's greatest wood tone on that instrument. You don't hear that wood in what most clarinetists play today, but I love it—and miss it.

Bechet was never a very outgoing man, yet he took Johnny Hodges under his arm and taught him everything. Johnny's approach to saxophone was very much in that direction, anyway, so it was easy for him to absorb from Bechet, whom he loved and really idolized.

Speaking of those two reminds me of when I was writing *The New Orleans Suite* in 1970. After the premiere in New Orleans, I added four portraits, of Bechet, Louis Armstrong, Mahalia Jackson, and Wellman Braud. I was writing the portrait of Bechet for Johnny Hodges to solo on when a phone call announced that Johnny had just died of a heart attack during a visit to the dentist.

FLETCHER HENDERSON

When I was just a scuffling, little piano player around Washington, I was playing in a joint called Jack's on Seventh Street and Fletcher Henderson came in with Hawk (Coleman Hawkins). They were playing in the city with Bessie Smith, and they came by to visit. I was honored to have these celebrities with me, and everything was going along fine until a fight started in the place. It began with a little throwing of things, and ended up with gun shooting and Fletcher, Hawk, and me under the bandstand. I don't remember any more about our first meeting.

Fletcher was a big inspiration to me. His was the band I always wanted mine to sound like when I got ready to have a big band, and that's what we tried to achieve the first chance we had with that many musicians. Obviously, a lot of other musicians wanted the same thing, and when Benny Goodman was ready for a big band, he sent for Fletcher Henderson to do his arrangements. That was consistent with good taste, and I am always glad to be identified with those who have good taste.

Another time I ran into Fletcher was one Sunday out in Salt Lake City. Fletcher and his kid brother, Horace, had a place out on the highway, a kind of roadhouse. We were playing in the area, and they came to see us. "Come on over," they said, "we're going to cook dinner for you today."

I was busy, locked up in the room writing *The Liberian Suite,* and they kept calling all day long. So finally, when I got through late at night, I went out there, and we had dinner and fun. Fletcher was a wonderful guy and an important influence. I was *there* when he won the famous battle of Big Bands with King Oliver at the Savoy on another Sunday night. When the King of the Gladiators is getting ready to square off on a night like that, you get off if you're not already off! You blow your gig that night. It's more important to be there. The kid on the corner knows that it is always more important to know what's happening than it is to make a living!

OTTO HARDWICK

Otto Hardwick was known as the little brother of John Hardwick in Washington, D.C., during the '20s. I think John played banjo, and he always felt responsible for watching over him. Otto was considered to be a nice kid, and to have music potential. I forget exactly when, but on one of those occasions when the more mature saxophone players were all engaged, we turned to him. Of course, his first appearance was a real surprise to all of us. He read very well and played even better, so he was no longer looked on as too young to be called for a job, and he was called on more and more often. I had the good fortune to be a friend of his, so he gradually became like my first chair saxophone around Washington. And then one day he, Sonny Greer, and I came to New York. He was with us at the beginning of our engagement at Barron's.

Otto, or "Toby" as he liked to be called, was Mr. C Melody himself, and nobody ever quite captured the overall illusion of his sound. His tone was one of my first outstanding sound identities. The C melody saxophone was his instrument, but later he added the baritone saxophone to his accessories. He was one of the first, if not *the* first, to do so, and he was an inspiration to other baritone players, notably Harry Carney, who was soon to be acknowledged as the symbol of the baritone saxophone. When Harry heard Toby play baritone, he ran, not walked, to the nearest baritone saxophone, went to work mastering it, and has never looked back.

Toby never went too far out of his way for anything good or bad. I think he felt that if he just sat patiently, what was good for him would fall into his lap. He loved everybody and hated nobody. His father and mother were wonderful people, and they owned property in Maryland, so Toby's background was solid and he never felt insecure, a wonderful feeling for any human being.

When Toby left New York and went back to Washington, it was not because he could not get a job, but to be with and look out for his people. He had no complexes. I always say that when an artist puts down his instrument, on which he has acquired great skill, to take on a relatively menial job, he is a man of unusual quality. Toby was a big man, just like a friend of mine in Chicago, Jimmy Hilt, who was once a millionaire and in a boss situation. When his luck changed, and he lost everything, he did not complain and blame everybody else, but took it in stride with grace and authority, and became a captain of waiters in a big hotel. Toby had the same spirit, and it is clear there are not many of that caliber around, so it is easy to miss him now. I feel certain the just God will reward him. People all over the world still ask me, "What ever happened to Otto Hardwick?" It is impossible to evalute his importance in the establishment of our position in the music world. His record performances, for instance, were unique and unparalleled. God bless Otto Hardwick.

SONNY GREER

Sonny Greer was born in Long Branch, New Jersey. His father was an electrical engineer, and he was raised in a fine home. He had a brother and two sisters, and his mother's major aim in life was to raise her children properly. It was a wonderfully warm home, the food was wonderful, and I was like a member of the family. Instead of following in his father's footsteps, Greer apparently wasted his time banging on his mother's pots and pans, and he developed his own style of drumming from those bim-banging beginnings. Ironically, the pots-and-pans bit prepared him for the career he was eventually to pursue as a drummer. A natural supporting artist with his pots and pans, he kept time with horses trotting, people sweeping, and people digging ditches. He didn't indulge in such activities himself, but he kept time with those who did. He duelled and duetted with everything from clanging bells to windshield wipers, and he dug the value of teamwork all the way back. By adding his own embellishments, he developed what was later to be his *forte*. Everything in his life, I think, has always been done in a happy way, even though not according to Hoyle.

Sonny Greer, 1940: "His resources unlimited, he's good for no amount."

Elmer Snowden

Every young drummer who ever saw Sonny Greer in his heyday was awed and inspired by his equipment, and the pros still talk about it. There were chimes, gongs, tympani, cymbals it seemed by the dozen, tom-toms, snare drums, and bass drums, enough to equip the whole percussion section of a symphony. It was not only ornamental, for he used to get some crazy effects.

Greer was not the world's best reader of music, but he was the world's best percussionist reactor. When he heard a ping he responded with the most apropos pong. Any tune he was backing up had the benefit of rhythmic ornamentation that was sometimes unbelievable. And he used to look like a high priest, or a king on a throne, 'way up above everybody, with all his gold accessories around him, all there was room for on the stand!

Sonny Greer is an endless story, full of sparkles, *double entendres,* and belly laughs. Every now and then he would deliver a really sage line with all the dragging weight of expectancy that is usual when an oracle speaks. "Bread cast upon the sea comes back buttered toast," is one I hope to use in my next sacred concert.

When we were working at the M-G-M studios in Culver City, making *A Day at the Races* with the Marx Brothers, I got some extra work. It was to do a commercial. Ivie Anderson was with us, but Sonny Greer, who had always been our male vocalist, was given the responsibility of reading or singing the words. The name of the product was M.J.B. Coffee, and every time he got to it he would say M-G-M. That was one commercial we all but blew.

Greer is, always was, and I am sure always will be an optimist. "If there are three people going that way, and only two people this way, then there must be more happening that way than this way, so I'm going that way too." Always, that has been a part of his philosophy—at any time of the day or night.

ELMER SNOWDEN

When Elmer Snowden came to Washington in Joe Rochester's band, all the banjo and banjorine players were playing everything right, right on the nose, according to the city's disciplinary climate. It seemed that he was not playing according to Hoyle, yet he had something extra going on that really upset everybody in Washington—musicians and audience. He had a flair for soul, plus ragtime, and a jumping thing that tore us all up. He immediately became the No. 1 Banjorine Player, and he had a tremendous influence on all the local banjorinists, and a kind of fusion resulted that was really compelling, for he, too, got something out of their style. By combining his with theirs, he remained No. 1 until we went to New York. Before that happened, he had taken Sterling Conaway's place in a trio with Sonny Greer and me, and he later played with us at Barron's and at the Kentucky Club.

ARTHUR WHETSOL

Arthur Whetsol, the son of a Seventh-Day Adventist minister, was born in Punta Gorda, Florida, and raised in Washington, D.C. He came with us on our first venture to the main drag, and played at Barron's, the Kentucky Club, and the Cotton Club in New York. A great organization man, he would speak up in a minute on the subject of propriety, clean appearance, and reliability. If and when any member of our band made an error in grammar, he was quick to correct him. He was aware of all the Negro individuals who were contributing to the cause by *commanding respect*. He knew about all the Negro colleges, and he also knew all the principal scholastic and athletic leaders personally.

As a trumpet player, he had a tonal personality that has never really been duplicated. Sweet, but not syrupy, nor schmaltzy, nor surrealistic, it had a superiority of extrasensory dimensions. Both as a soloist and from the point of view of teamwork, he was a fine musician. Everything with him had to be of the best, and he was one of the really good readers.

He left us to go back to Howard University to study medicine. Although he loved his music, I think he felt called upon to pursue a career that was considered, in those days, more respectable. Bubber Miley took his place, but he returned to the band several times during summer vacations. As the band grew bigger, we used first two, and then three trumpets, so there was always a chair for Arthur Whetsol until he had to retire because of illness in 1937. He was one of those who could have had the shirt off my back had he needed it. He left behind an echo of aural charisma that I can still hear.

Los Angeles, August 1966: Brass section at private recording session with Juan Tizol sitting in. Trombones, left to right: Lawrence Brown, Chuck Connors, Buster Cooper, Juan Tizol. Trumpets, left to right: Cat Anderson, Mercer Ellington, Herbie Jones, Cootie Williams

JUAN TIZOL

Juan Tizol was born in San Juan, Puerto Rico, and suitably named after the saint, San Juan. He studied and mastered every instrument in the orchestra, but finally settled down to specialize on the valve trombone. He came to Washington, D.C., about 1920 in Marie Lucas' orchestra, and played the Howard Theatre and the T.O.B.A. circuit. When we decided to add a valve trombone,

55

Whetsol took the responsibility of convincing him to come and join us at the Cotton Club in 1929. He was a tremendous asset to our band, managed his finances well, and in 1941 bought some property in Los Angeles which he later sold at a handsome profit.

Soon he wanted to stay in Los Angeles, and everything went well until his wife, Rosebud—a Washington girl and a splendid cook—got sick. When it became really serious, and she was hospitalized, he buried his horn in a closet and stayed home rather than gamble on playing his music and running the risk of losing his wife. He could watch over her and be at her side whenever she might need help, or a word of prayer, or someone to call the doctor.

Tizol is a very big man, a very unselfish man, and one of the finest musicians I've ever known. He and Rosebud are very close, and I love them both. When I happened to be out there, and had some problems myself, I'd go visit, and they would feed me some of their good cooking and words of encouragement. I always left feeling better than when I went.

My mother always told me not to worry and, as I've said, there always seems to be someone on hand to point out the way for me to go. When I got to the next corner, there would be someone else standing there to tell me where to go. And this is how my whole life has been all along.

One of the major examples of this was when Johnny Hodges, Lawrence Brown, and Sonny Greer all left the band at one time in 1951. Soon after that I was in Los Angeles, and Juan Tizol and his wife, Rosebud, called and said, "Come on over to the house to dinner." They were ready to show me which way to go. "All you've got to do," Tizol said, "is to say the word, and take Louis Bellson, Willie Smith, and me, and we'll leave Harry James and come with you." This was the big solution.

Of course, I was wondering who this was going to affect and who was going to be offended, because I never made a practice of taking people out of the other bands, but this was a kind of dire emergency. The whole thing actually sounded too good to be true and it deserved much consideration. If I had been talking to people I didn't know, I would have thought there was a big swindle involved, but I knew Tizol and Rosebud so well. Quite apart from having Tizol back, Willie Smith was the world's greatest first alto man, and everybody was jumping up and saying, "Louis Bellson— there's no drummer like him!" So I told Tizol, "That's crazy, man!" And we did it, and it paid off.

It was a sensation in the whole music world, and it resulted in very positive publicity. Willie Smith, of course, gave an entirely different character to the color of the sax section. And Louis Bellson brought real precision into the band. Then, naturally, it made me happy to have Tizol's wonderful valve trombone back again with its warmth and melody. It was another one of those important intersections in my life.

What made it not too unethical to take these guys out of Harry's band was the fact that he had taken Tizol out of my band not so long before. I felt he would understand.

JERRY RHEA

Jerry Rhea was a dear friend who first came into the picture in Washington, where he was a T Street brother. He knew me well and would go to any length to support me. He was always there as witness or evidence, to be leaned on in any of my weakened positions, to defend me musically or personally, to provide inspiration with his "Baby, go! Baby, go!" or to hesitate in disagreement with what I might have said that was not fitting. He was there to stop me from doing something that could be harmful to me or someone we both liked, loved, or considered too precious to be without protection. Jerry had something intangible as a friend. He was a rare species of human being. He would have made a good judge. He was a man of love and love of God.

He went to New York before I did, so when I got ready to go he had the same attitude as Sonny Greer: "Oh, well, I'll take you kids up to the big city and let you look around." Although he was a drummer, he was apt to say he wasn't a musician, but he served the same muse. He was a patron, and he did many different things for a living. He tried to sing once, in a trio I had at the Cotton Club—he, Bobby Sawyer, and Benny Paine. They didn't sing *with* me. It was an act that filled a spot up there for some reason or other. Nobody will ever forget Jerry Rhea.

Duke Ellington, ca. 1925

Duke Ellington, 1925

James Edward Ellington, top; Duke Ellington, middle; Ivie Anderson, bottom

Act Two

Night Life

Night Life is cut out of a very luxurious, royal-blue bolt of velvet. It sparkles with jewels, and it sparkles in tingling and tinkling tones. Some of its sparkles are more precious than precious stones; others are just splashes of costume jewelry. Night Life seems to have been born with all of its people in it, the people who had never been babies, but were born *grown,* completely independent. Some of them were wonderful people, and some were just hangers-on of a sort. Some of them experienced untold misfortunes, and some of them were lucky. Some of them glittered in Night Life even more brightly than their names on the marquees. Some played sure things, others were inclined to gamble. There were a few hustlers, who depended upon finding suckers for survival. And there were some who were too wise to hustle, who only wanted to have enough money to be able to afford to be a sucker. Night Life had a song and a dance. Night Life was New York, Chicago, San Francisco, Paris, Berlin; uptown, downtown; Harlem, out South; anywhere where they wore that gorgeous velvet mantle.

But something seems to have happened to Night Life. The South Side is no longer self-supporting. Broadway is a one-way street, and they've illegalized the whorehouses in Paris. And so what have you got? Copenhagen? Nagoya looks like Rush Street on Saturday night, all night, every night. The Night Life hustler has gone, but he left his offspring with us. For example: a very good, reputable hotel has an ice machine within convenient reach of all its tenants, one or two machines on each floor. The ice, of course, is free, but you have to call room service to get a paper bucket to carry the ice to your room. This is fine, but you just couldn't have a man come all the way up from the kitchen, or wherever he is, and make that long trip just to bring you a paper bucket without the consideration of some sort of gratuity. Now could you? Of course not. So why make it appear that the customer is getting something free, when actually he is not? Well, that is a hustle.

I've worked nightspots ever since the beginning of my piano-plunking career, but I'm proud to say that I've never hustled a man. Back in the old days when I first came to New York, I worked at Barron's (Barron Wilkins' joint was at 134th Street and Seventh Avenue, and it was considered absolutely the *top* spot in Harlem), where they catered to big spenders, gamblers, sportsmen, and women, all at the peak of their various professions. People would come in who would ask for change for a C-note in half-dollar pieces. At the end of a song, they would toss the two hundred four-bit pieces up in the air, so that they would fall on the dance floor and make a jingling fanfare for the prosperity of our tomorrow. The singers—four of them, including Bricktop —would gather up the money, and another hundred-dollar bill would be changed, and this action would go jingling deep into the night. At the end of the evening, at 4 A.M. or maybe 6, when our bountiful patron thought we had had enough setting-up exercises picking up halves, he would graciously thank us and wish us good luck. With our "See you soon again, baby," we looked forward to, and wished for, his good health and happy return.

Bricktop, incidentally, knew us in Washington, D.C. She had worked with us in the Oriental Gardens, at Ninth and R streets, N.W., a place owned by Louis Thomas, one of my original employers. Bricktop thought we were very nice kids. There were five of us: Sonny Greer, Elmer Snowden, Arthur Whetsol, Otto Hardwick, and myself. When she heard we were unemployed in New York, she insisted that Barron hire us immediately, and that he did. Mr. Barron Wilkins was a beautiful man. He had lots of money, but he never hustled a customer. Of course, that was the general spirit of those times. People in that life did not so readily underestimate others, and for young kids like us, they had many suggestions for ways to get along in the world.

I shall never forget Bricktop's speech. "You know that you kids are making your living on tips," she said. (The salary was fifty dollars a week, but tips at around a thousand dollars a night, split nine ways, averaged over a C-note a day for each person.) "Always remember it," she continued, "and always be generous when tipping, because the man who depends mostly upon tips for a living is one of us. And our people are always generous when we tip."

New York City

New York City Ditty,
Song of the City
Win or lose,
Laughs or blues,
When you get down
To the nitty-gritty,
New York City Ditty
Comes on like Pretty!

New York is a dream of a song, a feeling of aliveness, a rush and flow of vitality that pulses like the giant heartbeat of all humanity. The whole world revolves around New York, especially my world. Very little happens anywhere unless someone in New York presses a button!

New York is its people, and its people are *the city*. Among its crowds, along its streets, and in its high-piled buildings can be found every mood, sight, and sound, every custom, thought, and tradition, every color, flavor, religion, and culture of the entire earth. It is as if each of the world's greatest chefs had sent a pinch of his nation's most distinctive flavoring to contribute to the richness of taste of this great savory *pot au feu* called New York.

The miracle of the city is that this concoction, with its multitude of dissimilar ingredients, can sometimes come to the boil, and sometimes simmer away contentedly on the back of the stove. Since it is at the mercy of so many cooks, it is often stirred up, and, too often, of late, over-seasoned by some heavy-handed pepper wielders. Yet this gorgeously aromatic pot never burns or sticks to the bottom! Instead, New York presents itself as a proper feast to each human being of healthy appetite who hungers for soul food. Whether his needs are nutritional or merely "gourmet," the hungry one is fed, for in New York it is all there on the menu, that something to satisfy every taste: exotic, traditional, or adventuresome. Perhaps it is at this very moment of finding his soul food listed on the menu that the next New Yorker is born. For the "real New Yorker" is not always born in New York, you know. He becomes one at the very instant when he discovers that his own ingredients are completely compatible with the city's soups and salads.

I am that kind of New Yorker, for I was born in Washington, D.C. And if I am asked to describe New York, I must think in musical terms, because New York is people, and that is what music is all about. This incredible city embraces all humanity within its structure, whether resident or visitor, and joins each new heartbeat with her own throbbing pulse. For personified, New York is a woman, and as such she is a little of everything. Certainly, she is a sophisticate. Sometimes she is a lady of the evening. To her cosmopolitan visitors, she is always a gracious hostess deferential to their differing points of view. And like a true Earth Mother, she rests but never sleeps. She is the last to retire at night and the first to rise with each new day, for she suffers from an exhaustingly active energy called Anticipation!

In his ideal image, the real New Yorker is seen at the newstand after midnight with the *News* under his arm, but it is also considered extremely prestigious to be seen reading the *Times* on the subway in the morning. On his way home from work in the later afternoon, always with the *Post* in his pocket, the New Yorker looks as though he has been some place, and knows it.

It is impossible to enter New York without feeling that something wonderful is about to happen. Whether you arrive by plane, ship, train, car or bus, bridge or tunnel, you feel the immediate excitement of starshine. For to this great city come the world's Beautiful People; men of wisdom and good intent; people of cultures older than our own, with highly cultivated tastes; creative geniuses in all fields of endeavor; exquisite women of fashion; great ladies of all ages, whose beauty lies in their genuineness; and all are essential parts of the melody line in this dream of a song that is New York. This is a city of talented performance. Everyone in New York is a performer, down to the most casual visitor. Perhaps Shakespeare had a vision of Manhattan in mind when he wrote that "all the world's a stage," for most certainly we all get caught up in the plot!

There is a kind of highly contagious fever of backstage communication about New York. The opportunities to rub elbows with the "stars" are so many and frequent that a little of that glamour dust of starshine clings to everybody. There are almost no "bit players" on Manhattan Island. Everybody is a star. If this statement seems extravagant, then just consider the taxi driver. No greater Solon exists than the New York cabbie. He knows something about everything, and his is the only gossip column worth reading. He is part of the pulse of the people, of the beat and throb of the city, for he knows, he really *knows* what is happening in New York, from his own point of view and everyone else's. He speaks a "people" wisdom and at the heart of this great cosmopolitan city is a vital, small-town "peopleness." Have you ever been in New York during a disaster or a blizzard? It becomes the friendliest place in the world! That blew fuse, the black-out, was the friendliest of all, because nine months later the stork flew in over the horizon with a bumper crop of babies.

So amid all her tickertape and traffic, New York is the dream of a song. New York is a place where the rich walk, the poor drive Cadillacs, and beggars die of malnutrition with thousands of dollars hidden in their mattresses.

In 1972, I was honored by being appointed official host of New York's Summer Festival. Gloria Swanson was its hostess and Bernadette Allen its Queen. These charming associates made the whole thing a delightful experience, and it was such an inspiration that I came up with a new number, for which I wrote these lyrics:

> *New York, New York!*
> *New York, New York!*
> *New York is a summer festival!*
>
> *New York is a song,*
> *New York is a dance,*
> *New York is a summer, fall, winter, spring,*
> *Summer romance!*
>
> *Subway flights . . .*
> *Broadway brights . . .*
> *Lights and sights . . .*
> *A million delights.*
>
> *Thrill-filled thrill,*
> *Sugar Hill still*
> *Washington Heights . . .*
>
> *New York is a glitter,*
> *New York is a glamour,*
> *New York is a sun-swept, star-lit, moonshine,*
> *Super grand-slammer!*

New York, New York!
New York, New York!
New York is a summer festival,
And it's best of all,
Lovers' festival,
Summer festival,
Dancing, romancing . . .
NEW YORK!

The Big Apple

Fats Waller came to Washington in the spring of 1923 and played for Clarence Robinson in a burlesque show at the Gaiety Theatre. Sonny Greer, Toby Hardwick, and I had gotten to know him well when we were in New York with Sweatman, so now we had a chummy exchange.

"I'm quitting next week," Fats said. "Why don't you all come up to New York and take the job? I'll tell 'em about you."

We jumped at the opportunity and were all on edge until the time came to go. Sonny and Toby went ahead of me by a few days. When I called to find out if everything was straight, they assured me that it was.

"Everything's okay," they said. "Don't worry about nothin', man."

Because I had a gig waiting for me, I felt entitled to travel in style. I hopped a train, took a parlor car, ate a big, expensive dinner in the diner, and got a cab at Pennsylvania Station to take me uptown. With these expenses, and tips in proportion, I had spent all my money by the time I reached 129th Street.

Sonny Greer was waiting, and the first thing he said as he opened the cab door for me was, "Hey, Duke, buddy, give us something! We are all busted and waiting for you to relieve the situation." By "something," he meant money, but it was too late.

"Sorry, I'm broke too," I said. "I blew it all on the trip up from Washington."

Everything had gone wrong, and there was no job. Yet there were friends waiting to help us and to show me the way. Willie "The Lion" Smith was one of them, and Freddie Guy used to let us sit in for him at the Orient and, most important, split the tips.

It was a very hot summer, and I remember how we had to ride that subway every morning to get downtown to audition in the Strand Building, where nearly all the agents seemed to be. We had no luck there and it was Bricktop, the famous Bricktop (Ada Smith), who finally pulled us out of the hole we were in.

The Washingtonians were different in several ways. We paid quite a lot of attention to our appearance, and if any one of us came in dressed improperly Whetsol would flick his cigarette ash in a certain way, or pull down the lower lid of his right eye with his forefinger and stare at the offending party. Whetsol was our first unofficial disciplinarian, and he carried himself with dignity befitting a medical student of lofty ambitions. His tonal character, fragile and genteel, was an important element in our music. As a result of playing all those society dances in Washington, we had learned to play softly, what is sometimes known as under-conversation music. Toby also contributed much to this by playing sweet and straight on his C-melody saxophone. A lot of chicks wanted to mother him, and every now and then he would submit, so over the years he was in and out of the band rather unpredictably. Elmer Snowden was the businessman of the group, and eventually he got so good at business that he went his way, and we had to get Freddie Guy to take his place.

During my first few months in New York, I found out that anybody was eligible to take songs into the music publishers on Broadway. So I joined the parade and teamed up with Joe Trent, a nice guy who was familiar with the routines of the publishing world. He liked my music and he was a good lyricist, so he took my hand and guided me around Broadway. We wrote several songs together and auditioned every day in one publisher's office or another and, as was normal, had practically no success, until one day when we demonstrated a song for Fred Fisher. He was not only a publisher, but a wonderful song writer himself. He wrote "Chicago," and he was always an inspiration to me.

"I like it," he said, after listening to our song. "I'll take it."

"You know, of course, that we want a fifty-dollar advance," Joe said.

"Okay," Fred Fisher replied. "Give me a lead sheet and I'll sign the contract."

"Give the man a lead sheet," Joe said, turning to me.

I had never made a lead sheet before, nor tried to write music of any kind, but it was 4:30 P.M. and I knew the checkbook would be closed at five. So, in spite of ten pianos banging away in ten different booths, I sat down and made a lead sheet. It was satisfactory. We got the money, split it, and then split the scene. I had broken the ice and at the same time gotten hooked on writing music. (Write on!) The next day, and for many to follow, we were back in our old rut—peddling songs and failing to find any buyers.

One day Joe Trent came running up to me on Broadway. He had a big proposition and there was urgency in his voice.

"Tonight we've got to write a show," he said. *"Tonight!"*

Being dumb, and not knowing any better, I sat down that evening and wrote a show. How was I to know that composers had to go up in the mountains, or to the seashore, to commune with the muses for six months in order to write a show. The next day we played and demonstrated our show for Jack Robbins, who liked it and said he would take it.

"You know we have to get five hundred dollars in advance," Joe said.

"Okay," Robbins said. "Tomorrow."

The true story behind this is that Jack Robbins pawned his wife's engagement ring to give us our five-hundred-dollar advance. The show, *Chocolate Kiddies,* went into rehearsal, after which it went to Germany, where it played for two years in the Berlin Wintergarten. Jack returned to the U.S.A. a millionaire, a lord of music. He published several of my piano solos around that time, such as "Rhapsody Junior" and "Bird of Paradise," which Jimmie Lunceford later recorded after Ed Wilcox and Eddie Durham had orchestrated them.

However, in 1923 we were not exactly thinking in terms of millions, although the engagement at Barron's had brought us to the attention of a lot of people prominent in show business. In the fall of that year we went to the Hollywood Club downtown, at Forty-ninth and Broadway. After the first of several fires, it became the Kentucky Club, and we stayed there four years. It was a good place for us to be, because it stayed open all night and became a rendezvous for all the big stars and musicians on Broadway after they got through working. Paul Whiteman came often, and he always showed his appreciation by laying a big fifty-dollar bill on us.

It was at the Kentucky Club that our music acquired new colors and characteristics. First we added Charlie Irvis, a trombone player nicknamed "Plug" because of the unusual mute he used. Then, when Artie Whetsol went back to Washington to continue his studies at Howard University, we got Bubber Miley, the epitome of soul and a master with the plunger mute. After Irvis left to join Charlie Johnson's band, Joe "Tricky Sam" Nanton came in, and he and Bubber became a great team, working together hand in glove.

71

They made a fine art out of what became known as jungle style, establishing a tradition that we still maintain today.

Sonny Greer was in his element here, and he was known as The Sweet-Singing Drummer in those days. After the band had played the show twice—usually at midnight and 2 A.M.—as well as some dance music, I would send them home and Sonny and I would work the floor. I had one of those little studio upright pianos on wheels that you could push around from table to table, and Sonny would carry his sticks and sing. Answering requests, we sang anything and everything—pop songs, jazz songs, dirty songs, torch songs, Jewish songs. Sometimes, the customer would respond by throwing twenty-dollar bills away from him as though they were on fire. When business was slow, we'd sing "My Buddy." That was the favorite song of the boss, Leo Bernstein, and when we laid that on him he was expected to throw down some bills too.

Sonny always had an eye on the entrance stairway. (The Kentucky Club was a downstairs joint.) He was always ready to give a prosperous-looking customer a big hello, and if he could catch him as he came in, he would introduce him to the manager. "This is my *man*," he would say. "Take care of him!" More than likely the guy would slip him a sawbuck.

We might leave the club with a hundred dollars each in our pockets, but by the time we got home we would have blown it all, because we had to go from joint to joint to be received, and to find out what was happening. When we walked into one of those after-hours joints, all the chicks would stand up and holler, "Sonny, baby!" When he heard those broads holler, his feet would leave the ground, and he'd say, "Give everybody in the house a drink!"

My initial encounter with Irving Mills occurred during my first six months in New York. He was known as the last resort for getting some money by those who had been peddling songs all day without success. I first heard of him secondhand, and one day I joined a group of five or six songwriters. The personnel varied, but they would get together, each with a lead sheet of what they considered rather ordinary blues under his arm, and head for Mills Music. The procedure, they explained, was to sell those blues outright to Irving Mills for fifteen or twenty dollars. It was very simple—no hassle. Just give him the lead sheet, sign the outright release, pick up the money, and go. This happened nearly every day. I am sure some of them, after many of these visits, sold the same blues turned around. There is no telling or any way of knowing just how many Irving Mills amassed, but it was a good way for us to end the business day. After I was working regularly, those dollars did not mean so much to me, because after working through the night I'd always have a roll to break before I got home.

Later on, Irving Mills recorded one of those blues he had bought, released it, and had a big hit. The irony of it was that the cat who wrote it blew his top, completely forgetting the fact that he had sold this same blues who knows how many times? "The lowdown so-and-so only gave me twenty dollars," he complained.

Years after that, Cootie Williams went down to sell a number, and Irving asked him what it was.

"Just a blues," Cootie answered.

"Oh, no," Mills cried as he hit the ceiling. "I own *all* the blues!"

He used to come to the Kentucky Club often, and one night he said he didn't know what we were doing with our music, but he liked it and would like to record some of it with our band. We jumped at the chance, and this was really the beginning of a long and wonderful association. The procedure was usually the same. "Have four numbers ready for recording at 9 A.M. tomorrow," he'd say. We'd do that, and he liked what we did, and interest grew. It was a very good thing for us. He had the contacts, and I liked to write music—and play it, too. The rather short time allotted didn't bother me. Because I loved doing it, I just went ahead and did it. We seemed to be recording once a week, sometimes three or four times a week, sometimes with our regular group, and sometimes with singers or other musicians. It didn't matter which to me, because I was getting my kicks writing and recording, and some of the tunes were beginning to show up well in the sales department. All that activity was good for both Irving Mills and me, because I was in the environment I wanted to live in, recalling some of our old licks and experiments with new ideas and devices. We recorded for almost every existing label under different names: Duke Ellington on Victor, the Jungle Band on Brunswick, the Washingtonians on Harmony, the Whoopee Makers on Perfect, Sonny Greer and His Memphis Men on Columbia, the Harlem Footwarmers on Okeh, and so on. Most of the records were instrumentals, and they sold very well.

An episode from those early years, one that I never forget, is of quite a different kind. It happened in Pittsburgh, where Fletcher Henderson's band and ours were both playing at the same time. Liquor drinking among the musicians was done from the gladiator perspective, in just the same way as

The Washingtonians at Orchard Beach, August 1926. Back row: Rudy Jackson, Percy Glascoe, Fred Guy, Toby Hardwick, Duke Ellington; front row: Sonny Greer, Edgar Sampson, Joe Nanton, Bubber Miley

when they challenged each other on their instruments. There were many who had big reputations, whose status was determined by the amount of liquor they drank, and accordingly there were many contests.

Rex Stewart, who was then with Fletcher, ran into Tricky Sam (Nanton) of our band one afternoon.

"Hey, Tricky," he said, "I hear you can drink some liquor."

"Yeah, and I heard you got that reputation too."

They decided to meet that night after their respective gigs and have it out. I heard about the duel and said I would come along and be there—up on Wiley Avenue at Willie Cleveland's bar—to act as referee. All was agreed, and we three converged on the bar after our gigs.

74

Tricky and Rex shook hands, stood up to the bar, where Rex, with rather sophisticated flair, ordered half a pint of gin. "The same for me," Tricky said. "I'm the referee," I announced, "so I'll take a half pint, too." When served, Rex saluted, Tricky saluted, and then both turned their bottles up and drank them empty. I watched closely to make sure that everything was done according to the imagined rules, and then I drank my half pint.

Now there are certain things a contestant does, and certain things a contestant does not do in bouts of this kind. For instance, after emptying the half pint, the contestant does not make a face, nor does he take a chaser. He smiles cordially and possibly reaches for a cigarette, always maintaining an expression as though he had just had a sarsaparilla. It went on like this all night until nine in the morning when I, the referee, having drunk each time the same amount as the contestants, had both of them in tow, all but carrying them.

There I was with two bombed gladiators on my shoulders to be delivered to two different hotels. Courtesy demanded that Rex be delivered first, and I was staying at the same hotel as Tricky. By the time I got Tricky home, I was exhausted, so I left him at the bottom of the stairs and went up three flights to the floor where the rest of the cats in our band had rooms. When I told them what had happened, and where Tricky was resting, Bubber Miley went and got a fire bucket full of water. You could look over the banister and see Tricky sprawled out at the bottom of the stairs. Bubber leaned over and let the whole bucketful go. The water hit Tricky smash-dash in the face, shocked him awake, and he tried to *swim* out of it!

I don't drink booze any more. I retired undefeated champ about thirty years ago, and now I call myself a "retired juicehead." I drank more booze than anybody ever.

Another incident in the '20s that comes to mind was when we played Newport, Rhode Island, for the very first time, many years before they ever had jazz festivals up there. We had Bubber Miley, Tricky Sam, Toby Hardwick, Mac Shaw on bass, and Sonny Greer, and all we played was "swing soul." A gentleman had been wheel-chaired into the hall, and halfway through the dance he jumped up and started doing his thing! Everybody in the dance hall was quite shocked, because his daughter said her father had not been out of that wheel chair for twelve years.

The next big step was when we went into the Cotton Club on December 4, 1927. We had to audition for this job, but it called for a band of at least eleven pieces, and we had been using only six at the Kentucky Club. At the

The first Cotton Club band, 1927: Duke Ellington, Joe Nanton, Sonny Greer, Bubber Miley, Harry Carney, Rudy Jackson, Fred Guy, Nelson Kincaid, Ellsworth Reynolds

time, I was playing a vaudeville show for Clarence Robinson at Gibson's Standard Theatre on South Street in Philadelphia. The audition was set for noon, but by the time I had scraped up eleven men it was two or three o'clock. We played for them and got the job. The reason for that was that the boss, Harry Block, didn't get there till late either, and didn't hear the others! That's a classic example of being at the right place at the right time with the right thing before the right people.

If you ask Irving Mills, he will most likely confess that he is the man who:
(1) insisted that I make and record only my own music;
(2) got me into the Cotton Club, the RKO Palace, and *The Black and Tan Fantasy* movie;
(3) had big fights with record companies to get the black artist into hitherto all-white catalogs;
(4) fought with the Dillingham executives to have us play in concert with Maurice Chevalier;
(5) achieved our entry into picture houses, which we pioneered for big bands regardless of race;
(6) arranged our interstate tours of the South and Texas in our own Pullman cars;
(7) triumphantly secured my entrance into ASCAP;
(8) took us to Europe in 1933, where we played the London Palladium and met members of the British Royal Family on several occasions.

Irving Mills, in short, was a man with plenty of initiative. He started out singing and plugging songs from nine to five; then he would go to the movies and sing with the slides; and after that he would go to dance halls and sing with a megaphone. As his world expanded, his roles as manager and impresario became more important, but his roots were always in music publishing. He went by ear and vibrations. He could feel a song. He'd take a good lyricist, tell him, "Now this song needs something right here," and the cat would go over it, and it would come out perfect. He was a clever man.

So far as we were concerned, the engagement at the Cotton Club was of the utmost significance, because as a result of its radio wire we were heard nationally and internationally. In 1929 we appeared simultaneously at the Cotton Club and in Florenz Ziegfeld's *Show Girl,* which had a Gershwin score and introduced "An American in Paris" and "Liza." This was valuable in terms of both experience and prestige. The following year, Irving Mills succeeded in arranging for us to accompany Maurice Chevalier at the Fulton Theatre and play a concert selection of our compositions. This was about the only time I ever used a baton! In 1930, too, we went to Hollywood to appear in *Check and Double Check,* a film featuring the then-popular radio team of Amos 'n' Andy. The big song in it was "Three Little Words" by Harry Ruby and Bert Kalmar, but an instrumental of mine called "Ring Dem Bells" also became very popular. It was taken up by other bands, and for a considerable time it was a much-requested item. We hired Cab Calloway's

77

In Hollywood, 1930

band to play for us in the Cotton Club while we were away. We were going out to make some money, and the condition under which we could go was that we paid him.

Later that year, in the fall, we had a six-piece recording date. Mills never lost his liking for the original small-combo sound, even when the big band had made its mark. On this occasion, as usual, the night before was the time for me to write and think music. I already had three tunes and, while waiting for my mother to finish cooking dinner, I began to write a fourth. In fifteen

On the RKO lot for filming *Check and Double Check,* Hollywood, 1930: Joe Nanton, Juan Tizol, trombones; Freddy Jenkins, Cootie Williams, Artie Whetsol, trumpets; Duke Ellington, conductor; Sonny Greer, drums; Fred Guy, banjo; Wellman Braud, bass; Harry Carney, Johnny Hodges, Barney Bigard, reeds

minutes, I wrote the score for "Mood Indigo." We recorded it, and that night at the Cotton Club, when it was almost time for our broadcast, Ted Husing, the announcer, asked, "Duke, what are we going to play tonight?" I told him about the new number, and we played it on the air, six pieces out of the eleven-piece band. The next day, wads of mail came in raving about the new tune, so Irving Mills put a lyric on it, and royalties are still coming in for my evening's work more than forty years later. Husing, incidentally, was a beautiful cat with an up-to-the-minute awareness then known as "hip." He was radio's No. 1 announcer, and he did a great deal for us.

When we had made "Black and Tan Fantasy" with the growl trombone and growl trumpet, there was a sympathetic vibration or mike tone. That was soon after they had first started electrical recording. "Maybe if I spread those notes over a certain distance," I said to myself, "the mike tone will take a specific place or a specific interval in there." It came off, and gave that illusion, because "Mood Indigo"—the way it's done—creates an illusion. To give it a little additional luster for those people who remember it from years ago, we play it with the bass clarinet down at the bottom instead of the ordinary clarinet, and they always feel it is exactly the way it was forty years ago.

The Cotton Club was a classy spot. Impeccable behavior was demanded in the room while the show was on. If someone was talking loud while Leitha Hill, for example, was singing, the waiter would come and touch him on the shoulder. If that didn't do it, the captain would come over and admonish him politely. Then the headwaiter would remind him that he had been cautioned. After that, if the loud talker still continued, somebody would come and throw him out.

The club was upstairs on the second floor of the northeast corner of 142nd Street and Lenox Avenue. Underneath it was what was originally the Douglas Theatre, which later became the Golden Gate Ballroom. The upstairs room had been planned as a dance hall, but for a time the former heavyweight champion, Jack Johnson, had run it as the Club De Luxe. It was a big cabaret in those days, and it would seat four to five hundred people. When a new corporation took it over in the '20s, Lew Leslie was put in charge of producing the shows, and the house band was led by Andy Preer, who died in 1927.

Sunday night in the Cotton Club was *the* night. All the big New York stars in town, no matter where they were playing, showed up at the Cotton Club to take bows. Dan Healy was the man who staged the shows in our time, and on Sunday night he was the m.c. who introduced the stars. Somebody like Sophie Tucker would stand up, and we'd play her song, "Some of These Days" as she made her way up the floor for a bow. It was all done in pretty grand style.

Harlem had a tremendous reputation in those days, and it was a very colorful place. It was an attraction like Chinatown was in San Francisco.

"When you go to New York," people said, "you mustn't miss going to Harlem!" The Cotton Club became famous nationally because of our trans-continental broadcast almost every night. A little later, something similar happened with Fatha Hines at the Grand Terrace in Chicago. But in Harlem, the Cotton Club was the top place to go.

The performers were paid high salaries, and the prices for the customers were high too. They had about twelve dancing girls and eight show girls, and they were all beautiful chicks. They used to dress so well! On Sunday nights, when celebrities filled the joint, they would rush out of the dressing room after the show in all their finery. Every time they went by, the stars and the rich people would be saying, "My, who is *that?*" They were tremendous representatives, and I'm darned if I know what happened to them, because you don't see anybody around like that nowadays. They were absolutely beautiful chicks, but the whole scene seems to have disappeared.

The nucleus of the band was the group I had had at the Kentucky Club. Harry Carney had joined us during the summer, and he went in with us. We also had Ellsworth Reynolds, a violinist who was supposed to be the conductor, but he really wasn't as experienced in show business as we were after playing all those shows downtown in the Kentucky Club. So I started to direct the band from the piano, without baton or any of that stuff, for I understood what they were doing more than anyone else in the band.

The music for the shows was being written by Jimmy McHugh with lyrics by Dorothy Fields. Later came Harold Arlen and that great lyric writer, Ted Koehler. They wrote some wonderful material, but this was show music and mostly popular songs. Sometimes they would use numbers that I wrote, and it would be these we played between shows and on the broadcasts. I wrote "The Mystery Song" for the Step Brothers in rehearsal. It was part of their act, not part of the show. The different acts were presented individually as well as in the ensemble. After the Step Brothers came the Berry Brothers, and later on the Nicholas Brothers.

Sometimes I wonder what my music would sound like today had I not been exposed to the sounds and overall climate created by all the wonderful, and very sensitive and soulful people who were the singers, dancers, musicians, and actors in Harlem when I first came there.

During the prohibition period, you could always buy good whiskey from *some*body in the Cotton Club. They used to have what they called Chicken Cock. It was in a bottle in a can, and the can was sealed. It cost something like ten to fourteen dollars a pint. That was when I used to drink whiskey as though it were water. It seemed so weak to me after the twenty-one-year-old corn we had been accustomed to drinking down in Virginia. That was strong enough to move a train, but I paid no attention to this New York liquor. I just drank it, never got drunk, and nothing ever happened.

The episodes of the gangster era were never a healthy subject for discussion. People would ask me if I knew so-and-so. "Hell, no," I'd answer. "I don't know him." The homicide squad would send for me every few weeks to go down. "Hey, Duke, you didn't know so-and-so, did you?" they would ask. "No," I'd say. But I knew all of them, because a lot of them used to hang out in the Kentucky Club, and by the time I got to the Cotton Club things were really happening! I had some funny experiences in Chicago, too.

It was in that city, when we were playing the Oriental Theatre, that Irving Mills came to me one day with an original idea. He was always reaching toward a higher plateau for our music.

"Tomorrow is a big day," he said. "We premiere a new long work—a rhapsody."

"Really?" I replied. "Okay."

So I went out and wrote *Creole Rhapsody,* and I did so much music for it that we had to cut it up and do two versions. One came out on Brunswick and the other, longer one, on Victor. Irving almost blew his connection at both companies for recording a number that was not only more than three minutes long, but took both sides of the record. That was the seed from which all kinds of extended works and suites later grew.

After getting us into a legitimate Broadway theatre with Maurice Chevalier, Irving Mills was not satisfied until he had us play at the Palace Theatre, which was then a regular showcase for big acts. When we were appearing there, we were doubling at the Cotton Club—and sometimes "tripling" in the record studios.

Irving's next coup was an engagement at the London Palladium, which he arranged in association with the British bandleader, Jack Hylton. The Palladium was then regarded as the Number One variety theatre in the world. We sailed from New York on June 2, 1933, on the *Olympic.* Crossing the Atlantic for the first time was an exciting experience for all of us. There were many delegates aboard from all over the British Commonwealth, and they were going to a big conference in London. We played a concert and made some valuable friends among them.

Duke Ellington and his orchestra arrive at Southampton, England, 1933. Back: Bessie Dudley, Bill Bailey, Sonny Greer, Fred Guy, Harry Carney, Toby Hardwick, Barney Bigard, Spike Hughes, Cootie Williams, Wellman Braud, Johnny Hodges, Joe Nanton, Lawrence Brown, Ivie Anderson. Front: Derby Wilson, Freddy Jenkins, Jack Hylton, Duke Ellington, Irving Mills, Juan Tizol, Artie Whetsol

We had a terrific reception at the Palladium. Ivie Anderson broke it up every time with "Stormy Weather"; Bessie Dudley danced and shook to "Rockin' in Rhythm"; and we played "Ring Dem Bells" and "Three Little Words" to tie up with the Amos 'n' Andy movie. We always got a good response to "Mood Indigo," too. But the "jazz" critics were not satisfied, and we had to give a special concert one Sunday in the largest cinema in Europe, the Trocadero at the Elephant and Castle. It was organized by the *Melody Maker,* a music magazine, and the audience was almost entirely composed of musicians, who came from all over the country. We were to avoid "commercial" offerings on this occasion, and apparently we lived up to expectations, because Spike Hughes, the foremost critic at that time, didn't criticize us at all. Instead, he criticized the audience for applauding at the end of solos in the middle of the numbers! That's how serious it was.

We were absolutely amazed by how well informed people were in Britain about us and our records. They had magazines and reviews far ahead of what we had here, and everywhere we went we were confronted with facts we had forgotten, and questions we couldn't always answer. Nevertheless, the esteem our music was held in was very gratifying. A broadcast we did for the B.B.C. provoked a lot of comment, most of it favorable. Constant Lambert, the most distinguished British composer of that period, had written an appreciation of some of our early records years before. Now his beautiful Eurasian wife inspired a new composition when she referred to "Mood Indigo" as "Rude Interlude." I guess that had something to do with my American accent!

Lord Beaverbrook, who owned one of the most important London newspapers, threw a big party to which the Prince of Wales and the Duke of Kent were invited. We were invited too, and Jack Hylton's Empress Club band played until we got through at the Palladium. We arrived about midnight, along with Lord Beaverbrook's daughter and the younger set. It was all very colorful and splendid. Members of the nobility, members of Parliament, and delegates to the imperial conferences, all in formal dress, mingled happily. There was a generous buffet, and the champagne flowed freely.

Prince George, the Duke of Kent, requested "Swampy River," a piano solo I had a hard time remembering, but I was flattered, especially to have him leaning over the piano as I played it.

Later, the Prince of Wales had some kind words to say about us. When he suggested we have a drink together, I was surprised to find he was drinking gin. I had always thought gin rather a low kind of drink, but from that time on I decided it was rather grand. He liked to play drums, so he paid Sonny Greer a lot of attention, too. This is how Sonny remembers the evening:

"As soon as we had got the band set up, the Prince of Wales came over and sat down beside me Indian fashion. He said he knew how to play drums, so I said, 'Go ahead!' He played a simple Charleston beat, and he stayed right by me and the drums through most of the evening. People kept coming up and calling him 'Your Highness,' but he wouldn't move. We both began to get high on whatever it was we were drinking. He was calling me 'Sonny' and I was calling him 'The Wale.'"

I think the Prince of Wales really did like us, because he came to hear us again in Liverpool, when he was up in that area for the races at Aintree. He was loved by the day people and the night people, the rich and the poor, the celebrities and the nonentities: he was truly the Billy Strayhorn of crown princes. Sonny Greer always tells another story about when we were in Paris, and I hope I will not be thought immodest for including it here.

"We were playing a concert at the Salle Pleyel," he says. "During the half-hour intermission, they had a buffet table set up backstage with all kinds of food and drink. The aristocracy all came back to see Duke, and during this intermission a duchess lost a big diamond ring. Everybody stopped eating and drinking to look for it. After about ten minutes, when it was still not found, she told everybody to forget it. 'I can always get diamonds,' she said, 'but how often can I get a Duke Ellington?'"

The atmosphere in Europe, the friendship, and the serious interest in our music shown by critics and musicians of all kinds put new spirit into us, and we sailed home on the *Majestic* in a glow that was only partly due to cognac and champagne.

On our return, we played the Chicago Theatre during the World's Fair of 1933–34 where Sally Rand was just getting started on her road to fame, and then went down to Dallas. Now I had always resisted propositions to tour the South, but Irving Mills came up with an attractive offer to play the Interstate Circuit of theatres and picture houses all through Texas. I still had my British accent, and it showed to the Texans, but they were very nice about it, and did not let on whether they thought it natural gas or put on. It didn't last long, anyway, for the Texas way of speaking came upon me through natural absorption. I had had experience of traveling before but the Texas thing was bigger, broader, and a little more flamboyant. So in a few days I was together with the people, and down, as we say, and sounding like a Texan.

We played four shows a day, and dances after the theatre several times a week. The people had obviously been waiting for us. We made a lot of friends down there, and the climate and environment were conducive to the kind of musical dreaming I most enjoy. After that, we made yearly tours in the southern part of the country, spreading out to include Oklahoma, Louisiana, Alabama, Georgia, North and South Carolina. In order to avoid problems, we used to charter two Pullman sleeping cars and a seventy-foot baggage car. Everywhere we went in the South, we lived in them. On arrival in a city, the cars were parked on a convenient track, and connections made for water, steam, sanitation, and ice. This was our home away from home. Many observers would say, "Why, that's the way the President travels!" It automatically gained us respect from the natives, and removed the threat and anticipation of trouble. When we wanted taxis, there was no problem. We simply asked the station manager to send us six, seven, or however many we wanted. And when we were rolling, of course, we had dining-car and room service.

In 1935, on one of these one-nighter tours of the South, after I lost my beautiful mother, I found the mental isolation to reflect on the past. It was all caught up in the rhythm and motion of the train dashing through the South, and it gave me something to say that I could never have found words for. I reflected, and I wrote music, and it came out as *Reminiscing in Tempo,* which eventually ran to four record sides, two more than *Creole Rhapsody.* This meant that Irving Mills had twice as much trouble with the record companies, who threatened to throw us out of the catalog! That was unimportant to me, because I had written my statement. Hearing it constituted my total reward, and in it was a detailed account of my aloneness after losing my mother:

Dangling out there somewhere in a wilderness of the unknown, with no desire for adventure, where things and creatures that I neither saw nor heard were moving around . . . My ambition was dribbling away. Soon there would be nothing. I was not sure where I was. After my mother passed, there was really nothing, and my sparkling parade was probably at an end . . .

Every page of that particular manuscript was dotted with smears and unshapely marks caused by tears that had fallen. I would sit and gaze into space, pat my foot, and say to myself, "Now, Edward, you know she would not want you to disintegrate, to collapse into the past, into your loss, into lengthy negation or destruction. She did not spend all the first part of your life preparing you for this negative attitude." I believed I could hear the words, her words, and slowly—but never completely—I really did straighten up.

Earlier that year, when we were in Durham, North Carolina, Ed Merritt had a party for us, after a dance one night, up in the North Carolina Mutual Building. There were two girls I knew from before, and who had had a falling out with each other, because one had taken the other's boy friend. So I sat the girls one on each side of me, played piano as a sort of peacemaker, and dedicated a new song to them. They loved it, hummed it together, and for a moment everything was all right. Later, it was entitled "In a Sentimental Mood."

Another hit, "Solitude," had come about in somewhat the same way as "Mood Indigo." We had arrived in a Chicago recording studio in September 1934, in the same situation, with three numbers ready and a fourth needed. The band ahead of us went into overtime, which gave me an opportunity to do my fourth number. So, standing up, leaning against the studio's glass enclosure, I wrote the score of "Solitude" in twenty minutes. After we played and recorded it the first time, I noted that everybody in the studio was moved emotionally. Even the engineer had a tear in his eye.

"What's the title?" somebody asked.

" 'Solitude,' " answered Artie Whetsol, who had played so soulfully on it.

In 1936 we played two weeks at the Texas Centennial, a wonderful exposition with exhibits representative of the accomplishments of *all* the people of Texas. I was particularly impressed by the Negro building, and its real credits and acknowledgments. I was honored with a Certificate of Accomplishment, and I was very proud of it, because it was not awarded on a segregated basis. Texas, they said, was Western, not Southern.

We went back to the Cotton Club in 1937, and by then it had moved downtown to Broadway and Forty-eighth Street. "Caravan" was our big number that year. Juan Tizol's first strain and that Puerto Rican influence gave us a new dimension. In later years there were two other hit versions of "Caravan," by first Billy Eckstine and then Ralph Marterie's band out of Chicago. In each case, "Caravan" was the launching pad and vehicle to flights of popularity on the national and world charts.

Irving Mills had set up his own recording company at the end of 1936, and we began recording for both his labels, the big band on Master and the small groups on Variety. British bands, recorded in London, always seemed to have a special kind of resonance and echo, and Irving was attracted by this. One day, when we were recording a new tune called "Empty Ballroom Blues," we decided to try to get this effect. So he, we, and the engineers all began experimenting. Before the session was finished, we had a microphone put in the men's john, and there we found the effect we wanted! It was the first Echo Chamber, I think, and it has become a major recording device since then. I wonder who ever got the registered patent rights on that idea.

We were back downtown at the Cotton Club again in 1938, but this time

Henry Nemo and I wrote the *Cotton Club Revue*. We had a wonderful cast and it was a fine production. The score included "If You Were in My Place," "I'm Slapping Seventh Avenue with the Sole of My Shoe," and "The Skrontch." "I Let a Song Go Out of My Heart," written in a little Memphis hotel, was originally in the show, but Irving Mills decided it should come out and be replaced by something that had to do with Hawaii. So Nemo and I wrote "Swingtime in Honolulu." But the band played "I Let a Song" on the radio every night, and so did Benny Goodman from the Pennsylvania Hotel. He also recorded it, and "I Let a Song" got to be the big number that year.

After we left the Cotton Club, we went touring, and when we came back to New York we went into the Apollo Theatre on 125th Street. In preparing my big song of the season for the Apollo, I decided to do a new arrangement with rather a strong countermelody. Opening day, I soon learned that the audience, as always, wanted to hear the version they had heard on the air. So we took out the new chart after the first show and went back to the old arrangement, and that's the way it stayed. The following year, 1939, the new arrangement was reworked and recorded as "Never No Lament," which brings us to another, later story.

In 1943 we were playing the Hurricane Club on Forty-ninth and Broadway in New York. We had a sixth-month contract, but it was at a sacrifice and represented no profit to me, except that we could broadcast seven nights a week. By now, "Never No Lament" had lyrics by Bob Russell, had become "Don't Get Around Much Anymore," and had been recorded, before the union ban on recording came into force that year, by the Ink Spots and Glen Gray. RCA Victor was on its collective toes and had released the instrumental, "Never No Lament," under the new title. It was doing very well, too, but I didn't know how well.

Midway through the Hurricane engagement, I found myself a little short of cash, so I went up to the William Morris Agency—apparently cool, and not overly condescending—for the purpose of borrowing five hundred dollars. While I was exchanging greetings with some of the executives, an office boy passed and saw me.

"Oh, Mr. Ellington," he said, "I have some mail for you, too."

"Is that so?" I said disinterestedly.

He handed me about a dozen envelopes, which I proceeded to peel through casually until I came to one with a transparent window from RCA Victor. I opened it and took a quick glance at the check inside. The figure $2,250 is what I thought I saw as I slid it back in the envelope. To myself I said, "Hey, if this is $2,250, I don't need to make this touch up here, but maybe my eyes deceived me and it's really $22.50." So I pulled the check out again and it said $22,500! By the time I got my head back in my collar I was at the elevator exit on the first floor rushing to get a taxi. Man, what a surprise! What a feeling! I could breathe without inhaling or exhaling for the next three months!

When this happened, incidentally, I was already with the William Morris Agency. Irving Mills and I had come to the parting of the ways some years before. He gave me his 50 percent of Duke Ellington, Inc., in exchange for my 50 percent of Mills-Calloway Enterprises, Inc. We dissolved our business relationship agreeably and, in spite of how much he had made on me, I respected the way he had operated. He had always preserved the dignity of my name. Duke Ellington had an unblemished image, and that is the most anybody can do for anybody.

Dramatis Felidae

WILLIE "THE LION" SMITH

The Lion—Willie "The Lion"—Willie "The Lion" Smith—what a wealth of subject tingle! Would that I were sufficiently prolific to expound on the endless excitement and adventure of my first meeting and total exposure to this melodic, harmonic kaleidoscope.

Sonny Greer and I were real tight buddies and, naturally, night creatures. Our first night out in New York we got all dressed up and went down to the Capitol Palace. Greer had always told me that he and The Lion were real buddy-buddies and that we would not have to worry about anything where spending money was concerned (we had none); so down the steps of the Capitol Palace we started.

My first impression of The Lion—even before I saw him—was the thing I felt as I walked down those steps. A strange thing. A square-type fellow might say, "This joint is jumping," but to those who had become acclimatized —the tempo was the lope—actually everything and everybody seemed to be doing whatever they were doing in the tempo The Lion's group was laying down. The walls and furniture seemed to lean understandingly—one of the strangest and greatest sensations I ever had. The waiters served in that tempo; everybody who had to walk in, out, or around the place walked with a beat.

Downstairs, Sonny took the lead waving at people, people I know he did not know, but some of them figured, I suppose, "Well, maybe I know that cat from some place," and waved back, and some even invited us for a drink, which of course we always accepted. When Greer got to The Lion (incidentally, The Lion was from Newark and Greer from Long Branch), Greer upped and said, "Hey, Lion, you remember me, Jersey-boy Sonny Greer"—he then proceeded to rattle off a few names of hustlers, pimps, etc.—from Long Branch.

Willie "The Lion" Smith

"I want you to meet the Duke," said Sonny. "He is just a yearling, you know. Hey, Duke, come on over, shake hands with Willie Smith The Lion, my man."

The Lion extended his hand and said, "Glad to meet you, kid," and, looking over his shoulder, "Sit in there for me for a couple of numbers. D-flat. As one of those Western piano plonkers just fell in, I want him to take the stool so I can crush him later," he added.

This was the big thing about The Lion: a gladiator at heart. Anybody who had a reputation as a piano player had to prove it right there and then by sitting down to the piano and displaying his artistic wares. And when a cat thought that he was something special, he usually fell into that trap (or, you might say, into the jaws of The Lion) and he always came out with his reputation all skinned up, covered with the lacerations of humiliation, because before he got through too many stanzas The Lion was standing over him, cigar blazing.

Like if the player was weak with the left hand, The Lion would say, "What's the matter, are you a cripple?" Or, "When did you break your left arm?" Or, "Get up. I will show you how it is supposed to go."

The Lion has been the greatest influence on most of the great piano players who have been exposed to his fire, his harmonic lavishness, his stride—what a luxury! Fats Waller, James P. Johnson, Count Basie, Donald Lambert, Joe Turner, Sam Ervis, and of course I swam in it. Most of it still clings—agreeably. Even Art Tatum, as wonderful as he was—and I know he was the greatest— showed strong patterns of Willie Smithisms after being exposed to The Lion. I have never heard anybody accompany a singer like The Lion (they used to sing twenty or thirty choruses, each one different), and every supporting phrase that Willie played fit like a glove and drove her into her next melodic statement.

For me, the biggest moment at the White House birthday dinner in 1969 was when I saw my man, The Lion, sitting there at the concert grand piano with his derby on, playing behind the President of the United States. He is wonderful, and I love him. I can't think of anything good enough to say about The Lion, Willie "The Lion," Willie "The Lion" Smith.

MEXICO

George James was known in Harlem as "Mexico." He was born in the South, but at one time he had fought in Mexico as a mercenary. He had a little after-hours spot on 133rd Street in the late '20s, and it was very popular. No matter how late we musicians worked on our regular gig, Mexico's was always open afterwards. It was a real after-after-hours joint. Willie "The Lion" Smith played there, so it was a natural place for all piano players to hang out.

Mexico made his own booze and some of his intimate friends were allowed to stay after he closed to watch him make it. His special, a very strong one, he called "99," because it was not quite hundred-proof. After we had watched him make it, we were allowed the privilege of tasting it. After sampling "99" through the several stages of its brewing, the tasters would be quite smashed. Ah, but it was an honor to get loaded during the process.

Mexico's was the scene of many battles of music. Every Wednesday night there would be an open blowing competition. A different instrument was featured each Wednesday. One week it would be cornets, another alto saxophones, a third clarinets, and so on, until it became the turn of the tuba players. The joint was so small, only one or two tubas could be in the place at one time. The other tubas had to line up on the curb outside, and wait for their turn. Virtuoso combat was the most popular form of sport for the professional musician in those days. I shall never forget the night Fats Waller, James P. Johnson, and The Lion tangled there. Too bad there were no tape recorders in those days.

JAMES P. JOHNSON

My first encounter with James was through the piano rolls, the Q.R.S. rolls. Percy Johnson, a drummer in Washington who told me about them, took me home with him, and played me "Carolina Shout." He said I ought to learn it. So how was I going to do it, I wanted to know. He showed me the way. We slowed the machine and then I could follow the keys going down. I learned it!

And how I learned it! I nursed it, rehearsed it . . . Yes, this was the most solid foundation for me. I got hold of some of his other rolls, and they helped with styling, but "Carolina Shout" became my party piece.

Then James came to Washington to play Convention Hall. It holds maybe four or five thousand people. I was always a terrific listener. I'm taller on one side than the other from leaning over the piano, listening. This time I listened all night long. After a while my local following started agitating.

"You got to get up there and play that piece," they said. "Go on! Get up there and cut him!"

So, you know, I had to get up on there and play it.

"Hey, you play that good," James said. We were friends then, and I wanted the privilege of showing him around town, showing him the spots, introducing him to my pals, the best bootleggers, and so on. That, naturally, meant more leaning on the piano. Afterwards, we were fast friends, and James never forgot.

Later, when I showed up in New York, I found him there, and I met Lippy, too. Lippy was his dear friend, his pal—his agent, you'd have said, except he never took that 10 percent. James was doing pretty good. He'd written the show *Running Wild*—not the tune but the show—and that's where "Charleston" was born. So he wasn't hungry. But he never lost contact with his foundations, with the real, wonderful people in Harlem. Harlem had its own rich, special folklore, totally unrelated to the South or anywhere else. It's gone now, but it was tremendous then.

So there in that atmosphere I became one of the close disciples of the James P. Johnson style. Some nights we'd wind up—James, Fats Waller, Sonny Greer, and I—and go down to Mexico's to hear The Lion. I was working and would buy a drink. Tricky Sam had likely stayed up all night to help make it. Tricky was Mexico's official taster. So we would sit around, and during intermission I would move over to the piano. Then it would be Fats. Perhaps he'd play "Ivie." (He dedicated that to Ivie Anderson, I think.) Afterwards, he'd look over his shoulder jovially at James and call, "Come on, take the next chorus!" Before you knew it, James had played about thirty choruses, each one different, each one with a different theme.

By then The Lion would be stirred up. James had moved into his territory and was challenging. "Get up and I'll show you how it's supposed to be done," he'd say. Then, one after the other, over and over again they'd play, and it seemed as though you never heard the same note twice.

James, for me, was more than the beginning. He went right on up to the top. You know, he ordinarily played the most, and in competition a little bit more. You couldn't say he cut The Lion. It was never to the blood. With those two giants it was always a sporting event. Neither cut the other. They were above that. They had too much respect for each other. They played some impossible things, toe to toe, a saber in each hand—*En garde!*

Other times, Lippy and the bunch would get together, get James cornered, find a taxi, or maybe walk over to someone's house, and ring the bell. This would be 3 or 4 A.M. People stuck their heads out of windows, ready to throw a pot (flowerpot, maybe).

"Who's that down there?" they'd growl.

"This is Lippy," the answer would be. "I got James with me."

Those doors flew open. Lights switched on. Cupboards emptied, and everybody took a little taste. Then it was me, or maybe Fats, who sat down to warm up the piano. After that, James took over. Then you got real invention—magic, sheer magic.

James he was to his friends—just James, not Jimmy, nor James P. There never was another.

DON REDMAN

Don Redman always stood very tall in our field. His talent was simply in inverse ratio to his short stature. He played on one of our earliest record sessions, at a time when we were at the Kentucky Club with six pieces and the date called for ten. He was already then a forerunner, a wonderful writer and arranger. He wrote songs like "Cherry" and "Save It Pretty Mama" and his ideas have been copied and applied right on down the line, like those of Fletcher Henderson, whose band he was in during the '20s.

When he became director of McKinney's Cotton Pickers, I admired him from a distance, but then he got his own band at Connie's Inn and became a competitor, a fact I didn't appreciate at all. He was *tough* competition, as anyone who ever heard his "Chant of the Weed" must know. Twenty-one years after he wrote it, I asked him to do the arrangement for us to record, and it still sounded tremendous.

Everybody loved Don Redman, and I don't wonder he and Louis Bellson always got along so well when they were working together.

WILL MARION COOK

Will Marion Cook, His Majesty the King of Consonance . . . I can see him now with that beautiful mane of white hair flowing in the breeze as he and I rode uptown through Central Park in the summertime in a taxi with an open top. It was always when I was browsing around Broadway, trying to make contacts with my music, that I would run into Dad Cook.

Will Marion Cook, song maker

"Going uptown?" I would ask.

"Yes."

Then we would decide to stop in at one of the "friendly" publishers, and Dad would always cause a furor when he walked into one of those places, because everybody downtown in the music world knew that he was "the most" in learning. He knew enough about music to have had occasion to correct several of the masters abroad. When he first returned to New York and did a concert at Carnegie Hall, he had a brilliant critique next day in a newspaper.

The reviewer said that Will Marion Cook was definitely "the world's greatest Negro violinist."

Dad Cook took his violin and went to see the reviewer at the newspaper office.

"Thank you very much for the favorable review," he said. "You wrote that I was the world's greatest Negro violinist."

"Yes, Mr. Cook," the man said, "and I meant it. You are definitely the world's greatest Negro violinist."

With that, Dad Cook took out his violin and smashed it across the reviewer's desk.

"I am not the world's greatest Negro violinist," he exclaimed. "I am the greatest violinist in the world!"

He turned and walked away from his splintered instrument, and he never picked up a violin again in his life.

But back to my story and the friendly publisher . . .

"Let me have twenty dollars on account," Dad would say. "I want to buy a hat while I'm down here."

I knew he didn't want a hat, because he never wore one. Further, he probably had no real business deal going with that particular publisher at that time, but the cats in the music business just wanted to be on the right side with Dad. It was considered a prestigious relationship.

Of course, I was a sort of hanger-on. Several times, after I had played some tune I had written but not really completed, I would say, "Now, Dad, what is the logical way to develop this theme? What direction should I take?"

"You know you should go to the conservatory," he would answer, "but since you won't, I'll tell you. First you find the logical way, and when you find it, avoid it, and let your inner self break through and guide you. Don't try to be anybody else but yourself."

That time with him was one of the best semesters I ever had in music.

WILL VODERY

Will Vodery was Florenz Ziegfeld's Number One orchestrator from 1905 until the end of the glorious Ziegfeld era. When Ziegfeld left Broadway and went to Hollywood, Vodery went with him.

Vodery was the best pal of Bert Williams, the brilliant Ziegfeld star whom so many copied. They were regularly seen together during the Ziegfeld period. Handsome, debonair, and always in gentlemanly attire, they were respected by everyone as they walked through the downtown streets. They patronized any place they chose in that Glitter Belt, even sometimes in company with those gorgeous Ziegfeld beauties, and there was no sweat, no color compromise!

Will Vodery got us the gig in *Show Girl* at the Ziegfeld Theatre simply by mentioning my name to Flo Ziegfeld. It featured Ruby Keeler and Jimmy Durante, and had a George Gershwin score. It was a splendid show. A ballet was set to "An American in Paris," and "Liza" was premiered in it.

We were featured in "Liza" and a couple of other numbers on stage. My mother came up to New York from Washington, and brought my sister Ruth with her, just for the purpose of seeing me in the show. It was the first time she had ever seen me on stage, and I can see her now, waving her handkerchief the whole time we were out there.

Will Vodery was a very strict and very precise musician. He would stand up and write an orchestration without a score, and guarantee every note. Sometimes he would bring one of his very legit arrangements and make the cats in our band play it, and play it as though they too were legit. He used to give me valuable lectures in orchestration.

During the rehearsals for *Show Girl,* when cuts and adjustments were being made, there was an abrupt change from one key to another. Vodery picked up the parts one at a time, and then distributed—without a score—a twelve-tone chord that was probably the most consonant twelve-tone chord ever.

Boss musician, baby!

CHARLIE SHRIBMAN

Charlie Shribman started his business career as a shoeshine and newspaper boy. He worked his way up in a few years to where he owned a bowling alley in Salem Willows, Massachusetts. Then he got another bowling alley somewhere else, and more bowling alleys, until he was in a position to buy a ballroom in Salem Willows. After that he got more and more ballrooms, although the one in Salem Willows was always his pet. He didn't own all the ballrooms in New England, but he had a very good association with the people who owned those that he did not.

The time came when Charlie Shribman heard a big band, and ever after that he dedicated himself to supporting, patronizing, and subsidizing—not one, but all of them.

After enjoying the lucrative benefits of the holidays and New Year's Eve in the bustling boroughs of The Big Apple, the smart boys in the nightclub business of those days knew that the immediate future on the business horizon was not too bright. Sometimes they had the misfortune to dream of a holocaust, a dream so realistic that they would feel obliged to discontinue business. (I imagine that the insurance company was usually in that dream too.)

Charlie Shribman heard that we were out of work after January 1, 1924, but he didn't mention this fact, or that the Kentucky Club had burned down. Everybody in the world knows that nobody needs the responsibility of booking a band in January right after the holidays, but Charlie Shribman claimed he was in a pinch, stuck out there in Salem without a band, and would we please do him a favor and come out and work for him six weeks around New England. After that, for several years, we moved into Salem early every January, and again every summer. Salem became our home base for lengthy periods as we worked around the New England territory.

That was how it was with all the bands Charlie Shribman got to hear about. Later on, Mal Hallett, who lived up there, became his Number One, steady band attraction. Every time a band was organizing and just getting together, Charlie would send for them and keep them working, sometimes for a year. In one case, he nursed a band for two years, and soon afterwards it was the biggest band in the country. Yet Charlie Shribman never owned a piece of any band or anybody.

All those New England gigs were promoted and financed by Charlie and his brother Sy Shribman. I cannot imagine what would have happened to the big bands if it had not been for Charlie Shribman.

CHICK WEBB

I made Chick Webb a bandleader when I was working at the Kentucky Club. As I've said, that club was a kind of center for after-hour activity. When some of the boys around downtown decided to open up a new joint, they would stop by and tell Sonny Greer and me, "We need a band." Or, "We need a piano player." Or it might be a drummer, a trumpet player, or a singer. This particular night, a guy came in and said, "Hey, we need a band! We're going to open up a place tomorrow night, and we need some waiters, too." Sonny and I assured him everything would be all right. "Don't worry about it," we said. "They'll be there!" We went uptown and hired five or six musicians, and Chick was one of them.

"Now, you're the bandleader," I said to Chick.

"Man, I don't want to be no bandleader," he answered.

"All you do is collect the money and bring me mine."

"Is that all I have to do?"

"Yeah."

"Okay, I'm a bandleader."

I was there at his opening night, and it was on that engagement that the dancing waiters got started.

As a drummer, Chick had his own ideas about what he wanted to do. Some musicians are dancers, and Chick was. You can dance with a lot of things besides your feet. Billy Strayhorn was another dancer—in his mind. He was a dance-writer. Chick Webb was a dance-drummer who painted pictures of dances with his drums. Way back, at the Cotton Club, we were always tailoring orchestrations to fit the dances. If you listen to the figures in some of Strayhorn's pieces, like "U.M.M.G.," those are dances—tap dances maybe—and you can't mistake what they essentially are. The reason why Chick Webb had such control, such command of his audiences at the Savoy ballroom, was because he was always in communication with the dancers and felt it the way they did. And that is probably the biggest reason why he could cut all the other bands that went in there.

COUNT BASIE

When I play Paris, Hugues Panassié comes to the concerts and always puts his bid in for the piano player to open up his left hand on something like "Carolina Shout." I naturally acknowledge the request, but first I tell this little story:

When I first came to New York, Count Basie was playing piano over on

Count Basie

Fifth Avenue between 134th and 135th at a place called Edmond's. It was owned by a man named Edmond who was supposed to be the brother of Barron Wilkins. I used to go over there every night and stand on the opposite side of Fifth Avenue and listen to Count Basie wail. It was wonderful except for the fact that I was too young to be allowed into a place like that. One day, I shed my adolescence by putting on long pants. They thought I was a grown man and let me in. I fooled them, and I'm glad, because I finally got to stand alongside the piano and watch the great Count Basie.

LONNIE JOHNSON

Lonnie Johnson helped bring about one of my giant steps on milestones established by men sound of ear and skilled to thrill through the climate they created with their music magic. I have always felt indebted to him because his guitar added a new luster to my adolescent orchestral attempts on the records we made in 1928. He was born in New Orleans, and he must have been a good man, because he spoke only good about other men, and I never heard anyone speak anything but good of him. God bless Lonnie Johnson.

MACEO PINKARD

Maceo Pinkard was the first to take me to a studio for the purpose of recording our group. When I think of how wonderful those men of that period in New York were, and of the way in which they received me, I always feel a glow of gladness and gratitude.

Maceo Pinkard allowed me to pal around with him on Broadway, just as though I were really somebody too. I was with him in 1925 on one of the days that I think were very important in the history of Tin Pan Alley. It was the day he wrote "Sweet Georgia Brown." He played it, and looked to me for my reaction. How about that? "It's great," I said, and I sat with him in his office while he made the lead sheet and piano copy. The next day, it was printed, published, and on the street. I heard it on Broadway before anybody but Maceo Pinkard.

PAUL WHITEMAN

Paul Whiteman was known as the King of Jazz, and no one as yet has come near carrying that title with more certainty and dignity. He gave up his position with the Denver Symphony to organize and lead a class jazz band. Despite his classical background, he didn't have a snooty bone in his body.

Now there have been those who have come on the scene, grabbed the money, and run off to a plush life of boredom, but nobody held on to his band like Paul Whiteman did. He was always adding interesting musicians to the payroll, without regard to their behavior. All he wanted was to have those giant cats blow, and they blew up a storm. He brought them in from all over the country, stars of the years that followed, like Tommy and Jimmy Dorsey, Jack and Charlie Teagarden, Red Nichols, Bix Beiderbecke, Miff Mole, Eddie Lang, Joe Venuti, Roy Bargy, Chester Hazlett, Bill Challis, Ferdie Grofe, and Red Norvo, not to mention singers like Bing Crosby and Mildred Bailey. As we said in "A Drum Is a Woman," he "dressed her in woodwinds and strings" and made a lady out of jazz.

We knew him 'way back when we were at the Kentucky Club, which stayed open as long as the cash register rang. It was the after-hours hangout for all the musicians who played in the plushier Broadway places. Paul Whiteman came often as a genuine enthusiast, listened respectfully, said his words of encouragement, very discreetly slipped the piano player a fifty-dollar bill, and very loudly proclaimed our musical merit. I remember the first night Bix Beiderbecke came to New York to join him at the Palais Royal, just around the corner from us. After their gig, they all came down to listen to our six-piece band. We must have been saying something, for they kept coming back.

In 1939, Paul Whiteman organized what I think was considered his most successful concert. He had a forty-three-piece orchestra, all hand-picked musicians, none but the best. And he chose several people—Roy Bargy was one, I remember—to write original compositions connected thematically or otherwise with bells. I was honored to be included among them, and my work was "The Blue Belles of Harlem." I think the title is self-explanatory, but I remember that it was written when we were somewhere in Kansas, during the period when Strayhorn, Jimmy Blanton, and Ben Webster were new with us, and it was all bubbly, boiling . . .

LUCKEYETH ROBERTS

When I was a kid, I used to go to the Howard Theatre almost every day to hear the good music. One of the big talents to appear there was Luckeyeth Roberts. He had such a spread to his hands that he could stretch a twelfth flat with either one, and he would throw them up in the air when playing piano in a flashy, acrobatic manner that I copied at Mrs. Dyer's.

He liked what we were doing with our five-piece band at Barron's in Harlem. He liked it so much, he gave us his time. He would come over there in the afternoon when we were rehearsing and hold sessions of lectures, demonstrations, questions and answers. All of it was vitally instructive to us, but he said it was fun for him to go through the musical possibilities of a five-piece band.

He was another one of the Beautiful People, who gave us a shove and a kiss of good luck on our road to every place we've been since 1923. In addition to his prowess at the keyboard, he was a success in the society world as a bandleader, wrote the music for several Broadway shows, and had a big hit in "Moonlight Cocktail." A Quaker from Philadelphia, he never touched liquor in his life, but he used to own a bar on St. Nicholas Avenue.

GEORGE GERSHWIN

When I saw the movie based on the life of George Gershwin, I remember feeling a little annoyed about the way it depicted an aspect of him I certainly never encountered. He was shown as a man and artist of temperament who was somewhat rude at times.

I never heard of this in his lifetime, and I was very close to many people who were as close to him as they could be, and they could not recall this side of him either.

He was not the kind of guy who would be in Row A, ready to take a bow on opening night. In fact, when several of his most successful shows opened, he could be seen dressed like a stagehand, who could get in the front or backstage door. In a sports shirt, with no tie, he would humbly take his place in

With W. C. Handy, composer of *St. Louis Blues*

the standing-room area. If you didn't know him, you would never guess that he was the great George Gershwin.

He once told Oscar Levant that he wished he had written the bridge to "Sophisticated Lady," and that made me very proud.

BUBBER MILEY

Bubber Miley was from the body and soul of Soulsville. He was raised on soul and saturated and marinated in soul. Every note he played was soul filled with the pulse of compulsion. *It don't mean a thing if it ain't got that swing* was his credo. Before he played his choruses, he would tell his story, and he always had a story for his music, such as: "This is an old man, tired from working in the field since sunup, coming up the road in the sunset on his way home to dinner. He's tired but strong, and humming in time with his broken gait—or vice versa." That was how he pictured "East St. Louis Toodle-oo."

Both Miley and Whetsol painted pictures in music, one in one style and one in another. They spoke different languages, and though the listener didn't understand their language, he *believed* everything they had to say.

Bubber was born in South Carolina, but his family moved to New York when he was quite young, and he was raised there. His growl solos with the plunger mute were another of our early sound identities, and between 1925 and 1929 he laid the foundation of a tradition that has been maintained ever since by men like Cootie Williams and Ray Nance.

JOE "TRICKY SAM" NANTON

Tricky Sam, Joe Nanton, was a youngster who made it to all the joints around Harlem where you could hear the music people insisted on calling jazz. He had really never had his coming-out party, and he had never found a place to fit on a full-time basis. Nor had he found a true running mate. He'd carry his horn around from one joint to another, and get to play a chorus here and a chorus there.

Joe "Tricky Sam" Nanton

Before Tricky joined us, Charlie Irvis, who was known as Charlie Plug, was our original trombone player down in the Kentucky Club. He was called Plug because of the device he used on his horn. In those days they manufactured a kind of mute designed to make the trombone sound like a saxophone. The sax was still regarded as new then. Charlie had dropped this device and broken it, so he used what was left of it, rolling it around the bell of his trombone. He couldn't use it the way it was intended, because of the part broken off, but he'd get this entirely different, lecherous, low tone, and no one has ever done it since. You might say that there was really a lost art.

When Charlie left and we got Tricky, it was exactly the opposite, because everything he did was up the top of the horn. Luckily we had Bubber Miley as his plunger mate. Tricky had been using the plunger before, and he had all those sounds, but they were a little too sophisticated to be appreciated by the average listener who would walk into a jam session. By sophisticated, I mean that he had had to devise a technique, because those sounds had to be precise. There were certain distances the plunger had to be away from the mute inside the bell, and there was the matter of when you squeezed it. There were certain tones and a certain pitch that were relevant. All these people were valuable to me, because each one's effective range or scope was limited.

You take a guy using a thing like Charlie Irvis did: you had limitations on how far he could go with it before it became ugly or uninteresting. The same applied with Tricky at the top of the horn. You take the limitations on how many notes you can make effectively, and you have a little problem with your writing. In other words, you have to write to fit the limitations. But any time you have a problem you have an opportunity. It was all a matter of the kind of sound you wanted to make with the available equipment. If you had just seven good tones, those were the tones that had to be used, no matter how many tones were within the compass of the instrument.

Bubber Miley was the right mate for Tricky. "Now you've got it," he'd say, and we gave Tricky the opportunity to play more. Instead of just playing a chorus, and then packing his horn and leaving, he had a chance to develop his "tricks." That's what we called them, and he was "Tricky" because he wasn't stupid. When he played his thing, that was the end of it. He didn't stay there and mess around trying to blow someone else's thing. What he was actually doing was playing a very highly personalized form of his West Indian heritage. When a guy comes here from the West Indies and is asked to play some jazz, he plays what *he* thinks it is, or what comes from his applying himself to the idiom. Tricky and his people were deep in the West Indian legacy and the Marcus Garvey movement. A whole strain of West Indian musicians came up who made contributions to the so-called jazz scene, and they were all virtually descended from the true African scene. It's the same now with the Muslim movement, and a lot of West Indian people are involved in it. There are many resemblances to the Marcus Garvey schemes. Bop, I once said, is the Marcus Garvey extension.

Bop was likened by many people, in certain of its aspects, to modern European music. The Europeans who went to Africa came back with "modern" art. What is more African than a Picasso? And what the bop musicians were doing was parallel to African art, if not to African music.

Coda: In 1971 we were in Las Vegas at the same time as Louis Armstrong. We went to hear him one night, and Tyree Glenn, his trombonist, played a chorus on "Mood Indigo" that was absolutely identical with Tricky's.

FREDDY GUY

Freddy Guy was born in Georgia, but he had been in New York most of his life when he joined us in 1925, and he knew Harlem backwards and forwards. He was rather a serious type of fellow, and was always giving us advice, but his guitar was a metronome and the beat was always where it was supposed to be. He was a good man at managing finances, too. Herman Stark, the manager of the Cotton Club, used to say to me, "You are going to be a very famous star, but Freddy Guy is going to wind up with the money."

We first met him when he was the leader of a small band that played in a joint on 135th Street owned by Earl Dancer. He had Fats Waller in the band, and a beautiful chick named Angelina Rivera, who was a fine violinist. They allowed us the privilege of sitting in and participating in the music and the tips. All over Harlem there were only great, hospitable people to welcome us to New York.

HARRY CARNEY

Harry Carney was just seventeen years old when he first came with me in '27. He owned a car and all his own instruments, and already had six thousand

Harry Carney, 1963

dollars in the bank. He started playing with us while on his summer vacation, which, of course, was the time of year when he made all of his money. Through systematic saving, he should be in very good shape now.

A very well-behaved, well-organized young man, he was immediately nick-named "Youth" by Sonny Greer. He invited us to his home in Boston, where, he claims, Freddy Guy and Duke Ellington conned his beautiful mother, Mrs. Jenny Carney—a lovely lady, and a good cook known for her warm hospitality—into letting him come with us instead of going back to school. He's a little fatter now, but he still looks like his nickname.

Harry has always had a driving passion for driving, but he never lets any-body else but Harry Carney drive his car. As far back as I can remember, he has been driving it, and sometimes, when we're doing one-nighters, the dis-tances between dates have been pretty long. This fact has only seemed to com-pound his passion, and I love to drive with Harry. He is not the world's greatest speed king, but he observes a very sound system of rules, of dos and don'ts. In other words, he is very careful, not for his own safety, but be-cause, I think, he just doesn't want anything to happen to that car. Up until right now, I don't know of anyone else who has ever driven one of Harry Carney's cars.

We make good time, but if I see him begin to rub his left leg, I know he's beginning to get a little sleepy. So I open my window wide and let the cold morning air hit him in the back of the head. That annoys him, and when he is on the verge of becoming a little evil he says, "I'm all right, man. You can close that window."

We make good traveling companions, because he always has his mind on his driving, and I, of course, am the navigator, the World's Greatest Number One Navigator. I know just about all the major roads to any place in the United States and Canada, and I don't do too badly overseas, either. For ex-ample, I keep my map ready for checking and double-checking routes, and if, say, I'm en route from Baton Rouge to Fort Polk at two o'clock in the afternoon, and the sun is blazing in the right-hand window of the car, I know that we are traveling northeast instead of northwest as we should be. That's how the World's Greatest Number One Navigator operates.

Harry Carney doesn't talk much while he's driving, so this gives me lots of time to establish mental isolation for thinking, planning, and writing my words and music. Dashing through the night, many observations are made and many inspirations are felt, some of them from great distances away.

When we were going west once on Route 40 out of Reno, after a very silent period between us, we drove into a clear, open area, and there, looking in a northwesterly direction, I saw it, high in the sky. "Harry, have you ever seen a moonbow?" I asked. "No-o-o-o," he answered. "Well, look up over there," I said. Harry looked and said, "Hey, what is that?" I had neither seen one before nor ever heard of one before, but I had put a name to it, and there it was, just like a rainbow after a rain. But it was not a rainbow, because it didn't have all the colors in it; what it did have was all the various shades and tints of the night sky. When we checked on it the next day, they said, "Yes, that was a moonbow."

One evening we were a little late leaving Tampa, Florida, en route to West Palm Beach to make a gig. The weather was wonderful and it was just about sunset when, halfway across Florida, we passed a bird. We didn't see it, but we heard its beautiful call. I asked Harry if he heard it and he said, "Yeah." We were a little too pushed for time, and going too fast to stop or go back and thank the bird, so I pulled out my pencil and paper and wrote that lovely phrase down. I spent the next two or three days whistling it to the natives, and inquiring what kind of bird it could have been that sang such a beautiful melody. Finally, I was convinced it had to be a mockingbird. I made an orchestration around that melody, titled it "Sunset and the Mocking Bird," and included it in *The Queen's Suite* as one of the "beauty" experiences of my life. Another number that went into the same suite was written after experiencing a different display of beauty.

We came out of Cincinnati late one night, took a road to the east on the South Shore of the Ohio River, and got lost while searching for the country club we were supposed to play. We ran into an area where the sultry moon was half-hidden by the trees it silhouetted. We stopped short, for there in this huge arena, with the trees as a backdrop, were, it seemed, millions of lightning bugs, dancing in the air. It was a perfect ballet setting, and down below in a gully, like an orchestra pit, could be heard the croaking of frogs. The number this inspired was called "Lightning Bugs and Frogs," and I included it in *The Queen's Suite,* too.

I've seen the Northern Lights many times, but one night in Canada, when Harry Carney and I were en route from Three Rivers, Quebec, to North Bay, Ontario, on Route 17, we saw the greatest display of all.

It seemed to us as though we were two short men standing behind two tall men at a magnified Radio City while a stage production was on. We could not see the players, only shadows and reflections of performers passing back and forth before a brilliantly lit backdrop. You could see the course of the prima donna, the prima ballerina, the heavy, and all the dancing and show girls, many of them in formation. It was the greatest stage production I've ever seen, and it went on and on until I had occasion to get out of the car. While standing there, I looked up, and straight up over my head the same thing was going on. It was eerie, and rather terrifying. I rushed back to the car.

"Let's go, Harry," I said. "The same thing is going on overhead. Let's get out of here!" And we did, but fast!

Billy Strayhorn did not see this, but he wrote the music after I told him about it. It turned out to be a wonderful piece and it was included in *The Queen's Suite*. We recorded the six movements of this suite, but only one copy was pressed, and that was presented to H.M. Queen Elizabeth at Buckingham Palace.

"Northern Lights," to me, represented majesty, whereas "Le Sucrier Velours" represented beauty. That is the name the French have for a bird whose song is sweet as sugar and who feels as soft as velours. Another movement, "Apes and Peacocks," was inspired by reading in the Bible about the Queen of Sheba and all the gifts she brought to King Solomon. Besides all that wealth of gold, silver, and ivory, there were apes and peacocks. To us, apes and peacocks seemed like the splendor of all time. The sixth movement, "The Single Petal of a Rose," represented wonder.

Half the time on our trips Harry and I arrive at the city or town where we are to play that night thinking the other knows the place where the gig is, or has an itinerary in his pocket. Every now and then it happens that neither of us knows nor has an itinerary with him. "No sweat, baby!" I say, and we drive into a gas station, where Harry says, "Fill it up." After I've stretched my limbs, I ask the attendant, "Do you know where Duke Ellington is playing tonight?" Usually the man answers, "Oh, over at the Auditorium, three blocks down this way to the red light, turn left, then first right, and straight ahead—you can't miss it." So we just go and follow the directions, and we're cool, but feeling it was a good thing we picked that gas station for information. We had been doing this sort of thing with good results down through the years until one night, a couple of years ago, we arrived in, I think it was, Santa Rosa, California. We pulled into the gas station with the same routine up to, "Where's Duke Ellington playing tonight?" The cat with the gas hose turned and said, "Who? Who's he?" When we explained, he said, "I don't know anything about a dance or a concert here tonight." And there we were, standing there, feathers peeling off one at a time.

"Oh, no," Harry said, "you don't suppose we goofed on the name of the town?"

"There's only one way to find out," I said. "Call Ruth or Cress Courtney." So I went to the telephone to call my sister in New York.

All this time, cars were coming and going, and as they stopped for gas we'd give them the same question: "Where's Duke Ellington playing tonight?" Most of their responses were something like, "Duke Ellington? I didn't know he was playing here tonight." Then Ruth answered the telephone and we got the directions. So I turned to the cat at the gas station and said, "We're playing at the Fair Grounds." "Oh, that's it, is it?" he said. "Right catty-corner across the street." What a relief!

But the Fair Grounds were very dark—no lights in sight. After finally finding an entrance gate, we drove in, and around, and around, and around. Nobody, but nothing, until eventually we were about to pass another car going in the opposite direction. Both cars honked their horns, stopped, let their windows down.

"Do you know where . . . ?" Harry began.

"That's what we want to know, Harry," the other driver interrupted. It was Ralph Gleason, of the San Francisco *Chronicle* at that time. We laughed, turned around, and both cars continued their search until suddenly—there it was!

Duke Ellington? Who's he? Duke who?

BARNEY BIGARD AND WELLMAN BRAUD

Barney Bigard and Wellman Braud, when they were in the band, were a fountain of stories about New Orleans. Both of them were from there, and now and then they would take off in their French patois. Naturally, they both claimed Creole heritage, and they would elaborate on all the things that the New Orleans Chamber of Commerce would have liked to have heard. They would talk of Old Days, even before their time, calling names, very colorful names, like Buddy Bolden and King Oliver, and they would have a lot to say about the marching bands and the Second Line. Even today, one never hears too much about the Second Line, which is the name given to fans who dance attendance on the bands as they proceed through the streets.

Everything they talked about and played was the purest old jazz, and they were forever making comparisons between the New York cats and the jazz clan of New Orleans. It all sounded so good and so romantic that I was ready to catch the next train. Finally in the middle '30s we went to New Orleans, and it was very much like they had said, so we felt rather at home with the crayfish and gumbo filé.

Because Bigard and Braud were in the band with us, thousands of people were at the station in New Orleans when the train arrived. The two musicians had first-name exchanges with the crowd, and we felt it was because of them that we were received with such warm hospitality.

Bigard and Braud also made many valuable suggestions in regard to music, particularly about style and tempos, so that we felt we were benefiting from a very informative semester. They were both major contributors to our budding style. They executed their background obligations most fittingly, and both were fine soloists. To me, they were organization men plus.

When Mr. Braud joined us in 1926, he was already a celebrated veteran of New Orleans jazz, and a clean, neatly dressed coach who knew all the answers. He and Freddy Guy were the two Big Daddies. As a bass player, he believed in crowding the microphone, and when you got ready to blow a chorus Mr. Braud would already have established so compelling a beat that you could not miss.

Barney Bigard joined us in 1927 when we augmented the band for the first engagement at the Cotton Club. I had heard him for the first time when he was playing for King Oliver in a battle of music with Fletcher Henderson at the Savoy. He is a very original and imaginative clarinet player, and he gave our band another of its distinctive sound identities. Like several of the best clarinet players from New Orleans, he was taught by Lorenzo Tio, Jr. He always played the Albert system, and he had that woody tone which I love on the instrument. He was invaluable for putting the filigree work into an arrangement, and sometimes it could remind you of all that delicate wrought iron you see in his hometown.

Johnny Hodges playing soprano saxophone and Harry Carney, ca. 1940

JOHNNY HODGES

As a youngster, Johnny Hodges was a saxophonist in Boston whose style, in the estimation of all other alto saxophonists, was unique. Even now, I have never yet met and don't know of a saxophonists who didn't say he was knocked out by Johnny Hodges. As I originally told Stanley Dance years ago, "Johnny Hodges has complete independence of expression. He says what

he wants to say on the horn, and that is *it*. He says it in *his* language, which is specific, and you could say that his is pure artistry. He's the only man I know who can pick up a cold horn and play in tune without tuning up. And I've heard plenty of cats who can't play in tune after they tune up all day."

When he left the Black and White Club in Boston, his first big job in New York was with Chick Webb. This did not bring out the real "soul" potential, for Chick came to me and said he thought Johnny would be better in our band where he would have more freedom of expression. So after Rudy Jackson had left, we had a meeting of the band to decide whether to get Buster Bailey or Johnny Hodges. Buster was regarded as just about the top clarinetist at that time, 1928, but Barney Bigard voted him out and Johnny Hodges in!

So we sent for the New Blood—young, untapped, etc.—and no decision could have been better, for with more freedom of expression Johnny developed into the most outstanding name in the band, not only in the United States, but throughout the world. His sultry solos were not done in an attempt to blow more notes than anyone else. He just wanted to play them in true character, reaching into his soul for them, and automatically reaching everybody else's soul. An audience's reaction to his first note was as big and deep as most applause for musicians at the end of their complete performance. Audiences acted as though they understood and agreed with him, showing this in responses that ranged from grunts, oohs, and aahs to "Yes, daddy!" These responses were never too loud to prevent their hearing the next note he played.

He was a combination of himself and Sidney Bechet, who loved him and always encouraged him. His tonal charisma is difficult to describe, but he always referred to it as "the kitchen." If someone else played something in his style, he would say, "All right, come out of the kitchen!"

Irving Mills soon recognized an unusual quality in his playing, and he had us make some small-band record dates with Johnny Hodges, as well as with Cootie Williams, Rex Stewart, and Barney Bigard, those wonderful individuals. All through the years that followed, Johnny did recording dates on his own with many different combinations. Eventually, Norman Granz signed him up for Verve, and some fine albums were produced on that label with accompanying artists like Wild Bill Davis and Fatha Hines.

On May 11, 1970, I was thinking about how I could persuade him to get his soprano saxophone out once more to play on "A Portrait of Sidney Bechet" in *The New Orleans Suite*. The telephone rang and I was told that he had just died at his dentist's office. This is the eulogy I wrote that night and it still captures best my feelings about him.

Never the world's most highly animated showman or greatest stage personality, but a tone so beautiful it sometimes brought tears to the eyes—this was Johnny Hodges. This *is* Johnny Hodges.

Because of this great loss, our band will never sound the same.

Johnny Hodges and his unique tonal personality have gone to join the ever so few inimitables—those whose sounds stand unimitated, to say the least—Art Tatum, Sidney Bechet, Django Reinhardt, Billy Strayhorn . . .

Johnny Hodges sometimes sounded beautiful, sometimes romantic, and sometimes people spoke of his tone as being sensuous. I've heard women say his tone was so compelling.

He played numbers like "Jeep's Blues," "Things Ain't What They Used to Be," "I Let a Song Go Out of My Heart," "All of Me," "On the Sunny Side of the Street," Billy Strayhorn's "Passion Flower" and "Day Dream," and many more.

With the exception of a year or so, almost his entire career was with us. Many came and left, sometimes to return. So far as our wonderful listening audience was concerned, there was a great feeling of expectancy when they looked up and saw Johnny Hodges sitting in the middle of the sax section, in the front row.

I am glad and thankful that I had the privilege of presenting Johnny Hodges for forty years, night after night. I imagine I have been much envied, but thanks to God . . .

May God bless this beautiful giant in his own identity. God bless Johnny Hodges.

COOTIE WILLIAMS

Chick Webb came running up to me one night in the Rhythm Club, and he said, "Hey, man, I got a hell of a trumpet player for you. He was with me for a while, but he's too much for me. Fletcher (Henderson) heard him and hired him, but that style don't fit Fletcher's band. He's a hell of a player, man, and for you he'll be a bitch!"

"Well, what do I do," I asked, "how can I hear him?"

"You can't hear him," Chick said, "because Fletcher don't give him any solos. So if you want him, he wants to come with you."

Of course, I trusted in Chick's taste and his evaluation of our kind of

Freddy Jenkins, 1932

musician without question. After all, he had already recommended Johnny Hodges, and we had had so much success with *his* sound.

So I said, "I want him. Send him to me. What's his name?"

"Cootie Williams."

"Okay, he can start work tomorrow night."

"It's a deal," Chick said, "'cause Fletcher don't mind. He has no value with him."

It was 1929 when Cootie came into the band, and he soon became one of our most outstanding soloists. He began to use the plunger mute, one of our major tonal devices, and he used it very well, right up to one night eleven years later, when he took me for a ride all around Chicago in his car. He wanted to tell me that he had a very lucrative offer to go with Benny Goodman for a while. "Well, okay," I said.

But lucky boy me! The next night we went to a nightclub and heard Ray Nance. Well, what can I tell you?

FREDDY JENKINS

Freddy Jenkins came to us from Wilberforce University in 1928. He had no bad habits and, thanks to his college years, he was a perfect gentleman who dropped the right names of all the "right people" in Ohio. He was a good reader, but he developed an extra dimension that earned him the nickname of "Posey." It really began with his sitting at the end of the trumpet section. He brought us a new kind of sparkle: his every move was a picture, in the groove, and right on top of the action. Even a cliché in his solos had an extra unique flare, a personality play. He was total "theatre"—*le plus jambon.* He dressed flashily, almost foppishly, and gained the attention veteran vaudevillians strove for—and bragged about whenever they attained it. Posey's showmanship was unforgettable. People still ask, "Whatever happened to that wonderful, left-handed trumpet player who used to sit out there at the end?" He never lived in any of the many violent ways open to musicians, but he had to be seen, standing on the corner at all hours of the day with his big cigar, saying, "What's happening, man?"

This routine was not good for his health, and so in 1938 he had to leave us and go into the hospital. But sick as he was, he regularly called to find out how all the other cats were. Now and then he was told that this one or that one had a cold, or something minor wrong with him, and Fred would say, "Oh, that poor guy, I'm so sorry!" He, seriously ill in the hospital, worried about some cat who had a temporary sneeze.

He got well, however, and whenever we went anywhere near Fort Worth, Freddy Jenkins would always show up to greet us looking better than all of us put together. Out there, he has been a disc jockey; he has been in real estate and insurance; he has been in politics and held a government position; and altogether he has a record I would be proud to have. I hope Fort Worth is good to him for another thirty years. I love a self-sufficient man. He never asks for help, and he puts on a front so worthy of a man—a real man. As Buster Cooper would say, "He must have been born grown." Yes, a Big Man, he makes four-foot-ten look like ten-foot-four!

LAWRENCE BROWN

Lawrence Brown was born in Lawrence, Kansas, and he acquired a wonderful background in all kinds of music—classical, radio, television, show music, gospel, spiritual, pop, and so-called jazz. He had been playing in Les Hite's band with Louis Armstrong at Sebastian's Cotton Club in Los Angeles before he joined us in 1932, and he had quite a reputation as a kind of "strolling violin," going from table to table playing very soft, beautiful melody.

As a soloist, his taste is impeccable, but his greatest role is that of an accompanist. The old-timers used to say, "Soloists are made, but accompanists are born." Lawrence Brown is the accompanist *par excellence*. During the many years he was with us, records prove that his solo performances had the widest range from classical standard up to, around, and above the jet-swept contour of the vision we almost hear.

IVIE ANDERSON

In 1931 we were booked to play the Paramount-Publix Circuit's (Balaban & Katz) Oriental Theatre in Chicago for the first time. The producer thought it would enhance our show if we were to add a girl singer. Now in the late

'20s and early '30s, May Alix had a very good name as an attraction. She had had several very successful records with such greats as Louis Armstrong and Jimmie Noone, singing such songs as "Big Butter and Egg Man" and "My Daddy Rocks Me." We had the choice of May or Ivie Anderson, and we agreed after some discussion that instead of picking the girl with the Big Record we would use Ivie. I wondered why, without challenging the decision (since they were paying), and soon I learned that Ivie was chosen because she was of darker skin. Well, I am one of those people who never consider color important. What was important in this instance was the sound and ability of the singer.

Although Ivie was not well known at that time, I soon found that she was really an extraordinary artist and an extraordinary person as well. She had great dignity, and she was greatly admired by everybody everywhere we went, at home and abroad. She became one of our mainstays and high-lights, and she gave some unforgettable performances. She stopped the show cold at the Palladium in London in 1933. Her routine normally consisted of four songs, but while she was singing "Stormy Weather" the audience and all the management brass broke down crying and applauding. The brass came backstage to say, "Don't let her sing anything but 'Stormy Weather.' Even she couldn't follow that!" Tears streaming down her cheeks, Ivie did the most believable performance ever. This was topping our eight weeks of playing "Stormy Weather" at the Cotton Club for Ethel Waters, for whom the song had been written by Harold Arlen and Ted Koehler.

In addition to her great singing, Ivie was also considered a good-luck charm. We opened at the Oriental Theatre on Friday, February 13, 1931, and we broke the all-time house record. We returned to the Oriental on Fri-day, March 13, 1931, and broke that record, too. At the Palladium, our act was No. 13 on the bill.

They still talk about Ivie, and every girl singer we've had since has had to try to prevail over the Ivie Anderson image.

REX STEWART

Although he was born in Philadelphia, Rex Stewart came out of the same Washington school system that I did, and his intellectual ambitions were typical of the Washingtonian of that time, when people believed that if you were going to be something, you ought to learn something and know something. Some people learn from going to college, others from just reading. Some learn from conversation. All my musical education, for example, was received orally. When they asked you questions, they *knew* if you knew what they had taught, but if you brought them papers . . . well, somebody else might have written them for you!

Rex Stewart had been taught the responsibility of commanding respect for his race and to this end he maintained an offstage image very deliberately. It was a dignified, decent-sort-of-chap image, and he never strayed far away from it, so that he was always posing to some extent and never really relaxed. It is possible that tensions and conflicts came from this and were apparent in his music, but he was an exciting player who made a big contribution during the years he was with us—1934–45. He was extremely versatile and we made use of his virtuosity on "Trumpet in Spades" and "Boy Meets Horn." His half-valved effects on the latter have never been forgotten, but he should not be judged only by demonstrations of that kind. There was another, less spectacular side to him that was also very valuable.

Since I refer to it often, I should say that commanding respect, in my view, is a social credit that will never become outdated, unless one is blinded by the blazing light of apparent freedom and overemphasized equality, the sugar-substitute meringue of what is actually being served to those who don't believe they are getting it.

RICHARD BOWDEN JONES

We all called him "Jonesy," and he was our first band boy. Born in Chester, Pennsylvania, he came to New York and worked his way up to bus boy at the Cotton Club. This fact alone proves that he was a man of forethought, because people who work as waiters, cooks, dishwashers, and bus boys always know where they are going to eat—dishwashers and bus boys particularly. They recognize that as a major factor in their security. Also, all bus boys at that time participated in a percentage of the waiters' tips.

Jonesy had a personality of his own, too, and when big spenders wanted their champagne opened in the manner that makes the popping of the cork a salute in itself, Jonesy could make the cork pop louder and fly higher than any of the waiters. When Legs Diamond came to the Cotton Club to celebrate, he wanted everybody in the joint to know that his table was where the action was, and every time Jonesy popped a bottle of champagne for him he'd give Jonesy a sawbuck.

On nights like that, Jonesy went home loaded, or, rather, he left the Cotton Club loaded, because if the waiters declared a poker game, Jonesy went along, to lose a little sometimes and win a little sometimes. If anybody hit the numbers, those waiters would *always* declare a poker game, usually at the flat of Kid Griffin, Sonny Tate, Sharkey, or Jack Sheppard. I was one of those who liked hanging out with waiters, mainly because they were so hip, but that was also one of the reasons I usually went home broke.

Jonesy was a wonderful cat. I loved him, and he was always ready to do anything to help us. He first got into our world by helping us load instruments on the many nights we did benefits. We were sort of hooked on each other. When we got ready to leave the Cotton Club in 1931, Jonesy went to Herman Stark, the manager, and said he was quitting to go on the road with us. Stark hit the ceiling, but eventually relented, and Jonesy stayed with us until we lost him in Los Angeles.

It was a great loss, for he really took care of business, and he was much more than a band boy. A couple of times he had to act as my bodyguard, and he did that, but good. I don't know how I would have managed without him. God bless our Jonesy.

Act Three

The City of Jazz

The City of Jazz is a place in which certain people live. Some are on their way out, while many others are on their way in. Some are rushing to get there, but others appear reluctant and are cautious in their approach. Still others claim they are afraid, and hesitate to expose themselves in this place where they feel so strange, this strange place where the most solid citizens are so hip, or slick, or cool. These hesitant ones fear they will feel like country folk in the metropolis, or like people on the Chinatown bus tour. They wonder if they will be taken for suckers or squares.

My experience on my many visits to and from the city (I do one-nighters, you know) has convinced me that its people are all very nice human beings. There are those who work for the city (the players), those who work at the city (the analysts), and those who just enjoy it (*these* are my people).* The citizens of all three groups are more concerned with what they like than what they dislike. All of them, too, assume that they know one another. For instance, when they meet for the first time they embrace warmly like old college chums.

In the city's public square, you find statues of heroes. Some are of those who built the walls, like Buddy Bolden and King Oliver. They appear to have been sculptured in bars, after-hours joints, and houses of ill-repute. Some are of those who fought to save the city, like Fletcher Henderson and Paul Whiteman, and they are identified with the world of ballroom palaces. Some are of those who went down swinging, like Bix Beiderbecke and Chick Webb, and who were decorated posthumously for heroic performances above and beyond the call of duty. Last, in the same concert halls where they play the

---

* Some other Foundation Members of the "Love You Madly Club": Coots Bussard, Ted Travers, Fred Wyatt, Bob Smith, Ken Jones, Cal Bailey, Sue Harbin, Torchy Pechet, the Lowell Cuzzens, Dr. L. Young, Dr. Herbert Henderson, Louis Ventrilla, Aaron Bridgers, the Pharrs, the Diamonds, Bob and Evelyn Udkoff, Jimmy Jones, Dee and Liz, and the daughter of W. E. B. Dubois.

masterworks, are statues of some of the great ones who long defended the walls, like Bechet, Armstrong, and Hawk.

This City of Jazz does not have any specific geographical location. It is anywhere and everywhere, wherever you can hear the sound, and it makes you do like this—you know! Europe, Asia, North and South America, the world digs this burg—Digsville, Gonesville, Swingersville, and Wailingstown. There are no city limits, no city ordinances, no policemen, no fire department, but come rain or come shine, drought or flood, I think I'll stay here in this scene, with these cats, because almost everybody seems to dig what they're talking about, or putting down. They communicate, Dad. Do you get the message?

Villesville is *the* place—*trelos anthropos!*

Chicago

Chicago always sounded like the most glamorous place in the world to me when I heard the guys in Frank Holliday's poolroom talking about their travels. The way dining-car waiters and Pullman porters spoke of the city as "Chi-kor-ga" fascinated me, and they told very romantic tales about the nightlife on the South Side.

By the time I got there in 1930, it glittered even more, but we were there only one day to play the Savoy ballroom before going on to the West Coast to do the Amos 'n' Andy picture. When I came back on Friday, February 13, 1931, to play eight weeks in Balaban and Katz theatres, I saw it good and really got the vibrations.

The most impressive aspect, I think, was that the South Side was *together*. It was a real us-for-we, we-for-us community. It was a community with twelve Negro millionaires, no hungry Negroes, no complaining Negroes, no crying Negroes, and no Uncle Tom Negroes. It was a community of men and women who were respected, people of great dignity—doctors, lawyers, policy operators, bootblacks, barbers, beauticians, bartenders, saloonkeepers, night clerks, cab owners and cab drivers, stockyard workers, owners of after-hours joints, bootleggers—everything and everybody, but *no* junkies.

Chicago then was all that they had said in the poolroom: the Loop, the cabarets, the biggest railroad center in the world, beaches that ran along Lake Michigan the full length of greater Chicago, city life, suburban life, luxurious neighborhoods—and the apparently broken-down neighborhoods where there were more good times than any place in the city.

In those days, glaring accounts of the gangsters and Al Capone came over the radio and filled the newspapers. I was introduced to Sam Ablon, a cat who was supposed to be one of the big, mob guys, and we became chummy. He used to pick Sonny Greer and me up after our show, and we'd sit around and

At the Fulton Theatre, 1930: Joe Nanton, Juan Tizol, trombones; Freddy Jenkins, Cootie Williams, Artie Whetsol, trumpets; Duke Ellington, piano and conductor; Sonny Greer, "the sweet-singing drummer"; Fred Guy, banjo; Wellman Braud, bass; Harry Carney, Johnny Hodges, Barney Bigard, reeds

drink all night long. He'd get juiced, and we'd get juiced, until the point was reached where it was really time to go home.

"Well, all right, man," we'd say. "We'll take you home, Sam. Ain't nobody goin' to bother you!"

We used to play theatres in Chicago like the Oriental and the Regal, but I remember that once we were out at the Paradise on the West Side, and it was the custom then for anybody who had his name up in lights to be challenged. When I got there, the manager, Sam Fleischnik, told me that I had had some visitors.

"Some of those gang punks were here this morning," he explained, "and

1935, left to right: Cootie Williams, Wellman Braud, Toby Hardwick, Duke Ellington, Lawrence Brown, Joe Nanton, Rex Stewart, Artie Whetsol, Sonny Greer, Harry Carney, Barney Bigard (top), Johnny Hodges, Juan Tizol, Fred Guy

they said for Duke Ellington to send out five hundred dollars or don't come out. You know what I told 'em?"

"No, what?"

"I told them all the boys in the band carried pistols. Each and every one had a gun, and we would shoot it out with them."

"You must be out of your mind," I said as I recovered from that.

After we had finished our four shows that night, we were on our way back to the South Side when a car pulled up alongside us at a red light. They trained a strong spotlight on us, and we were scared stiff.

"Sorry," a voice said, "but we are looking for somebody."

It was a police car, and as it pulled away we breathed big sighs of relief. But my troubles were not over. When we arrived at our hotel, the Trenier Hotel out at Oakwood Boulevard and South Parkway (I think it is now called the Ritz), a little kid stopped me on the sidewalk and said, "Duke, there's a couple of gangsters waiting for you in the lobby."

I was scared again, but it was cold outdoors, and I said to myself, "Well, hell, it's no use my standing out here." So with my best stiff upper lip, I walked into the lobby, recognized nobody and was recognized by nobody. I got on the elevator and went upstairs to my room, where I took off my coat after closing the door, and sat down. "If there's going to be any trouble," I thought, "why get trapped up here all by myself?" So I went back down to the lobby, where there were a lot of people talking and relaxing. I spotted two guys who had the appearance of those the kid had mentioned, so with upper lip up stiffer, I walked over to them.

"Hi," I said, smiling. "You looking for me?"

"Who are you?"

"I'm Duke Ellington."

"Hey, Duke, don't you remember me? I'm Mike Best's brother."

"Sure, man, how are you?" I said, although I had never seen either of them before in my life. "Good to see you."

After some more jive of this kind, one of them says, "We need a favor. Our buddy got bumped off yesterday, and we want two hundred dollars to ship his body home."

"Man, Mike Best's brother can have anything I've got. Come by the theatre tomorrow. I don't have any loot on me at the moment."

"Oh, we can't do that," they said, interrupting me. "This is urgent. We've got to have it now."

"Well, wait a minute," I said. "Maybe I can borrow it at the desk."

I went over to the front desk and spoke to Phil the cashier, who was the brother-in-law of Ed Fox, the man who ran the Grand Terrace next door.

"Phil, I need a couple of hundred dollars."

"Two hundred!" Phil said, startled. "What can you do with a couple of hundred tonight? You're invited next door to the Grand Terrace as our guest, and you can't spend a dime in there."

"Oh, some friends want a little favor," I said.

"Friends?" Phil said. "Where'd you get friends? You ain't been in Chicago five minutes. How'd you get that kind of friend so quick? Where are they?"

"Those two cats over there."

"Them two bums!" Phil exploded, peering over his glass enclosure. "Okay, tell 'em to wait a minute while I go next door a..d get it from Joe Fusco."

When those two cats heard the name of Joe Fusco, they almost broke that big front door down dashing out to the street. So then I went over to the Grand Terrace and listened to Fatha Hines's band for the rest of the night.

After I got back to my room, I called Mike Best at the Cotton Club and told him about my visitors.

"My brother is in South America," he said, "and if he ever came to you for money he'd want twenty thousand dollars. He wouldn't want any two hundred. Hold on a minute . . ."

He put Owney Madden on the other telephone, and I told him about what had happened. "Don't worry about it, Duke," he told me. "I'll make a call and straighten it out. You won't have any more of that kind of trouble."

The next day, when I went to the theatre, the whole stage crew was waiting at the stage door, salaaming and saying, "Why didn't you tell us you *know* people?" It seemed Owney Madden had called Al Capone, who issued an order: "Duke Ellington is not to be bothered in the Loop."

But after the first show, those two cats called up and said, "Duke, couldn't you please let us have twenty dollars. We've got to leave town. The Loop is too hot."

"Sure," I said. "Come on over."

"Oh, no," the cat said. "Send it down to the front lobby by your manager, but don't tell anybody else, please. Thanks."

135

Toronto

In 1940 something happened that I have never forgotten. It was during the period when we used to play "locations" more often. That is, engagements where you worked four weeks or so in the same club. The money was often far from the greatest, but in addition to easing up on the travel there was the big advantage of a regular radio broadcast. The air time could be used by a band to plug its new music, and it was more or less a sure thing that, after you had aired a particular song every night for four weeks, there would be some reaction from the public. Having been raised in the Irving Mills tradition, I knew how important it was to pick out something recently recorded and released, so that it had a good chance of being ballyhooed.

Places like the Cotton Club in New York, the Cotton Club in Los Angeles, and the Congress Hotel in Chicago were convenient for sitting down for a while, but on this occasion we were in the College Inn of the Sherman Hotel in Chicago. Songpluggers representing the various music publishers were making the normal requests. Although I had a lot of my own stuff to plug, during the fourth week I decided I could relent a little. There were more than twenty of these songpluggers, some of them good friends, and all of them, I decided, pretty nice guys.

"All right, fellows," I said to them one day, "tonight we do it. Tonight I'm going to put everybody's song on the air!"

I made out the program, and it was very tight with more than twenty numbers to be played in an hour. Broadcast time came, and we went on the air with everybody's music but mine. All the pluggers were very happy about it, but then came a long telegram which read, in essence:

IF YOU EVER PLAY A PROGRAM LIKE THAT AGAIN, WE ARE GOING TO TUNE YOU OUT AND NEVER TURN YOU ON AGAIN.

SIGNED THE MUSICIANS OF LOCAL 149, A.F.M.,
TORONTO, ONTARIO, CANADA.

This was an awful blow to me, because by doing the songpluggers a favor I had let down some of my dearest friends.

Toronto was a unique place in those days. Artistic perspectives were adjusted to a strong natural state of individuality. Everybody in Canada seemed to listen to what they individually enjoyed, and nobody could tell them what to like, or what was popular, or what was the In thing. Even today, it is very hard to brainwash Canadians.

On top of that, starting with my first visit to Canada, when we were playing the Shea Theatre in Toronto, I had made two close friends in Jack Barker and Robert Favreaux. Both were painters and fine artists, and I spent much of my time with them when in Canada. Their constant warnings had to do with condescending to commercial music. I should not, they insisted, be influenced by anybody, by any music, or by anybody's taste but my own. My main fear was how I could face them after the Local 149 telegram. But they were true friends, and I was well received as always by them, and they allowed me to sit and drink their gorgeous Canadian rye all night while benefiting from their critique of my recent recordings.

We have always had a lot of friends in Toronto. I remember Helen Oakley and her brother taking me out to their house during one of our first visits to the city. Their mother was very proud of her garden, but displeased by her daughter's lack of interest in it.

"The trouble with Helen," she said to me, "is that, no matter how much she knows about music, she doesn't know one plant from another."

"Well, if you told her that that one was in E flat," I said, "I'm sure she would remember it."

There is a funny twist to that story. Nowadays, her English husband complains that he often does not get his afternoon tea at the proper time because Helen is so busy pruning her shrubs and rosebushes.

Mrs. Anger and her son, Ron, are also among our most loyal friends and supporters. They never miss our appearances in Toronto, and the city's chapter of the Duke Ellington Society has always owed a great deal of its health to them.

In addition to its sensitive audience—and maybe because of it—Canada has developed many brilliant musicians. I had an opportunity to show my appreciation of these great artists in 1967. Louis Applebaum, who was for many years musical director at the Stratford Shakespearean Festival, Stratford, Ontario, asked me if I would be willing to be "exploited" on behalf of Canadian composers.

"Sure," I said. "What do you want me to do?"

He explained that they wanted me to play piano with two hand-picked groups performing compositions by Ron Collier, Norman Symonds, and Gordon Delamont. The project was fostered by the Composers, Authors and Publishers Association of Canada (CAPAC) and the Canadian Association of Broadcasters (CAB), the primary objective being to make the work of Canadian musicians better known. Ron Collier conducted and the results of two record sessions were later issued on a Decca album entitled *Duke Ellington North of the Border*.

I thought it was very much worth while, because I am well aware that a problem of communication exists between Canada with its twenty-one million people and us, the big neighbor to the south, with our two hundred and three million. Canada has a character and a spirit of its own, which we should recognize and never take for granted.

London

London was the first city we went to on the other side of the Atlantic, and in 1933 we could not have had a better steppingstone to Europe. Being able to speak the language was a big help, although I had some doubts about that during our first week at the Palladium. There was a Cockney comedian on the bill with us—I think his name was Max Miller—and he used to have the whole house in an uproar. I would stand in the wings, and at first I did not dig what he was doing, but then I began to understand his slang, and friends explained some of the finer points of his humor, which, when you were with it, was really down.

There are many reasons why I love London. First I think of the people I have met there or who live there: H.M. Queen Elizabeth II; the Duke of Edinburgh; Princess Margaret; the Duke of Windsor, when he was Prince of Wales; Prince George, the Duke of Kent, who was tragically killed during World War II; the Earl of Harewood and his brother, the Hon. Gerald Lascelles, and Mrs. Lascelles. Their kindness, and their interest in what we were doing, meant a lot to us. There was a consistency in their attitude from 1933 right on up to our last visit. It was in London, too, in 1933, that I first met my good friend, the Maharajah of Cooch Behar, who was then at school in England. He is the Django Reinhardt of maharajahs.

Then there are our many personal friends, like Renée and Leslie Diamond, Mips and Sinclair Traill, Betty and Max Jones, and the great Duggie Tobutt, who did so much to make us comfortable when we were touring the island. We also enjoyed the friendliest of relations with many fine musicians, beginning with Jack Hylton in 1933 through to Johnny Dankworth at the present time.

Besides these people, and London Bridge, and Waterloo Bridge, and Chelsea Bridge, and Piccadilly, and Mayfair, and Hyde Park, and hotels like the Grosvenor, the Dorchester, and the Savoy, and the acclaim I have repeatedly received in the city, I love London for quite another reason.

To me, the people of London are the most civilized in the world. Their civilization is based on the recognition that all people are imperfect, and due allowances should be and are made for their imperfections. I have never experienced quite such a sense of *balance* elsewhere. What is cricket, and what is not, is very well understood by everybody. And hysteria is something you may sometimes hear about there, but you never are exposed to it except at a very great distance. Self-discipline, as a virtue or an acquired asset, can be invaluable to anyone.

Paris

When I was in Paris in 1970, I was invited to do a television show. I hadn't the foggiest notion of what I was to do until I arrived at the station, where I was told very politely, but rather vaguely, that perhaps I could play some piano and talk about Paris in between. The lights went on, and there I sat at the piano with no lead or anything. So I announced who I was, what I did for a living, and drifted into playing and talking about my first visit to Paris in 1933. I apologized for not being able to speak in French, and I dropped names like crazy, beginning with Bricktop's, and going on from there to mention several famous restaurants.

To me, I explained, the people in it are always what make a city, although this does not mean that I am not susceptible to the sights, sounds, scents, and, shall we say, sustenance of one like Paris. Far from it. I continued in this strain:

Among those I think of as citizens of Paris was Django Reinhardt, a very dear friend of mine, and one whom I regard as among the few great inimitables of our music. I had him on a concert tour with me in 1946, so that I could enjoy him the more. He was not billed because he was booked after the tour had been sold and the advertising was out. I always said that Django was a great believer, because a believer is an optimist who thinks of tomorrow, and one of Django's favorite sayings was, "Tomorrow, maybe . . ."

Then, of course, there was Sidney Bechet, who worked with us in 1926, and who much later, after World War II, made his home in Paris, where he became a great popular star. He was another of the inimitables.

I have always had good luck in Paris and with people who come from there. The first time I ever conducted with a baton was when our band accompanied the first personal appearance of another inimitable, Maurice Chevalier, in New York at the Fulton Theatre in 1930. Nearly forty years

With Bert Ambrose and Django Reinhardt, 1946

later, he remembered that occasion when they were celebrating my birthday at a party in the Alcazar in Paris.

"You have brought back my youth to me," he said, smiling. Then he presented me with the straw hat he was wearing.

"It is an honor to wear this straw hat," I said, "the symbol of Maurice Chevalier, whose shoes no one else in the world can fill."

It was an expansive and expensive affair with a real Parisian flavor. Baron Edmond de Rothschild and Salvador Dali were there. A huge cake—*en forme de camembert géant, trois mètres de diamètre*—was lowered from the ceiling, the first time nearly on my unsuspecting head! The second time, it made a safe descent, and out from it stepped *trois danseuses nues,* to everybody's intense satisfaction. After that, I was presented with more than two hundred roses by different artists and guests, one at a time. It was a moving and charming gesture. As *Le Figaro* put it next day, they were convinced that "when one has a flower in the hand, one no longer needs to speak English."

In 1960, I was in Paris for eight weeks to write the music for *Paris Blues.* This was the film in which Louis Armstrong, Paul Newman, Sidney Poitier, Joanne Woodward, and Diahann Carroll appeared. Jean Vilar of the prestigious Théâtre National Populaire had another assignment for me. He invited me to do music for *Turcaret,* a classic play by Lesage that had not been performed since 1709. That was a ball, and I recorded it with a band of French musicians. I thought it was great, and we have tapes of it, so someday perhaps we can release it.

Another invitation that I appreciated very much was to play at the Christmas Eve mass in the enormous Palais de la Défense. I played "Come Sunday," the spiritual theme from *Black, Brown and Beige,* and I am glad to say that everybody seemed to find it appropriate to the occasion.

Billy Strayhorn loved Paris and always named it among his very favorite places. On this television program, I played his "Lotus Blossom," which he always claimed I played better than he did. He was a very gracious man, but I am sure his friend Aaron Bridgers plays it better than I do. Aaron is one of our New York people who made his home in Paris. There is a whole group of good piano players there. Every time I go, I have Raymond Fol write something for me. And then there is Claude Bolling. I never forget Claude for the time I made a new arrangement at the last minute on something somebody had requested. He came out of the audience afterwards, and he was very polite.

"There's a change in the harmony," he said, "and I really don't understand why." He was right. It was in the second bar of "Magenta Haze."

I was not embarrassed. Never get embarrassed by what friends say. Any time friends have to be careful of what they say to friends, friendship is taking on another dimension.

While Billy Strayhorn was in the hospital in New York, I was in Paris again, and one night we made a tape with Joe Turner and all the other good pianists, each of them playing two compositions. It was wonderful, because I felt I was bringing Billy a piece of his favorite city. All his colleagues, friends, and fellow pianists participated in this. They stayed up till eight in the morning after working all night long. We hope to take that beautiful tape and sell it, and use the money to establish a Billy Strayhorn scholarship in Paris. When that comes out, it will make Billy happy, and he will smile again, as I am sure he did when we set up the first Billy Strayhorn scholarship at Juilliard in New York.

Whenever I play a concert in Paris—and we have been playing concerts there since 1933 at the Salle Pleyel and 1939 at the Palais de Chaillot—Hugues Panassié demands that I go 'way back and play James P. Johnson's "Carolina Shout." Of course, I used to do that when I had a terrific left hand, but my left hand is relatively unrehearsed nowadays, and it shows badly when either Joe Turner or Claude Bolling are around, because they do it *beautifully*. However, we always give Hugues Panassié credit for writing our trombone parts when we play in Paris!

Another great Parisian is Charles Delaunay, who gave me the opportunity to play and record with the Paris Opéra Orchestra when we were recording for his label. This was the first time we had really recorded with the symphony. It was a glorious affair playing with all those wonderful musicians, playing just exactly as we wrote it, and with me conducting! It was just too much!

Talking about such fine people and such happy happenings, I felt I got through my television show rather creditably, but no sooner was I out of the studio than I remembered several other important people, notably Stephane Grappelli, the violinist and Django's partner. That was inexcusable, because I had recorded him with two other violinists, Svend Asmussen from Copenhagen, and our own Ray Nance. So I went back in the studio and added these names. "Cool," I thought, "I haven't missed anybody this time."

The very next day, as I was leaving Paris, I was absolutely horrified when another great name came into my mind. I had left out a little chorus girl who first went to Europe in a show I wrote so many years ago. Who do you think it was? Nobody but Josephine Baker! I was so disgusted with myself, I just about dropped my tools.

I immediately tried to figure out a way to redo by long distance, but no dice! Here I am, still biting my fingernails and kicking myself! She had sent her chauffeured Rolls to take me out to her beautiful château, and she had heaped goodies on me as though I were really somebody.

The only way I can account for that gaffe is that I was welcomed and feted on Josephine Baker's estate with such grace and honest-to-goodness hospitality, and made to feel so much at home, that I just simply forgot this one-in-a-million great lady was *not* the pretty girl next door.

So I hope I have not lost my license to give Josephine Baker four kisses and a dozen roses for each one. She is so beautiful.

I guess I am just a pedestrian at heart!

Act Four

Satin Doll

Formative Years Adjusted

Gus Greenlee's nephew was tending bar in Pittsburgh, and he told me of a friend of his who wrote music "real good." I hear this many times a year, but he was a friend and I agreed to listen.

"Bring him to the theatre," I said, "between shows."

I went back to partying until it was almost time for the first show, and then went straight to the theatre without sleep. After the show, I headed for my dressing room to lie down and rest.

Greenlee arrived ten minutes later with his young man who could write music. I didn't get up, but continued lying on the bed. In a very wide-awake voice, I told them to come on in.

"Have him play on the piano over there," I said, smiling.

So this young man sat down at the piano, and I couldn't believe what I heard. It was wonderful. I didn't lie there any longer, but jumped up, *really* wide-awake.

"Hey, play that again!"

On and on, a real marriage of words and music . . .

"What did you say your name was again?"

"Billy Strayhorn."

"Man, you're great!"

Encore after encore, compliment after compliment, until it was almost time for my second show.

"Why, young man, I'm going to bring you to New York, and you will be my lyric writer. I'm mad about what you're doing. Don't forget to give me your address and phone number. Soon . . . you and I in New York."

I probably took longer than I realized sending for Strays, but this very bright young man showed up again in my dressing room one day when we were playing the Adams Theatre in Newark, New Jersey.

"You don't get away again," I said. "I take you with me tonight." And so I did.

I took him to 381 Edgecombe Avenue, and said, "This is my home, and this is your home. I'm leaving for Europe in a few days, but you stay here with my son, Mercer, and my sister, Ruth. They'll take good care of you."

We left on March 23, 1939, for Le Havre on the French ship *Champlain*. We had very rough seas all the way. The *Champlain* tossed up and down on the Atlantic, first the front end out of the water, and then the back end. You could hear the propeller spin and scream, and then the boat would slap back on the sea with a bump and a crash. You had to hold on every minute of the day.

The band acted brave, drank the booze, and went on down to their sleeping deck to bed. Rex Stewart and I didn't act so brave. We weren't scared either—just observant. Our drink was champagne and cognac, half and half. When the bar was ready to close, we would order enough to last all night if necessary. When the boat tossed with an extra flip, we would salute one another and drink a toast.

Nearly everybody in the band was a crazy gambler except Lawrence Brown. Cootie Williams, Wellman Braud, Johnny Hodges, Ivie Anderson—all were astute and serious players in their different ways. We played poker all day and all night. When the other cats finally went to bed, Rex and I would still be up playing head-and-head poker. One night, I remember, I was winning and had all the money in front of me when Rex said, "I've got an idea for a new tune."

"Let's go over to the piano and see how it sounds," I said.

I liked the idea, and we developed it, and it turned out to be a very good number, which we titled "Morning Glory."

When we were all finished with music, we returned to our table to continue the game. Rex sat down in the chair in front of all the money, and I sat down where there was little or nothing. We discussed this and decided there must have been some kind of mistake. Then we wandered out on deck.

We went up to explore the wheelhouse, and the Captain's and officers' quarters, but there was nobody to be found anywhere up there. This struck us as extraordinary.

"How do you like that?" we said. "There's nobody guiding the ship in the middle of the night!"

So we had to stay up and watch until daylight, and only then sometimes go to bed. When we told the cats in the band that there was nobody in the wheelhouse, they all promptly got stoned. We did our night duty every night thereafter until we arrived in Le Havre.

It was April when we got to the Netherlands, and the tulips were just breath-taking. I had never seen such a beautiful place before. We had some cause for concern, however, because we had heard that the Hitler regime did not like jazz, and on our train trip from Holland to Denmark we had to go through Germany.

Because we were all well aware of the tension, we deliberately kept our cool. Cootie Williams had his record player with him, and he was sitting minding his business when a couple of German kids came into his section of the train.

"Is this your record player?" they asked. "And are these jazz records? Please, may we play them?"

"Go ahead," Cootie said. "Help yourself."

They jumped at the chance, and they played those records all day with the volume turned up loud enough to wake people in other parts of the train.

We had to change trains in Hamburg, and there was a six-hour layover. We were a party of twenty black people who, according to rumor, were thought less of there than in the U. S. South, but it was strange how they just ignored us. The merchants were civil enough, and we got on our train to Denmark without incident. Part of the train, I remember, was put on a ferry to cross over to Copenhagen.

I stayed at the Palace Hotel, right across from Copenhagen's City Hall. They had a carillon in the tower, and I sat up all one night listening to them ring it, not only on the hour, but on the quarter hour, half hour, and three-quarter hour as well, and different each time. It was wonderful, and I especially liked one wild interval change.

Rex Stewart and a couple of other cats in the band always used to keep a carton of Tums handy. After the first two or three days in Sweden, they were complaining about the cold food for breakfast, but they decided to stay with it and be polite. A few days later, I found a couple of big packages of Tums discarded on the restaurant table, and it turned out that the cold Swedish food they had been turning their noses up at had actually cured their need for Tums!

We went to Stockholm and about twenty other cities in Sweden. Our impresario was Baron Lennart Reuterscholl, and we opened at the Konserthus in Stockholm. I shall never forget my birthday there. The celebration started at 8 A.M. with the entire Grand Hotel staff—from manager to dishwasher—marching through the sitting room and into my bedroom, greeting me, and then on out and down the stairs. The procedure called for me to get out of bed, slip into my robe without dressing, and fall in at the end of the line. The column continued on down the stairs to the ground floor and into the main dining room, where breakfast was waiting. There were drinks, toasts, and the singing of good wishes. This went on all day, with flowers arriving every minute—large pieces, small pieces, all gorgeous. The celebration went on through our two evening concerts—one at 6 P.M., the other, I think, at 9 P.M.—flowers and greetings flowing in all the time. Some of the floral pieces were so big they had to be carried by two men. At intermission, the entire audience stood and sang the Swedish equivalent of "Happy Birthday" and after that they brought out ten tiny little girls who sang it in English. This really broke me up, and I had tears in my eyes before they finished. After the demonstration had been repeated at the nine o'clock concert, we went out on the town. At every nightclub we went to, the audience stood up and sang that wonderful song. And this went on till eight o'clock the next morning, when we wound up at the home of Baron Reuterscholl.

It was a glorious spring that year, and only one thing spoiled it. All through the day the Swedish people had the radio on, listening to Hitler threaten them and the world. When we asked what he had said, they simply shrugged their shoulders. It was all so mysterious that Rex and I wanted to take the first ship home.

We came back eventually on the *Île de France,* and when I returned to 381 Edgecombe Avenue I discovered that Strays and Mercer had been going through my music scores. Strays said he thought he would be able to do a little orchestrating. I took it in tempo until one day when we were caught in a cramp for a number on a record session the following morning. I gave the job to Strays, and he came up with this wonderful sound that knocked everybody out.

"What!" they said. "You mean this little child did that?"

Then Sonny Greer dubbed Strays "Swee' Pea," because in size he resembled Swee' Pea in the comic strip, and he stayed Swee' Pea until one night in Rochester, New York, where Sonny Greer took Strays out and got him juiced. I saw his condition when they returned and was a little alarmed.

"What have you done to this boy?" I asked Sonny.

Strays was wearing my hat, which I had asked him to take back to the hotel after the dance. At this point he came out from under the hat and said in a very hip manner, "I don't dig you, man!"

From that night on, Strayhorn was more than an accessory to me.

Two other additions to the band around this time were also of great importance. Ben Webster was really saying something on that tenor saxophone, and I thought it was a most fitting thing for us to do, to get him. We got him, and immediately the sax section became more mature, with a grip on getting-togetherness it had never had before.

Strays and Ben almost forcibly drew my attention to Jimmy Blanton, who revolutionized bass playing, and meant a great deal to the band. All in all, when we went out to the Coast at the beginning of 1941 we were in very good shape.

Before that, however, a good friend of mine named Edmund Anderson came over with Ted Grouya and their new song entitled "Flamingo." I listened and liked it, and gave it to Strayhorn right away so that he could prepare it for Herb Jeffries to sing. The orchestration he did on "Flamingo" was, in my opinion, a turning point in vocal background orchestration, a renaissance in elaborate ornamentation for the accompaniment of singers. It soon caught on and became a big hit. Since then, other arrangers have become more and more daring, but Billy Strayhorn really started it all with "Flamingo."

In 1939, I had signed to write music exclusively for Jack Robbins, who by then owned several publishing companies. The contract was for three years, and in that time I probably gave them more music than anybody else had written for them in ten years.

Almost simultaneously, I went with the William Morris Agency for booking the band. They did the usual things—one-nighters—which took us into some of the most beautiful parts of the country on the West Coast I had ever seen. While driving along the south shore of the Columbia River east of Portland, Oregon, we had a good view of the mountains on the north shore. They had the most voluptuous contours, and to me they looked like a lot of women reclining up there. "Warm Valley" came directly from that experience.

We played a lot of spots around Los Angeles, and were for a long time in the Casa Manana, which was originally Frank Sebastian's Cotton Club, and

At Puyallup, Washington, Festival of Daffodils, 1940. Back row: Rex Stewart, Cootie Williams, Wallace Jones, Joe Nanton, Juan Tizol, Lawrence Brown, Fred Guy, Billy Strayhorn; front row: Sonny Greer, Duke Ellington, Johnny Hodges, Barney Bigard, Ben Webster, Toby Hardwick, Harry Carney, Jimmy Blanton

later the Meadowbrook. During this period—1940–41—we produced some very good music. Because of the ASCAP-BMI fight, I could not play any of my own compositions, and this prompted the great activity of Billy Strayhorn, Juan Tizol, and Mercer Ellington, which in one way or another led to "Take the 'A' Train," "Perdido," "Daydream," "Things Ain't What They Used to Be," and a number of instrumentals that have become standards.

There is just one sad memory from that time. I had made a date to meet my Los Angeles doctor, Dr. Gordon, Dexter Gordon's father, in the bar of the Dunbar Hotel on Forty-first and Central at four o'clock Christmas morning. A friend came in right on the hour and told me the doctor couldn't make it, because he had just died of a heart attack. That completely ruined my chances of a happy Christmas celebration.

The band attracted a wonderful audience and made us extremely hot on the West Coast. At the same time, I was getting mixed up with some of the Hollywood writers whose sympathies fitted into my scene and scheme, and this all led to *Jump for Joy*.

Dramatis Felidae

BILLY STRAYHORN

Billy Strayhorn was always the most unselfish, the most patient, and the most imperturbable, no matter how dark the day. I am indebted to him for so much of my courage since 1939. He was my listener, my most dependable appraiser, and as a critic he would be the most clinical, but his background—both classical and modern—was an accessory to his own good taste and understanding, so what came back to me was in perfect balance.

In music, as you develop a theme or musical idea, there are many points at which direction must be decided, and any time I was in the throes of debate with myself, harmonically or melodically, I would turn to Billy Strayhorn. We would talk, and then the whole world would come into focus. The steady hand of his good judgment pointed to the clear way that was most fitting for us. He was not, as he was often referred to by many, my alter ego. Billy Strayhorn was my right arm, my left arm, all the eyes in the back of my head, my brainwaves in his head, and his in mine.

Our rapport was the closest. When I was writing my first sacred concert, I was in California and he was in a New York hospital. On the telephone, I told him about the concert and that I wanted him to write something. "Introduction, ending, quick transitions," I said. "The title is the first four words of the Bible—'In the Beginning God.'" He had not heard my theme, but what he sent to California started on the same note as mine (F natural) and ended on the same note as mine (A flat a tenth higher). Out of six notes representing the six syllables of the four words, only two notes were different.

Now I only hope that my representation of him will have the dignity with which he represented me. Our theme is his "Take the 'A' Train," and I

With Billy Strayhorn, 1959

With Billy Strayhorn at a recording session, 1965

can still hear his voice clearly clearing up any point of indecision with his watchword: "Ever onward and upward!" Many people are indebted to Billy Strayhorn, and I more than anybody.

It was early in the morning of May 31, 1967, when my sister, Ruth, called, crying, and told me Billy Strayhorn had just passed in the night. I was in Reno, and I don't know what I said, but after I hung up the phone I started sniffling and whimpering, crying, banging my head up against the wall, and talking to myself about the virtues of Billy Strayhorn. Why Billy Strayhorn, I asked? Why? Subconsciously, I sat down and started writing what I was thinking, and as I got deeper and deeper into thinking about my favorite human being, I realized that I was not crying any more. It seemed that what I was doing was more important than anything, so on and on I wrote. When it was finished, I called Ruth and read it to her over the phone. Then I called all my friends of the clergy who had been praying for him ever since they heard he was sick in the hospital. I told them the bad news and asked them to continue to pray for him.

This is what I wrote that May morning:

Poor little Swee' Pea, Billy Strayhorn, William Thomas Strayhorn, the biggest human being who ever lived, a man with the greatest courage, the most majestic artistic stature, a highly skilled musician whose impeccable taste commanded the respect of all musicians and the admiration of all listeners.

His audiences at home and abroad marveled at the grandeur of his talent and the mantle of tonal supremacy that he wore only with grace. He was a beautiful human being, adored by a wide range of friends, rich, poor, famous, and unknown. Great artists pay homage to Billy Strayhorn's God-given ability and mastery of his craft.

Because he had a rare sensitivity and applied himself to his gifts, Billy Strayhorn successfully married melody, words, and harmony, equating the fitting with happiness. His greatest virtue, I think, was his honesty, not only to others, but to himself. His listening-hearing self was totally intolerant of his writing-playing self when, or if, any compromise was expected, or considered expedient.

He spoke English perfectly and French very well, but condescension did not enter into his mind. He demanded freedom of expression and lived in what we consider the most important and moral of freedoms: freedom from hate, unconditionally; freedom from self-pity (even throughout all the pain and bad news); freedom from fear of possibly doing something that might

159

At Leeds Festival, 1958. Left to right: the Hon. Gerald Lascelles, Al Celley, Billy Strayhorn, Duke Ellington, the Earl of Harewood

help another more than it might himself; and freedom from the kind of pride that could make a man feel he was better than his brother or neighbor.

His patience was incomparable and unlimited. He had no aspirations to enter into any kind of competition, yet the legacy he leaves, his *oeuvre,* will never be less than the ultimate on the highest plateau of culture (whether by comparison or not).

God bless Billy Strayhorn.

Billy Strayhorn belonged to the Copasetics, a club organized mostly by tap dancers. As I've always said, he was fundamentally a dancer himself (how well his composition, "U.M.M.G.," demonstrates this!), so he naturally gravitated toward this club where he had a lot of friends. The membership consisted of: Charlie Atkins, Paul Black, Buster Brown, Ernest Brown, Louis Brown, Roy Branker, Honi Coles, Chink Collins, Charles Cook, Emory Evans, Billy Eckstine, Francis and Frank Goldberg (twins), Milton Larkin, LeRoy Myers, Pete Nugent, Phace Roberts, John Thomas, Elmer Waters, Eddie West, Charles Penelton, Bubba Gaines, Charlie Shavers, Dizzy Gillespie, and B. B. King. At the annual show they put on, everybody danced—Billy Eckstine, and even Billy Strayhorn, who had written the music.

Billy became the president of the Copasetics, and it is consistent with his enchanting spell that they refused to have anyone else as president after they lost him. The title of president was permanently retired in his honor, and thenceforward the vice-president presided. Henry Phace Roberts is v.-p. as this is written.

RAY NANCE

Ray Nance never played a bad note in his life, so this makes him unique among artists who practice freedom of expression in music. Singer, violinist, cornetist, and dancer, he is consistently a gas! Despite his brilliant solos, he never got a swollen head. He played his section parts with dedicated teamwork, too, and never demanded any special recognition for his outstanding performances in the band. Many is the time, when other members fell short, that he jumped into a substitute spot. I don't think he ever joined the gang very much in their after-hours activities and pleasures, but when he worked he worked beyond the limit, sometimes even beyond the call of duty. He is a pure artist at heart, and no trumpet player ever takes an ad-lib chorus on Billy Strayhorn's "Take the 'A' Train" without falling back on some of the original licks introduced by Ray Nance on the first recording of it.

I knew all of his wonderful, hospitable family very well in Chicago, where he was born and raised. He joined the band in 1940 and was with us over twenty years. What else can I tell you about a man short of stature who towers ten feet above his colleagues and competitors. There's really only one Ray Nance.

Willie Cook, Lawrence Brown, Ray Nance (the "pep" section)

BEN WEBSTER

After he had made a record date with us in 1935, I always had a yen for Ben. So as soon as we thought we could afford him, we added him on, which gave us a five-piece saxophone section for the first time. Although Barney Bigard used to play tenor saxophone, clarinet was his main instrument, so Ben Webster was really our first tenor specialist and soloist. His splendid performances on "Cottontail," "Conga Brava," "All Too Soon," "Just a-Settin' and a-Rockin'," and "What Am I Here For?" were a sensation everywhere, and he soon became a big asset to the band. His enthusiasm and drive had an especially important influence on the saxophone section.

His influence didn't end when he left either, because when Paul Gonsalves came into the band he knew all of Ben's solos note for note. Besides Paul, we now have Harold Ashby as well, and "Ash" is both a Webster protégé and a disciple.

The last time I saw Ben Webster was in Europe, where he now lives. He proudly showed me a photograph of himself on skis, but one thing about it struck me as a little strange.

"How is it, Ben," I asked, "that your skis are pointing *up* the mountain?"

JIMMY BLANTON

In 1939 we were playing the Coronado Hotel in St. Louis. After the gig one night, the cats in the band went out jumpin' in the after-hours joints. They landed up in a hot spot on the second floor of Jesse Johnson's restaurant, where they heard and jammed with a young bass player—Jimmy Blanton. Billy Strayhorn and Ben Webster dashed over to my hotel and came into my room raving about him. I had to get up and go with them to hear him, and I flipped like everybody else. It seemed that Jimmy had done most of his playing with his mother, a pianist, and his big band experience was limited. But we didn't care about his experience. All we wanted was that sound, that beat, and those precision notes in the right places, so that we could float out on the great and adventurous sea of expectancy with his pulse and foundation behind us.

We talked him into coming down to the hotel the next night to play a few things with us. He was a sensation, and that settled it. We had to have him, and he joined the band, although our bass man at the time was Billy Taylor, one of the ace foundation-and-beat men on the instrument. So there I was with two basses! It went along fine until we got to Boston, where we were playing the Southland Cafe. Right in the middle of a set, Billy Taylor packed up his bass and said, "I'm not going to stand up here next to that young boy playing all that bass and be embarrassed." He left the stand, left us with Jimmy Blanton, and went on out the front door. I think it takes a big, big man to acknowledge the facts and take low.

Jimmy Blanton revolutionized bass playing, and it has not been the same since. No one had played from the same perspective before. He playd melodies that belonged to the bass and always had a foundation quality. Rhythmically, he supported and drove at the same time. He was just too much.

We were doing wonderfully with him. He had given us something new, a new beat, and new sounds. We made records of just bass and piano, and altogether it was a great period. Then he got sick, with TB.

164

Duke Ellington (piano); Wendell Marshall (bass); Sonny Greer (drums); Lawrence Brown, Quentin Jackson, Tyree Glenn (trombones); Jimmy Hamilton, Johnny Hodges, Ben Webster, Russell Procope, Harry Carney (reeds); Al Killian, Shorty Baker, Francis Williams, Shelton Hemphill, Ray Nance (trumpets)

It was in Los Angeles, when we were playing *Jump for Joy*. He and Billy Strayhorn were sharing a room. One day he came home, packed up his things, and told Strayhorn he had a chick he was going to live with. He wasn't actually going to live with anybody, and he didn't even tell Strayhorn that he was sick. He had gone to the doctor, and the doctor had told him, and to avoid exposing Strayhorn to it he packed up and made this excuse.

When he got *very* sick, and the whole thing came out and everybody knew what was going on, I tried to do something about it. I called doctor after doctor until I found out who the top people on TB were in Los Angeles. I made a date and took him down to the big city hospital, where there were three beautiful, young specialists. They all knew him; they were fans of his, and they talked about his music.

"I'm getting ready to leave town," I said. "Will you take care of him?"

"Yes, we will," they said. "Leave him right here. He'll just have to stay in the ward a couple of days or so until we can get him a room." A room at wherever it was they sent their people to for special care. He hadn't been there two days when some cat went down and said to him, "Why, the idea of Duke leaving you here in the ward!" He packed him up and took him out somewhere near Pasadena, I think it was, somewhere along a railroad siding. It was supposed to be a recuperating place, and each patient had his own little square box to live in. I don't think the place was big enough to have a bathroom.

When I got back to town, there he was, on his cot. They had nothing there, no X-rays or anything. "Well, you can't move him," they said, and he should have been moved a month before I got there. I took one look and knew he was gone. It was just horrible that a man's life should have been wasted that way. If that cat hadn't been so smart, and stomped his authority around, the doctors in the hospital would have had him in a very highly specialized place as we had planned. I felt terrible about it. I knew his mother, and this was almost the first time he had ever played with anybody but his mother, down there in Tennessee.

HERB JEFFRIES

Herb Jeffries was a kid we knew around Detroit. When he got involved in a series of movies as a singing cowboy, he became known as the "Bronze Buckeroo." His style inclined to the falsetto then, but it was very well accepted. We knew his family, and one day we agreed that he would come with us just for the fun of it, expenses, and a little plus. While he was with us, we played quite a few theatres and picture houses. Between shows, while everybody else was playing poker, Herb would be ad-libbing and doing imitations all over the place. He did all the singers of that time, as well as Amos 'n' Andy, and one day he was doing his interpretation of Bing Crosby, when Strayhorn and I both said in unison, "That's it! Don't go any further. Just stay on Bing."

So he did that, and Herb's imitation of Bing was the foundation until Herb's own singing self took over. I think he just forgot he was imitating

Bing, and he has been there ever since. As I've noted, when Edmund Anderson gave us a copy of his and Ted Grouya's new song, "Flamingo," in 1940, Strayhorn wrote a great arrangement for it, Herb sang it, and it became a big hit. We still get requests for it. The years went by and after we heard Herb at the Ruddy Duck in Sherman Oaks we didn't see him again until 1972 in Honolulu, where he joined Tony Watkins on stage for "One More Time."

LENA HORNE

Lena Horne is such a delicate beauty. When she decided it was show business for her, before she became of age, she had to be accompanied by her mother when she came to work at the Cotton Club. From bandstands with Charlie Barnet, she went on to movies, and always with a dignity that gained respect. When she moved into Broadway plays, she turned down hundreds of lucrative contracts because she would not play the part of a maid, a whore, or any of the other stereotypes.

When I introduced Billy Strayhorn to her, they immediately recognized their affinity as kindred spirits, and she and her late husband, Lennie Hayton, always kidded him by calling him their son. An American standard, and the essence of total agreeability, she is what most eligible women would like to be. She may well have been the inspiration for my song:

> *Oh, gee, you make that hat look pretty!**
> *Oh, gee, you make that perfume smell good!*
> *You glide like a mellow ditty,*
> *Won't you be my bride? You know you should.*
> *Oh, gee, you make your silence sing!*
> *And when I touch you I feel like a king,*
> *My heart just giggles and skips a beat.*
> *Oh, gee, you make those kisses taste sweet!*

MARY LOU WILLIAMS

Mary Lou Williams made a special contribution to our cause, especially during the time she and Shorty Baker were married. They brought Al Hibbler to

* I inherited the first line from my father.

Mary Lou Williams

us at the Hurricane Club one night. When they were in Pittsburgh, Mary Lou's hometown, they would go with Billy Strayhorn to hear Erroll Garner at the little old place where he was playing. We really had to do a job on him to get him to come to New York.

"Man, you *gotta* get out of here!"

"Naw, man, I can't leave from here. I can't make it in New York."

Finally he came, however, and took over, took over Fifty-second Street.

Mary Lou Williams is perpetually contemporary. Her writing and performing are and have always been just a little ahead throughout her career. She did one of our most important arrangements on Irving Berlin's "Blue Skies," which we recorded as "Trumpet No End," and it has always been one of our standard high spots. Much of her time is now devoted to work in the religious field, but her music retains—and maintains—a standard of quality that is timeless. She is like soul on soul.

ART TATUM

I first met Art Tatum in Toledo, Ohio, which was his home and base at the time. Friends had been talking about him, telling me how terrific he was, yet I was unprepared for what I heard. I immediately began telling him that he should be in New York. Quite a lot of what he was doing was taken right off the player-piano rolls, and I felt that the action and competition would do much good in helping to project that part of himself which was covered up by the carbon-copy things he did so perfectly. Also, I knew that once in New York he would be drawn into the Gladiator Scene with some real bad cats. I could just see The Lion, cigar in the corner of his mouth, standing over him while he played, and on the verge of saying, "Get up! I'll show you how it is supposed to go."

Tatum agreed with me and said he was going to hit the Apple one day, but he wasn't going to rush it, nor, as Ben Webster used to say, "run out there and get all skinned up." When eventually he started out for New York, he stopped on the way in Cleveland. There he got himself a job in an after-hours joint called Val's in the Alley. It was really in the alley, off an alley that was off another alley. He stayed there quite a long time. Val had a piano that was so old and beat-up that Tatum had to learn to play everything up toward the treble end. But it had a most compelling sound, and the action was obviously just right, because Tatum loved that piano even after he went to New York. Famous as he became, and deserved to be, he would always return to Val's in the Alley to play that piano. When he was playing the RKO Palace in Cleveland, he would rush out and make a dash for Val's in the Alley after doing four or five shows a day, which was customary in picture houses in those days. It was the same when he worked one of the plush hotel jobs in that city. He would end up sitting in Val's, and playing for kicks all night.

His first visit to New York stirred up a storm. In a matter of hours, it got around to all piano players—and musicians who played other instruments, too —that a real Bad Cat had arrived and was threatening the position of The Lion, James P. Johnson, Fats Waller, etc. Though he challenged them, they loved him, and this kind of association with fellow musicians is a big and profound subject that is impossible to explain.

The funny part of it was that Tatum heard, listened to, and enjoyed these encounters. After hearing The Lion and being so close to him, I'll always say that you could hear his influence in Art Tatum's playing for the next two years. Tatum was Boss, but he had a deep appreciation of all the other beautiful things in the Top Drawer.

Billy Strayhorn loved Tatum, and he spent much time with him, because he didn't have to make all those one-nighters as I did. Strays could play some of Tatum's devices that were usually considered inimitable. And would you believe that the great Art Tatum sometimes got up from the piano and asked *me* to play? Well, people, when I grow up, you'll see.

One night in Los Angeles, some friends from San Francisco and I were roaming around, and we wound up in an after-hours joint on Adams Boulevard called Brother's. Who do you think had stopped by after his job and seated himself at the piano? Nobody but my man Tatum. He was in his usual rare form, and doing all of the most impossible high and harmonic changes. Strays was with us, and our friends from San Francisco, Mr. and Mrs. Archibald Holmes. After meeting Art and conversing with him, she hit on the subject of Bach, because she had been studying his music. Something in Tatum's playing moved her to utter the next thing to a challenge. "Well, Mr. Tatum, do you know any Bach?"

"A little," Mr. Tatum answered, and then proceeded to execute a parade of Bachisms for the next hour. After getting her breath, the lovely lady said, "Thanks. I guess I'll keep my big mouth closed now!"

CHARLIE BARNET

Charlie Barnet has always been a wonderful friend to me. Because of his musicianship, good judgment, and good taste, he has always had people working for him whose potential was immense. Some who come to my mind are Lena Horne, Kay Starr, Judy Ellington, Clark Terry, Billy May, Andy Gibson, Willie Smith, Al Killian, and Spud Murphy. At the same time, he constantly bolstered my ego by playing a book almost full of our compositions. The arrangements of our things—no copycat versions—were done to fit the Charlie Barnet band, and they were suitable for whatever occasion he played.

If he heard we had a layoff in his territory, during those times when his band was not organized and working, he would—and still does—call my agent and say, "I want Duke's band to play a party for me." Actually, it would be a party for us, for there was no set order of playing—just play when we felt like it. And then, between "sets," we would join the party and ball it up like guests of honor.

One night, at one of these parties, he had signs posted up in the lobby of the country club where we were supposed to be working. They read: *No Requests. No Melancholy Baby. No anything but Duke Ellington.* He had an electric board fixed backstage, and he sat at it himself and blended the lights to fit the mood of the music. I should add that the guests (or the other guests) were nothing but the top guests of our mutual music world—Stan Kenton, Billy May, etc.

MRS. FITZPATRICK WHITE

Ever since I was a child, I've always had a profound interest in the Bible. As I've often said, every time I read the Bible I learn, or suddenly understand something that I thought I had learned. It seems, too, that there is always some dedicated person who seeks me out, or comes visiting, and talks about it.

One of these occasions occurred when we were playing the theatres around the country. A wonderful lady came backstage and asked to see me. She was Mrs. Fitzpatrick, a widow who later married Paul White, one of our feature artists in *Jump for Joy*. When we sat down to talk, she told me she was there as a representative of Jehovah's Witnesses, and she asked if I would like to hear their interpretation of biblical teachings, particularly with reference to Armageddon. I found it all very interesting and instructive, so I encouraged her to come back again at any time. I told her she was always welcome unannounced. She showed up in many places, and after her visits I always felt rewarded and more secure. All of what she had to say was stimulating, and I still somewhat expect the time of Armageddon to come to pass.

Her husband, Paul White, is still around, and the last time I saw him was in Europe, but unfortunately we lost her. I always feel that she is sitting in some quiet place waiting for Armageddon. God bless Mrs. Fitzpatrick White, a simply wonderful and gentle lady.

Act Five

Jump for Joy Extension

In 1941 a team of scholarly Hollywood writers decided to attempt to correct the race situation in the U.S.A. through a form of theatrical propaganda. This culminated in meetings at which the decision was made to do *Jump for Joy,* a show that would take Uncle Tom out of the theatre, eliminate the stereotyped image that had been exploited by Hollywood and Broadway, and say things that would make the audience think. The original script had Uncle Tom on his death bed with all his children dancing around him singing, "He lived to a ripe old age. Let him go, God bless him!" There was a Hollywood producer on one side of the bed and a Broadway producer on the other side, and both were trying to keep him alive by injecting adrenalin into his arms!

The financial backers were all top-bracket film people, such as Joe Pasternak, John Garfield, William S. Burnett, Mario Castelnuevo, Ed Fishman, Bob Roberts, George Quince, and Al Barber.

Jump for Joy was premiered at the Mayan Theatre in Los Angeles early in the summer of 1941. The audience itself was of unusual composition, for it included the most celebrated Hollywoodians, middle-class ofays, the sweet-and-low, scuffling-type Negroes, and dicty Negroes as well (doctors, lawyers, etc.). The Negroes always left proudly, with their chests sticking out.

The original program—see pages 177–179—shows who was involved in the production. Working with those writers was a very interesting experience for me. The show was never the same, because every night after the final curtain we had a meeting up in the office. All fifteen writers would be present whenever possible, and we would discuss, debate, and make decisions as to what should come out of the show the next night. We were always on guard against the possibility of chauvinism creeping in, of saying the same things about other races we did not want said about Negroes, so sometimes we had to take a successful sketch out because it leaned too far toward delicate susceptibilities. One of our funniest sketches had three colored guys sitting on a table in a tailor shop, sewing, and singing Jewish songs. It was a show-stopper, but it had to come out.

The show was done on a highly intellectual level—no crying, no moaning, but entertaining, and with social demands as a potent spice. Anyone who attended those backstage meetings for twelve weeks got a full college education in social significance. The show was a smash during its three-month run, but along came World War II to scoop up most of our young show-stoppers.

Avanelle Lewis Harris, who has been in the theatre since she was six years old, when she worked for Mack Sennett, recently wrote some of her memories of *Jump for Joy:*

"The most exciting experience of my life in the theatre was the opportunity to be a member of the cast in the musical *Jump for Joy*. I did not know how far ahead of its time it was until I read the script. It was the first legitimate show to be created and produced on the West Coast. The importance of its message caused a wave of enthusiasm throughout the cast, which was well aware of its controversial impact. Everything, every setting, every note of music, every lyric, meant something. All the sketches had a message for the world. The tragedy was that the world was not ready for *Jump for Joy*.

"How I remember the opening—'The Sun-Tanned Tenth of the Nation!' And the finale of the first act was 'Uncle Tom's Cabin Is a Drive-In Now':

> *There used to be a chicken shack in Caroline,*
> *But now they've moved it up to Hollywood and Vine;*
> *They paid off the mortgage—nobody knows how—*
> *And Uncle Tom's Cabin is a drive-in now!*

"They made us take the opening of the second act out of the show. It was called 'I've Got a Passport from Georgia (and I'm Going to the U.S.A.).'"

AMERICAN REVUE THEATRE

(WALTER JURMANN, Chairman)

PRESENTS

DUKE ELLINGTON

in

A Sun-Tanned Revu-sical

"JUMP FOR JOY"

with

DOROTHY DANDRIDGE

IVY ANDERSON

HERB JEFFRIES

Music by

Duke Ellington and Hal Borne

Lyrics by

Paul Webster

Sketches by

Sid Kuller   Hal Fimberg

Staged by

Nick Castle

Costumes. Scenery, Lighting

Rene Hubert

Sketches Directed by

Sid Kuller   Everett Wile

Additional Lyrics and Music

Sid Kuller. Otis Rene, Langston Hughes, Charles Leonard, Mickey Rooney,
Sidney Miller, Ray Golden, Richard Weil

Entire Production Supervised by

Henry Blankfort

PROGRAM

ACT I.

1. **SUN-TANNED TENTH OF THE NATION**
   Lyrics by Paul Webster   Music by Hal Borne and Otis Rene
   First Drummer . . . . LeRoy Antoine
   Second Drummer . . . . Edward Short
   Third Drummer . . . . Sonny Greer
   Duke Ellington at the Piano
   Ivy Anderson, Dorothy Dandridge, Herb Jeffries, Roy Glenn,
   Rockets, Hi-Hatters, Choir, Ensemble.

2. **AL GUSTER**
   "Stomp Caprice"   *Music by Mercer Ellington*

3. **BROWN-SKINNED GAL IN THE CALICO GOWN**
   Lyrics by Paul Webster   Music by Duke Ellington
   The Boy . . . . Herb Jeffries
   The Girl . . . . Dorothy Dandridge
   Calico Girls — Artie Brandon, Lucille Battle, Avanelle Harris,
   Doris Ake, Myrtle Fortune, Suzette Johnson.
   Dance by . . . . The Hi-Hatters

4. **HUMAN INTEREST**
   By Hal Fimberg
   Charlie . . . . Pot
   Smithers . . . . Roy Glenn
   Baltimore . . . . Skillet
   Ohio . . . . Pan
   Old Man . . . . Wonderful Smith

5. **BLI-BLIP**
   Lyrics by Sid Kuller   Music by Duke Ellington
   Girl . . . . Marie Bryant
   Boy . . . . Paul White

6. **I GOT IT BAD AND THAT AIN'T GOOD**
   Lyrics by Paul Webster   Music by Duke Ellington
   Ivy . . . . Ivy Anderson
   A Friend . . . . Alice Key

7. **WONDERFUL SMITH**

8. **CINDY WITH THE TWO LEFT FEET**
   Lyrics by Paul Webster   Music by Hal Borne
   Schoolboy . . . . Paul White
   Cindy . . . . Dorothy Dandridge
   First Sister . . . . Avanelle Harris
   Second Sister . . . . Lucille Battle
   Fairy Godmother . . . . Evelyn Burwell
   Prince Charming . . . . Al Guster
   Jitterbugs—Rockets, Hi-Hatters, Artie Brandon, Myrtle Fortune,
   Millie Monroe.

9. **POT, PAN AND SKILLET**
   "Bugle Break"--Subtle Slough   Music by Duke Ellington

10. **FLAME INDIGO**
    Garbo
    Lyrics by Paul Webster   Music by Duke Ellington

11. **MAD SCENE FROM WOOLWORTH'S**
    Langston Hughes and Charles Leonard
    Cornelia . . . . Ivy Anderson
    Woman . . . . Avanelle Harris
    First Salesgirl . . . . Suzette Johnson
    Second Salesgirl . . . . Alice Key
    Manager . . . . Al Guster
    Passerby . . . . Wonderful Smith

12. **SHHHH! HE'S ON THE BEAT!**
    By Sid Kuller and Hal Fimberg   Music by Duke Ellington
    Proprietor . . . . Roy Glenn
    Waitress . . . . Marie Bryant
    Bartender . . . . Wonderful Smith
    First Couple . . . . { Hyacinth Cotten
                                                           { Andrew Jackson
    Seocnd Couple . . . . { Artie Brandon
                                                           { Henry Roberts
    Third Couple . . . . { Clarence Landry
                                                           { Udell Johnson
    Fourth Couple . . . . { Avanelle Harris
                                                           { Pot
    Cop . . . . Pan

13. **I'VE GOT A PASSPORT FROM GEORGIA**
    Lyrics by Paul Webster and Ray Golden   Music by Hal Borne
    The Traveler . . . . Paul White

14. **GARBO AND HEPBURN**
    By Sid Kuller
    Garbo . . . . "Garbo"
    Hepburn . . . . Marie Bryant

15. **THE EMPEROR'S BONES**
    Lyrics by Paul Webster   Music by Otis Rene
    The Guide . . . . Roy Glenn
    Tourists—Artie Brandon, Louise Franklin, Patsy Hunter, Edward
    Short, Lawrence Harris.
    Hi-Hatters and Rockets

16. **CYMBAL SOCKIN' SAM**
    Lyrics by Sidney Miller   Music by Mickey Rooney
    The Girl . . . . Dorothy Dandridge
    Sam . . . . Sonny Greer

17. **UNCLE TOM'S CABIN IS A DRIVE-IN NOW**
    Uncle Tom . . . . Roy Glenn
    Aunt Jemima . . . . Evelyn Burwell
    Waitress . . . . Ivy Anderson
    Second Waitress . . . . Marie Bryant
    Pot, Pan and Skillet, Hi-Hatters, Rockets, Ensemble

ACT II.

1. **JUMP FOR JOY**
   Lyrics by Sid Kuller & Paul Webster   Music by Duke Ellington
   Singer, Herb Jeffries. Choir, Rockets, Hi-Hatters, Ensemble.

2. **VIGNETTES**
   By Sid Kuller
   By Sid Kuller
   First Couple . . . . { Dorothy Dandridge
                                                         { Herb Jeffries
   Second Couple . . . . { Marie Bryant
                                                          { Udell Johnson

3. **OLD-FASHIONED WALTZ**
   Lyrics by Sid Kuller   Music by Duke Ellington
   Singer . . . . Herb Jeffries
   Couples: The Hi-Hatters, Suzette Johnson, Millie Monroe, Ava-
   nelle Harris.

4. **WE AIM TO PLEASE**
   By Hal Fimberg and Sid Kuller
   Laughin' Andy . . . . Roy Glenn
   Ever Joyous . . . . Paul White
   Customer . . . . Skillet
   "Smilin' Franky" . . . . Al Guster

5. **IF LIFE WERE ALL PEACHES AND CREAM**
   Lyrics by Paul Webster   Music by Hal Borne
   First Couple . . . . { Dorothy Dandridge
                                                         { Herb Jeffries
   Second Couple . . . . { Marie Bryant
                                                          { Paul White

6. **RENT PARTY**
   By Sid Kuller
   Hostess . . . . Ivy Anderson
   The Duke . . . . Duke Ellington
   Sonny Greer, Ray Nance, Ben Webster, Joe Nanton, Jimmy Blan-
   ton, Rex Stewart, Roy Glenn, Henry Roberts, Suzette John-
   son and Ensemble.
   Concerto for Clinkers . . . . Music by Duke Ellington

7. **THE FINISHED SYMPHONY**
   By Richard Weil
   Tiger . . . . Roy Glenn
   Rough-house . . . . Pan

8. **CHOCOLATE SHAKE**
   Lyrics by Paul Webster   Music by Duke Ellington
   Bartender . . . . Paul White
   Boy . . . . Al Guster
   Girl . . . . Ivy Anderson
   Cigarette Girl . . . . Marie Bryant
   Rockets, Hi-Hatters, Ensemble

9. **HICKORY STICK**
   Lyrics by Paul Webster   Music by Hal Borne
   Singer . . . . Dorothy Dandridge
   Dancer . . . . Pete Nugent

10. **RESIGNED TO LIVING**
    By Hal Fimberg
    Gertrude . . . . Suzette Johnson
    Noel . . . . Al Guster
    First Caller . . . . Herb Jeffries
    Second Caller . . . . Henry Roberts
    Man . . . . Wonderful Smith

11. **NOTHIN'**
Lyrics by Sid Kuller and Ray Golden   *Music by Hal Borne*
Boy .... Paul White
Girl ....Ivy Anderson
Rockets, Hi-Hatters, Ensemble
12. **MADE TO ORDER**
By Sid Kuller
First Tailor .... Pan
Second Tailor ....Skillet
Customer ....Pot
13. **SHARP EASTER**
Lyrics by Sid Kuller   *Music by Duke Ellington*
The Loan Shark.......................... Herb Jeffries
The Streetwalker .... Marie Bryant
The Dandy ....Andrew Jackson
The Sweetman ....).............. Henry Roberts
The Wolf ...."Garbo"
The Customer ....Pot
The Tailors ....Pan and Skillet
14. Finale Entire Company.

DUKE ELLINGTON'S ORCHESTRA
Johnnie Hodge ....Alto Saxophone
Barney Bigard ....Tenor Saxophone
Ben Webster ....Tenor Saxophone

Otto Hardwick ....Alto Saxophone
Harry Carney ....Baritone Saxophone
Rex Stewart ....Trumpet
Ray Nance ....Trumpet
Wallace Jones ....Trumpet
Joe Nanton ....Trombone
Lawrence Brown .... Trombone
Juan Tizol ....Valve Trombone
Jimmy Blanton ....Bass Viol
Sonny Greer ....Drums
Freddie Guy ....Guitar

GIRLS OF THE ENSEMBLE
Artie Brandon, Lucille Battle, Avanelle Harris, Ethelyn Stevenson,
Myrtle Fortune, Alice Key, Doris Ake, Hyacinth Cotten, Millie Munroe, Frances Neely, Louise Franklin, Pasty Hunter.

CHOIR
Roy Glenn, Wesley Bly, Edward Short, Lawrence Harris, Louise
Jones, Anna Dent, Evelyn Burrwell, Eloise Flenoury, Le Roy Antoine

THE ROCKETS
Henry Roberts   Andrew Jackson

THE HI-HATTERS
Clarence Landry   Vernod Bradley   Udell Johnson

VOCAL ARRANGEMENTS

Hal Borne   "Jump for Joy" Number
Assisted by Eddie Jones   By Eddie Jones

MUSICAL ARRANGEMENTS

DUKE ELLINGTON, WILLIAM STRAYHORN, HAL BORNE

ASSISTANTS TO MR. CASTLE
Patsy Hunter   Joe Stevenson

ASSISTANTS TO MR. HUBERT
Denny Winter   Herman Cherry

Costumes Executed by Hogan-Anderson and Vessie Cardinal
Sets and Draperies by California Scenic and Costume Company
Lighting Equipment by L. A. Stage Lighting Company
Shoes by Capezio
Men's Clothes by Arno

FOR THE "AMERICAN REVUE THEATRE"

General Manager . . . . Henry Blankfort
Company Manager . . . . Everett Wile
Press Representative . . . . Nate Krevitz
Stage Manager . . . . Jack Boyd
Assistant Stage Manager . . . . Joe Stevenson
Carpenter . . . . Ernest Parks
Electrician . . . . Norman Peterson
Assistant Electrician . . . . Sammy Thompson
Properties . . . . Dolly Case
Wardrobe . . . . Don Rhoda
Casting Director . . . . Ben Carter

GLOSSARY

all reet . . . all right
all root . . . all right
short . . . cheap car
rubber . . . good car
vine . . . suit
hame . . . job
fly . . . fine
groovy . . . in t e know
square . . . not a the know
sport my hen . . . show off my girl
kitten . . . girl
beat . . . tired
cut out . . . have to go
knock a scarf . . . eat a good meal
solid . . . fine

murder . . . fine
banta . . . girl
jump . . . joyful
killer . . . dandy
cat . . . fellow
lush . . . sot
juice . . . liquor
charge . . . marijuana
charge water . . . liquor
blow my top . . . enjoy
flip my lid . . . enjoy
snap my cap . . . enjoy
bust my conk . . . enjoy
don't drape that on me . . . don't kid me

dig this . . . get this
dig you later . . . see you later
pins . . . legs
gams . . . legs
dresses . . . girls
pants . . . boys
chick . . . girl
K.M. . . . kitchen mechanics
Jack . . . name for any fellow
Mike . . . other name for any fellow
skin . . . palm of hand
ice . . . jewelry
furburg . . . town far away
put you on the air . . . give me a cigarette
waitress . . . aviator

After I signed up Joe Turner, we really had great blues in the show. I had stopped all the comedians from using cork on their faces when they worked with us. Some objected before the show opened, but removed it, and were shocked by their success. As the audience screamed and applauded, comedians came off stage smiling, and with tears running down their cheeks. They couldn't believe it. I think a statement of social protest in the theatre should be made without saying it, and this calls for the real craftsman.

(Years later, we did *Jump for Joy* again in Miami, where Billy Strayhorn represented me. It seemed for a time as if the entire financing was done by one millionaire talking a jillionaire into putting up all the money. As the show went into production, rehearsal, and opening, everything was fine, until a day came when we needed ten thousand dollars. I went to the meeting of the money men, and the millionaire went into his customary routine of telling the jillionaire what he thought should be done—such as the jillionaire coming up with another ten G's. "Now, wait a minute," the jillionaire replied, "I've put the last ninety thousand in, and now I think it's your turn!" He looked the millionaire dead in the eye. They were looking at each other when, suddenly, both turned as one and looked at me, as though they expected *me* to scrape up ten thousand dollars overnight. I got the hint, and split the scene. And that was the end of the 1958 version of *Jump for Joy*.)

When we came back east after *Jump for Joy,* everybody in the office was aware of our financial position. While we were playing the Regal in Chicago, I met Cress Courtney. The theatre had sent for somebody in my agent's office to come out and talk to me, because we were having a little difference of opinion about my closing number. I liked the idea of being different and closing my act with a slow, soft tune, maybe "Mood Indigo," or something like that.

Nat Kalcheim of William Morris, Inc., sent Cress out to talk to me. When he arrived, he was wearing a very pretty tie, which I admired. I settled for the tie and changed the closing number to something bright, fast, and loud. I did not see Cress Courtney again until I ran into him one night when I was doing the spots in New York.

The feeling of responsibility that *Jump for Joy* had aroused sustained itself, and one day William Morris, Jr., said, "I want you to write a long work, and let's do it in Carnegie Hall." So out came *Black, Brown and Beige,* which was premiered on January 23, 1943, at Carnegie Hall before a standing-room-only audience with overwhelming success. All proceeds from the concert, incidentally, went to the Russian war relief fund. I had started writing it in Hartford, Connecticut, when Frank Sinatra was just beginning as a single. (He was our supporting act at that time, but he immediately sprang into stratospheric stardom.) *Black, Brown and Beige* was fifty-seven minutes long, but when we recorded it we had to cut it to fit four sides of a 78 album.

I remember that Hartford engagement vividly for another reason. It was in December 1942 and between stage shows I would get my paper and pencil and go to the piano on stage and experiment and write. The light was not too good for writing music, and the movie they were showing was *The Cat Woman.* It was about a woman who used to change into a cat and do people in. Since I could see what was going on on the screen, it sometimes got pretty scary back there in the dark. But *Black, Brown and Beige* came off well nevertheless. Maybe Frank Sinatra had an in with my muse. Or could it have been the cat woman?

Hartford, incidentally, occupies a very significant place in my memory, and I recall a couple of fine musicians there: Lenny Berman, who played piano and did an orchestration of the National Anthem for me during World War II, and his brother, Tiny, a bassist.

Black, Brown and Beige was planned as a tone parallel to the history of the American Negro, and the first section, "Black," delved deeply into the Negro past. In it, I was concerned to show the close relationship between work songs and spirituals. "Work Song," used in many forms, recognized that a work song was sung as you worked, so that there was a place for the song and a place where you grunt. "Come Sunday," the spiritual theme, was intended to depict the movement inside and outside the church, as seen by workers who stood outside, watched, listened, but were not admitted. This is developed to the time when the workers have a church of their own. The section ends with promises. I felt that the kind of unfinished ending was in accordance with reality, that it could not be tied, boxed, and stored away when so much else remained to be done.

The second section, "Brown," recognized the contribution made by the Negro to this country in blood. We began with the heroes of the Revolutionary War, the first of three dances, "West Indian Dance," being dedicated to the valorous deeds of the seven hundred free Haitians of the famed Fontages Legion who came to aid the Americans at the siege of Savannah. We proceeded to the Civil War, and then to the lighter attitude prevailing after the Proclamation of Emancipation. "Emancipation Celebration" described the mixture of joyfulness on the part of the young people as well as the bewilderment of the old on that "great gettin' up mornin'." After years of hard work, when they were maybe all set to rest for their remaining days, how did the old people feel that morning when somebody came along and told them they were *free*? Moving on to the Spanish-American War, we pictured the homecoming of the decorated heroes, and then that offspring of romantic triangles which was and is "The Blues."

At Carnegie Hall, I introduced the third section, "Beige," by referring to the common view of the people of Harlem, and the little Harlems around the U.S.A., as just singing, dancing, and responding to the tom-toms. On closer inspection, it would be found that there were more churches than cabarets, that the people were trying to find a more stable way of living, and that the Negro was rich in experience and education. For instance, at this time there were forty-two Red Caps in New York's Grand Central and Penn Stations who had Ph.D.'s. The little waltz movement represented a bit of sophistication that was perhaps somewhat rough about the edges. "Sugar Hill Penthouse" evoked the atmosphere of a Sugar Hill penthouse in Harlem which could neither be understood nor appreciated unless one had lived there. (Later, I became more explanatory: "If you ever sat on a beautiful magenta cloud overlooking New York City, you were on Sugar Hill.") Coming more up to date, we found the Negroes struggling for solidarity, and in the confusion of it all, just as we were beginning to get our teeth into the tissue, we discovered that our country was in deep trouble again. So, just as always before, the Black, Brown, and Beige were soon right in there for the Red, White, and Blue.

Black, Brown and Beige provoked a good deal of controversy, but I had not realized what an impact this 1943 concert at Carnegie Hall had on the industry as a whole until I ran into Cress Courtney again. He was fully aware of it. We gave each other a big hello and a slap on the back, and suddenly he got the idea to put us into the Hurricane Club at Forty-ninth and Broadway for six months. He made a connection with Al Bordi, the booker for the Hurricane, and we were in. Dave Walper had just been given the place as a present. He was a great fellow, and we got along fine.

During our stay, William Morris, Jr., the head of the agency, told Cress

Courtney to look after me, because Willard Alexander was, after all, looking out for Count Basie in the same office. Six months of air time, with Cress driving all the way, put us right on top. He was young and energetic, but he just sat there (with "Don't Get Around Much Anymore" on the air every night) and told prospective buyers we were not available unless they wanted to pay five g's or four g's with a 60 percent privilege.

By the time we left the Hurricane Club, our radio promotion had jumped our asking price up four times. (Cute story, huh?) We had a wonderful four weeks at the Capitol on Fifty-first and Broadway with Lena Horne as co-star. (Beauty—I love her!) She was the new thing, right out of her first movie triumph. While we were there, I wrote *New World a-Comin'*. The title was suggested by Roi Ottley's best-selling book of the same name. Of course, we had our own annotation for the piece, a twelve-minute performance for piano with band.

It was premiered at Carnegie Hall on December 11, 1943. Ottley looked forward to better conditions for the Negro after World War II, his final optimistic statement being: "In spite of selfish interests, a new world is a-coming with the sweep and fury of the Resurrection." I visualized this new world as a place in the distant future where there would be no war, no greed, no categorization, no nonbelievers, where love was unconditional, and no pronoun was good enough for God. Later, the work was orchestrated for performance by the symphony, and I always remember that even Don Shirley, a pianist with prodigious technique, had trouble with a ragtime "lick" for the left hand.

The annual Carnegie Hall concerts were really a series of social-significance thrusts, or so I and many other people came to regard them, but the following year, on December 19, when Lauritz Melchior, no less, presented me with my portrait in oils, Billy Strayhorn and I presented our four-part *Perfume Suite*. The premise behind it was what perfume does to or for the woman who is wearing it, and each part portrayed the mood a woman gets into—or would like to get into—when wearing a certain type of perfume. Thus, "Under the Balcony Serenade" pictured a woman who feels, on wearing this perfume, that she is the better half of Romeo and Juliet. "Strange Feeling" has to do with the mental violence that comes with intentions, either to do or to be. "Dancers in Love" is naïveté, a stomp for beginners, where it is very difficult for the boy partner to determine what kind of perfume she is wearing, because they are dancing at such a great distance. This is not important to her, because she just wants to dance! The last is "Colorature," and here the attitude is that of a prima donna who feels she is always making an entrance.

By now, a "major" work was expected of us at every Carnegie Hall concert, and on November 23, 1946, we came up with *The Deep South Suite*. This was also in four parts, the first of which was entitled "Magnolias Just Dripping with Molasses." The Deep South is many things to many people, but here we were content to reproduce what might be called the Dixie Chamber of Commerce dream picture, with beautiful blue skies, Creole gals with flashing eyes, fried chicken, watermelons, and all those good old nostalgic memories. I described the mood as "Dixie flavor in a pastel (whispering) jump," and it was maintained till the last chorus, which we took out fortissimo. "Hearsay" was concerned with other things that were told about the South, things that were not at all in accordance with the Chamber of Commerce dream picture, things that were at times almost directly the opposite. "There Was Nobody Looking" illustrated the theory that, when nobody is looking, many people of different extractions are able to get along well together. It had to do, I explained, with a pretty little flower in the middle of a field and a small dog who was fascinated by the flower. As the puppy reached over to caress the flower, a light breeze blew it out of his reach, and every time he tried to touch it the flower was carried off in a different direction by the breeze. There was, nevertheless, no animosity or friction between dog and breeze, for each respected the other's right to court the flower. Moreover, the puppy and the flower were both too young to be influenced away from their natural tendencies, and, most important, there was nobody looking! The responsibility for telling this little parable in music devolved upon the piano player.

The last section of *The Deep South Suite,* and the only section ever publicly available on records, was "Happy-Go-Lucky Local." This told a story of a train in the South, not one of those luxurious, streamlined trains that take tourists to Miami, but a little train with an upright engine that was never fast, never on schedule, and never made stops at any place you ever heard about. After grunting, groaning, and jerking, it finally settled down to a steady medium tempo. The train had a Negro fireman who loved to pull the string that blew the whistle, and since he seemed to know every house, and to recognize someone watching him go by in every window—in every house and every window on *his* side of the tracks, that is!—he was forever pulling that string. He played tunes on the whistle, too—blues, spirituals, a little "Shortenin' Bread"—calling somebody as the train rattled along with more than a suggestion of boogie-woogie rhythm. Down in the South, they called the train No. 42, but we just called it the "Happy-Go-Lucky Local."

After the concert, we had a party up at Cress Courtney's house. William Morris, Jr., was there, and he really pitched a bitch. "You should've said it plainer," he kept insisting. "You should have said it plainer!" He was for out-and-out protest, but as with *Jump for Joy,* I felt it was good theatre to say it without saying it. That is the art.

The following year, I wrote the music for *Beggar's Holiday,* which was based on the English classic, *The Beggar's Opera,* by John Gay, a play first produced in London at the Theatre Royal in 1728. John Latouche did the book and lyrics, and it was a great experience writing with a man like him, a man who is so imitated today by other people writing shows. He was truly a great American genius, and he was recognized as such, but he was not an aggressive man and he took it all in his stride like a true artist.

Beggar's Holiday was about three-and-a-half hours long, or at least an hour-and-a-half longer than it should have been. And it was a long time before its time so far as social significance was concerned. Again it was a matter of saying things without saying them. If you had white and black people on the stage together at that time, one of them was supposed to call the other a bastard, or something. There was none of that in this show. People were cast according to their ability. Alfred Drake played the part of Macheath the mobster, and the chief of police and his daughter were both black. Mack and the colored girl fell in love. Now that's a silly show in 1947! There were no such things then.

It was a gorgeous play, and it had great people in it. Everybody who came out of that show seemed to become a great star. Valerie Bettis, the choreographer, was the big star of *Inside U.S.A.* the following year. Besides Alfred Drake, there were Zero Mostel, Bernice Parks, Avon Long, Mildred Smith, Jet McDonald, and Marie Bryant. Even the production team of Perry Watkins and John R. Sheppard, Jr., was biracial. Everything was done with the utmost artistic gentility. Latouche wrote and wrote, and nobody had a harsh word to say of anyone, until after the show had opened in New Haven and gone on to Boston, where I crept into a matinee.

At a meeting after the show, the director was still asking for more music, as he had been up to and through over fifty songs.

"What we need here is a song," he began right away.

"Well, listen now, I love to write music," I answered. "Let's put ten new songs in the show. I'll sit here and write 'em tonight. But here is a man (Latouche) who has written the lyrics for over fifty songs. I just saw the matinee, and I couldn't hear the words."

I was immediately challenged on that.

"Why couldn't you?"

"Well, the actors are not projecting, and the orchestra is too loud."

"Now, Mr. Ellington," the musical director protested, "you ordered these orchestrations made by your man, Billy Strayhorn, who . . ." (I had remembered what Will Vodery used to say: "When you write a score, don't ever arrange it." When you do, you are confined by your own personal prejudices.)

"Yes, but they're only notes on paper," I replied. "They can be played loudly or softly, and the orchestra is playing what is supposed to be an accompaniment, or under dialogue."

I got into a big thing about it, and they let that go by.

There was a section two hours into the show where they had a ten-minute soliloquy by Alfred Drake—just he and his pistol walking around—followed by a ten-minute, slow-moving ballet over the original set of fire escapes. (The same scenic director used practically the same set in *West Side Story*.)

"A high school play wouldn't put two slow-moving, ten-minute sequences back to back," I said. "Why can't they be separated?"

The New York program credited me with having written seventy-eight pieces of music, thirty-nine of which were ultimately used in the show. It enjoyed a tremendous *succès d'estime,* but the public was not really ready for it. I hope that if Perry Watkins succeeds in bringing the show back, the public will be ready now.

The year 1947 was also the year in which we were commissioned by the Liberian Government to compose a suite to commemorate its country's centennial as a republic. *The Liberian Suite* was premiered at Carnegie Hall on December 26, the day the big snow came. The ex-President of Liberia, Mr. E. V. King, was to be there, and at a rehearsal we had arranged in Nola studios. After the snow came, we began searching for Mr. King, and he was found way down on Fifth Avenue somewhere, looking at the snow. He had never seen snow before, and he thought it was the most beautiful thing, and he was just standing there looking at it fall! It kept on coming, too. The instruments had to be carried by hand from Nola studios to Carnegie Hall, because a truck couldn't make it. The performance that night, and the following night, had been sold out weeks in advance, but because of the snow there was scarcely anybody there. *The Liberian Suite* was recorded later, so it was not entirely eclipsed by the snow. In form, it consisted of an introduction, "I Like the Sunrise," dramatically sung by Al Hibbler, and five contrasting dances, whose moods and rhythms were related to what I knew of the Liberian past and present.

November 13, 1948, saw the premiere of *The Tattooed Bride* at Carnegie Hall, and for this I will refer you to the program notes, as follows:

"Described by the composer as a musical striptease, this is one of the most curious pieces of program music ever delineated by Duke. The story which it tells in music involves a week-end honeymoon spent at a seaside resort by an energetic young man and his bride. The young man apparently expends his energy through the medium of long hikes along the boardwalk, liberal bouts of swimming, and other recreational activities, after which he returns home and goes to sleep exhausted. After three nights of this sort of thing he declares that this is the best vacation he has ever had. At this point we might insert a row of asterisks, which would be the printed equivalent of Jimmy Hamilton's climactic, long-held note on the clarinet, indicating that the husband has finally found out that his wife is tattooed."

Earlier in the year, I had made the trip to Europe on which Jack Robbins accompanied us. He had sold his publishing companies to M-G-M, retaining 49 percent, and getting a job as president, or something like that. They paid him $100,000 a year, and he didn't even have to go to his office! One day, while I was playing the Paramount Theatre, Jack came in, and he was grinning.

"I've sold everything," he said. "I've got a million dollars tax free, and I have nothing else to do. Where are you going now?"

"I'm getting ready to go to Europe," I said. "Come on with me."

"Okay," he said. "Fine!"

So one fine day we sailed on the *Medea*, a brand-new Cunard ship on her maiden voyage, carrying two hundred and fifty first-class passengers. Jack and I used to play gin rummy all night, and at five o'clock every morning they would put on a crew of five to serve us breakfast, just Jack and me. After we had had our breakfast, I would go into the salon to sit at the piano and warm up my left hand, because what I was going to do at the Palladium in

London was to play piano solos, and as the featured artist I had to have my exercise. I would play and play until one by one the other passengers came in. We had a ball all the way over. Besides Kay Davis and Ray Nance, I had Hernandez, my barber, with me.

When we arrived in Southampton, it was raining like crazy. Somehow or other, we got moved around and separated, until finally we looked around and saw Jack Robbins out between the tracks with *all* the bags, carrying some and standing beside the others, out in the rain, while Hernandez and I were under shelter.

"Here I am, a millionaire," Jack said, "and I'm carrying the barber's baggage! What is this?"

Jack, Al Celley, my manager, and I shared an apartment on Curzon Street in London and we enjoyed ourselves. The group was rather successful at the Palladium, where we appeared as "variety artists." There was a squabble at that time between the British and American unions, and our full band could not play in England. I used a British rhythm section—Jack Fallon on bass, Malcolm Mitchell on guitar, and Tony Crombie on drums—and we played a few concerts after the Palladium appearance. A French impresario, Jules Borkon, came over, and he booked us for some concerts in Paris and around the Continent.

Then I came on back and got the band together, and didn't go to Europe again until 1950, when the whole band went. There was a bit of unrest in Paris at that time, and we encountered a very, very knowing audience at the Palais de Chaillot. This was the first time the band had been to Europe since 1939, and the Paris jazz enthusiasts are very knowledgeable. They don't want you to palm anything off on them. They had not heard all the stuff we had written year after year, from the beginning in 1943, when we had started writing a long work each year up to this time. So I was showing off with the band, and we were playing *The Liberian Suite*. At the end of one of the movements, or somewhere along the line, a fine young man came strolling down the aisle and up to the stage.

"Mr. Ellington," he said, "we came here to hear Ellington. This is not Ellington!"

With that, of course, we had to tear up all the programs and go back to before 1939, to "Black and Tan Fantasy" and that kind of thing.

On our return, on the *Île de France*, I wrote *Harlem,* which had been commissioned by the NBC Symphony during the time when Maestro Arturo

Toscanini was its conductor. A concerto grosso for our band and the symphony, it provides me with the opportunity to make some statements on the subject of Harlem, the music and the people. Here is how I saw it:

Harlem is a place, a place in New York City, bordered on the south by Central Park and on the north by 145th Street, the Harlem and East River on the east, and the Hudson River on the west. We were represented in Congress not long ago by a minister, a minister who was not only a minister, but a man involved in the interest and advancement of his people, his neighbors, his friends, his race. I do not speak of Adam Clayton Powell as a United States Representative or a Representative from Harlem in the past tense, for I feel that any progress made today or hereafter will rise upon the foundation bearing the charisma of his social demands. Adam Clayton Powell was the man who got his people together. His crowning achievement is recorded in the annals of history as the Emancipation of 125th Street. One day, Harlemites were only allowed to *spend* on 125th Street; the next day, they were drawing paychecks as clerks, salesmen, etc.!

We would like now to take you on a tour of this place called Harlem. It has always had more churches than cabarets. It is Sunday morning. We are strolling from 110th Street up Seventh Avenue, heading north through the Spanish and West Indian neighborhood toward the 125th Street business area. Everybody is nicely dressed, and on their way to or from church. Everybody is in a friendly mood. Greetings are polite and pleasant, and on the opposite side of the street, standing under a street lamp, is a real hip chick. She, too, is in a friendly mood. You may hear a parade go by, or a funeral, or you may recognize the passage of those who are making our Civil Rights demands. (Hereabouts, in our performance, Cootie Williams pronounces the word on his trumpet—*Harlem!*)

Harlem has its heroes, too. A long list of heroes . . . Jackie Robinson, Ray Robinson, Chief Justice Thurgood Marshall, Countee Cullen, Langston Hughes, Bill Robinson . . .

Up until 1950, the responsibility for answering charges of rape and murder Down South always fell in the lap of the NAACP. No matter how false the charges, no matter how bigoted the opposition, no matter how dangerous the mission, the head of NAACP had to get on a train, leave New York City, and go down there into that lions' den of terror. I remember when this was the duty of Walter White, the head of NAACP, who, incidentally (and this made it even worse), looked more Caucasian than the adversary. There he would

189

be, down there alone, without benefit of Federal troops, defending some poor Negro who had been accused of the most outrageous crimes. Walter White was lucky, after his stay and after the trials, to make it to the train, much less back to New York City. A brave man, Walter White, with a heart as big as all outdoors.

Then there was the late Hon. Dr. Ralph Bunche, the miracle man, who accomplished the impossible. Representing, I believe, the U.N., he went to the Near East and, through wisdom and understanding, convinced the Arabs and Israelis, for the one time in history, to stop warring on each other. If that is not accomplishing the impossible, then I hope something big and ugly bites me.

By 1950 everybody was giving concerts, and even a concert at Carnegie Hall no longer had the prestige value it had had in 1943, but our series there had helped establish a music that was new in both its extended forms and its social significance. I should also mention *"The Blue Belles of Harlem"* and *"Blutopia,"* both written for and premiered by Paul Whiteman; *The Tonal Group* ("Rhapsoditti," "Fugaditti," and "Jamaditti") prepared for the first Carnegie concert in 1946; *The Beautiful Indians* ("Minnehaha" and "Hiawatha") premiered at the second Carnegie concert in 1946; *The Manhattan Murals* (as seen from Billy Strayhorn's "A" Train, and written for Mayor Vincent Impellitteri), and the two-movement *Symphomaniac,* both performed at the November 1948 concert.

In 1955, I was commissioned by the eminent composer and conductor Don Gillis to write a piece to be played by the Symphony of the Air in concert with our band. *Night Creature* was the outcome, and it was subsequently performed not only by the Symphony of the Air, but also by the symphonies of Buffalo, Detroit, and New Haven, as well as by the National Symphony in Washington D.C. In 1963 we recorded the first and second movements with the Stockholm Symphony, and the third movement with the Paris Symphony. My annotation on *Night Creature* is as follows:

The first movement is about a blind bug who comes out every night to find that because he is king of the night creatures, he must dance. The reason he is king, of course, is that being blind he lives in night all day, and when night really falls he sees as well as anyone else, but with the difference that he is *accustomed* to not seeing. So he puts out his antennae and goes into his dance, and if his antennae warn him of danger, he pauses, turns in another direction, and continues bugging the jitterbugs.

The second movement is concerned with that imaginary monster we all fear we shall have to meet some midnight, but when we meet him I'm sure we shall find that he too does the boogie-woogie.

Night creatures, unlike stars, do not come *out* at night—they come *on,* each thinking that before the night is out he or she will be the star. They are the restless cool whose exotic or erotic animations, no matter how cool, beg for recognition, mainly from the queen, that dazzling woman who reigns over all night creatures. She is the theme of the third movement, sitting there on her high place and singing, 'I want to be acknowledged' (in D major), or 'Who but me shall be desired?' (in A flat), or 'Who has the taste for my choreography?' (in A minor). After having made each of her subjects feel that Her Majesty sings only for him or her, who is individually the coolest or the craziest, her high-toned highness rises and snaps her fingers. As they stomp off the handclapping, everybody scrambles to be in place, wailing and winging into the most overindulged form of up-and-outness.

Nineteen fifty-five was also the year we played a season in the Aquacades out on the site of the 1939 New York World's Fair. I had very little to do except play a piano solo, after which the house conductor took over and the cats had to blow. So I could go and get some work done at home. That was when I wrote my play, *Man with Four Sides.*

Nineteen fifty-six was an important year. The performance of *Diminuendo and Crescendo in Blue* (originally written in 1937) at the Newport Jazz Festival, with an epic ride by Paul Gonsalves on tenor saxophone, brought us renewed attention and the cover of *Time* magazine. It was another of those major intersections in my career. Another great opportunity occurred later in the year, when we presented *A Drum Is a Woman* on the "U.S. Steel Hour." This musical fantasy or allegory told the story of jazz in terms of the adventures of Madam Zajj and Carribee Joe, from the Caribbean to the moon via Congo Square and Fifty-second Street. It was in four parts with a dozen selections, two reprises, and a finale. Extra percussion, a harp, and the voices of Margaret Tynes, Joya Sherrill, and Ozzie Bailey were used, but what could not be experienced on the Columbia album was the radiant presence of Carmen de Lavallade, who danced so superbly in the television version.

Nineteen fifty-seven was the year of *Such Sweet Thunder,* which naturally grew out of our experiences at the Shakespeare Theatre in Stratford, Ontario, to which we were invited by Tom Patterson, who was in charge of the organization. Barbara Reid, who handled publicity, also helped make us feel we belonged there, and the warm welcome the band received from the audience was heartening indeed. But it was the performances Billy Strayhorn and I witnessed that really inspired *Such Sweet Thunder.* We read Shakespeare quite thoroughly afterwards, and drew our title from Act IV, Scene 1, of *A Midsummer Night's Dream:* "I never heard so musical a discord, such sweet thunder." The set of vignettes we subsequently presented in a Music for Moderns concert at Town Hall in April 1957 was enthusiastically received, the subjects including Othello, Caesar, Henry V, Lady Macbeth, the Three Witches, Puck, Hamlet, Romeo and Juliet. The explanation of how I feel about Shakespeare, written for the Stratford program, may be of interest here:

I have a great sympathy with Shakespeare because it seems to me that strong similarities can be established between a jazz performance and the production of a Shakespeare play—similarities between the producers, the artists, and the audiences. Basically, both groups face comparable problems in the reluctance of some participants to expose themselves and join the audience. Their hesitance is due, in both cases, to a misconception that the major supporters of both these artistic manifestations—Shakespeare and jazz—are the people who have invested time and money in becoming experts.

Many people feel this way about chamber music, too; they fear that as members of an audience, whether for Shakespeare, jazz or chamber music, their reaction will reveal them as insufficiently informed, or possibly unaware of the sensitivities one must acquire to savor completely the subtleties of a performance. In the case of a jazz listener, he may be caught sitting next to an enthusiast and will be ashamed to admit his lack of familiarity with the names of the exponents. In all cases, the newcomer is afraid he will be looked upon as a square. (Nobody knows what a square is—it's just that nobody wants to *be* one.)

Anybody who listens to a beautifully performed symphony for the first time gains something from it. The next time he hears it, he gains more; when he hears the symphony for the hundredth time, he is benefited to the hundredth power. So it is with Shakespeare. The spectator can't get it all the first time; repeated viewings multiply the satisfaction.

There is a perfect parallel with jazz, where repeated listening makes for enjoyment. The Stratford Festival, by tying in top-grade jazz with its Shakespeare productions each season, is showing its awareness of this.

There is an increasing interrelationship between the adherents to art forms in various fields. Contemporary jazz, for instance, has many enthusiastic listeners in its audience who are classical musicians of heroic stature. Indeed, some classical musicians in recent years have involved themselves with jazz as composers, soloists, or both. I am not pointing this out in any attempt to plead for tolerance, for jazz is not in need of tolerance, but of understanding and intelligent appreciation. Moreover, it is becoming increasingly difficult to decide where jazz starts or where it stops, where Tin Pan Alley begins and jazz ends, or even where the borderline lies between classical music and jazz. I feel there is no boundary line, and I see no place for one if my own feelings tell me a performance is good.

Any musician will agree that the final judgment of a musical performance lies in its immediate impact on the human ear, rather than in previous knowledge or academic study.

In the final analysis, whether it be Shakespeare or jazz, the only thing that counts is the emotional effect on the listener. Somehow, I suspect that if Shakespeare were alive today, he might be a jazz fan himself—he'd appreciate the combination of team spirit and informality, of academic knowledge and humor, of all the elements that go into a great jazz performance. And I am sure he would agree with the simple and axiomatic statement that is so important to all of us—when it sounds good, it *is* good.

Although we had participated in many films, shorts, and full-length features (*Check and Double Check, Murder at the Vanities, Belle of the '90s, Cabin in the Sky,* and *Reveille with Beverley*), it was not until 1959 that I was asked to do the score for a movie—Otto Preminger's *Anatomy of a Murder.* The shooting was done at Ishpeming, Michigan, and I went up there without Billy Strayhorn, but it all boiled down to the same thing whether he was there or not. He was always my consultant. He joined me when the Preminger organization arranged for me to have an apartment up on Sunset Boulevard. It was a penthouse apartment that had seven rooms, three baths, and a patio twice as big as the apartment itself. The location was wonderful and we had a magnificent view of Los Angeles, Beverly Hills, the Hollywood hills, everything. I spent most of my time walking around looking at the scenery. One night you would get one picture, the next night another. To anyone accustomed to observing beauty, it was a very interesting place for the scenic effects. I was sort of hooked. Strayhorn was hooked too, when he moved into this scene. He became the official cook, because we had a great big kitchen with lots of pots and pans. He would not allow anyone else to enter the kitchen, and he used to cook some great dishes. He even got himself a chef's hat. But there was one great meal he did not cook. When we returned from the studio one day, we found a gigantic pot sitting in front of the door. It was a real chef's cooking pot, about three feet tall. We took the top off and it was full of gumbo filé. We moved it inside and tasted on it. We invited people from miles around, and everybody was crazy about it. Herman McCoy, who was a chef, had brought it over, and left it when he found we were out. In fact, we spent almost the entire time there partying, enjoying ourselves, and enjoying the scenery, until one day a guy called up from the studio and said, "You know, Mr. Ellington, we are recording Friday." I think we had about forty-eight hours. So then the writing really started. It turned out all right, too, because we won awards with it.

The next movie assignment was for *Paris Blues* in 1960. The contract called for me to be in Paris twelve weeks, but while they were shooting the first four weeks, I was represented by Billy Strayhorn. To him, being in Paris on such an assignment was like champagne and caviar, or, if you prefer, pie and ice cream.

In 1966, I did the background score for *Assault on a Queen*. It was fun, but not so much as when you go on location while they are shooting. When I got this assignment, the shooting was finished. Frank Sinatra told me confidentially that he wanted to talk to me about certain music for the picture. So one night I flew over to Vegas for a visit and a conference, and all he said was, "When we open that safe door on the ship, I want you to *GO!*" We did. We made a track for that scene that was *really* going! I had taken eight of my guys out there, and augmented the group with about fourteen of those great Hollywood cats like Bud Shank and Buddy Collette. We put Jimmy Hamilton on clarinet with those two, and we did a track that was a chase. It was terrific. I still have a tape of it, and one day I am going to talk Reprise into releasing it. I know Sinatra was unhappy that they took it out and didn't use it. After we left, they brought in another cat who did the boom-boom-boom—the old bass walking thing. It had no chase in it. But maybe we overdid it. The music, of course, is supposed to be an accompaniment, and must not overshadow the picture. Then I don't think the director saw eye to eye with me, because after they showed me the picture the first time he asked what I thought of it, and I told him I thought it was one of the best westerns I had ever seen.

In 1969 we were engaged to do the music for *Change of Mind,* a picture with a provocative subject—the transplanting of a white lawyer's brain to a

At Leeds, 1958, with Queen Elizabeth II and the Duke of Edinburgh

black man's body. It was evidently not too popular generally, but the music incorporated in the score consisted of updated versions of material from the '30s, such as "Wanderlust," "What Good Am I Without You?" and a theme from "Creole Rhapsody" which we retitled "Neo-Creole."

Festivals of one kind or another had by now become the springboard for new works, much in the same way as our annual Carnegie Hall concerts had previously been. In 1958, I was invited to perform at the first festival of the arts in Leeds, England, where I had the great honor of being presented to Her Majesty Queen Elizabeth. Representatives of all the arts were drawn from all over the world, and at the festival's conclusion a magnificent banquet was preceded by a red-carpet reception. Her Majesty asked me when I first visited England. "Nineteen thirty-three, Your Majesty, years before you were born."

Inspired by this meeting, I composed and recorded *The Queen's Suite.*

The Newport and Monterey jazz festivals, as rather special occasions, have been the cause of our writing a lot of special material. In 1956 we wrote the three-part *Festival Suite* for Newport, the sections being entitled "Festival Junction," "Blues to Be There," and "Newport Up." *Toot Suite,* written for the 1958 festival season, consisted of "Red Garter," "Red Shoes," "Red Carpet," and "Ready, Go!" No wonder many people still refer to it as the *Red Carpet Suite.* In 1959 we prepared the three-part *Idiom '59* as our contribution to the outdoor activities. Then in 1960 we came up with *Suite Thursday* for the Monterey Festival that year.

This was in four parts—"Misfit Blues," "Schwiphti," "Zweet Zurzday," and "Lay-by"—and in them we tried to parallel John Steinbeck's story, "Sweet Thursday," which was set in Monterey's Cannery Row. Doc, the main character, had a theory that the octopus changed color in accordance with his moods and emotions. We felt that the people of Cannery Row changed their colors too. That is, the character you thought was a bum turned out to be an angel, and the horrible fellow, when dressed in some clean clothes, was found to be a real right guy, and so on. Certainly, as we indicated in "Schwiphti," Cannery Row had a tempo. The critics at the festival didn't dig the suite too well, but when the record eventually appeared there were a lot of reversed opinions. It wasn't the first time we had experienced that sort of thing!

Some of the special occasions happened in the record studio, as when we and the Count Basie band joined forces and did our thing together there in 1961. In 1962, Coleman Hawkins joined us for a session, and I joined Max Roach and Charles Mingus on another. On a third date that year, John

With Princess Margaret in London

Coltrane and I alternated with each other's rhythm sections. Both Rosemary Clooney and Ella Fitzgerald had recorded with us in 1957, and we had the pleasure of accompanying Ella for another album made on the Côte d'Azur in 1966. In 1961, I took Billy Kyle's place at the piano, when Louis Armstrong's group recorded two albums of my compositions.

Another important event in my career was the presentation of *My People* at the Century of Negro Progress Exposition in August 1963 at McCormick Place, Chicago. I was writing the music for this show and for the Stratford

Shakespearean Festival, Stratford, Ontario, production of *Timon of Athens* at the same time. This meant going to Stratford to work, flying into Chicago to rehearse the choirs of Irving Bunton and Charles Moore, doing my one-nighters with the band in between, dashing back to New York to work with the choreographers, Alvin Ailey and Tally Beatty, returning to Stratford, and so on and on. Working from all angles at once in music and the theatre was the greatest kind of fun for me. I wrote the music, words, and orchestrations for *My People,* directed it, and did everything but watch the loot, which was good for the pople who did. In Stratford, while the orchestra was rehearsing the music for *Timon,* I would watch Michael Langham direct the actors, and when I went to Chicago I would stand in front of my cast, extend my arm as Michael did, and make like a heavy director. It was a ball, too, when the two choreographers honored my request to be allowed to choreograph the opening.

When I first went to work in the McCormick Theatre, I was knocked out by the enormous size of the stage. I sat in the front row of the orchestra seats and looked up at the stage, to get the audience's view. The ninety-foot proscenium was sixty feet from floodlights to back wall; there was a fifteen-foot orchestra pit, and a seventy-five-foot arc to the ramp. Man, I thought, a hundred people on this stage will look like a quartet! But all problems offer the opportunity for invention, so now to figure out the solution. I sat and looked for a while, and then came up with an idea to fill this big stage (they were not spending any money for scenery). We would extend the sixteen-piece band just back of the apron, and behind the band we would have an elevation twelve feet high which would be carried all the way back to the back wall. On either side would be stairs running down behind the band.

For the opening, I would have a boy and a girl dancing at the extreme back end of the elevation—a sort of Afro dance. Then black out, fade up to green as backdrop silhouettes the dancers; fade up amber cross lights at the point where the boy is doing the head-rolling thing *à la* Geoffrey Holder; slow fade to black, and first slowly cross orchestra pit with ambers, purples, and reds, and then quickly bright up. Instead of two tiny figures in the distance, the audience was suddenly looking at forty-eight giant hands rising up out of the dark, towering over them on the orchestra pit elevator. Some were shocked by the silhouette and even cried out in fright. Thanks to Ailey and Beatty, Ellington had achieved a choreographic masterpiece on his maiden voyage.

To play *My People* I had this great band in which, if you notice, there are nine alumni:

Conductor—Jimmy Jones	3rd Trumpet—"Ziggy" Harrell
1st Alto—Rudy Powell	4th Trumpet—Nathan Woodard
2nd Alto—Russell Procope	1st Trombone—Britt Woodman
1st Tenor—Bob Freedman	2nd Trombone—John Sanders
2nd Tenor—Harold Ashby	3rd Trombone—Booty Wood
Baritone—Pete Clark	Bass—Joe Benjamin
1st Trumpet—Bill Berry	Drums—Louie Bellson
2nd Trumpet—Ray Nance	Piano—Jimmy Jones (Billy Strayhorn)

The same year, we set off on our exciting tour of the Middle East, India, Pakistan, and Ceylon. This was musically an inspiring experience, but Billy Strayhorn and I deliberately let several months go by before we set about writing our impressions. What was eventually entitled *The Far East Suite* included "Ad Lib on Nippon," a piece that displayed the virtuosity of John Lamb and Jimmy Hamilton, and was the result of our first trip to Japan in 1964. "Bluebird of Delhi" was originally named "Mynah" in memory of the bird that used to sing a pretty lick in Stray's hotel room. He was always talking to it—"How are you today?", "Good morning!", "Do you want something to eat?"—but the bird never answered him until he was leaving the room and Delhi. Then it sounded off the low raspberry you hear at the end of the number. Trying to express in music how we felt about Damascus, the Taj Mahal, Isfahan, and Mount Harissa near Beirut was a challenge we very much enjoyed.

Our first visit to the Caribbean was also inspiring, and we wrote a rather lighthearted salutation in the form of *The Virgin Island Suite* in 1965. Its four parts were entitled "Island Virgin," "Virgin Jungle," "Fiddler on the Diddle," and "Jungle Kitty." We have been warmly welcomed each time we have been to the West Indies. In 1969 we went to Jamaica and presented our sacred concert in the Roman Catholic cathedral, and Mayor Eric Bell gave me the key to the City of Kingston. It was very hot while we were there, and I think that was the only time the band was uniformly dressed in dashikis.

In 1965, I had two important meetings with the symphony. On July 28, I played with the Boston Pops Orchestra at Tanglewood, with Arthur Fiedler conducting. Richard Hayman, a master orchestrator, was responsible for the charts, and Louis Bellson and John Lamb were there to give me support. We did about a dozen of my numbers, including the march from *Timon of Athens,* as written for Alcibiades and his army in the 1963 production at Stratford, Ontario.

Three days later, I was at Lincoln Center for the premiere of *The Golden Broom and the Green Apple,* a new work specially written for performance by the New York Philharmonic Orchestra at the French-American Festival. It was a modern allegory in three stanzas, and it goes like this:

Stanza I: The Golden Broom

The Golden Broom is a reflection of the haze we enjoy in the spin of today's whirl, as our luxuriously appointed vehicle (designed originally for the Beautiful Rich City Witch) dashes through space with its vacuum jet stream magnetizing the golden gleam of material security.

Stanza II: The Green Apple

As we relax graciously, we love thinking that in spite of how far we have gone to acquire our position of advantage, we still have our Green Apple (naturally grown and owned by the Poverty Strick' Country Chick), the symbol of our potential, our virtues, our God-made and untouched purity.

Stanza III: The Handsome Traffic Policeman

In the third movement, we may find the symbol of ourselves in the very Handsome Traffic Cop, flashing his reds, greens, and ambers as he stomps his authority around the intersection, where the paths of the Beautiful Rich City Witch with her Golden Broom and the Poverty Strick' Country Chick with her Green Apple will sooner or later converge . . . and the decision has to be made. With only one ticket left in our book, which of the two ladies gets the ticket? (The reason that the Handsome Traffic Cop's book is so depleted and down to one ticket is that all the more desirable ladies prefer to commit their violations at his intersection.)

I had a triple role that night, because not only did I conduct *The Golden Broom and the Green Apple* and play the piano part in *New World a-Comin',* but I was also honored by being asked to act as narrator in Aaron Copland's *Preamble for a Solemn Occasion,* which was performed in memory of Adlai Stevenson.

The Latin-American Suite was unusual in that it was written while we were actually touring Latin America for the first time in 1968. I had originally agreed with impresario Gary Keys, who was responsible for the Mexican part of the tour, to present a new work in Mexico City. Some importance was attached to this, for he was making a film of the trip. My original idea was *The Mexican Suite,* but after it had become *Mexicanticipación,* our experiences in South America determined that those sections would have to become part of a larger *Latin-American Suite*. When finally complete, it consisted of "Brasilliance," in memory of Brazil; "Tina," an affectionate diminutive for Argentina, where we were greeted so warmly; "Latin American Sunshine," which we played everywhere, had to do with the warm smiles as well as the sun; "Eque" celebrated our first crossing of the equator; "Chico Quadradino" was an expression I picked up, and musically it portrayed a little Spanish square doing his thang; "Oclupaca" was for a place where we had a very happy time, and you may find you have been there too, if you try spelling it backwards; and last *The Sleeping Lady and the Giant Who Watches Over Her,* for the mountains that overlook Mexico City.

At the 1970 jazz festival in New Orleans, I presented part of what I later got in the habit of announcing as *The New New Orleans Suite.* The original five sections acknowledged various aspects of the city's past and present, such as the aristocracy and Jean Lafitte; that indispensable part of every street parade, the Second Line; the excruciating ecstasies one finds oneself suspended in when one is in the throes of the jingling rhythmic jollies of Bourbon Street; that omnipresent music, the blues; and, equally omnipresent, the religious element in New Orleans life. To these we added portraits of four New Orleans notables with whom we were well acquainted: Sidney Bechet, Wellman Braud, Louis Armstrong, and Mahalia Jackson.

In retrospect, it seems that 1970 must have been a busy year, because I was also working on a ballet score that had been commissioned by the American Ballet Theatre. Choreographed by Alvin Ailey, the ballet was premiered at the New York State Theatre on June 25, and it received enthusiastic reviews from, notably, Clive Barnes in the New York *Times.* It was entitled *The River,* and this is what the various movements mean to me:

The River starts as . . .

THE SPRING, which is like a newborn baby. He's in his cradle . . . spouting, spinning, wiggling, gurgling, squirming, squealing, making faces, reaching for his nipple or bottle, turning, tossing, and tinkling all over the place. When he hits the floor the first time out of the cradle, he is about to go into . . .

THE RUN. Although he can hardly walk, he now feels compelled to march like his little toy soldiers. Throwing his shoulders back, he marches forward until he is attracted by a pretty puddle, which momentarily becomes the object of his affection. Recalled to duty and the march, he sets forth again, and is happily making his way when, over his shoulder, he sees a big bubble bearing down on him. He scrambles to get out of the way and escape; and finally does so just as the big bubble sweeps by and passes on down the run. With that, he feels safe again and he gets up and continues the marching once more until it begins to grow boring; so now he is down on the floor in . . .

THE MEANDER, where he is undecided whether to go back to the cradle or pursue his quest in the wake of the big bubble. There he is, rolling around from one side to the other on the floor, up and down, back and forth, until he sees the door, the kitchen door, and looks out into that big backyard. "This must be the biggest world in the world," he says. "Look at all that space out there!" So he dashes out of the door, and now he is into . . .

THE GIGGLING RAPIDS, and he races and runs and dances and skips and trips all over the backyard until, exhausted, he relaxes and rolls down to . . .

THE LAKE. The lake is beautiful and serene. It is all horizontal lines that offer up unrippled reflections. There it is, in all its beauty, God-made and untouched, until people come—people who are God-made and terribly touched by the beauty of the lake. They, in their admiration for it, begin to discover new facets of compatibility in each other, and as a romantic viewpoint develops, they indulge themselves. The whole situation compounds itself into an emotional violence that is even greater than that of the violence of the vortex to come. The lake supports them until, suddenly, they are over the top and down . . .

THE FALLS. The falls always looks the same at the top and always sounds the same at the bottom. You can always hear the voice of the spirit that has gone over the falls and into the whirlpool, yelling and reaching to get back up the falls to regain the place of serenity that is the lake. But what is to follow is . . .

THE WHIRLPOOL itself, an experience in which, of course, you must really immerse yourself to appreciate the hazards. From the whirlpool we get into the main train of . . .

THE RIVER, which gallops sprightly and, as it passes several inlets, broadens and loses some of its adolescence. Becoming ever more mature, even noble, it establishes a majestic wave of monumental cool as it moves on with rhythmic authority. At the delta, there are two cities, one on each side, and there is always something on one side of the river that you cannot get on the other. Sometimes it's bootleg booze, or hot automobiles, or many other things. For our cities, we have picked . . .

THE NEO-HIP-HOT COOL-KIDDIES COMMUNITY and, on the opposite bank . . .

THE VILLAGE OF THE VIRGINS, whose riparian rights are most carefully preserved. The river passes between these two cities and goes plunging into . . .

THE MOTHER, HER MAJESTY THE SEA. At this point, the river is no longer a river. It has passed its point of disembarkation and here we realize the validity of the foundation of religion which is the HEAVENLY ANTICIPATION OF REBIRTH. The mother, in her beautiful romantic exchange with the sun, gives up to the sky that which is to come back as rain, snow, or fog on the mountains and plains. So the next time we see it, it is like a newborn baby . . .

THE SPRING. This materialization proves the validity in our HEAVENLY ANTICIPATION OF REBIRTH.

For the Monterey Festival in September 1970 we prepared a suite called *The Afro-Eurasian Eclipse*. The foundations of this were laid the previous December when we were playing Caesar's Palace in Las Vegas. After our second show ended at three-fifty every morning, I would rush up to my room and turn on the television to catch shoot-'em-ups, old movies, old two-gun reruns, and other repeats that were years old. After that would come the Sunrise Semester—writing music—and then more television watching. On December 31, Marshall McLuhan was being interviewed, and he made a statement that impressed me very much. "The whole world," he said, "is going oriental, and nobody will be able to retain his identity, not even the orientals."

Traveling so much as we do, I could understand what he meant. I had seen saris on the Côte d'Azur, British musicians playing the sitar, and everywhere a trend toward the exotic. Youngsters—the women and the would-be young men—were dressing in oriental styles everywhere you turned. The beards, the long hair, and the fact that many Americans have taken to Eastern religions, were all consistent with McLuhan's statement. The food on the table, and the way it was served and eaten, also often pointed to the same conclusion. When I first went to Japan, I noticed at once how the twain seemed to have met there. Japanese architecture had much in common with American and European, just as Japanese jazz musicians had much in common with their American counterparts. In a nightclub, I heard a girl singing an English song with perfect enunciation, and then I discovered she didn't have the foggiest notion of the meaning of the words she was singing. Elsewhere, I have described the problems we had in locating any traditional Japanese musician to play for an American television team.

When we went on to Australia and New Zealand, the McLuhan statement was still hanging in the back of my mind, and it was kept fresh by what we saw as we constantly traveled the world. In Australia, we encountered not only the kangaroo, but the didjeridoo, too, a long, tubular instrument played by a beautiful black man, an aborigine. In 1971 we recorded the suite, which covered the whole scene—African, Indian, occidental, soul, etc.

In 1971 we wrote two more suites. *The Goutelas Suite,* premiered at Lincoln Center on April 16, expressed some of my admiration for Goutelas and the people responsible for its restoration. *Togo Brava!* was presented for the first time at the Newport Jazz Festival in July. In 1967 the Republic of Togoland released a set of four postage stamps dedicated to the twentieth anniversary of UNESCO. Each stamp bore the likeness of a musician, the four chosen being Bach, Beethoven, Debussy, and myself—a rare honor, indeed, to be in such company! Our humble suite was just a token of gratitude and appreciation.

As we prepared for the longest tour in the band's history—five weeks in Russia, five weeks in Europe, and three weeks in Latin America—the rest of 1971 seemed potentially rich in inspiration.

Doctors and Surgeons

I have been very, very lucky with my doctors, and particularly with my surgeons. The very first operation I had was for a hernia, when I was eighteen years old in Washington, D.C. Dr. Cuthbert, the doctor my father used to work for, selected all of our specialists. He was right there in the operating room when Dr. Mitchell was operating. They talked to me throughout the entire operation, which was done with a local anesthetic. "My, Edward," they would say, "you've got such a fine . . . look at that! . . . and what's this? . . . isn't that wonderful?" And so on. They were talking about all the gems and healthy organs I had inside me, and all I could say was, "Yes . . . yes . . . yes . . ." After doing my operation, Dr. Mitchell went away to become Surgeon-General of the United States Army, so I had really made a brilliant debut.

When I first came to New York, Binga Desmond was my doctor. I am quick at grabbing a doctor, so I took a hangnail, or something that was troubling me, for him to look at.

"Oh, nothing much," he said, "I'll just dress it."

"Well," I said, "you have a very beautiful nurse. Let's let her dress it."

"Sure, okay," he said. The nurse happened to be his wife.

So I'd go every day, and she'd dress it. He didn't look at it for four or five days, but when he did he said, "Hey, man, this thing is turning green. I think we're going to have to cut off a piece of it!"

"Doctor," I asked, "who's going to cut it off, and when?"

"You're going to have at least one joint cut off," he said, "maybe two."

It was the forefinger of the left hand, and I was still saying, "Well, who's gonna . . . who do you think . . . ?"

He sent for a friend, a surgeon, and he came around and looked at it, and said, "Yeah, I think we're gonna have to . . . But I'd rather see it in daylight."

"Binga, *who* is the best surgeon in New York City?" I asked after he had gone.

"Oh, that man who's down here from *Virginia,*" he said, to scare me away. "He's really the best, but you know . . ."

"Call him up," I said, "and see what he's doing right now."

As luck would have it, Dr. Tom Russell was in, and he said, "Well, send him on down."

When I walked into his place on East Seventy-seventh Street, he was standing there with his scalpel in his hand, just like a guy walking around the house with his trumpet in his hand, looking for something to jam on. He was waiting for me, and he welcomed me back in another room, where he took my finger and held it up under a light right over our heads.

"What is this I see?" he said, touching my finger with the scalpel, and before I knew what was happening he was chopping at it, cutting away some of the skin.

"Hey, tell me, how did you happen to come to me?" he asked.

"I asked Dr. Desmond who the best surgeon in New York City was, and he said you were."

He kind of smiled at that, and said, "Well, you're a lucky man, because not everybody knows what to do about these fingers. There are a lot of nerves and muscles and blood vessels, and that sort of thing." All the time, for about twenty minutes, he kept whittling away at my finger until it was about half its normal size. He took the whole nail out, and did the entire thing without any anesthetic, as I stood there watching him, and feeling nothing, absolutely nothing. It was like getting a manicure.

Afterwards, whenever I mentioned this cat's name to doctors they would say, "Whoo . . . he's the best!" This was in the '20s.

Ever since 1937, when he came down to the Cotton Club one night to treat Toby Hardwick's asthma, Arthur Logan has been my doctor. The great thing about Arthur Logan, I think, is that he is approachable at any time, and his special virtue is that he cannot cure everything. He is the first to send you to a specialist, to the top specialist in the particular area in which your ailment falls. And he has sent me to some *great* specialists.

The first operation he arranged for me—again for hernia, on the other side —was in 1938. He got Dr. Louis Wright, who is an amazing man and well known to all the top physicians and surgeons in New York. When they went into somebody and found a hopeless case, they would sew him up quick and send for Louis Wright. He is one of the greatest, recognized Negro surgeons, and he has operated all over town and saved a lot of lives. He did a magnificent job on me, so that I was out on time and soon back at work.

The next time I needed surgery was in 1948 when I was in Washington, playing the Howard Theatre, and I had a pain in the side and back. I went to some friends down there who examined me thoroughly and took X rays. The pictures were wonderful, and the result of their diagnosis was that I should have a kidney taken out immediately. At that point, I called Arthur Logan.

"You better come down here and see what's going on," I said. So he came down and examined me.

"Well, I'm not sure," he said after a moment of hesitancy.

My sister, Ruth, came down too, and they were both in my dressing room at the Howard Theatre.

"Arthur, if it were you," she asked, "where would you have it done?"

"Well, I live in New York," he began.

"Edward, you live in New York too," Ruth said, "so we leave tonight for New York!"

Arthur brought the pictures with him, and we went to New York and up to the Columbia-Presbyterian Medical Center, where we had a date with Dr. Cahill, the head of the Urology Department. He and Arthur went in a room with the pictures and came out again in about ten minutes.

"It's a benign cyst on the outside of the kidney," Dr. Cahill said. "I'll take it off Monday, and it won't come back."

"Now, doctor, you don't suppose that maybe . . . ?" I began.

"You're the maestro on the piano, but I'm the maestro up here," he answered, "and I tell you that when I take it off it won't come back."

Monday came, and he did the operation. While I was convalescing in the hospital, Cress Courtney, my manager, wanted to know about a date at the Paramount Theatre, whether we should keep it or cancel it. Ella Fitzgerald was to be on the bill with us.

"Dr. Cahill," I said, "I've got a date about nine days from now, and I want to know whether I should cancel it or keep it."

"Oh, I think a man should work," he replied. "I'm not in favor of a man laying off too long. I would say that you'll be all right."

So we kept the date in, and I went to the Paramount soon after the operation. I had to go to the hospital every day for Dr. Cahill to dress my wound, and after about the third or fourth day he said, "Well, you're all right, I guess. What time do you do your show?"

"I've done three shows already, doctor," I replied, "and I've got three more to do. I'm here between shows."

He almost dropped his instruments. "I thought you had one show a day," he said. Luckily, everything went along fine.

In 1958, however, I was getting a different kind of pain. Arthur Logan gave me the diagnosis, said it was my gall bladder and that the simplest thing would be to take it out. "When?" I asked.

"Oh, any time in the next year and a half," he answered.

"What are the hazards?"

"Well, if one of the stones should happen to slip down, then, of course, you would have a little pain."

"Doctor," I said, "let's do it Monday!" That was about three days away.

So he got Dr. Samuel Standard, a great man, at New York University Hospital, downtown. Shortly before the operation, I had told a good friend of mine in Washington, Dr. Clark, about it. "Well, listen," he said, "don't rest up for it. Work right up to it, and keep yourself active all the way through when you're to have any kind of operation on the stomach."

I did two benefits the night before I went into the hospital, one at the Waldorf and the other at the Astor, and I went directly from the Astor at about eleven o'clock at night. They operated on me at about eight the next morning, and twelve hours later the nurse came in and said, "Sit up on the side of the bed, put your feet in your slippers, and walk over there by the door. I'll help you."

"Hey," I said, "you know I just had my operation this morning."

"I know," he said. "Don't worry."

I was out real quick. As a matter of fact, nine days later I was working with the band and m.c.-ing the Washington jazz festival. Different people are affected differently by that operation, but I didn't even have to have the tubes up the nose that are usually obligatory. Some years later, I met one of the doctors up at Jackie Robinson's place in Connecticut.

"How did you come out?" he asked. "I was on the team when Dr. Standard operated on you."

"All right. I had no trouble at all."

"Do you have to watch your diet?"

"No, I eat anything I want."

"You're very lucky, because some people have a lot of trouble. Some people, for example, can't eat ice cream afterwards."

It was the same doctor who told me that they always overload the patient with massive doses of Vitamin C after all major surgery. It was just about the time I was getting on the vitamin kick, because of what all these medical people had told me, and when I heard this I said, "Oh, really, doctor?" And it has been me and Vitamin C ever since.

I always keep in mind, too, what Arthur Logan told me once. He said that the bug disease kills more people than any other disease in the world, and that it is therefore important not to let anything bug you. This is very closely related to one of my pet theories: that selfishness can be a virtue.

One night in San Francisco, I was a guest at dinner with Dean C. J. Bartlett, the Reverend Canon John S. Yaryan, the late Bishop James A. Pike, and their families, when a lady with whom I was talking said, "That was selfish of me." I forgot what she had done, but, because of my theory, I felt obliged to demur politely.

"Selfishness," I said, "can be a virtue." She was somewhat surprised and I continued, "Selfishness is essential to survival, and without survival we cannot protect those whom we love more than ourselves."

To finish with my hospital adventures: I had to go back to Paris in 1963, where I had a very busy time. Not only were we doing the usual concerts with the band, but I was also acting as a record producer for Reprise Records. I made albums with some of the wonderful people who were there then: the Paris Symphony Orchestra; Bud Powell; Dollar Brand and Bea Benjamin; Ray Nance, Stephane Grappelli, and Svend Asmussen, the fiddlers three; and that glorious person, Alice Babs, who came down from Sweden. I worked very hard for all of a week. After being closed up in the recording monitor rooms, and then walking out into the damp Paris air, and going to the Crazy Horse, and to see Hazel Scott, I guess I was exposed to something when my resistance was low. I began to feel a little bad; I had aches and pains and thought I had a cold. So I called up my doctor in Paris, Dr. Dax.

"Listen, doctor, I know it's four o'clock in the morning, and I don't expect you to get out of bed and come out, but I'd like to come over to your house and let you . . ."

"Fine," he said. "Come on over."

So I went over to his place and he examined me.

"Well, gee, you've got pneumonia. Go home now. I'll come get you in the morning and take you to the hospital."

After four days in the hospital, they had a kind of party in my hotel when I came out. All the musicians around town were there. Hazel Scott brought me a bank as a present, and in it I put one bill from every country I had recently been in. I still do that, and it's the only time I've ever collected anything. Of all things to be collecting—money! Particularly money of no value, just little bits and pieces.

I Miss

I miss John Popkins' old Hickory House, because in addition to the prime steaks there he used to have wonderful music by extraordinary pianists like Don Shirley, Mary Lou Williams, Billy Taylor, Marian McPartland, Joe Shulman, George Shearing, Eddie Thompson, Frank Froeba, Peter Nero, Joe Bushkin, Ray Bryant, Junior Mance, John Bunch, Monty Alexander, Toshiko, Jutta Hipp, Ralph Sutton, Martial Solal, Joe Castro, Marty Napoleon, Bill Evans, and so many more who are pretty big names today.

I miss Bop City and Bud Powell, who created a wave that was never appreciated artistically as I thought it should have been.

And the Metropole, which had an atmosphere of its own that was strongly directed toward Dixieland, and featured artists like Red Allen and Lionel Hampton.

And Fifty-second Street, which was the all-time Cool Street with Coleman Hawkins, Dizzy Gillespie, Charlie Parker, Lady Day, Art Tatum, Don Byas, Ben Webster, Oscar Pettiford, and so many greats who so definitely influenced the avant-garde.

And Café Society with Hazel Scott, Teddy Wilson, the Kraft Sisters and Josh White.

And Minton's, the home base of Thelonious Monk, Bird, Charlie Christian, and all the great cats who mastered the idiom.

Of course, if you say those were the days, you may sound a little fogyish, but—and I'm sorry—that was truly *un climat extraordinaire*.

What Is Music?

What is music to you?
What would you be without music?

Music is everything.
Nature is music (cicadas in the tropical night).

The sea is music,
The wind is music,
Primitive elements are music, agreeable or discordant.

The rain drumming on the roof,
And the storm raging in the sky are music.

Every country in the world has its own music,
And the music becomes an ambassador;
The tango in Argentina and calypso in Antilles.

Music is the oldest entity.

A baby is born, and music puts him to sleep.
He can't read, he can't understand a picture,
But he will listen to music.

Music is marriage.

Music is death.

The scope of music is immense and infinite.
It is the "esperanto" of the world.

Music arouses courage and leads you to war.
The Romans used to have drums rolling before they attacked.
We have the bugle to sound reveille and pay homage to the brave warrior.

The Marseillaise has led many generations to victories or revolutions;
It is a chant of wild excitement, and delirium, and pride.

Music is eternal,
Music is divine.

You pray to your God with music.

Music can dictate moods,
It can ennerve or subdue,
Subjugate, exhaust, astound the heart.

Music is a cedar,
An evergreen tree of fragrant, durable wood.

Music is like honor and pride,
Free from defect, damage, or decay.

Without music I may feel blind, atrophied, incomplete, *inexistent*.

I Really Never Miss

The cats who come into this band are probably unique in the aural realm. When someone falls out of the band—temporarily or permanently—it naturally becomes a matter of "Whom shall we get?" or "Whom can we get?" It is not just a matter of replacing the cat who left, because we are concerned with a highly personalized kind of music. It is written to suit the character of an instrumentalist, the man who has the responsibility of playing it, and it is almost impossible to match his character identically. Also, if the new man is sufficiently interesting tonally, why insist upon his copying or matching his predecessor's style?

In other words, if we are completely satisfied with the horse and buggy, why invent an automobile or airplane? In the first place, when a man is needed, I personally scarcely even know which way to look for a replacement. I haven't the slightest idea whether the grass next door is greener or leaner. So someone suggests So-and-so, and we send for So-and-so, and get him. We play together a day or two, and then I inquire whether or not the new cat likes what we are doing, having already watched his reaction in the band. If he likes it, he is invited to stay.

As a rule, he is usually a very good man for our purposes. He's a good musician, neat, clean, and with good manners and stage deportment. Of course, he has his own idea of the dramatic aspects of his sole responsibility.

Everybody agrees he's a nice guy until one day, sooner than expected, one of his other selves breaks through, or one of his more eccentric sides shows. Then I confess, or one of the other cats in the band hollers, loudly, "Duke, you never miss!"

Our new man has come home to the home of homies. He manifests his acceptance of the honor bestowed upon him, and settles down to the prospect of welcoming the next new So-and-so.

Ah, you don't know how refreshing it is to keep such a high batting average—on wigs! Oh, doesn't he look sporty, wearing his hat on the side? He is not wearing his hat on the side. He is not wearing his hat at all. He just looks that way because his wig slipped.

Dramatis Felidae

CAT ANDERSON

Cat Anderson joined the band in Philadelphia in 1944. He had had a good musical education and had really mastered the trumpet. Because of the attention he had devoted to high-note technique, he was always given the responsibility of a Babe Ruth when the bases were loaded. All the other cats would do their individual thing, playing true to their tonal personalities, and then for the highspot, for the screeching, clear-over-the-wall, clean-the-bases job, here would come Cat and his acrobatics beyond the limits of the instrument. He did this with an over-500 batting average, but in spite of his heavy role he always made time and would usually be first man on the stand. Never a no-show artist, for a while he became an essential ingredient—*le super grand splang de l'acrobatique.*

JOYA SHERRILL

I first met Joya Sherrill backstage at the Paradise Theatre in Detroit during 1941. I asked her recently to refresh my memory with some details of our very happy musical association, and she remembers it like this:

"I had written a set of lyrics to 'Take the "A" Train,' and had come to the theatre to sing it for you. I had no thought of singing with your band, but only hoped you would like the lyrics I had written.

"You called Billy Strayhorn to the piano. He played, I sang, and you listened. After I had finished, you asked me to sing something else, and I sang three other songs.

Marie Ellington, Joya Sherrill, and Kay Davis

"'That's very good,' you said. 'I like that. Where are you working?'

"'I'm not working anywhere. I'm still in school.'

"'Well, keep in touch with me,' you said. 'I can always use a good singer.'

"I thanked you, but really thought you were just being nice. I put no stock in the idea of singing with your band. Aside from the excitement of meeting you and telling all my school friends about the experience, I truly dismissed it from my mind.

"A few months later, a call came to me one evening in Detroit from Pittsburgh, from 'Duke Ellington.' I shall always remember *exactly* what you said.

"'I've been thinking about you,' your first words were. 'Sing something for me.' I was so excited, tears were streaming down my face, and I tried to think of a song to sing.

"'Sing something bluesy,' you said.

"I sang a few bars of 'I've Got a Guy.' It was a long-distance call and I thought I should be brief. 'Sing the rest of it,' you said. So I finished the song, and I remember word for word what you said then:

"'I would like to use you to broadcast and record. Your diction is perfect and you articulate so well. When will you be finished school?'

"'In June,' I replied.

"'Well, I'm rather forgetful, so let me know when you're out of school, because I want you to join the band.'

"This was the first time I realized I might really be going to sing with your band, and I started planning my life accordingly. My family was opposed to show business and explained to you that the only way I could go was if my mother went with me. So mother traveled with me.

"I opened in Chicago at the College Inn in the Hotel Sherman, July of 1942. Ivie Anderson, I shall never forget, was still with the band. You called me to sing 'Mood Indigo' (it was Ivie's song), and she pulled me back before I walked out to sing, and said, 'Sing it *good*, or I'll come behind you and sing it too!' I was terrified, but determined to do a good job.

"I sat on the bandstand by Freddy Guy each night, and during the two months we worked there he told me about everybody who came in the place, so I got a small education.

"It was at the College Inn that I met Richard Guilmenot, whom I married in 1946. Mother wanted to go to Detroit one weekend to see my daddy, and you told her not to worry, that you would look after me while she was away.

So I met Richard at the club that very evening. He wanted to take me out and, although I did not date as yet, I wanted to go out with him. I asked you if it would be all right. You were sweet and replied, 'What do you think your mother would say?' I said, 'I really don't know.' Then you told me, 'If there's any question in your mind, don't go. It's not that important.' I didn't go, but we married two years later.

"After we left Chicago, I went on tour with the band. There was a ban on recording at that time, but as soon as it was lifted in 1944 I recorded 'I'm Beginning to See the Light.'

"Marie Ellington had been brought to your attention by Freddy Guy, and she joined the band in Ohio. She was married to Spergan Ellington, an Air Force pilot who later was killed. Soon after that, we became a threesome when Kay Davis joined the band at the Royal Theatre in Baltimore. Kay was from Evanston, Illinois, and the three of us became the best of friends, and are still to this day."

What Joya doesn't say, of course, is that she did such a good job on "I'm Beginning to See the Light" that we have been playing it ever since. It is a tribute to her diction and articulation, too, that when I ask them to join in singing it with us, audiences all over the world seem to know the words.

KAY DAVIS

Kay Davis was an honor student of Northwestern University, where she studied opera and majored in music. She had perfect pitch, could sight-read, and had all the gifts, so we decided to use her voice as an instrument. This was in addition to her interpretations of regular songs with words, and it proved very successful on several numbers. I shall never forget her first Carnegie Hall appearance in January 1946. Subtitled "A Blue Fog You Can Almost See Through," "Transbluency" was a last-minute kind of composition, and the two featured musicians (Jimmy Hamilton on clarinet and Lawrence Brown on trombone) had to have music stands at the mike, because it had been completed too late for them to memorize. So we put Kay's part on a music stand at the mike, just like those of the musicians, and the performance was a smash.

She came with me and Ray Nance when we played at the London Palladium and toured Europe in 1948. Her wordless vocals reminded a lot of our older fans of the early records we made with Adelaide Hall.

Of course, I was very lucky to have three such singers as Kay Davis, Joya Sherrill, and Marie Ellington all at one time, but there is a sad corollary to be detailed: all three were pretty, all three married, and all three left me.

MARIE ELLINGTON

Marie Ellington was so pretty that it took a while for audiences to realize that she was presented for the purpose of singing rather than just to be looked at! Then, when they became aware of her lovely, sultry voice, they simply surrendered.

Nat "King" Cole took one look at her, scooped her up, carried her off to the preacher, married her, and took her home to his beautiful Beverly Hills love nest, where she listened to his love songs for the rest of his life.

JIMMY HAMILTON

Jimmy Hamilton was born in South Carolina, like Cat Anderson and Rufus Jones, but he was raised in Philadelphia. He joined us in 1942 when we were in the Hurricane Club on Broadway. He had been playing in Dave Martin's trio in Brooklyn, but, after sitting in with us for a couple of days, he decided to join us. However, he had to make a slight compromise. His main instrument was clarinet, and his double had been alto saxophone, but now he had to make a switch, because our book called for clarinet doubling tenor. That he managed this perfectly was typical of Jimmy. He usually manages anything musical that he sets his mind to, and there, I think, is the key to any attempt at describing him. He has the capacity to discipline himself and the diligence to study in order to learn. He practices endlessly and scarcely ever gets away from the school rules. You might say that he is a tutor-rooter, and a credit to his tutor!

His solid musical foundation supports him when he arranges and composes. Although he has strong classical tendencies on clarinet, he always more or less leaned toward the funky on tenor—until he heard Harold Ashby, and then you could tell how much he liked Ash.

He's a nice guy, with patience and a dry sense of humor, and he's easy to get along with. If he believes something, or in something, neither hell nor high water will change his belief. He was very important to us throughout the twenty-five years he was in the band.

PAUL GONSALVES

Paul Gonsalves is a nice, easygoing guy from a beautiful family in New Bedford, Rhode Island. His mother is beautiful, his sisters and brothers are beautiful, and all of his children are beautiful. In fact, he is blessed with nothing but beautiful relatives. He had good musical education, has great solo taste, and plays with profound authority. But he is shy, hates microphones, and loves *au naturel*. We call him "the strolling violins," because he will take his horn and walk over to a group, or do his whole solo to one child in the audience.

He wants to be liked by everybody, and doesn't want anything from anybody except a kind word and a water chaser. He will stand around and talk and socialize with people all night, whether or not he knows them, and always he says, "They're some beautiful cats, man."

He has respect for respect, but never makes demands for himself. There is never an evil thought in his mind. In fact, his purity of mind suggests to me that he would have made a good priest. His punch line, of course, is "Jack Daniels," but that is just a kind of façade.

SHORTY BAKER

Harold "Shorty" Baker came into the band in 1942 to give us our first trumpet section of four. He joined Ray Nance, Rex Stewart, and Wallace Jones, and with his phenomenal phrasing and tone control he was an immense asset. He ad-libbed hot or blues as though he were recalling some beautiful dreams of St. Louis, his home and birthplace. His way of playing a melody was absolutely personal, and he had no bad notes at all.

RUSSELL PROCOPE

Russell Procope was a kind of child wonder. He was taught violin at first, but when he heard Fletcher Henderson's band he was attracted to jazz. The urge grew stronger when his schoolmate Benny Carter got an alto saxophone. He was also drawn to the clarinet, first by the playing of Buster Bailey with Fletcher; then by Omer Simeon's when he worked with him in Jelly Roll Morton's band; and after that by Barney Bigard's when he heard him in King Oliver's and our band. So you see why even today he is a master of the old New Orleans style on the Albert system clarinet!

He worked a while with Chick Webb until he became first alto in Benny Carter's place with Fletcher Henderson. There he was alongside such idols of his as Coleman Hawkins, Buster Bailey, and, later, Hilton Jefferson. In 1938 he became a part of one of the most outstanding of all combos, John Kirby's. Kirby and Buster Bailey had been with him in Henderson's band, and with Charlie Shavers, Billy Kyle, and O'Neil Spencer they were a smash hit everywhere. After World War II he came with us in 1946, and he has been with us ever since.

Russell Procope grew up through all this to be a man of dignity and gentility, of clean and gentlemanly appearance. What is more, he became a conscientious, all-around musician, one always to be depended on.

BETTY ROCHÉ

Betty Roché was an unforgettable singer. She came with us during our Hurricane engagement in 1943, and she sang almost anything that was suggested or requested. She learned new songs so quickly, and they always came off as Betty Roché originals. She had a soul inflection in a bop state of intrigue, and it was presented to the listener in a most believable manner as by a little girl with an adult delivery. The recordings she did with us are still considered great, and they still have the luster of originality. Many of the phrases she came up with, along with the words she added, would have been considered good as instrumental licks. Her treatment of "Take the 'A' Train," for example, is as classic as the original Ray Nance trumpet solo. She was the first to sing "The Blues" in *Black, Brown and Beige* (at Carnegie Hall in January, 1943), and every word was understandable despite the sophisticated hip and jive connotations. She was thirty years ahead of her time. She never imitated anybody, and she never sounded like anybody but Betty Roché.

AL HIBBLER

I first met Al Hibbler in Little Rock, Arkansas. I knew he was a singer but had never heard him sing. Our paths crossed several times before 1943, when we were playing the Hurricane Club at Forty-ninth and Broadway. Mary Lou Williams and Shorty Baker came up and told me that Al Hibbler was downstairs in the Turf, and that there was a possibility of getting him to sing for us. So they brought him up, and he sang something. I naturally liked it, but the thought of adding to the payroll was a cause of concern, and a smart business mind would not have considered it. But me—well, my ear makes decisions.

"Great," I said. "I like it. You just started work."

It was much easier than I thought it would be for Hib to learn songs, but that was because he has ears that see, and so miracles happened. He learned song after song, and soon he was our major asset—truly a profitable investment, both dollar-wise and for luxury of keeping my ear in deep fat. He had so many sounds that even without words he could tell of fantasy beyond fantasy. Hib's great dramatic devices and the variety of his tonal changes give him almost unlimited range. His capabilities are so many, but I should mention first his clear, understandable enunciation. He can produce a whispering, confidential sound, or an outburst that borders on panic. He will adopt a nasal tone at just the right word and note, or affect a sudden drop to what sounds like the below-compass bass. Cries, laughs, and highly animated calls—he uses them all to make the listener see it as he sees it. Sinatra calls Albert Hibbler and Ray Charles his two ace pilots.

I learned a lot from Al Hibbler. I learned about senses neither he nor I ever thought we had. And I think that he learned some little things from me. On a train one day he was listening to a football game on his radio, something he had done many times before. I felt an opportunity and said, "Do you understand the exact position of the players on each team?" After a pause and a thought, he said, "Well, not really." So I explained how the eleven men of each team faced one another, marked their positions with hands and fingers on his thigh, and after a while he knew and understood it, I think, as well as I did. Maybe by now he's got the outstanding play of the century in his head. Do you know a team that might need a coach or quarterback?

I remember that Hib and Laura, his sweetheart, had a split-up, and that we didn't see her very often afterwards. But one day she came visiting backstage. Hib was in his dressing room 'way across the stage. The picture was on, so it was dark back there, but something happened then that nobody understood. Several days later it came out when somebody asked, "Hib, have you seen Laura lately?" "No," he answered, "I haven't seen her, but I know she was backstage here the other day. I can tell anytime she is within twenty feet of me."

WINI BROWN

Wini Brown's father was one of the intellectual waiters who graduated from the old Cotton Club. He was intelligent and hip, as all of the Cotton Club waiters were in those days. He had two lovely daughters and two handsome sons, and they lived across the street from us up on St. Nicholas Avenue. When Wini became a chorus girl at the Cotton Club, she was so young she had to have her mother bring her to work and come back at the end of the show to take her home. Wini first married Stepin Fetchit and then, in 1944, when we were playing in the Hurricane, she was in a Broadway show called *Early to Bed*. One night the entire cast came to the Hurricane for one of their celebrations, and Wini, always a put-on artist, took her turn singing. She got such a good audience reaction that, when I went over to congratulate her and give her good wishes, I invited her to join the band. She was a beautiful chick and she copped out by saying, "You've got to be kidding! I'm not a singer, I'm a dancer."

Nevertheless, she opened with us our first night out of town at the Downtown Theatre on State Street in Chicago. Dusty Fletcher was on the bill too, I remember. Everything was going fine until a very famous young doctor, Midi Lambright, married her and dragged her off to Cleveland.

With Louis Bellson and Willie Cook, 1970

LOUIS BELLSON

Louis Bellson (Louis Balassoni) is so handsome a cat that when he's on the stand the chicks don't see anybody but him. Chicks come, wait, and hope, but he is not very forward with the girls.

He took us, the entire band and show—Nat Cole, Sarah Vaughan, Patterson and Jackson, Timmie Rogers, Peg Leg Bates, and I don't know how many others—to his house one night when the *Big Show of '51* played Moline,

Illinois. His beautiful mother, who is as cute as can be and whom everybody calls Curly, served an Italian dinner of endless courses. Patterson and Jackson, the heavy boys of the eating league, were filled to overflowing and knocked out 'way before the last course. I paced this gorgeous feast with the proper salad punctuations, of course, and came off champ. Everybody else thought every course was the main course. I was alone with—and ate—the dessert. It was the greatest reception since Mrs. Carney laid the band out, stuffing them with Boston-type food. What a wonderful family!

Louis Bellson is the epitome of what Paul Gonsalves means when he says, "He's a beautiful cat, man!" For in spite of his outrageous beauty, Louis Bellson is truly a beautiful person. With never a thought about getting even or getting the better of any man, he has the soul of a saint. There is nothing too good for someone he likes, and I don't know anybody he doesn't like, or anybody who doesn't like him. He and Billy Strayhorn were very good buddies, when he was with us as a musician.

Supporting or solo, he is the epitome of perfection, a brilliant performer. We really felt it when he had to quit to go and organize a band to back up his lovely wife, who, as you must know, is sometimes known as Pearlie Mae, the inimitable Pearl Bailey.

We are proud indeed to have been the first to present him as a *musician extraordinaire* in an entire fifteen-minute feature. Then, too, he keeps coming back with great big bands, for which he writes the orchestrations. We are still getting requests for his "Skin Deep" and "The Hawk Talks."

JIMMY WOODE

Jimmy Woode joined us in Boston in 1955, temporarily, because our regular bass man, Junior Raglin, was sick. He was recommended to us by George Wein, whose regular bass player he had been for gigs around Boston.

"Good bass player," we said, "reading or faking."

Then I became aware of his sensitivity. No matter which way we turned, melodically or harmonically, Jimmy Woode was right on top of it. When we realized that he was really with us all the way, we knew he was well worth considering for the regular spot.

He was another teammate whose constant intent was "give to." A musician with this intent, like all good musicians who know their instruments according to Hoyle (and all the other ways), enjoys the sensitivities we depend upon when aural compatibility is the foundation of the final product at the ear of the listener.

Jimmy Woode was born in Philadelphia, and his father was a music teacher. He was always a solid believer in the theory that when your pulse and my pulse are together, we are swinging, with ears, eyes, and every member of the body tuned in to driving a wave emotionally, compellingly, to and from the subconscious.

SAM WOODYARD

Sam Woodyard, who came into the band in 1955, was born in Elizabeth, New Jersey. He is a real easy-to-get-along-with type of cat. He doesn't want to outdo or do anybody out of anything. He just wants to be *in there,* giving with his body, his soul, his mind, his pulse, his instrument, his drums. No crash bang, never overpoweringly loud, volume just where it should be—*in there.*

When he is playing, he just about has an affair with his drums, an observation that was the inspiration of *A Drum Is a Woman.* He lives "It Don't Mean a Thing If It Ain't Got That Swing," and if it ain't swinging he'll tag along with respect and sympathy, but without sympatico.

Sometimes we would write something that seemed or was expected to be below bland, but when Sam added his thing to it, immediately it took on a new dimension, exotic, zesty, or maybe lecherous soul. Sam the Man, who began with his hand on the plan for the stand of his drums—exotic as the tabla, lecherous as the cuica, his elbow on the snare drum.

He was one of three heroes whose performance lifted an exhausted audience around two o'clock in the morning at the 1956 Newport Jazz Festival, when policemen were stalking, stomping, and threatening a curfew two hours too late. George Wein was walking up and down in front of the stage, walking in time to the music, with his face serious on the police side and smiling on our side. Paul Gonsalves, Jimmy Woode, and Sam Woodyard lifted that stone-cold audience up to a fiery, frenzied, screeching, dancing climax that was never to be forgotten. One lovely society matron broke through her veneer of discretion, and jumped her thing for all twenty-seven choruses, adding a cherry and whipped cream topping to our sundae morning.

JIMMY GRISSOM

Jimmy Grissom sang with the band in the early '50s, and was a hit in the blues segments of *My People,* the show we presented in Chicago in 1963, where he sang with all the believable nuances expected of a blues singer. He always looked very young, yet when he sang the blues you had to believe that he had suffered every incident in the heartbreaking lyrics. In addition to that, he had a street-scene, jive quality that demanded his recognition as a worldly man who had given his heart in vain. I was lucky enough to get him through a disc jockey in Fort Worth.

JOHN SANDERS

John Sanders was always, as musician, man, and ambassador, a major credit to our band, right from the beginning when he joined it in 1954. A valve trombonist, he played solos that were the nearest we ever had to Tizol's originals. He was a brilliant musician and an irreplaceable aide when we were orchestrating *en masse* with a devastating deadline at our heels. In addition, he was a gentleman in every sense of the word—in manners, ethics, and appearances.

I love John Sanders and think that just about everyone else who knows him loves him for the great human being that he is. He is from a beautiful, gentle, educated family. His total intent is absolute, unadulterated good, and I tried but could not find a better or more fitting word than that—*good.*

In 1965 he decided to enter the priesthood, and in 1973 he was ordained in the Diocese of Bridgeport. I was extremely touched by a compliment he paid me in the June 1972 report of the Pope John XXIII National Seminary, Weston, Massachusetts, where he was studying. I hope I will not be thought immodest by including it here, but it exemplifies John's generosities, apart from anything else:

"While Duke is one of the great creative people of our times, he is above all a very fine human being. You could tell by the way he treated the men in the band and his audiences that he lived by the Gospel message. He never once was above anyone—everyone mattered to him, from celebrities to the average person who would ask for one more number beyond time to quit. No one-night-stand ever was unimportant to Duke."

WILLIE COOK

Willie Cook has always been potentially the best first trumpet player in the business, but from time to time romance has had a stronger appeal than running all over the world doing one-nighters and all that jazz. He has been in and out of the band many times since 1951, but whenever he returns he gives a brilliant performance. His taste as a soloist is quickly proved to anyone who listens to his records.

At one time we had Willie Cook, Shorty Baker, Clark Terry, and Ray Nance sitting side by side in our trumpet section . . . Too much!

CLARK TERRY

The first time I ever heard about Clark Terry was when Charlie Barnet told me about him. Charlie was raving: "Clark Terry is the greatest trumpet player in the world. You wait and see. Or better still, go get him for your band, but hurry, because soon everybody is going to be trying to get him." I considered myself lucky indeed to get him in 1951.

Like Shorty Baker, Clark is from St. Louis, a city that seems to specialize in producing fine trumpet players. Although I don't think he has had the recognition he deserves, there is one area I know where he is very much appreciated. He is a busy man, but he always finds the time to help the college bands around the country, and I am sure many a youngster has been inspired by him both as a man and as a musician.

When a trumpet player imitates Louis Armstrong, Louis gets the credit. When a trumpet player decides that his style is to be built on Dizzy Gillespie's, Dizzy gets the credit. The same thing with those saxophone players who copied Coleman Hawkins and Charlie Parker. But today, although I hear a whole new world of flügelhorn stylists formed behind Clark Terry, I hear none of the prime authorities on the subject say, "Clark Terry did this sixteen years ago." If this is not recognized soon, he could grow up to be the Barzillai Lew of the flügelhorn.*

ERNIE SHEPARD

We were playing a joint in Seattle in 1962, and everything was going smoothly until our bassist, Aaron Bell, decided to tell me that he would have to leave the band in a day or two. I'm in Seattle and really stuck for a bass player, so I had to act quickly. I got on the phone and called Pat Willard in Los Angeles, asked whom she knew who might be available and free to leave immediately. She gave me a few names, and I called three or four, but all I got from them was a lot of jive, like, "Man, you see I've got these studio obligations, and some very lucrative gigs, too, so I would have to get the kind of unheard-of money you wouldn't believe!" The last name on the list was Ernie Shepard.

"What are you doing?" I asked. "Where are you working?"

"Nowhere, man," he answered. "I ain't doin' nothin'!"

With that and his tone of voice, I felt that I had finally gotten lucky. We soon reached an understanding about the money and had everything straight.

"There'll be a ticket waiting for you at the airport tomorrow," I said. "Get up here as quickly as possible."

Well, Shep arrived on time, and the minute he played the first number I knew I had hit the jackpot. Such sensitivity, such taste, even in numbers where there was no bass part. He reminded me of Blanton with an added bop flair. This was one of the real, big rewards in my career.

Later, he told me he had not been well. So when we got to New York the first thing I did was to rush him up to my doctor, Dr. Arthur Logan. He gave him a complete checkup, called me and said, "When you leave for Europe in a week or two, you cannot take this man with you. He's got too many things medically wrong with him." The bottom dropped out of my hopes.

* Although not as well known as Crispus Attucks, Barzillai Lew was a black soldier from Chelmsford, Massachusetts. As drummer and fifer, he fought in the French and Indian War and also served throughout the Revolutionary War on the American side. (Editor)

With Ernie Shepard, Colombo, Ceylon, 1963

"But, Doctor," I said, "this man is not the man he was when he first came with us. He is involved totally with the music, and that's got something to do with what's happened to him. He is a very content man now."

"Well," Dr. Logan said, "I'm just telling you." And he rattled off a long list of ailments, any one of which could wash him away. But I believed in the way Shep was acting. He was an optimist, and it isn't easy to kill an optimist.

"Please," I begged. "I'll watch over him and see that he gets his checkups. The slightest change—I'll fly him right back to you."

Then I talked it over with Shep, and he agreed that he was happy, and would not let anything or anybody bug him.

"Okay," Arthur Logan said. "Maybe a miracle will happen."

231

With that, we left for Europe. Shep got better and better, and played better and better. Dr. Logan said he never would have believed it.

Shep became one of our most outstanding members. Everybody in the band loved him and wanted to play solos with him. He was a wonderful rhythm-section teammate for Sam Woodyard and me. We really had a ball, and everything was fine until he fell in love in Germany, and decided to make it his home. The whole thing added about ten years to the life of a man who was just sitting out in Los Angeles waiting for his number to be called.

We still have a recording I love to listen to now and then when I have the time—and a machine. It's just Shep singing and accompanying himself on the bass.

JOE TURNER

When we were playing the Booker T. Washington theatre in Kansas City, we went to hear Joe Turner sing the blues every night, all night. Pete Johnson was playing piano for him, and it was a great kick. So when we did *Jump for Joy* at the Mayan Theatre in Los Angeles in 1941, I sent for Joe Turner and signed him up. I got so much pleasure listening to him break it up that I completely forgot I had him under contract. He still has a tremendous track record. Right on!

JIMMY RUSHING

Although he was born in Oklahoma City, Jimmy Rushing was a true representative, the Senator, from the Kansas City jazz-blues community you found around Eighteenth and Vine, where Joe Turner was Mayor, Pete Johnson the Majority Leader, Julia Lee the Corporation Counsel, Walter Page the School Superintendent, Bennie Moten the Treasurer, Jay McShann the Commissioner of Public Works, Harlan Leonard the Chairman of the Board of Estimates, and Piney Brown the Public Health Superintendent. Jimmy was closely identified with my very dear friend Count Basie, who is the

Swinger of the Swingingest, or the Swingingest of the Swingers. Naturally, Jimmy fit right into his band context, because their pulses were together.

Jimmy was a great artist, an original, and, as Pastor Gensel said at his funeral service in 1972, he still retained a childlike—not to be confused with childish—quality right through to the end of his long professional career. That, of course, was virtue manifesting itself.

We never were able to hear enough of him. He recorded with us once, and on several occasions he came by where we were playing and sat in with us. But never often enough! That's it, the whole story of Jimmy Rushing. He wasn't an aggressive man, so there was never enough heard of him.

STEPIN FETCHIT

Stepin Fetchit played comedy parts in many pictures, but none could have been staged so hilariously as a real-life sketch he accidentally put on for me and the night crowd in Los Angeles one night. Stuff Crouch's joint was one of the leading late-hour spots then. It was at Central Avenue and Forty-first Street, on the second floor, and when I happened to wander up there I ran into Step.

He was in a wonderful, hospitable mood, and he received me with open arms.

"Come in and be my guest," he said. "Stuff, give my man anything he wants. It's on me!" Then he turned and said, "Duke, I want you to meet my bodyguard. Man, I've got a bodyguard. This is Mr. So-and-so, my bodyguard."

Right after that a great big cat moved in to shake my hand, saying, "Mr. Ellington, I'm glad to shake your hand, but I'm sorry to tell you that I had to slap one of your boys the other night."

This was really bad news, because this fellow had a reputation for knocking people down—a one-punch man. So I responded with a smile, hoping he was joking, and asked, "Which one?"

"That drummer of yours, Sonny Greer," he said. "He's too fresh. He got out of line with me and I had to slap him."

At this point, Step stepped in and interrupted: "Now these gentlemen are from the East Coast, and when they come out here to California we have to be nice to them."

"I don't have to be nice to nobody who gets smart with me," the big cat says, "or anybody I think is out of line."

"You should be ashamed of yourself going around hitting people," Step said. "I know somebody who might punch you in your nose."

"Who?" the other guy asked, glaring.

Step stepped back and gestured to his bodyguard, who received the presentation speech with proper aplomb and bowed from the waist, but the big cat started to swing on him and Step right away. There was no fighting back. Step and his bodyguard turned on the fan and blinded the spot. Down on their hands and knees they went, under the tables and chairs, to the exit and down the stairs, with the big bad cat right on their respective Daniels.

JIMMY JONES

Jimmy Jones is a close member of our musical family. Outside of our original version, he and Toby Hardwick were the first to do "Come Sunday." I have had many different associations with him, the most notable being when we did *My People* in Chicago in 1963. I could not be there during the entire run, and he took over many of my responsibilities, played the piano and directed the orchestra. Then, when we were touring with Ella Fitzgerald, he was acting as her pianist, conductor, and orchestrator.

He extended his scope so much as an arranger that he ended up out in Hollywood, doing that picture stuff, but I hope his ability as a pianist won't be lost to us. From the time he came to New York with Stuff Smith in 1944, he worked with many famous names and became recognized as one of the truly professional dependables. As Paul Gonsalves would say, "Beautiful cat, man!"

LOUIS ARMSTRONG AND JOE GLASER

Louis Armstrong and Joe Glaser; Joe Glaser and Louis Armstrong. Don't put the cart before the horse, they say, and at first glance you might think Louis was the horse doing all the pulling while Glaser was in the driver's seat of the cart. Obviously, a cart is a most convenient place to stash the gold.

With Louis Armstrong at the Rainbow Grill, New York City, 1969

Then you realize that in spite of how well Joe Glaser did for himself, Louis still ended up a very rich man, maybe the richest of all the "trumpet Gabriels." This is not a fact to be ignored, for what more can one man do for another: Joe Glaser watched over Louis like the treasure he was, and saw to it that his partner was well fixed for the rest of his life.

Joe Glaser never let anybody book Louis but Joe Glaser, thus automatically eliminating all dipsies. He gave personal attention and direction to all his business, and nobody represented by his agency—Associated Booking Corporation—came before Louis. Nobody could get a job before him, the

Number One, the Number One Man, Louis. So I think Joe Glaser deserves a salute in recognition of the state of security he obtained for Louis, who really didn't have to work. The fact that he did work showed how it is when a musician is married to his horn. (No offense to Louis' wonderful wife, Lucille, who also watched over him, sick or well.)

Louis Armstrong was the epitome of jazz and always will be. He was also a living monument to the magnificent career of Joe Glaser.

At Christmas, Joe gave everybody he represented sweet and tinkling cash presents. He paid the sidemen in Louis' band the kind of money musicians would like to be making today. They were carefully selected musicians, however, men who would enchance the image of Louis Armstrong. And Joe had his own personal physician travel with Louis all over the world, to insure against those little things that traveling people are exposed to, from the common cold on up. So you see that Joe used money generously to protect his partner, and Louis was more partner than most people suspect.

I loved and respected Louis Armstrong. He was born poor, died rich, and never hurt anyone on the way.

ELLA FITZGERALD AND NORMAN GRANZ

We had the great privilege of recording a collection of our compositions with Ella Fitzgerald for Norman Granz's Verve label. Billy Strayhorn and I wrote a four-part *Portrait of Ella Fitzgerald* and introduced its various sections with the following observations:

"While Billy Strayhorn sets the mood (at the piano), we gather the material for our musical portrait of Ella Fitzgerald by allowing our imagination to browse through her family album. We see there many people, pretty people, strong people, sturdy, solid people—people and events of great dignity and distinction, and all with a beat! As we turn the pages, we observe that she is of 'Royal Ancestry,' and in our first movement we try to capture and convey some of the majesty of Her Majesty.

"As the inspection of our royal subject gains momentum, we imagine we have been granted a confidential glimpse into her diary, and the more we leaf through the pages the more we realize that this is a personality of wonderful warmth, and that she is 'All Heart.'

Ella Fitzgerald

"Ella Fitzgerald is a great philanthropist. She gives so generously of her talent, not only to the public, but to the composers whose works she performs. Her artistry always brings to mind the words of the Maestro, Mr. Toscanini, who said concerning singers, 'Either you're a good musician or you're not.' In terms of musicianship, Ella Fitzgerald is 'Beyond Category.'

"In our musical search for a tonal portait of Ella Fitzgerald, we find a melodic parallel in which royal ancestry, greatness of heart, and talent beyond category are the principal components in the quest for 'Total Jazz.'"

The following year we went to Europe for Norman Granz for the first time. He did it very well, represented us beautifully as an impresario, and left me feeling very much indebted to him. He took us back several times after that, and in 1966 we went with Ella Fitzgerald, which was a bang.

Norman Granz is one of those guys I have spoken of as encountering at the various intersections of my road through life, guys who have been there to point out the way. He got some very good deals for me, too, like the Francis Sinatra picture, *Assault on a Queen.* They were not talking as much money as he was thinking, but he got it, and fairly quickly, too. It was one of those situations where someone says, "That's it, or nothing!" He kept cool, called up an hour later, and the price was up $15,000, or something like that.

The representation he gave me was great. It makes a lot of difference when the man who is doing the talking for you is a millionaire. He had no dipsies. Everything had to be cleared through him and he took full responsibility. Although he was acting in effect as my manager, he never took a percentage or a fee. I was happy with him, but then Cress Courtney came back into the picture.

One of the highest honors paid me was when Norman Granz presented us at the St. Tropez Art Festival in 1966 along with Ella Fitzgerald and a host of top masters in their own different fields. I had the enormous pleasure of appearing in a film made at this time with Joan Miró, the great Spanish painter, at one of the world's finest museums, La Fondation Maeght, in St. Paul de Vence.

FRANK SINATRA

A unique individual, a *primo* nonconformist *assoluto,* Frank Sinatra never wanted to be like anybody else, I think, other than perhaps his parents. I first met him when he was with Tommy Dorsey. They all came down one night to the College Inn at the Sherman Hotel in Chicago where we were playing, and I think it was just about the time he was ready to split the Dorsey gig. I could tell that by the way Tommy said good night to him!

The next time we met was when he was doing a single on the bill with us at the State Theatre in Hartford, Connecticut. He was young, crispy-crunch fresh, and the girls were squealing then. He was very easy to get along with, and there were no hassles about his music.

From that time on, Sinatra just went ever upwards, and everybody knows about him as an artist. Every song he sings is understandable and, most of all, believable, which is the ultimate in theatre. And I must repeat and emphasize my admiration for him as a nonconformist. His first really big booking was when he played the New York Paramount for $15,000 per week. The chicks were screaming, but he didn't act like a celebrated swoon weaver. I don't know of anybody else who would have done anything to jeopardize his position so soon after reaching a peak of success, but Francis Sinatra decided—I'm sure against the wishes of his advisors and yes-men—to do what is usually considered dangerous and damaging to a budding career. He went ahead and made a tour of racially disturbed high schools in New York City preaching race tolerance. He's an individualist, and he never trails the herd. Nobody tells him what to do or say.

Some time later, he felt that a syndicated columnist had spoken out of turn. So what did Francis do? He slugged the cat, and then went on and upwards to still greater heights.

Back in the '50s, we were playing Las Vegas when some of my cats were nabbed in a raid. The newspapers played it up as a big thing. What did Francis do the very next night? He came to visit and hear our show. He brought a party of thirty people, and they gave us the bravos of the giants. After that, the good citizens forgot about the raid.

More recently, we were both playing in Vegas, and he was having a birthday party at the place where he was appearing. I asked permission from the management where we were to go over and play a few numbers for Francis. No sweat. We went and had a ball. Who do you think had the most fun? Nobody but Paul Gonsalves. He had to be carried out bodily. I thanked Francis and told him it was the best party he ever gave for Paul Gonsalves!

ORSON WELLES

When we reached Los Angeles in 1941, we were involved with *Jump for Joy* and a strong social-significance element, which was now entering everything we did in music. *Jump for Joy,* as mentioned, was written by fifteen Hollywood writers, and financed by a lot of Hollywood actors and writers, and patronized by many different Hollywood types and groups. They used to keep on coming back to the Mayan Theatre, where the show was presented. Orson Welles came one night and left word for me to come to his office at RKO next morning. He wanted to talk to me about doing a picture. So I was in his office promptly at nine o'clock. I should have known better, because I've never been anywhere else on time in my life. I sat there for an hour or so, and finally he came in.

"I'm sorry to be late," he said. "We saw the show last night, and it's great!" Then he went right through it. "The overture should be done with the band on stage instead of in the pit. One man should come out alone, and then the others, one by one, until the whole band is on the stage." He went through the show from the first curtain to the last curtain, blow by blow, every number, every sketch, all of it coming out of his mind without notes—and he saw it once! It was both a review and a mass of suggestions. It was the most impressive display of mental power I've ever experienced— just pure genius.

After getting through the show, he said, "What I really want to talk to you about is that I want to do the history of jazz as a picture, and we'll call it *It's All True*. I want it to be written by Duke Ellington and Orson Welles, directed by Duke Ellington and Orson Welles, music written by Duke Ellington . . ." There must have been a dozen such titles and credits. "While you're thinking about this," he continued, "you're on salary at a thousand dollars a week, and if you don't take it you're a sucker!"

"I accept," I said.

I collected up to $12,500, for which I wrote a total of twenty-eight bars, and it was supposed to represent Buddy Bolden. I tried to recapture some of it in *A Drum Is a Woman,* but I'm not sure of the relationship between them, because a lot of time elapsed between *Jump for Joy* and *A Drum Is a Woman*.

The project was going along well. A lot of research people were hired. I had fifteen million assistants, people of great significance in the literary field, and all that sort of thing. And Duke Ellington was the Number One everything in every department. I was almost the Number One photographer, too. Then Orson had a big dispute with RKO about another picture he was doing in South America, and the company junked all of his projects. He left them with a lot of film on their hands, which, I understand, they couldn't put together without him. That was the end of *It's All True*. No filming was done—just a lot of research.

The next time we worked together was when I was in Paris and he wanted me to write the music for a play he was doing there. It was a play to launch Eartha Kitt, and I think he was playing the part of Faust himself. Some good music went into that, and we recorded some of it. One number is called "Orson." There was a point in the play where Mephistopheles had promised Faust everything.

"What I want," Faust said, "is Helen, Helen of Troy."

"It's all arranged, don't worry about a thing," Mephistopheles said. He had his bargain all arranged, and he turned and said, "Helen, stand up!"

That was when a little girl sitting on the curbstone and eating an apple stood up—Eartha Kitt! That was the beginning, in Paris, of Eartha Kitt on a higher level.

I think this was right after *A Drum Is a Woman* was released, because I met Orson Welles on a train going to Chicago, the Twentieth-Century Limited. I looked up and here he was coming aboard. I told him about it, and said he should see it or hear the record. Then he told me about his play. It must have been 1957. In doing the background music for a thing like that it is always a kick matching moods.

JO JONES

Jo Jones* was the driving force behind our big success at Newport in 1956, the man with a blueprint for a bouncing, boiling bash, the man in the pit with the git-wit-it git. Out of sight of the audience, in the pit in front of the grandstand, slapping a back beat with a newspaper, talking to us, he prodded us into a *Go, Baby!* drive that developed into the rhythmic groove of the century, with Paul Gonsalves down front at the microphone.

I don't know what would have happened if Jo Jones had taken over at the drums, but what he did, when he did it, and where he was doing it, must have been the most fitting position for him when that night caught fire.

If we had had Count Basie at the piano, and Freddie Green on guitar . . . Well, I don't know, maybe we might have scorched the moon.

---

* Jo Jones fought in the percussion section under the banner of the illustrious Count Basie Original Big Jazz Band. Jo, Freddie, and Count (rhythm section) made that band swang its assoff.

JOE WILLIAMS

When we returned from the Orient in 1972, we had the pleasure of working with Joe Williams for a week in Detroit. I first heard him in Chicago. He was singing around for a while with Jimmy Noone, and at that time he was a very good ballad singer. He sang beautiful sweet songs, and whatever he sang he sang magnificently, but he never got a real good break.

Singers in those days were all considered band singers, and then in 1943 the A.F. of M. had a recording strike. All the record companies decided to record singers without musicians, or with scab musicians, or with vocal groups, or by overdubbing old band charts. This immediately caused people to think of nothing but singers, and from that day on singers have been topping bands.

Joe Williams was still waiting for his break when he turned to the blues. He was no imitator of other blues singers, but he sang real soul blues on which his perfect enunciation of the words gave the blues a new dimension. All the accents were in the right places and on the right words. When he joined Count Basie in 1954, he soon had a smash hit with "Every Day," and another blues by Memphis Sim called "The Comeback." He sang Leroy Carr's "In the Evening" and Pete Johnson's "Roll 'Em Pete," and had another hit in "Alright, Okay, You Win." Since those days with Count Basie, he's been going stronger and stronger. Held higher and higher every day in the ear of the listener, he ain't looked back since. As Billy Strayhorn used to say: "Ever onward and upward." Every day.

CHARLES MINGUS

Alan Douglas of United Artists arranged a record date in 1962 on which I was to play with two fine musicians, two men of imagination, whose normal personalities were as far apart as the North and South poles. Charles Mingus and Max Roach were both leaders of their own groups, but what was wanted now was the kind of performance that results when all the minds are intent on and concerned with togetherness. Nothing should be overdone, nothing underdone, regardless of which musician was in the prime spot as a soloist.

Douglas, the producer, wanted me to write all the music for the date. We called a meeting in my office one night to discuss the material, which I had composed but had not written down. I went through a series of demonstrations at the piano for them. I wanted it to be the kind of fun date that is just about the next thing to what is generally accepted as jamming. They listened and talked, and the titles, even without the music, helped to adjust their perspectives. The next time we met was at the recording session itself.

One of the numbers recorded was approached something like this: I announced the key signature and continued into the annotation. " 'La Fleurette Africaine,' " I explained, "is a little African flower. The piece should be executed from the African philosophical point of view, with which it is concerned. The jungle, to Africans, is a place deep in the forest where no human being has ever ventured, and this little flower was growing right in the middle of it, miles away from human eyes in the central part of the jungle that is God-made and untouched. The little flower just grew prettier and prettier every day."

They both gave a nod of understanding. I went to the piano and called to the engineer, "Roll it!" Roach's rhythmic embellishments could not have been more fitting, nor have sounded more authentic, while Mingus, with his eyes closed, fell into each and every harmonic groove, adding countermelodies as though he had been playing the number all his life. It was one of those mystic moments when our three muses were one and the same. There was just one take, and I was thrilled.

A funny thing happened in the middle of that session, however. Mingus started to pack up his bass, so I asked what the trouble was and where he thought he was going.

"Man, I can't play with that drummer," he said.

"Why, what's wrong?" I asked.

"Duke, I have always loved you and what you're doing in music, but you'll have to get another bass player."

"What, you mean just like that, in the middle of a date? Come on, man, it can't be that serious!"

But he finished packing up his bass and went out to the elevator door. I followed him there, and after he had rolled off a few more beefs, and when he was in the elevator about to push the button, I said, quietly and slowly:

"Mingus, my man, United Artists gave you a full-page ad in the Christmas *Billboard*. It was beautiful."

"Yeah."

"You know," I continued, "if Columbia Records had spent that kind of money on promoting me, I would still be with them today."

He picked up the bass, came back into the studio, and we recorded very happily from then on until the album was completed.

DIZZY GILLESPIE, MILES, AND 'TRANE

When a lady in the audience once complained that she didn't understand what Miles Davis was playing, he responded with one of the sage statements on the art: "It took me twenty years study and practice to work up to what I wanted to play in this performance. How can she expect to listen five minutes and understand it?"

So true, so universally true. One more for Miles!

The only time I had the privilege of working with John Coltrane was on a record date. It was a very interesting session. We recorded some of his tunes with his rhythm section, and some of mine with my rhythm section. No hassle, no sweat—John Coltrane was a beautiful cat. The date flowed so smoothly we did the whole album in one session, and that is rare. I loved every minute of it.

I always liked the bop, and I am proud to say that the fabulous, flamboyant John Birks Gillespie worked in our band once, for four weeks. Diz played with us at the Capitol Theatre in 1944, when we had the gorgeous Lena Horne on the bill. Of course, I'd known him for quite a while before that, because I was an avid visitor on Fifty-second Street. I don't think I missed going there a night after we finished work at the Hurricane on Broadway. All the greats were performing—Art Tatum, Coleman Hawkins, Billie Holiday, Slim and Slam, and so many more. Bobby Short was too young, and was still in Los Angeles, but Mabel Mercer—all the way from Bricktop's in Paris—had her own joint on the same side of the street as the 21 Club, Les Extrémités, Ils Touchent. But I can always say that Dizzy Gillespie, one

Dizzy Gillespie

of the original pioneers of the bop, worked with us. He also played on rather an unusual album of ours called *Jazz Party*.

FRANK HOLZFEIND

Frank Holzfeind was not a swinger or a hip, nightlife kid, but an accountant, a fine family man, and a person with a taste for what he considered listenable music. He opened the Blue Note in the basement of a building in Chicago and started booking in bands, combos, singers, and groups of all sizes, primarily because they did something that he enjoyed. He never booked anything in the Blue Note that would interfere with his jollies of sitting there with martinis. In fact, I have known him to turn down attractions that were sure-shot money-makers in favor of an act that was not too hot at the time monetarily. Why? Because he was going to enjoy listening to it. And this policy was very successful until he had to move to another spot around the corner on Dearborn Street.

Then and there he became the target of agents, managers, and yes-men who all claimed to be in the In. When he said he liked Dave Brubeck, and wanted to book him in the Blue Note, they told him he was crazy. Nevertheless, he brought Brubeck in and he became a big hit, but then the agents priced him out of reach and reason for a spot the size of the Blue Note.

While it was open, between 1949 and 1960, I always called the Blue Note the Metropolitan Opera House of Jazz. We enjoyed a beautiful relationship with Frank Holzfeind, and we played there many times. For years, we would go in there for four weeks in the summer and for the month of December through Christmas and New Year's, and I always remember how Two Ton Baker would play Santa Claus the Sunday afternoon before Christmas Day. In addition to being the great musician he is, Two Ton Baker was the perfect host. In size and personality, he was the perfect Santa Claus. He would sit and play piano, and give presents to the kids, and everybody came and brought their children. They loved Two Ton Baker.

We'd go in there during the summer, too, often for a month at a time, and sometimes for a period between those two bookings, which was most agreeable to Frank and me. He says I was "the all-time champ" at the Blue Note, playing it seventeen times for a total of forty-five weeks. George Shearing was the runner-up with thirty-two weeks. There'll never be another patron of our particular art like Frank Holzfeind of the artistic heart.

Due to an A.F. of M. ruling, Chicago has always had a five-day work week. Monday and Tuesday were our off days, but Frank Holzfeind used to have folk musicians and singers on Mondays, and I think this was the beginning of the big days for folk music. His top folk artist was Burl Ives, and this is proof of Frank Holzfeind's taste, for Ives subsequently went on and up to international heights.

Christmas at the Blue Note, Chicago

IRVING TOWNSEND

Irving Townsend is a very sensitive musician. He plays clarinet in a trip symphony, one of those groups which include doctors, lawyers, and accountants who worked their way through college as professional musicians and who like to get together once or twice a week to try out their chops. He is now executive producer for Columbia Records on the West Coast.

As an a. and r. man, he is wonderful. He has a full knowledge of the mechanics of the business, and he also has such understanding that he seems to know what the artist is trying to get without going into a long-winded rigmarole of rules and regulations, and without being swayed by what some other artist did last week. I love him and his whole beautiful family. We are indebted to him for having produced many of our favorite and most satisfactory records.

GEORGE WEIN

George Wein was well raised and well educated in the Bostonian manner on a rather well-to-do level by his beautiful mother and prominent, physician father. Born rich, he never had any kind of money problems, and he knew and understood the meaning of love. He studied piano and grew interested in jazz, when he became aware of the importance of the left hand in the ragtime-jazz idiom. Having long since gained the confidence of Boston businessmen, it was easy and logical for him to be the one to open jazz joints in the city, first in the Buckminster Hotel, then in the Copley Square Hotel, and then in the Bradford Hotel. His rooms in these hotels bore such names as Storyville and Mahogany Hall, so it was also quite logical that he should end up in charge of the New Orleans Jazz Festival in 1970. In the meantime, of course, he had gone on and on to the Newport Jazz Festival, which automatically established itself, mainly because jazz buffs came from everywhere to hear all the top musicians, as well as singers like Frank Sinatra and Mahalia Jackson, in the natural setting of the highest society.

From Newport, George branched out to other festivals around the country—jazz, folk, and pop—and then internationally, so that today his name and enterprises are known all around the world. He has done a lot of good and made a tremendous contribution to the welfare of all of us who fight under the banner of jazz. Personally, he is one of the good guys, and no matter how successful he is in business, he still likes to sit down at the piano and open up his left hand—even in the presence of The Lion!

JIMMY LYONS

The impresario *assoluto* of the Monterey Jazz Festival is Jimmy Lyons, a fine man, and a good friend to us. He was a disc jockey from 1948 to 1952 on KNBC in San Francisco, and during 1952–53 on KGO. He then moved to

Monterey to live, and that gorgeous part of the country was obviously an inspiration to him. He commuted to San Francisco, broadcasting on KGO again in 1956–57, and then on KFRC from 1961 through 1965. Beginning in 1958, commuting and moonlighting, he also produced the Monterey Jazz Festival each year. He has done a magnificent job, and he has really accomplished much for the artist. We always look forward to playing the Monterey Jazz Festival. It is not a carbon copy of the one at Newport, but a festival with a character all its own. We hope it has continued success under Jimmy Lyon's direction. He's good, and he should be proud of what he has achieved.

TIMME ROSENKRANZ

Baron Timme Rosenkranz was of noble Danish blood, but he was not known to us by his formal title in Harlem, on Broadway, the Champs Élysées, State Street, or Central Avenue. To us he was known simply as Timme.

Although he was an artist in his own right, a writer, a poet, and a wit *extraordinaire,* you will not find volumes of his works that are truly representative of his literary stature. The reason for that is that he was a very unselfish man who always dedicated himself to the great musicians he loved and to the music they played. There is therefore no way now of properly evaluating this man's potential, because his patronage of music consumed most of his time.

We are thankful to Timme Rosenkranz, and may God bless him and minimize the grief of his relatives, who may be assured of the great love felt for him by all of us, his friends.

TONY BENNETT

According to Frank Sinatra, Tony Bennett is the greatest, and if Frank Sinatra says that Tony Bennett is the greatest, including himself, then Tony Bennett must be saying something, and if nobody else is listening, *I* am.

Tony Bennett is the most unselfish performing artist today. He gives credit to everybody with him, including the fourth triangle player. Tony is a Christian, and he lives as one. Father Jack Morley is always there at all his openings to give his blessing. Tony's beautiful mother is there too, to give support to

With Tony Bennett

her son, along with his sister, Mary, and family—Mr. and Mrs. Tom Chiappi and their daughter, Nina, that is. They are all wonderful optimists, and by now you must know what I think of optimists.

Tony Bennett is truly a thrill to listen to, and on at least a couple of occasions his generosity has broken the record. For instance, he hired me and my band to play a tour with him a couple of years ago, and his respect for me told him to give *me* top billing. Well, to my knowledge, nobody ever gives away top billing, particularly when they are buying the package and paying top salaries. I believe the same thing happened when he went on tour with Count Basie.

I was at Tony Bennett's opening night at the Copacabana, and after the show many of his friends went to the 14 Hotel next door to pay their respects. One of them was Al Hibbler. Hib had been Tony's guest that night and the Copa people had shown him real hospitality, serving him anything and everything he wanted. So by the time the show was over, Hib was loaded with love and enthusiasm. He went next door to tell Tony how great he was, and to show his appreciation he decided to sing a few songs for Tony.

Tony listened very graciously and approvingly, and this went on and on until Hib had him cornered and was giving him a person-to-person recital of some of his most effective devices. By now, it was very late, and in spite of his exhaustion Tony was still listening with amazing interest. The situation was getting to be a little awkward, because Tony was never going to say, "Well, fellows, let's go home!" I went over to Hib, put my arms around him, and said, "Come on, Hib, let's go to the happening, man! I've got a limousine outside, and I know a place that's jumpin'. Let's ride."

Hib reluctantly agreed. We told Tony, his family and friends good night, went out, and got in the car. Now I had to think up what to do with Hib, who was alone. Then I had a hot idea and said to the chauffeur, "Jilly's!"

When we got there, who do you think was having a big party in the back? Nobody but Francis (Frank Sinatra).

"Hib, here's Frank," I said. "Francis, you know Al Hibbler."

"Why, that's my man," said Frank, getting up to welcome him. "Hib is my pilot."

After the greetings, Hib decided to do another recital, and he repeated his whole post-Copacabana act. It went on and on again until some man who lived near Hib in Jersey said, "I'm an upstate neighbor, and if he's going home I'll be glad to give him a lift."

"It's getting pretty late, Hib," I said. "Let's go home."
"Okay."
Coda: And we all lived happily ever after.

COLEMAN HAWKINS

Coleman Hawkins was one of the real masters of the tenor saxophone. Everybody who wanted to blow the instrument in his day wanted to blow like Coleman Hawkins. I don't know of anybody who really *tried* to avoid sounding like him. There are quite a few around today who will play you identical Hawk solos, and just about everybody in the world knows his "Body and Soul." When he was with Fletcher Henderson's band, he made that band a real challenge to us. I am very glad we were able to make the album together in 1962.

His "Body and Soul," his version of it, was one of the first that came to my mind a few years ago when Their Majesties the King and Queen of Thailand visited President Johnson at the White House. I was honored then by being asked what music I would suggest be given His Majesty as representative of American jazz. At the time, I was out at Lake Tahoe, and I thought for a second and said, "Well, if it were for me, I'd like to have lead sheets on all the great solos jazz musicians have made on popular tunes, like Hawk's 'Body and Soul,' Jack Jenney's 'Stardust,' Ray Nance's 'Take the "A" Train,' Lawrence Brown's 'Rose of the Rio Grande,' and I don't know how many by Johnny Hodges."

"That's a fine idea," they said. "How'll we get them?"

There was nothing out there in Lake Tahoe, so I called Dick Vance in New York, told him the names of songs and soloists, and told him to get the records and make lead sheets from them. I also told him there was only three hundred dollars in it, but advised him to do it as good p.r., anyway. They were printed up and bound in a special volume to be presented to His Majesty. Mrs. Johnson's secretary (Mrs. Bess Abel or Mrs. Barbara Keehn) asked Dick if he and his wife would like to come to the party, and he, of course, said they would love to do that. So he went to the boss of the joint in New York where he was working and asked if he could take that particular night off to go to the White House. The boss raised hell and said, "You're

With Coleman Hawkins

lying. You've got another gig. No, you can't take off!" So Dick Vance had to
call back the White House and say, "Will you please mail me the invitation
so I can show it to my boss." They did that, and he got the night off.

I was standing on the South Lawn talking to His Majesty when Dick and
his wife came around a corner toward us. Dick was in his tuxedo and his wife
was wearing a beautiful evening gown.

"Ah, Your Majesty," I began, "this is Dick Vance . . . Mrs. Vance . . .
His Majesty the King of Thailand. Dick Vance used to . . ."

"Dick Vance!" said His Majesty. "I know who Dick Vance is. He used to
wail with Chick Webb!"

"Oh, baby," I thought to myself, "this is a real hip king!" For Dick Vance
was not one of the featured trumpets in Chick's band, and those most people
know about are the ones who take the solos.

Coleman Hawkins ought to have been there that night too.

With Billy Eckstine, 1952

BILLY ECKSTINE

Billy Eckstine lit a fire around the in-crowd of Broadway, Fifty-second Street, and Harlem. He was a master of the true, nightlife meaning of Hip, the original, traditional meaning. At once the coolest and the hippest, he was just a little too much for the undown people. His romantic meanderings with melody were strictly for those of us who dug his sensuous semantics. Eckstine-style love songs opened new lines of communication for the man in the man-woman merry-go-round, and blues *à la B.* were the essence of cool. When he made a recording of "Caravan," I was happy and honored to watch one of our tunes help take him into the stratosphere of universal acclaim. And, of course, he hasn't looked back since. A remarkable artist, the sonorous B.

He worked with us at the New York Paramount once, and it was a ball hearing him five shows a day. There was also a little thing going on between B. and me. For four weeks, neither of us wore the same suit twice. He flattered me by ordering his valet to call Los Angeles and have two more trunks shipped out immediately. By the third week, people were buying tickets just to see the sartorial changes.

Recently, he sang with us in a sacred concert at Temple Emanuel in Beverly Hills. Being the superb dramatic director that I am, I decided to close the first half with B. singing "Come Sunday." The reaction was indescribable. The audience applauded, gave him a standing ovation, shouted for more—the World's Greatest First Act Curtain!

B.'s from Washington, D.C., so we have a relationship that's like homey dahomey. He had his own band once, and in spite of the fact that it was a good band, I suspect his balladeer image somewhat affected his bandleader charisma. His style and technique have been extensively copied by some of the neocommercial singers, but despite their best efforts he remains out front to show how and what should have been done.

MAHALIA JACKSON

Bill Putnam, founder, builder, recording engineer, and President of Universal Recording Studios in Chicago, was having a party on a yacht one evening out on Lake Michigan. There were a lot of bigwigs from the Loop there, and a representative of Columbia Records came up to me, all glowing.

"Say, you must hear this new girl we've got signed up!" he said.

"Who's that?"

"Mahalia Jackson."

"Oh, yeah, she's a good cook."

"No, she's a singer."

"I know," I said, "but she's a good cook, too."

She was the best, a great cook. I had been to her house several times before ever she signed with Columbia, and she always had fine soul food out there.

One of the memorable occasions was when we made "Come Sunday" with her in 1958. Billy Strayhorn was down in Florida, but I had told him the key and he sent the arrangement. Ray Nance was there with his violin, and it all came off well.

The next day, however, she came by when we were recording some other selections. "Mahalia, listen, we want to try something different," I said. "We're not going to play, and we're going to put the lights out, and I want you to sing 'Come Sunday' just by yourself." Columbia still has that tape, of Mahalia singing in the dark all by herself.

"Duke," I remember her complaining, "you're trying to make an opera singer out of me!"

This encounter with Mahalia Jackson had a strong influence on me and my sacred music, and also made me a much handsomer kid in the Right Light.

Act Six

Civilization

When I really settled down to read and to think about what I was reading in the Bible, I found many things that I had been feeling all my life without quite understanding them. On becoming more acquainted with the word of the Bible, I began to understand so much more of what I had been taught, and of what I thought I had learned about life and about the people in mine. What I had learned in school became clearer to me—the appraisal of situations, what to expect, what not to expect. Like a child, I had always believed that nothing was impossible until it could be proven impossible. I had optimism to the Nth degree. Pessimism is unfortunately for the sick of mind, for those who have complexes. I have found that all human beings have limitations, which is something everyone should take into consideration. We should recognize that everybody is capable of making a mistake, and we should not raise any more hell about somebody else's mistake than we expect to be raised when we make one. Who does not make mistakes? Who is not limited? Everybody but God.

Suspicion and accusation have driven many people to do things they never originally thought of doing, and they have driven others to make their grand stand for right, to refuse to participate in actions they thought unworthy of themselves and the reputations of their families. Unconditional love not only means *I am with you,* but also *I am for you, all the way, right or wrong.* Two should be as one. After all, another turn of the time wheel, and either one can be in the reverse position.

The mind not only acts, it also reacts, sometimes in rebellion. If and when someone makes a mistake, he is always the first to know. He is also very much aware of the possibility of its getting back home. Given the chance to minimize the damage, or correct it completely, he may win the undying love of the one he loves the most. And there is nothing *greater!*

Seeing God

If you can see by seven caroms to the seventh power, then you can see God. If you could see total carom, to total power, you would be thought to be God. And since you can't do either, you are *not* God, and you cannot stand to see God, but if you happen to be the greatest mathematician, you will discover after completing carom that God is here with you.

So be wise and satisfied with the joy that comes to you through the reflection and miracle of God, such as all the wonders and beauty we live with and are exposed to on earth.

There have been times when I thought I had a glimpse of God. Sometimes, even when my eyes were closed, I saw. Then when I tried to set my eyes—closed or open—back to the same focus, I had no success, of course. The unprovable fact is that I believe I have had a glimpse of God many times. I believe because believing is believable, and no one can prove it unbelievable.

Some people who have had the same experience I have had are afraid or ashamed to admit it. They are afraid of being called naïve or square. They are afraid of being called unbrainwashed by the people who brainwash them, or by those they would like to be like, or friendly with. Maybe they just want to be *in*. Maybe it's a matter of the style, the trend, or whatever one thinks one does to be acceptable in certain circles.

There was a man who was blessed with the vision to see God. But even this man did not and does not have the power or whatever it takes to show God to a believer, much less an unbeliever.

The Sacred Concerts

In 1965, I was invited by Dean C. J. Bartlett and the Reverend John S. Yaryan to present a concert of sacred music in Grace Cathedral, San Francisco, as part of a year-long series celebrating the completion and consecration of that great Episcopal cathedral atop Nob Hill. I recognized this as an exceptional opportunity. "Now I can say openly," I said, "what I have been saying to myself on my knees."

A new venture of that kind could not be begun without a certain amount of trepidation, because of the possibility of misunderstanding or misinterpretation, and I tried to explain my approach beforehand. The gist was that in this world we presume many ambitions. We make many observations such as (a) everyone's aloneness (there really are no categories, you know. Everyone is so alone—the basic, essential state of humankind); (b) the paradox that is communication—the built-in answer to that feeling of aloneness.

Communication itself is what baffles the multitude. It is both so difficult and so simple. Of all man's fears, I think men are most afraid of being what they are—in direct communication with the world at large. They fear reprisals, the most personal of which is that they "won't be understood."

How can anyone expect to be understood unless he presents his thoughts with complete honesty? This situation is unfair because it asks too much of the world. In effect, we say, "I don't dare show you what I am because I don't trust you for a minute but please love me anyway because I so need you to. And, of course, if you don't love me anyway, you're a dirty dog, just as I suspected, so I was right in the first place." Yet, every time God's children have thrown away fear in pursuit of honesty—trying to communicate themselves, understood or not—miracles have happened.

As I travel from place to place by car, bus, train, plane . . . taking rhythm to the dancers, harmony to the romantic, melody to the nostalgic, gratitude to the listener . . . receiving praise, applause, and handshakes, and at the same

261

time doing the thing I like to do, I feel that I am most fortunate because I know that God has blessed my timing, without which nothing could have happened—the right time or place or with the right people. The four must converge. Thank God.

For instance, my being invited by Dean Bartlett and the Reverend John S. Yaryan to participate at Grace Cathedral, San Francisco, and by the Reverend Dr. Bryant M. Kirkland and the Fifth Avenue Presbyterian Church, New York City, and then by the Reverend Dr. George W. McMurray and Mother A.M.E. Zion Cathedral in Harlem, whose Cathedral Choir joined me in a homecoming Concert of Sacred Music.

I am not concerned with what it costs. I want the best of everything possible. I want the best musicians, the best singers and coaches—amateurs or professionals—and I want them to give the best they have. I want all the help I can get and to say what I hope I am good enough to say because this is the performance of all performances—God willing.

Wisdom is something that man partially enjoys—One and only One has all the wisdom. God has total understanding. There are some people who speak many languages. Every man prays in his own language and there is no language that God does not understand.

The great organ accompanies worship—sometimes the symphony or part of the symphony—and what could seem more suitable than a harp sole? It has been said once that a man, who could not play the organ or any of the instruments of the symphony, accompanied his worship by juggling. He was not the world's best juggler but it was the one thing he did best. And so it was accepted by God.

I believe that no matter how highly skilled a drummer or saxophonist might be, if this is the thing he does best, and he offers it sincerely from the heart in—or as accompaniment to—his worship, he will not be unacceptable because of lack of skill or of the instrument upon which he makes his demonstration, be it pipe or tomtom.

If a man is troubled, he moans and cries when he worships. When a man feels that that which he enjoys in his life is only because of the grace of God, he rejoices, he sings, and sometimes dances (and so it was with David in spite of his wife's prudishness).

In such a program, you may hear a wide variety of statements without words, and I think you should know that if it is a phrase with six tones, it symbolizes the six syllables in the first four words of the Bible, "In the

Concert at Sacred Heart Cathedral, Newark, New Jersey, October 4, 1968

beginning God," which is our theme. We say it many times . . . many ways.

The concert was performed for the first time on September 16, 1965, and it was successful beyond my wildest dreams, both in San Francisco and at a subsequent performance in the Fifth Avenue Presbyterian Church of New York on December 26. *Duke Ellington Talked to the Lord in Grace Cathedral Last Night,* read headlines above a UPI report in hundreds of newspapers across the country. "These were musicians offering what they did best—better than any others in the world—to the glory of God," said the *Saturday Review* in an article entitled "The Ecumenical Ellington."

Baby Laurence rehearsing for the Sacred Concert, Orange, France, 1970

Tony Watkins at the Sacred Concert, Orange, France, 1970

Even more gratifying to me was the understanding approval of religious leaders. In a preface to the San Francisco program, Dean Bartlett wrote: ". . . is liturgical worship the only form of public prayer? We believe not! Among other forms surely must be included all expressions of the creative and performing arts, *especially* where such expressions are offered consciously by the artists and performer *'to the service of'* God."

All the members of the band played in character. Cootie Williams growled, Cat Anderson sent notes flying around the roof, Louis Bellson made an elegant percussion declaration, Harry Carney stated the theme with power and dignity, Johnny Hodges "sang" "Come Sunday" as only he could, Paul

Gonsalves swung, and Tony Watkins wound it up with his *a cappella* delivery of "The Lord's Prayer." Choirs and three featured singers—Jon Hendricks, Esther Merrill, and Jimmy McPhail—gave it impact, but I think what registered most with many people was the dancing of Bunny Briggs, who was out front in the climactic spot for "David Danced Before the Lord with All His Might."

When we did it in New York, we had Brock Peters in Jon Hendricks' place, and he did a very impressive job on "In the Beginning God." This was the occasion, too, when Lena Horne sang "A Christmas Surprise" with Billy Strayhorn at the piano. The lyrics were by Dean Bartlett.

The following year, when we were in England, I was invited by Canon (now Bishop) Simon Phipps to give a performance of the Sacred Concert in Coventry Cathedral. Built since the World War II bombing, it is a very impressive modern edifice with a striking tapestry by Graham Sutherland behind the high altar.

We gave this concert in many different cities before congregations of all denominations, from Cambridge, Massachusetts, to Cambridge, England, until in 1968 the opportunity occurred to me, suggested by the Reverend Canon Weicker, to present an entirely new one at the Cathedral Church of St. John the Divine in New York by invitation of Bishop Horace W. B. Donegan.

The experiences encountered in the course of giving nearly fifty performances of the previous concert had naturally given me fresh insight into the way people were thinking and reacting. Some people ask me what prompted me to write the music for the sacred concerts. I have done so not as a matter of career, but in response to a growing understanding of my own vocation, and with the encouragement of many people, among whom I must name Bishop Horace W. B. Donegan, Canon Edward N. West, Canon Harold Weicker, the Reverend John S. Yaryan, Dean Bartlett, Pastor John Gensel, Father Norman O'Connor, Dr. Sandford Shapiro, the Reverend Henry Jesse, Jr., Father Egan of Ireland, Frank Salisbury of the Christian Scientist Church in Tucson, the Reverend Nicholas Freund, the Reverend E. Franklin Jackson, the Reverend Jerry Moore, and Geoffrey Holder. It was Father Yaryan who suggested that we use "Father Forgive," as in Coventry Cathedral, and we have put it into the middle of a song called "Don't Get Down on Your Knees to Pray Until You Have Forgiven Everyone." Many other suggestions have come from the little book put out by the Episcopal Church called *Forward*. The pay-off statement in the selection, "Freedom," comes from it.

Joe Morgen, Stanley Dance, and Tom Whaley at a Sacred Concert rehearsal, New York City, January 1968

I have been very fortunate to have been accepted on this team of dedicated men and women who work ceaselessly in the ecumenical movement to bring peace to the world we live in now, and to secure our future down at the end where all ends end. As human beings, we do not have adequate words for description beyond that point. How can a man make a blueprint with specifications that re-create his Creator? But these dedicated people have grace, humility, and profound understanding. They honored me by granting me the privilege of performing this new concert, a sequel to the series which began in Grace Cathedral, San Francisco, and was later performed in cathedrals, churches, and temples throughout the world, including the Fifth Avenue Presbyterian Church in New York, Trinity Cathedral in Phoenix, and Temple Emanuel in Beverly Hills.

These concerts are not the traditional mass jazzed up. I have not as yet written music for a mass, although I have been commissioned by Father Norman O'Connor to do so. But since this is not a jazz mass, I should very much like to make my point of view clear.

I think of myself as a messenger boy, one who tries to bring messages to people, not people who have never heard of God, but those who were

Performance of the Sacred Concert at the Cathedral of St. John the Divine, New York City, January 19, 1968

more or less raised with the guidance of the Church. Now and then we encounter people who say they do not believe. I hate to say that they are out-and-out liars, but I believe they think it fashionable to speak like that, having been brainwashed by someone beneath them, by someone with a complex who enjoys bringing them to their knees in the worship of the nonexistence of God. They snicker in the dark as they tremble with fright.

It has been said that what we do is to deliver lyrical sermons, fire-and-brimstone sermonettes, and reminders of the fact that we live in the promised land of milk and honey, where we have prime beef and 80-percent-butterfat ice cream. I am sure we appreciate the blessings we enjoy in this country, but it wouldn't hurt if everyone expressed his appreciation more often.

We shall keep this land if we all agree on the meaning of that unconditional word: LOVE.

These thoughts were amplified in the lyrics of the various songs that were embodied in the concert. The solo singers and the choirs were given even more responsibility than in the first concert, and at St. John's we had Alice Babs, Devonne Gardner, Tony Watkins, and Jimmy McPhail in solo roles, and three choirs: the A.M.E. Mother Zion Church Choir directed by Solomon Herriott, Jr.; the choirs of St. Hilda's and St. Hugh's School directed by William Toole, and men of the Cathedral choir under Alec Wyton, who also played an impressive, specially composed piece on the organ as an introduction to the whole concert. Because I regard this concert as the most important thing I have ever done, I am including here the routine and lyrics in full.

PROGRAM OUTLINE FOR THE SACRED CONCERT

INVOCATION
ORGAN PROLOGUE
OPENING THEME: PRAISE GOD   featuring solo instrumentalist

SUPREME BEING   The Choir, Orchestra and solo instrumentalist

(A section of cacophony represents the scene before the Supreme Being created order.)

Recitative:
Supreme Being
There is a Supreme Being
There is One
Only One
One
Supreme Being.
Out of lightning, thunder,
Chaos and confusion,
The Supreme Being
Organized and created,
Created and organized
Heaven and Earth.
For darkness was upon the deep
And the earth was without form.
Light—good
Darkness—good
Day—good
Night—good
Evening—good
Morning—good
Firmament—firmament
Waters—good
Dry land—good
Earth—sea—grass—herb—fruit tree
Delicious!
The great light and the lesser light,
Sun—Moon
Moving creatures of the sea,

Fowl of the air,
Cattle and the creeping thing,
Beast of the earth,
And last but not least,
The most perfect creature,
Man—in the image of God,
Male—Female
To dominate.
Man to dominate over land—sea—sky—bird—beast—fish—serpent—lobster—
shrimp—oyster—terrapin—snail—swine—APPLE TREE

SONNET OF THE APPLE (Solo Recitative for Little Boy.)
I shall never forget the Apple Tree.
Oh yes! I was there.
Don't you remember me?
I was the apple.
There I was suspended in mid-air,
The leaves rustling in the breeze.
'Twas such a lovely day.
I was swinging.
Ripening in peace and quiet,
And who do you think came crawling down that limb?
That little old serpent.
He beguiled her,
He mesmerized her,
Hypnotized and coerced her.
That cute little old snake made that pretty lady
    Bite me,
And things really ain't been the same since.

Heaven and Earth—sun—moon—land—sea—sky—bird—beast—fish—serpent
To be dominated over by God's most perfect creation,
Man—in the image of the Supreme Being.
But, with domination came responsibility.
Domination—responsibility—and accounting to the
Supreme Being.
The immortal Creator and Ruler of the Universe,
Eternal and All Powerful
Supreme Being,
GOD.

SOMETHING ABOUT BELIEVING featuring soloists from the Choir in speaking roles

Song
Something 'bout believing that keeps unfolding,
Something 'bout believing that makes my soul sing,
Something 'bout believing that keeps me holding
On to GOD Almighty.
Something 'bout believing that helps my mending,
Something 'bout believing that there's no ending,
Believing all the way because I'm depending
On the GOD Almighty.

    I don't light a lamp to see the Sun,
    Don't need proof of GOD,
    Because I know that there ain't a-gonna be but One.
Something 'bout believing in the creation,
Something 'bout believing the information.
Something 'bout believing there's just one nation,
Under GOD Almighty.

    I want to be hip, I want to be cool,
    I got to be with it all the way,
    Because I ain't about to be no fool.
Something 'bout believing that's greater than pleasure,
Something 'bout believing that's more than treasure,
Something 'bout believing that's beyond measure,
Just one GOD Almighty.

Recitative:
I know that you know,
The Bible says it's so.
There is much mystery in the history,
To be exact, accept the fact,
An example or two is here for me and you.

Song
Animals, birds and fish,
Have senses much keener and stronger.
And scientists do the difficult today,
And even the impossible just takes a little longer.

Recitative:
If you believe this,
What's to keep me from believing that?

Song
Something 'bout believing that keeps me going,
Something 'bout believing my faith is growing,
Something 'bout believing that keeps me knowing,
I'll see GOD Almighty.

Recitative:
Silliest thing ever read,
Was that somebody said,
"GOD is dead."
The mere mention of the first word,
Automatically eliminates
The second and the third.

ALMIGHTY GOD   featuring solo vocalist

Almighty GOD has those angels,
Away up there above,
Up there a-weaving sparkling fabrics
Just for you and me to love.
Almighty GOD has those angels,
Up in the proper place,
Waiting to receive and to welcome us,
And remake us in grace.
  Wash your face and hands and heart and soul,
  'Cause you wash so well.
  GOD will keep you safely,
  Where there's no sulfur smell.
Almighty GOD has those angels,
As ready as can be,
Waiting to dress, caress and bless us all
In perpetuity.

THE SHEPHERD (WHO WATCHES OVER THE NIGHT FLOCK)   featuring solo instrumentalist

(A portrait of the Reverend John G. Gensel, Lutheran Pastor to the Jazz Community, who has made so many sacrifices to help the night people.)

HEAVEN   featuring solo vocalist and instrumentalist

Heaven, my dream,
Heaven, divine
Heaven, supreme

Heaven combines
Every sweet and pretty thing
Life would love to bring.
Heavenly Heaven to be
Is just the ultimate degree to be.

IT'S FREEDOM   the Choir, Orchestra and solo vocalists

Song:
Freedom, Freedom, Freedom, Freedom,
Freedom, Freedom, Freedom, Freedom.
To be contented prisoners of love,
Or to reach beyond our reach,
To reach for a star,
Or go about the business of becoming
What we already are.
Freedom, Freedom, Freedom, Freedom.

Freedom, Freedom,
Freedom's what you thought you heard.
Freedom, Freedom,
Freedom's not just one big word.
Freedom, Freedom, a perfect healing salve.
Freedom, Freedom, it's what you've got to have.
Freedom, Freedom,
Freedom's good both night and day.
Up and down and all around
And all the way,
Give me Freedom.
Freedom, Freedom must be won,
'Cause Freedom's even good fun.

Recitative:

Freedom	Forrettighed	
Liberté	Frihet	
Libertad	Svoboda	
Liberta	Tavesoubl Ba	
Liberdade	Eleitheria	
Libertas	Jiyuna Koto	
Freiheit	Jiyu	
Vrijdom	Tzu Yu	
Vrijheit	Uhuru	
Frihed	Chofesh	Freedom

Song:
Freedom is sweet, on the beat,
Freedom is sweet to the reet complete.
It's got zestness and bestness,
Sugar and cream on the blessedness,
No more pains, no more chains,
To keep free from being free.
Freedom is sweet fat, and that's for me.

(The Choir, Orchestra and soloists are employed in this composition's eight segments, one of which, "Sweet, Fat and That," was suggested by an old lick of Willie "The Lion" Smith, who helped us when we came to New York in 1923. We end with a statement of the four freedoms by which I think Billy Strayhorn lived: freedom from hate unconditionally; freedom from self-pity; freedom from fear of doing something that would help someone more than it does him; and freedom from the kind of pride that could make a man feel that he was better than his brother.)

Song:
Freedom, Freedom, Freedom, Freedom,
Freedom, Freedom, Freedom, Freedom.
To be contented prisoners of love,
Or to reach beyond our reach,
To reach for a star,
Or go about the business of becoming
What we already are.
Freedom, Freedom, Freedom, Freedom.

(INTERMISSION)

MEDITATION   featuring the composer at the piano

THE BIGGEST AND BUSIEST INTERSECTION   featuring the percussion section (A fire-and-brimstone sermonette)

(In life, we have to make a decision every two or three minutes, whether we are going straight ahead, or left, or right, or make a U turn. This happens at every traffic intersection. In Denver, they have one with five points, and at the Arc de Triomphe in Paris there are so many outlets that it is terribly confusing if you are not familiar with it. Down at the end where all ends end, there is an intersection with millions of outlets. If you've been a "good boy" and have made it all the way to the gate, almost, you still have to go through this last, final intersection. The pavement is slippery, and there are all kinds of pitfalls, potholes, booby traps, and snares. The commercials that the representatives of the opposition are doing are outrageous. They even have cats who come up just as you see the reflections of the golden streets and are about to put your hand on the gate. "Baby," they whisper, "I know it looks pretty in there, but you should see how those chicks are swinging down where we are!" They always whisper, you know, but you have to watch it right up to the very last second, because it is the largest, loudest, fastest, and most insidious intersection, down at the end where all ends end, just before the beginning.)

T.G.T.T.   featuring solo vocalist

(*T.G.T.T.* means *Too Good to Title,* because it violates conformity in the same way, we like to think, that Jesus Christ did. The phrases never end on the note you think they will. It is a piece even instrumentalists have trouble with.)

DON'T GET DOWN ON YOUR KNEES TO PRAY UNTIL YOU HAVE FORGIVEN EVERYONE   featuring solo vocalist

Song (Theme)
Don't get down on your knees to pray
Until you have forgiven everyone.
Don't get down on your knees to pray
Until you have forgiven everyone.

Recitative:
Have you forgiven the sinner
Who kept you from being winner?
And the one who stole your bulging purse?
Have you lost the rancor
In your heart for the hanky-panker?
Or for him, is there still a little curse, or worse?

Song
(Theme)

Recitative:
Life is much too short
To waste on negative thought
For the one you think might harm you next.
Don't dream of him with snakes,

276

Forget mistakes he makes,
And throw away that dirty little hex.

Song
(Theme)

Recitative:
Have you forgiven your lover,
And the one whom you discovered,
Coveting the loved one you adore?
Have you done the thing that's right?
Do you pray for them at night?
Or is hatred seeping through your every pore?

Song
(Theme)

Recitative:
Does your anger run so rife,
That you'd like to use your knife?
Don't do it! 'Cause you'll wind up in the clink.
And after you've calmed down cool,
You'll find that gossips talk the fool,
And nothing's on the brink of what you think.

Song
(Theme)

Recitative:
It's harder to defeat
Than it is to spell,
Revenge is not sweet,
It's bitter as Hell.

Song
(Theme)

Recitative:
May your prayers be answered,
And your blessings multiplied,
But don't dare pray for that
Which you have caused to be denied.

Song
(Theme)

FATHER FORGIVE   vocal soloist and the Choir

Choir
Father Forgive, Father Forgive
Soloist—Recitative:
The hatred which divides nation from nation,
race from race, class from class.
Choir
Father Forgive, Father Forgive
Soloist—Recitative:
The covetous desires of men and nations
to possess that which is not their own.
Choir
Father Forgive, Father Forgive
Soloist—Recitative:
The greed to exploit the labors of
men and lay waste the earth.
Choir
Father Forgive, Father Forgive
Soloist—Recitative:
Our envy of the welfare of others.
Choir
Father Forgive, Father Forgive
Soloist—Recitative:
Our indifference to the flight of the
homeless and the refugee.
Choir
Father Forgive, Father Forgive
Soloist—Recitative:
The lust which uses for ignoble ends,
the bodies of men and women.
Choir
Father Forgive, Father Forgive
Soloist—Recitative:
The pride which leads us to trust
in ourselves and not in God.
Choir
Father Forgive, Father Forgive, etc.

DON'T GET DOWN ON YOUR KNEES TO PRAY UNTIL YOU HAVE
FORGIVEN EVERYONE (Reprise)   the Orchestra featuring vocal soloist

Orchestra
(Theme)

Soloist—Recitative:
Have you given GOD the break,
To heal your worst mistake,
By letting GOD within
Forgive you from your sins,
As on your knees you pray,
"Father, love me, so I may love today."

Song
(Theme)

(I am grateful to my friend, the Reverend Harold H. Weicker, for contributing this last Recitative)

PRAISE GOD AND DANCE   by the entire company and featuring vocal soloist

(This has the same theme as the opening selection, PRAISE GOD. It is
based on the 150th Psalm, the last Psalm of the Psalter, and I am indebted
to Maria Dance for bringing it to my attention.)

Praise God with the sound of the trumpet
Praise God with the Psaltery and harp
Praise God with the sound of the timbrel
And Dance, Dance, Dance, Dance.

Praise God with the sound of the stringed instruments,
The organ, the cymbal, the loud, high sounding cymbals,
Let everything that has breath, Praise God.
Praise the Lord, praise ye the Lord,
Praise God and Dance, Dance, Dance, Dance, Dance, Dance.

ASSISTANTS TO MR. ELLINGTON
    Thomas L. Whaley   Mercedes Ellington
    Mercer Ellington   Geoffrey Holder
    Herman McCoy   Herbie Jones
    Stephen James

St. John's is reputed to be the biggest cathedral in the world, and it was packed with over seven thousand people on January 19. They gave us a wonderful reception and their excitement as two companies of dancers swung down the aisle in the finale, "Praise God and Dance," was tremendous.

I had persuaded Alice Babs to come over from Stockholm, and her superb interpretations of "Almighty God Has Those Angels," "Heaven," and "T.G.T.T." enchanted everyone. The complete confidence I had in her was more than justified. Not only did she read the difficult "T.G.T.T." at sight, but her helpfulness and ardor were an inspiration to all the other performers. Cootie Williams' performance of "The Shepherd" was also received with great acclamation, despite the unusual idiom he employed. I am sure that few church congregations can have been familiar with the use of the plunger mute, but this one took it in stride.

The press also approved, and glowing accounts subsequently appeared in, among other publications, the *Daily News,* the New York *Times,* the *Christian Science Monitor,* and the *Saturday Review.* Bishop Donegan expressed his view to a UPI reporter: "A cathedral should be a place where creative people can express themselves, as well as a place where those who appreciate creative people can gather."

We gave two more performances in Connecticut, where, instead of the dance companies, Geoffrey Holder danced alone to great effect. We then succeeded in recording the whole production before Alice Babs was obliged to return to Sweden.

It has been performed many times in this country since then, as well as in Toronto. When we did it in San Francisco, a tremendous dance group headed by Sheila Xorego appeared with us. In Europe, where Alice Babs rejoined us, it was given before five thousand people in the Church of Saint Sulpice, Paris, performed in Stockholm and in Barcelona's ancient Church of Santa Maria del Mar. The audience in Barcelona entered into the spirit of the finale, burst into the aisles, and joined in the dancing. The following year, 1970, we again performed it in France, this time at Orange, where Baby Laurence danced.

Tom Whaley usually goes ahead to rehearse the choirs affiliated with the places of worship where we are playing. I would really like to list all the choirs and choir directors who have cooperated with us with so much good will. Right from the beginning, when Herman McCoy was a great help to me, this has been one of the most encouraging factors. A friend of

Geoffrey Holder at New Britain, Connecticut, Sacred Concert, 1968

Tony Watkins from Philadelphia, Roscoe Gill, would also help with the rehearsals, and he often sang in what we called the "choirette."

The choir in Barcelona, which later came to sing with us in Orange, had a flavor all its own because of the way its members pronounced the English words. They were Roman Catholics, of course, and when I heard them singing in the ancient Roman amphitheatre in Orange with Alice Babs from Stockholm, Tony Watkins from Philadelphia, and our band of musicians from all over the U.S.A., before a perceptive and very appreciative French audience—then I felt the ecumenical spirit was really working.

Endorsements by the clergy were heartening. They made me feel the concerts had been effective, and that we were getting somewhere. A girl confirmed it for me one day when she came up and said, "You know, Duke, you made me put my cross back on!"

Mrs. Ethel Rich, Professor of Speech and Drama at Milton College, Wisconsin, is the wonderful lady who was instrumental in my being awarded an honorary degree as Doctor of Humanities. More important, I think, is the way she seemed to sense my role in sacred music. I had written a couple of background scores for her production of T. S. Eliot's *Murder in the Cathedral,* and given her permission to use some of the music originally written for the Shakespearean Festival at Stratford, Ontario.

From the first day we met at the University of Wisconsin, where we were playing a concert or a prom, and where I was introduced to her by Paul Eduard Miller, she has religiously sent me every issue of *Forward,* a publication of the Episcopal Church. Ever since I saw the first copy, this little book has been my daily reading. It is very clear, easy to understand, written in the language of the ordinary man, and always says things I want to know. It is extremely instructive, and it has played a great part in the adjustment of my perspective on the approach to the relationship between God and the human being. So I am profoundly indebted to Mrs. Rich and the booklet she sends regularly four times a year.

Forward may, in fact, help me reach the point where I can feel convinced that I have seen the more eligible light of semantics I so desperately need to think in terms of writing music for a mass. One may be accustomed to speaking to people, but suddenly to attempt to speak, sing, and play directly to God—that puts one in an entirely new and different position!

About the time of my first encounter with Mrs. Rich, I met Pastor John Gensel, whose Lutheran church my sister, Ruth, regularly attends. I went to

With Pastor John Gensel

his church and found that music was not confined there to the more or less solemn kind usually heard in churches. Pastor Gensel had recitals and music that were, I sensed, much more appropriate to the jazz musicians with whom he was involved. This led to the observation I made in connection with the first sacred concert: that every man worships in his own language. And I *know* that there is no language God does not understand.

In addition to this, Pastor Gensel often went without, denying the needs of his own family, and even using money earned by his beautiful wife as a schoolteacher, in order to pay the rent, or doctor's bills, or to buy food for some of the less fortunate night people. That is why we saluted him with a tonal portrait as "The Shepherd Who Watches Over the Night Flock." His is pure humanism and the type of unselfishness that mark a man as a true representative of God.

Canon Harold Weicker was not only the one who suggested that we do our second Sacred Concert, but he did all the leg work, made the contacts, and stimulated the enthusiasm of Bishop Horace W. B. Donegan at the Cathedral Church of St. John the Divine in New York. He did such a wonderful job that I just floated into it, started writing, and sent to Stockholm for Alice Babs. When I called and told her what I wanted to do, the answer was an emphatic yes. Regarding the money she would have, she said to me, "You just take care of the expenses—no salary."

To have constantly the good fortune of a musical relationship with people like this could do but one thing for me: it made me write what I wanted to write, as I wanted to write it, without fear of questionable performers. And so it was that she came, and was a sensation—a *believable* sensation. Over seven thousand people crammed into St. John's on that night of January 19, 1968. I don't know how many were turned away, but many people stood outside the church and absorbed the beautiful spirit of the occasion.

Canon Weicker, I must not forget, also contributed one of the verses in "Don't Get Down on Your Knees to Pray Until You Have Forgiven Everyone."

The Reverend Gerry Miller, who was the chief clergyman in Minneapolis, requested that our Sacred Concert be performed in his city. It was there, in Dr. Chester Pennington's Methodist Church on Hennepin Avenue that we witnessed the first audience participation in our rendition of the 150th Psalm. After our soprano had sung the words, the whole production started to jump, and the entire audience participated in the dance routine that followed. They did not get up and jump all over the church, but they sat in their chairs and followed Tony Watkins and the principals in their hand dancing. It was glorious to see, and you could feel a wave of worshipful feeling all through the church. The same thing happened again in Milwaukee, and from then on we encouraged the audience to join in the hand dancing, because it seemed so right, so worshipfully committed.

In both Paris and Barcelona the Swingle Singers were part of our Sacred Concerts. The capper was the concert we did in Barcelona, where Alice Babs rejoined us. She took ten curtain calls, and when we went into the hand-dance bit the audience rose up and seemed on the verge of dancing down the aisles with Tony Watkins. The choir there was the greatest, and our sacred concert hit a new and unforgettable high.

Acclaim

The Pulitzer Prize music committee recommended me for a special award in 1965. When the full Pulitzer committee turned down their recommendation, Winthrop Sargeant and Ronald Eyer resigned.

Since I am not too chronically masochistic, I found no pleasure in all the suffering that was being endured. I realized that it could have been most distressing and distracting as I tried to qualify my first reaction: "Fate is being very kind to me; Fate doesn't want me to be too famous too young."

Let's say it had happened. I would have been famous, then rich, then fat and stagnant. And then? What do you do with your beautiful, young, freckled mind? How, when, and where do you get your music supplement, the deadline that drives you to complete that composition, the necessity to hear the music instead of sitting around polishing your laurels, counting your money, and waiting for the brainwashers to decide what rinse or tint is the thing this season in your tonal climate?

Dramatis Felidae

BROCK PETERS

Brock Peters, a thespian of heroic proportions, has been thrilling audiences throughout his career on stage and screen with one sterling performance after another. We had the good fortune to have him in our first Sacred Concert, *In the Beginning God,* which was premiered in September 1965 and recorded in December of the same year.

One example of how well he can act that I always remember was when he played an African witch doctor in the Broadway play *Kwamina.* The male protagonist was the son of the chief of the tribe, and he got a big build-up while away at school in England long before his entrance. He was a nice, young, brownskinned man in love with a lovely English girl. When he arrived back home, he was received in the embrace of the lovely ofay chick—in a series of embraces, in fact. But after the chicks in the audience had had a half-hour peep at Brock Peters' multiple virility-plus, the nice-looking, brownskinned young man's protagonist image paled. They could not believe that Brock was not the protagonist, and I swear it seemed as though the lovely Caucasian chick could feel the tepidity by automatic comparison. It is impossible to appear, believably, more virile on stage than Brock Peters. He was so great he ruined the show. He is another of those who possess the essence of good theatre—believability.

ALICE BABS

In 1963, I found myself in Paris with an unusual contract that gave me authority to act as a. and r. man for Reprise Records and record six or seven people of my choice. The first one I got was Alice Babs, for she is probably the most unique artist I know. She is a coloratura soprano, an unlimited soprano. She sings opera, she sings lieder, she sings what we call jazz and blues, she sings like an instrument, she even yodels, and she can read any and all of it! No matter how hard the intervals, when you hand her the music, she sight-reads and sings it as though she had rehearsed it a month. Every word comes out perfectly enunciated, understandable and believable. Alice Babs is a composer's dream, for with her he can forget all the limitations and just write his heart out. When I persuaded her to come down from Stockholm to Paris, we made a wonderful record with her and four French horns. It never came out here, but the Swedes made sure it was issued in their country.

She is just one of the rare people, one of the rarest artists. Whenever I get an opportunity to do anything I feel is out of the ordinary, I think of her. So when I got ready to do my second sacred concert in 1968, where I had to go up over the top of the first, I sent to Sweden to bring her to New York. There were a couple of things in that concert which required real musicianship, which had to be read and executed just as they were planned, and she was the one I had complete confidence in to do that. She is a terrific musician, and when I look at the pictures of her taken in the Cathedral Church of St. John the Divine—why, I think she looks like an angel! She is a beautiful person who has overcome the problem of singing as pretty as she looks. In referring to her, one never says, "There are just a few left," because she was probably the only one born.

TONY WATKINS

Tony Watkins was brought to me by Mrs. June Read, the wife of an eminent lawyer in South Jersey and the mother of two of the nicest kids I've ever met, a boy and a girl, now both young adults. Mrs. Walter N. Read is a lady who lives on top of a lot of responsible effort, civic and otherwise. She and her daughter, Karen, both spun away from a statement I made when the family came to one of our concerts in Princeton. What I said was that Mrs. Read was a patron of the arts at the hightest cultural level. "Not so," she replied. "I just put on my track shoes and keep going." The truth is that she has helped to build more schools, more hospital wings, volunteered in more clinics, tended

With Tony Watkins

more sick, and influenced more trends of thought in the educational systems in the Delaware Valley than anyone I know. In addition, she has taken many children under her wing and more or less adopted them. The Reads live in New Jersey, but it is the kids in Philadelphia who have ability that constantly concern her.

Two of these Philadelphia kids arrived in New York with Mrs. Read one day—Tony Watkins and Devonne Gardner. Her purpose was to have me hear them sing. When I heard Tony sing his version of "The Lord's Prayer," I was amazed and thrilled. It is to me the one standard performance, and so strong that I have given Tony Watkins the heavy responsibility of closing all our sacred concerts by singing it *a cappella,* without electronic amplification.

Of course, Tony has lived and sung in church all his life, so he is 100 percent soul. His beautiful mother is a source of stability, and she keeps her husband and daughters serenely afloat on a feeling of security. The Watkins family is wonderful, a wonderful haven for a child to come from and know that it is always there. Tony's baby sister, although still very young, already sings up a blue streak.

On those occasions when I bring new girl singers into the band, Tony takes them under his wing, and then, on his arm, escorts them around to hear all the other singers in town. He makes them feel that they are at home from the first meeting, and that is something seldom encountered by new singers. He is my most gracious host to them. He even invites them to come on stage and dance with him during his turn. He is totally unselfish, and some day soon he will be a very important name in the whirl. That's my aim.

Off stage, in the dressing room, or at a party or reception after a concert, Tony sometimes decides to do an opera, singing all the parts and characters himself, alone. On a plane, he is liable to get permission from the chief stewardess to make the regular speeches over the loudspeakers. He just seems to be unlimited.

When he goes to a theatre or nightclub to see another singer, he then becomes not an actor but a reactor. Why, anybody would think he was a paid claque! When he reacts, he injects the audience with his enthusiasm, too, and they join in and make an act that is not all it should be a smash success. That facet of Tony Watkins shows his humanitarianism. He wants everybody to get rave reactions. He joined us on the occasion of our first concert at Grace Cathedral in 1965, and now he is still a young enthusiast, although maybe just a little more mature.

He covers a very wide range of material when put to it: "The Lord's Prayer" or "Come Sunday"; "Solitude" in both ballad and soul-stealing form; "It Don't Mean a Thing If It Ain't Got That Swing" as an up-tempo gallop à la Broadway musical; and on gospel songs he is immediately transformed into a jackleg preacher. He knows all the generation-gap yappings and he rocks the enth. I plan to create a part for him that will employ his complete range.

TOM WHALEY

Tom Whaley has a specific place in our organization as choirmaster and copyist. Chairman of the Board is not a good enough title for him. He is one of the main arteries, and there's an entirely different atmosphere when he is around. He will speak very loudly about anything that does not sound right, or about anybody who isn't playing right. As I grow up, he gets to be a little more respectful toward me—now and then. But he'll holler in a minute, and pack up and walk out! Yet he is one of the real contributors: a very loyal friend; a man of great energy and dignity; and a man who is exceptionally healthy, thank God, for if he were not healthy he couldn't keep drinking that hundred-proof bourbon.

The only time anybody has ever howled Tom Whaley down was when we went to Dallas a few years ago, and we were in the house of our good friend, Mrs. Eva Dixon. When he got ready to sit down, he went into his bag and brought out his pint of hundred-proof whiskey, and set it on the table. Then Eva came out and said, "What is this man doing, bringing whiskey into *my* house, and putting it on *my* table? I'm a poor widow woman, but can't nobody give *me* nothing!" Tom had only a pint, and Eva had a buffet of quarts! Oh, man, she read him, as I've never heard anyone read Tom Whaley before or since! He took low, too.

Act Seven

C Jam Blues

San Francisco

San Francisco is where I premiered my very first Sacred Concert, which was presented at Grace Cathedral on September 16, 1965, as a result of an invitation from Father John S. Yaryan, Dean C. J. Bartlett, and Bishop James A. Pike of the Episcopal Diocese of California, to do a service of worship to God through the natural medium of our various talents and skills in the tonal personality of our music, and with words from our perspective.

Do you know that the lights and shadows—in fact, the whole scene in the Bay Area—change every second? Atop the Mark Hopkins Hotel and Fairmont Tower, it's like a carousel of mirrors reflecting tonal images against counter reflections, so that even the little men who work so diligently inside the music box for their soul food on Fillmore—even they are stricken with the pungent joy, the joy that sustains itself even after the removal of the outer glitter of glamour.

San Francisco is one of the great cultural plateaux of the world, one of the really urbane communities in the United States, one of the truly cosmopolitan places, and for many, many, many years it always has had a warm welcome for human beings from all over the world.

I might mention that my first visit to San Francisco was in 1932. Ivie Anderson, our singer who came from Gilroy, filled us in about all the surrounding territory before we arrived, and hers was a very detailed, inside fill-in. Then I met Henry Starr, a man of parts, a gentleman, a former athletic hero, a wonderful pianist, a believable vocal performer of songs, who had his own radio show and was the outstanding personality of San Francisco in that day. He showed me everything—Fisherman's Wharf, Twin Peaks, the Top of the Mark, the Presidio, and Oakland.

What would San Francisco be without Oakland? I remember one day when we were coming from Oakland on the ferry, and I looked up as two sea gulls were flying over. I heard one of them say to the other, "Hey, isn't that the Duke?" The second sea gull looked down and said, "It sure is. Well, what're we waiting for?"

Henry gave me a guided tour of San Francisco, the only *complete* tour of any city I have ever had in my life. I am the world's worst sightseer. When I was a kid, I used to run up the Washington Monument just to win a race. I live in New York City, but I have never been to the Statue of Liberty, and even though I perform in Paris every year, I have never visited the Eiffel Tower. I did go to see the Venus de Milo when she was on exhibition at the museum in Kyoto, Japan, but I am such a bad sightseer that when I was in India—and this is the worst confession—I didn't even see the Taj Mahal.

Billy Strayhorn loved San Francisco, and I am very happy to say that it was *I* who took *him* on his first guided tour when he went there with us in 1940. It is proof that the city really is an aesthetic center because Strayhorn loved it. And, after I had the honor of conducting him around this beautiful city, he became a much greater authority on the subject than I.

He went to see the Taj Mahal!

But I have had my tour of San Francisco. I have had the thrill of being presented in concert by the Patrons of Art and Music in the main gallery of the Palace of the Legion of Honor. I have had the pleasure of being exposed to some of the very top level people of this inspiring metropolis—Dr. S. I. Hayakawa, the world's greatest semanticist, and the very famous Alan Watts and his charming wife, who were most hospitable. I enjoy many, many good friends and loyal supporters like Sam Martin and his family, who are on hand to greet us at every date we play within a hundred-mile radius of San Francisco.

Today, the *Man* in San Francisco is Johnny Cooper, who holds forth at the Fairmont with his wonderful performance as a background for his very informative, very pleasant exchange with the friends who surround him at the piano.

And there is another great man, who, as a result of his superlative hospitality and grace, has brought about the production of one of the most talked-about programs in the history of television—the National Educational Television Network's Duke Ellington documentary, *Love You Madly,* filmed in San Francisco and wholly conceived by Ralph J. Gleason, then of the San Francisco *Chronicle* and KQED. The production, the direction, the writing, the editing, the photography, and the sound were all superb, but it was Ralph Gleason's grace and his unselfishness in interviewing that made this show unique. Both friends and critics have told me that this is the most honest public presentation of me that has been done. It's the greatest natural me they've ever seen. The credit is not mine. It all belongs to Ralph.

And there is one more person—Fran Kelley, musician, poet, songwriter, singer, orchestrator, manager, executive. This great woman with all these talents gave up running a radio station and record company in Los Angeles to pursue her spiritual quests in San Francisco. An original advocate of *Be,* it was she who stated years ago in some of her poems the absolute necessity of *being.* It was not a matter of dictating what or when one should be: the most important thing was to be.

I'm not sure San Francisco would be what it is today without Fran Kelley, the hippies, and the two Duke Ellington Days in Oakland.

Marvin Sachere of the University of California organized a unique event in September 1969 at Berkeley. This "celebration," or Ellington Symposium, included lectures, films, recordings, discussions, and a concert by the band. On the first day, the twenty-eighth, Ortiz Walton, Leroy Robinson, John Handy, Stanley Dance, Gunther Schuller, and John Lewis all spoke about our music. Charles Mingus brought his group for a musical demonstration. The following day, a collection of films in which we had appeared was shown, and then I made a brief appearance as a speaker before the enrolled students. In the evening, we played a special program, the first half of which emphasized material we do not often play, such as *Harlem, Black, Brown and Beige,* and excerpts from *The Deep South Suite.* Willie Cook played "Black Beauty," and we even tried our hands on a Mingus composition called "The Clown."

The following month, on the sixteenth, there was a happening of a different kind at Washington School in Berkeley. To celebrate the second year of complete desegregation in Berkeley schools, the principal, Dr. Herb Wong, had proclaimed it Duke Ellington Day, and when I arrived there I was met in the playground by first, second, and third graders, all waving placards and banners of welcome. A big one that I particularly remember said, "We dig you, Duke! Groovy. Room A." Inside the school, I saw their art work on themes such as "Mood Indigo" and "Take the 'A' Train." Across the street, in the Community Theatre, the Berkeley High School jazz band performed "Summer Song," a composition of student Robbie Dunbar. And in the evening we gave a concert there. The whole day really got to me.

Hooked

Much of the adventure in one-nighters is in the anticipation of approaching confrontations with one's self. When face to face with one's self, or looking one's self in the eye, there is no cop-out. It is the moment of truth. I cannot lie to me, or vice versa.

So the question is, was, and always will be: have we been true to ourselves? Did we compromise for the sake of monetary or material gain? Have we been too idealistic, as when we blew an opportunity that included bonus bundles? Just how far or how much should we bend in the interest of holding our position or an advantageous edge?

This is the kind of counterbanter we must contend with—no ifs, ands, or buts. The next time, of course, it will be different. The audience will have matured and we can allow our true artistic selves to come to the fore.

> *The cats all showed,*
> *The gig was blowed.*
> *Now that we've played,*
> *Goodbyes are bade.*
> *Oh, how we grieve*
> *That we must leave!*
> *Sorry we have to go-go-go!*

Are we leaving now to duck the responsibility of reacting sympathetically to the action whipped up in reaction to the action we have just laid down? Or to go in pursuit of our constant compulsion? Is this not a merry-go-round?

The constant chase, or being chased . . . the constant reaching for the melody that's right up there, so close you can almost see it . . . you grab at it, and think you've got it, only to find later that all you've got is a little piece of the tail!

So you're hooked on music. You think and anticipate music. You write music, play music, and listen to music. Your joy is music. You are lucky to be hooked on something you make a living by playing—and playing with—day after day, play after play, fifty-two weeks a year, in possibly the only band that doesn't take time off. This is probably the only group of people doing anything fifty-two weeks a year without weekends, holidays, or vacations, here and now in an age where most people who work a five-day week are talking about a four-day week, and four-day workers are demanding three-day weeks. You are most fortunate not to be one of those who do not enjoy what they do for a living. Don't you know that money is important to most people, and everything to some? And isn't it true when they say that anyone who makes a living doing what he doesn't enjoy is actually indulging in a form of prostitution?

Music to me is a sound sensation, assimilation, anticipation, adulation, and reputation. It takes me to new places and experiences. It brings me invitations to the most interesting occasions in North and South America, in Europe, Africa, Asia, and Australia. I get to smell things in India I couldn't smell anywhere else. I see skies in Sweden I could see nowhere else. I hear distant drums in Africa. I get a compelling urge from the *cuica* in Brazil. I see a flying saucer in Phoenix; a moonbow in Reno; snow and fog together in Toronto; snow and lightning accompanied by thunder in Chicago; four rainbows at once in Stockholm; and at precisely the hour and minute one year after Billy Strayhorn's demise, a celebration in the sky—a cloudburst on the New Jersey Turnpike like a testimonial to grief in the heavens.

Music is thus a key to great rewards in terms of experience. But when someone has to be told that he should study or specialize in music for the purpose of making a career—then I think more harm than good is done. Anyone who loves to make music knows that study is necessary. There are periods when music is a lucrative pursuit, but if money is the only reason for participating in it, then money can be more of a distraction than anything else. And I think this is true of every art form. Music—love it or leave it!

I have seen men on the bandstand so miserable it almost hurt me. There are many occupations they would enjoy more, but, no, in music they can make a little more money. Being away from home at the wrong hour, or out of town where they can't watch over things, eats them up with anxieties. Then, perhaps, the opportunity occurs to get what they call a studio job, and between television and recording it can add up to a considerable amount of money, but in such situations there is no real, personal relationship with music people. Someone brings in a chart. It is rehearsed, recorded, or given air time, and there it goes like the concern of whores:

> *I had my fun and here's your money!*
> *Now get the hell out of here!*

Servant or slave, monarch or monster, what has money got to do with music?

Notes on the State Department Tour, 1963

After thirteen different shots and vaccinations, we leave New York on September 6, 1963, for one of the most unusual and adventurous trips we have ever undertaken. We change planes in Rome and go on to Damascus, the first stop in a tour for the U. S. Department of State. Naomi Gilbert is the advance representative, Kenneth Oakley the State Department's representative and liaison officer, and Tom Simon the official assigned to travel with us.

Tom is young, new in the department, and on his first foreign-service trip. I am soon talking to him as though he were a relative, warning him against making the kind of mistakes that are all too easy, especially since the whole trip is east of Greece. If one is not socially aware, it is very easy to be caught in a position where one's chauvinistic shirttail is showing.

I drink my first Arab coffee and learn my first Arabic word, "Shookrum," which means "Thank you."

Damascus is the oldest continually inhabited city in the world, a fact immediately confirmed by the five senses. The main thoroughfare, "the street which is called Straight" of the Bible, runs from the West to the East Gate, and the atmosphere of the East is in its bazaars and that maze of tangled lanes which is the famous Hamidiyyah Bazaar. There are the smells of spices and garlic and exotic perfumes. There are marvelous brocades, oriental rugs, glass and copper trays, inlaid and engraved . . . The cats in the band go crazy about everything they see, and Billy Strayhorn was always at the head of the line. There are swarming masses of people everywhere, and the buses are jam-packed, but all the Moslem shops are closed on Friday.

Before going to bed, I learn about the long fast of Ramadan and the shorter feasts of Islam. After a good night's rest, I am rudely awakened by the all-time greatest noise of automobile horns. It seems as though every automobile in the city has converged on the intersection outside my window at six o'clock. If that noise could be properly orchestrated, sung, played, and recorded today, I am sure it would win a Grammy, an Oscar, or an Emmy.

Our first appointment is with His Excellency the United States Ambassador in Damascus, Ridgway B. Knight. When we arrive at the embassy, we are taken into the garden, a charming place shaded by lovely trees. It is here that the briefing session takes place. Some of the local customs are explained, and various dos and don'ts which we are expected to observe are enumerated. In this part of the world, it is considered insulting to show the soles of your feet when talking to a gentleman! Outside of our four concerts a week, every member of our company is expected to attend all the receptions and similar affairs. One notable point is that we are not required to restrain ourselves in the expression of our personal, political, social, or religious views. As citizens of a free country, there are no restrictions on our tongues. We are to speak as free men. They are very explicit in advising us that we should always say what we think in or out of favor of the U.S.

When the Ambassador finishes his speech, Paul Gonsalves gets up, goes over, and puts his arms around him. (We have been sipping our drinks meanwhile.) "Mr. Ambassador," Paul says, "you are absolutely right!" He then proceeds to make his own speech. His Excellency is astonished but feels it is wonderful and compliments Paul, telling him that he is a very good ambassador himself.

Everything else goes along fine in Damascus that week until I get hit by the "Thing." I call the doctor and he advises me that it is a very simple matter that will clear up in a few hours. I soon learn that one is very, very lucky to have the service of a physician who practices in the same vicinity as where your bug is born.

Off we go on the twelfth by special plane to Jordan. The country is strategically astride a major caravan route, and it has witnessed the passage of the leaders of great civilizations in ancient history. Not too much remains of ancient Amman. It was once a Roman city known as Philadelphia, and a Roman theatre built into the curve of a hillside is where we give our concert on Friday the thirteenth. It seats six thousand people, has excellent acoustics, and all kinds of outdoor festivities take place there.

Billy Strayhorn and I are house guests of a gracious host, Ambassador

In the Roman amphitheatre, Amman, Jordan, 1963. Cootie Williams in foreground

William B. Macomber. His English butler and huge dog are both very attentive and make us feel much at home. I am honored here by a dance with His
Majesty King Hussein's sister—a beautiful dancer.

Everybody drinks arak. The music of Jordan is haunting, formidable, beautiful, and compelling. It is here, I think, that we learn to love the Depke dance.
We have a wonderful visit in Amman.

Now we are in Jerusalem, the Old City, and from our hotel window at
night we can see the dark No Man's Land that separates the two parts of the
city, the Arab and the Israeli. We buy many Bibles with gold bindings as
presents for our relatives and good friends among the clergy.

The Old City is partly enclosed by a high wall that forms an irregular quadrangle two and a half miles around. Here are the holy places, the tomb where Christ was laid to rest, and the long Via Dolorosa from Pilate's court to Calvary. We drive out to the River Jordan, where it flows from Tiberias to the Dead Sea, and on our way we stop alongside the latter (twelve hundred feet below sea level) and go wading for a few minutes. I wonder if it is true, as somebody tells me, that a resort now stands on the original site of Sodom and Gomorrah?

Our first visit to Beirut is a six-hour layover between planes. The State Department officers have us check into the splendid Phoenicia Hotel. It is my lot to end up with rather an ordinary room at the back of the hotel. I call the front desk and say I would like to have a room on the seaside of the hotel, because it is my first visit to the Eastern Mediterranean.

"We don't have a room on the Mediterranean," the man says, "but we have a suite."

"That's fine," I say, "just what I want."

"But it's thirty-five dollars a day."

"Well, I'll take it."

This is when I first realize that the capitalistic United States did not invent money. And my new suite does not actually face the sea. I have to go out on the terrace and turn left to see it. Later, I discover that all the best suites face the swimming pool! In discussing this, I am informed that the hotel was not built in the position Mr. Edward Stone, the architect, had planned, and that when he found the best suites were overlooking the swimming pool he requested his name be removed as architect.

We leave for Kabul on September 17. A legendary land of high mountain ranges and fertile plains right in the heart of Central Asia, Afghanistan is said to have changed very little since Alexander the Great passed through on his way to India three hundred years before Christ. With Russia to the north, China to the east, and Iran to the west, it has always been a gateway to India. It is full of the antiquities of an old civilization, and many old-fashioned traditions remain. This is the land where polo was invented, and someone says it was originally played with a cow's head instead of a ball. There was always a great match on the King's birthday, and the players were highly skilled riders. During times of war, they would come by night, and reach down to pull up the tent pegs as they galloped past the enemy's encampment. And there would be the enemy, with the tent down over his head, helpless!

It is considered a good idea to get in the habit of closing the doors and windows of the hotel room at night, when the temperature drops quickly. Although there are many dogs in the streets, wolves can be heard howling outside the city. Something else that strikes us as strange is the fact that boys are still being used here for female roles in plays and sensuous dances.

The band is going crazy again, buying hats of karakul, Persian lamb, and leopard, not to mention all types of colored Afghan goods, carpets and rugs.

The reception arranged for us is a tremendous affair. The following members of the Royal Family are present:

Their Royal Highnesses The Victor of Kabul Lemar-i-Ali Marshal Shah Wali and Princess Safia;

H.R.H. Sardar Ahmed Wali and Madame Wali;

H.R.H. Sardar Abdul Wali and Madame Wali;

H.R.H. Sardar Wali Shah and Madame Wali Shah;

H.R.H. Sardar Zalmai Mahmud Ghazi and Madame Ghazi;

H.R.H. Sardar Sultan Mahmud Ghazi and Madame Ghazi.

Among the many high officials are the Minister of the Court, the Chief of the Royal Secretariat, the President of the National Assembly, the Vice President of the Senate, the Prime Minister, the Ministers of Finance, National Defense, Justice and Planning, the Chief of Staff, and the Commandant of the Royal Afghan Air Force. The diplomatic corps is very fully represented, among those present being the ambassadors of Bulgaria, Czechoslovakia, France, Germany, Great Britain, India, Indonesia, Iran, Italy, Japan, Poland, the U.S.S.R., and Yugoslavia. There is a large American contingent led, of course, by our own ambassador, as well as representatives of the press and various cultural officers.

When we play our concert in a large sports field—before a frankly curious audience—the Victor of Kabul, who once won a big battle with the British, is in the front row. As I do my finger-snapping bit at the end of the concert, I find that the Victor of Kabul's finger-popping pulse and mine are together. We are swinging!

Kabul is the last place on this tour from which I make an overseas telephone call home. It happens like this:

In my hotel room, I pick up my phone and say, "I would like to call New York City, please."

"Oh, yes, Mr. Ellington," the operator says. "Would you mind coming down here?"

So I go down to the lobby, and when I get there the man at the desk comes out, takes me over to the window, and points down the street to a building about two blocks away.

"You see that building right there," he asks, "the large one right on the corner?"

"Oh, yes."

"Well," he says, "you go down there, go up to the second floor, put the call in, and they will do the whole thing for you."

I go down to the building and tell the operator in charge what I want. He writes it all down very clearly and carefully, and then he tells me, "Very good, Mr. Ellington. Now you can go back to the hotel. We will call you."

Later in the day the hotel desk calls and says, "Mr. Ellington, your call to New York is ready."

"Okay," I say, "put it through."

"You will have to come down here," a new man on the desk says.

When I am once more in the lobby, he is pointing to that building two blocks down the street.

"You see that building down there? Well, you go right there and they'll have your call for you."

The plane that was originally to take us is canceled, so on the twentieth we wind up on an aged DC-3 out of Kabul en route to New Delhi. There are no stewardesses on this trip, just one very nice man who acts as steward. There is nobody on the plane but our company, so I push the back of the seat down in front of me and put my feet up. I am very comfortable and am really having a serene trip until the steward happens to pass by.

"Pardon me, but how high is that mountain over there?" I ask.

"Fourteen thousand feet," he answers.

"And how high is the one on this side?"

"Nine thousand feet."

"How high are we flying?"

"Five thousand feet."

We fly safely between the two of them and eventually stop for a coffee break—without coffee—at Amritsar.

Amritsar means full of nectar, and the city was established in the sixteenth century as the center of the Sikh religion. The Sikhs are easily recognizable.

With the brothers Greg and Steve Zorthian in India, 1963

They are tall, handsome, and dignified beyond words. They never cut their hair, and they wear a silver bracelet on their wrists.

After the coffee break, we reboard the DC-3 and find the whole front end of the plane loaded with freight. We don't have as much room to spread out as before, but we manage comfortably enough until we arrive in Delhi at two o'clock, where we are met by a lot of State Department and U.S.I.S. brass. I become, very luckily, a kind of personal protectorate of Barry Zorthian, Deputy Director of U.S.I.S. His wife and two little boys are absolutely wonderful. One gives me a golden, Indian necklace, the other a musical instrument.

At five o'clock there is a big press conference which I shall never forget. At first, everything goes along cozily in the sitting-room of my suite. Twenty to thirty ladies and gentlemen of the press are present, and Billy Strayhorn passes back and forth from this to the next room. After the conference has rolled along comfortably enough for about an hour, this cat with the "snake eyes" creeps out of a corner.

"Why," he asks, "doesn't the United States subsidize artists like Russia?"

"I don't quite get the meaning of the question," I answered.

"Russia, for instance, subsidizes the ballet."

"I suppose because ballet is a classical art, and to sustain the devices of an art hundreds of years old, as I believe ballet is, it is necessary that it be subsidized. In the United States, competition is in everything, and the tempo is so fast that artists, scientists, and everybody else are bent on discovering new devices."

I think I get away with that, and I go on to explain that it will be very difficult to make comparisons with the U.S. and other countries in the world because we speak different languages and have different values. In many ways the U.S. is like every other country in the world, but in others it is quite different. For example, practically every nation has its haves and have-nots, but the U.S. is the land of the haves and want-mores. There are thousands of people in the U.S. who were born in poverty and wound up millionaires or in very powerful political positions. It is a matter of opportunity, competition, and luck. All this annoys my questioner, and, judging by the looks on the faces of the other people in the room, I have won a little skirmish. So he comes back strong.

"What about the race question?" he asks.

"We have the same thing again," I reply. "Everywhere, there are many degrees of haves and have-nots, minorities, majorities, races, creeds, colors, and castes."

By this time, Billy Strayhorn has had more than enough. He stalks into the room. "I thought this conference had to do with music!" he blares at the press. Then he goes out the door into the hall.

"The United States has a minority problem," I continue after a pause. "Negroes are one of several minority groups, but the basis of the whole problem is economic rather than a matter of color."

While my opponent is busily thinking, I give him another opportunity by introducing another subject.

"The United States has an extremely accurate news service and the press enjoys almost complete freedom," I claim. "Did you, incidentally, hear about the five little girls who were burned up in that church down in Alabama the other day?"

"Yes," he says with great triumph.

"Well, that was only a couple of days ago, and I'm not sure anybody else would have let such news get out that quickly if it had happened in their backyard."

He has nothing to say to that, so I carry on:

"You have heard of the Reverend Martin Luther King, I'm sure."

"Yes," he says, with a measure of exultancy in his voice again.

"Let us say that he is the representative of an oppressed race of people. (Incidentally, I wrote the first published song that sang his praises, "King Fit the Battle of Alabam," a big choir-production number in my 1963 show, *My People*.) When I saw him just before I left Chicago a few weeks ago, he was coming down Michigan Avenue. I waved to him, and in order for him to say hello to me, he had to have his chauffeur stop this long Cadillac. An aide got out and opened the door, and two motor policemen in front of the car, and two more behind, had to stop so that he could get out and shake hands with me. This is the way the man lives and travels who is representing that oppressed race, so the standards are not the same every place in the world. They vary according to where you are."

On these State Department tours, you usually stay in one city for a week. You play three or four concerts, and the rest of the time you attend receptions, parties, and various functions. Because I am considered some sort of an expert on American music, additional performances are added now and then. We call them "Lecture Demonstrations," which means that some of the guys— not the full band—and I appear informally dressed and without orchestrations. I sit down, start playing the piano, and then the bassist and drummer come out. After that, several of the horn cats enter one by one and start doing solos. Immediately following each selection, I do some talking, and I usually begin like this:

"You probably heard of the word 'jazz.' It's all right if that is the way you understand or prefer it. We stopped using the word in 1943, and we much prefer to call it the American Idiom, or the Music of Freedom of Expression."

We go on to show that some things, actually written for specific people

Lecture demonstration, India, 1963

in the band, take into consideration their limitations as well as their out-standing gifts. Then the soloists demonstrate this, without music, so that it all appears ad lib, and sometimes the demonstrations are longer than the concerts. They are everywhere enthusiastically received, and many people consider them very informative.

The balls, parties, and receptions are something else, and we are guests at luncheons almost every day. The parties are usually in gorgeous gardens with beautiful people, beautiful women dressed in beautiful clothes and dripping with priceless jewels. People in high government and diplomatic positions

Sam Woodyard at an embassy party, India, 1963

are always there and, as I've said, the entire band is expected to show up at all these affairs.

This sometimes results in strange situations, because some people in the band, who we know have been leaning over bars for at least thirty years of their lives, consuming unlimited quantities of liquor—they find making these parties in the roles of representatives or guests something of a hardship!

They stand there in these glorious gardens, glass in hand, conversing with these very elegant and attractive people. Bearers impeccably dressed in white come and take the empty glass and put a fresh one in its place. (To think that this is a *dry* country!) Paul Gonsalves, always a very congenial guy, is also a great diplomat, and sometimes, from the way he goes on, you think it is he who is really representing the government. Sam Woodyard is another of the great men, another of those with great dignity. He may be leaning up against the wall with his first drink when he begins a conversation with some important minister, but after his glass has been refilled or replaced a few times he slides to the floor, never losing his poise or his drink, but with the glass firmly held at the end of an arm extended in the direction of the lucky person whom he is enlightening. Naturally, diplomats are supposed to have a certain amount of put-on, or a degree of façade, but these two musicians have none of that. They are just down cats, and everybody loves them. They are like the guests the perfect hostess leaves drinking her booze at the poolside after she goes to bed. She trusts them. She feels that they are friends, and these really are two friendly cats, baby. Harry Carney, now, is always a perfect gentleman, well dressed, well mannered, a Bostonian to the hilt. He, of course, is our senior senator, and is always loved and accepted at the highest level by everybody everywhere, in and out of the band.

While in Delhi, we have a very special musical experience. We are invited to the music department of the university, where they demonstrate all the indigenous Indian instruments. Then they take us to a dance recital, still within the university, where they do first a small ballet, and then a full, complete one. There are four major schools of dancing in India, three being in a sense counterparts of Western ballet. Folk ballet is quite different. In another part of the university, they demonstrate some rarer instruments, and we learn a good deal about the music itself. We are also given manuscripts, drums, a sitar, and a tabla.

Going to and from the university, I walk with no hat on, and the sun is very, very strong. To what degree it affected me, I don't know, but a day or so later I feel a little whoozy and know something is wrong. So we call the embassy doctor, who is really a surgeon.

"How soon do you play your concert?" Dr. H. K. Purcell inquires while taking my temperature.

"In about an hour, doctor."

"You don't have any temperature now," he says. "Do your concert and I'll see you afterwards."

So I go and do the concert, and the doctor sits out there in the front row enjoying every note. Immediately after the concert he comes backstage.

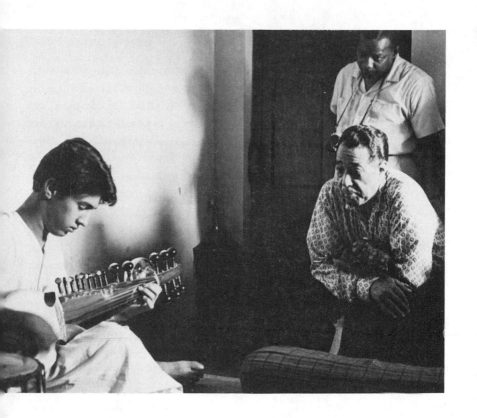

Watching a sitar player with Harry Carney in India, 1963

"Well, how do we find you now? Give me your wrist." After a pause, he says, "Hm, you have a temperature now. I must take you to the hospital."

I am extremely flattered to realize that this wonderful doctor had wanted so urgently to hear our concert! Anyway, they race me over to the Catholic hospital, the Holy Family Hospital, where I am soon ensconced in a very pleasant private room. The doctor turns me over to a specialist, an internist named Dr. Mathur, an Indian doctor who had done a six-year residency in Detroit General Hospital. He is just great, and he stays with me for about four days.

"Well, now I can go on my holiday," he says. "I'm going tiger-hunting in Bengal."

"What is this I have, doctor?" I ask.

"You have the three-day flu or virus."

"But, doctor, I've already had it four days!"

"You know how you theatrical people are!" he replies.

While I was in the Ashoka Hotel in New Delhi, there had always been flocks of eagles and hawks flying around outside my windows just like pigeons at home. Here in the hospital I have a friendly little lizard for company. He stays on the ceiling all the time with a very positive purpose—to eat any flies or insects that might eat me!

I have a lot of visitors. The Sister Superior, Sister Charles Salz, comes every day, and she is wonderful, so young, and with beautiful blue eyes. When she waves at the lizard, he doesn't move. I have with me a tape of *My People,* which I had recorded in Chicago with the original cast, and I play it for the sisters at just about the time the fever breaks.

Dr. Koto Matsudaira, the Japanese ambassador, sends me excellent steaks, and Lieutenant Colonel Louis Aebischer, our army attaché, flies to Pakistan to get more for me. Mrs. Chester Bowles comes to visit but unfortunately doesn't stay long, because I have neither the air-conditioner nor the fan on.

When I leave the hospital, I am the house guest of His Excellency, our ambassador in Delhi, Chester Bowles and Mrs. Bowles. The embassy mansion was also built by Mr. Edward Stone, the same architect who designed the Phoenicia Hotel in Beirut. The embassy office building and the ambassador's mansion are almost twin buildings, and very elegant in appearance. As a matter of fact, Embassy Row in New Delhi is a scene of real architectural splendor.

The sons and daughters of the American diplomatic whirl are having a party on Saturday night at the ambassador's residence, and they call up and ask me to come down and maybe play a tune or two. As always, I am like the girl in *Oklahoma!* and I can't say no. I go downstairs for the first time in four or five days, and afterwards I am so weak I can barely make it back to my bedroom. But the kids are marvelous and say I sounded great. By this time, of course, the band has gone on to the other cities we were scheduled to play, Hyderabad, Bangalore, and Madras.

The Barry Zorthians invite me out on a tour of Old Delhi, which I accept a little reluctantly, but after riding a while in their car I am very glad I made it. They give me a rundown on the various sights we pass, only to be corrected by their sons, two of the brightest boys I've ever encountered in my life. They speak the language; they know everything; and they do everything. We pass the buildings of the Red Fort with the monkeys on the roofs. We stop to speak to a group of Himalayan people who have come to Delhi and are sitting beside the road, very straight and quiet. They have enticing Himalayan articles for sale, and we buy some of their work. We go on to a government-controlled shop full of silk brocades, shawls woven from cashmere, printed textiles, and primitive jewelry. There are rough emeralds, sapphires, pearls, and an unbelievable place where they have rubies of all sizes and colors, some as large as pigeon eggs. We go over the entire building, which is several stories high, and many rooms wide. In one room the artisans are at work on ivory—very serious and intent, and putting much love into what they are doing. In another room they are working on sandalwood. At the end of the long visit to this establishment comes the *pièce de résistance,* or what we might call the First Act Finale. Lights are dimmed and extinguished until just one tiny light remains. Then they draw a curtain on a setting, and on the backdrop of this setting, gradually, as a result of the one very subtle light, we begin to discern the Taj Mahal coming into focus. The material of the backdrop looks like dark blue or black velvet, and the brilliant gems mounted before it form a perfect replica of the Taj Mahal.

With Billy Strayhorn at the piano, the band has been carrying on so well that it begins to look as though they don't really need poor little me at all. Here, for example, is a critique from the *Indian Express* of October 7 headlined ELLINGTONIANS STORM MADRAS:

All music is praise of the Lord. Jazz, which some people cannot or will not understand, the real jazz form of a spiritual soil, is truly the musical psalms of the twentieth-century man's torment in the tigerish growl of the trumpet. God's wrath and mercy are in the demonic drumbeat and the milksmooth sound of the saxophone.

Duke Ellington was far away in Delhi. Yet no one was more physically and spiritually present than the old master when the band gave its first performance before a packed audience at the Music Academy in Madras.

The Ellingtonians played with startling existentialistic freshness, heartfelt profundity and an interlinked unity of various individual skills. They played for the people in love.

The performance at Madras was a triumph for the band in its high-pressure harmony and hallelujah of groin-grinding surrealistic tension. It was not a one-man show; not merely the magical tantra of a trumpet solo by Cootie Williams, nor Sam Woodyard's voodoo at the drums, though he has a long way to go to catch up with Buddy Rich. It was a triumph for every player, each no less important than the other.

Highlights of the show: Sounds rising like the bubbles from a glass of champagne when Johnny Hodges swung his alto saxophone with a tingling titillation. A furore of fiery rhythm festooning the stage like the flickering glow of golden fireflies from the Rolf Ericson trumpet, and the grizzly bear growl of the Cootie Williams trumpet. A saxophone glimmering like a cigarette in the dark. A tender tragic lusciously lingering melody like a goodbye kiss from Billy Strayhorn at the piano. A Deepavali firecracker riot of cool raucous rhythm from Russell Procope and Cat Anderson.

The all-time favorite "Mood Indigo" was the mood of the century, purging the emotions in the classical manner through pitiful sounds, exalting its composer as the poet of the jazz world. Duke Ellington's orchestra played the poetry of jazz. We lost our hearts to "Take a Train" and remembered that line of T. S. Eliot's: "You are the music while the music lasts."

The band turned "Things Ain't What They Used to Be" into a rollicking lament over sheer joy of being alive. In "Eighth Veil" there was a pandemonium of pure disciplined jazz, and "Caravan" lit up the stage like Dante's Inferno. In "Diminuendo in Blue and Crescendo in Blue," Paul Gonsalves hypotized his audience and played like one possessed with the holy spirit of jazz.

Assessed by its three-star performance tonight, it would appear that Ellington and his boys are ready for a big break-through to new frontiers of jazz. Duke Ellington may yet compose the real jazz of the space age, which doesn't necessarily mean a series called "Rocket Launching Blues."

I arrive in Bombay a day ahead of the band and check into the Taj Mahal Hotel. They offer me a choice of suites. The first I look at is the Honeymoon Suite, 'way up on the top floor facing the Arabian Sea. It is actually a duplex, the bedroom on the upper level having wide-open windows in every wall. They were not built to have glass in them, and they stay open all the time. Birds are flying in and out of them. I don't know what kind they are, whether they are bats or eagles, but they are kind of large and probably a little far out for *un petit carré* like me. Another drawback is the fact that the bathroom is on the lower floor, and this is the cause of my definite decision to decline the suite. Imagine me going down a flight of spiral stairs in the middle of the night on my way to the bathroom!

They show me a couple of other suites, and I settle on one not so high up and far out. I am told that yet another mistake was made in the building of this hotel, and that the entrance, main façade, and magnificent garden face the city rather than the sea. I forget the name of the architect, but they say that when he came and saw what had happened he committed suicide. Great stories you hear in the East.

Being a chronic room-service type, I ring for my room boy right away and start inquiring about available food. I begin by reciting my favorites and get all the way down to chicken, but he responds to every item by shaking his head side to side. Although I am right here on the sea, he shakes his head again when I mention fish. Not knowing any better, I wind up eating lamb curry for four days, after which I discover that shaking the head from side to side means "Yes."

I go for a ride one day along the crescent-shaped drive by the bay that is known as the Queen's Necklace, because of the way it looks at night when all the lights are on. On the way up Malabar Hill to see the Hanging Gardens, we stop and get out of the car for a photographer who wants some pictures of me in a local setting. A man comes by to watch what we are doing. He has two little boys with him, his sons. This man is black, the blackest man I've ever seen in my life, and he has the most beautiful face I've ever seen. It is pure, completely positive, showing absolutely no sign of any susceptibility to any degree of negativity. There are no lines and no signs of anything in his face but innocence and virtue. I am told that they are members of the Hindu caste known as Untouchables.

There are a lot of people, too, who look like the Strayhorn family in this land, where so many races and religions are represented. I find the diversity endlessly fascinating. India's is one of the oldest civilizations in the world, and the mixing of different strains and the coexistence of different races has long been a source of wonder to foreigners. Indians explain their land as a kind of wall in which the windows are always open to receive fresh breezes. Its enormous population can roughly be divided today into four groups— Indo-Aryans in the north; Dravidians, the main, original stock (shorter and darker), in the south; Mongolians, mostly in the northeast; and primitive tribes in relatively isolated hill and jungle areas. The West has also left its mark on India, in one way or another, from the time of Alexander the Great's invasion right up to the long period of British domination.

There is a terrifying storm one day, and I sit and watch it through the window as it rages over the Arabian Sea. It is the greatest exhibition of its kind I've ever witnessed. Lightning blazes, thunder roars, rain deluges down, and after the storm there is the most extraordinary sunset. The whole sky over the Arabian Sea is cerise.

When I am strong enough to appear on stage, I am still too weak to do more than fifteen or twenty minutes, so I play only the medley and Billy Strayhorn plays all the rest of the concert. At a little reception afterwards, I learn of the black market for tickets. A lot of musicians write and telephone complaining about the impossibility of buying tickets. All musicians are brothers in arms and it distresses me terribly that they could not get in to our concert, so we go about the business of readjusting the conditions. I insist that from now on, no matter how limited the space, all musicians are to be admitted.

There are always surprises in Bombay. Harry Carney tells me that when he went down on the beach he saw I don't know how many turtles. They say some grow to weigh as much as three or four hundred pounds. When the eggs are laid, the mother digs holes or trenches deep in the sand and buries them for the purpose of protection, but large packs of dogs that roam the beaches dig them up and eat them. The baby turtle's chance of survival, of being hatched and born, is only 2 or 3 percent hereabouts.

Because of the absence of lemons, it is here that Harry really acquires the habit of taking his tea with lime. Somehow or other I fail to acquire any of the paintings from an exhibition in the hotel that had impressed me very much. Others are doing the acquiring, however. My barber, Roger Simon, for example. He is singing in every nightclub here, as in the other cities on this tour, and he is acquiring quite a reputation! Maybe this is how Rock gets around?

Before we leave Bombay, there is a big headline in the newspaper about an American engineer who was supposedly murdered in his sleep in Room 341 of the Grand Hotel in Calcutta, where we are going to stay. On arriving there, everybody says the same thing to the room clerk: "Don't give me Room 341."

Our concerts in Calcutta are played in the courtyard of the same hotel, which limits the audience to about a thousand, so many people who couldn't get tickets rent rooms in the hotel with windows overlooking the courtyard. You can see the heads of as many as eight or ten people in one room. Everything goes well, the people are wonderful, and Ali Akbar Khan, the famous Indian musician, presents me with two tablas during intermission. The informality which prevails is relaxed to the point where visitors arrive to see me as early as nine o'clock in the morning. We call the front desk, explain that I am still recuperating from my severe illness in Delhi, that I need all the rest I can get, and request them not to give out my room number in future. They are most understanding and cooperative, so much so that they send two of those handsome Sikhs in uniform, each with a gun on his shoulder, to stand on either side of my door! I know nothing about this until first Billy Strayhorn and then Harry Carney telephone, both a little put out, because the Sikh guards will not let them or anybody else pass. When I hear this, I open the suite door, and there are the two Sikhs, standing at attention and smiling. We shake hands. I don't dare offer them a drink, so we shake hands again.

Another day in Calcutta, a Catholic monk comes to visit me. He introduces a young Indian man as his assistant, and after welcoming them we sit down and have some tea. The monk tells me he is in a mission about three hundred miles away in the mountains. After an hour of conversation, he gives us his blessing, but before he goes I ask him to leave his address so that I can send him Christmas greetings. Afterwards, I look at his card and see, as someone had suspected, that he was from a leper colony. Having just managed to get out of the hospital, and still not having my full strength back, I alert the embassy and ask them to send their doctor. Because he has just taken a patient to England, they send a nice lady doctor instead. I explain to her about my visitor, and she tells me not to worry too much, for to do me any harm I would have had to be exposed to an active case. "Besides that," she continues, "I'm sure half the beggars in Calcutta are lepers anyhow." When I raise the subject of drinking water again, she shrugs that off with a smile too. "It's better just to believe that it's boiled, and enjoy it."

As I go out of the hotel each day, I notice a young boy with one leg parking the cars—quickly, but so efficiently. I admire his fortitude and the ease with which he does his job. It makes a big impression on me, and the day I leave I shake his hand and slip him a double sawbuck.

While we were still in Bombay, I got a telegram from my very good friend, the Maharajah of Cooch Behar, saying that he and his family were up in Kashmir and would like to come and see us in Calcutta. When they arrive, the entire balance of our stay is spent with him, the Maharanee, his beautiful wife, and his beautiful cousin. He also has with him another gentleman, a White Russian, who fled Russia at the time of the Revolution and opened a highly successful restaurant in Katmandu, Nepal. We enjoy this visit very much and one night, after our performance, there is an informal jam session in the hotel. When I walk in with the Maharajah and his family, we get a great welcome from mobs of friends.

From Calcutta, we go to Ceylon. After rather a bumpy trip, we arrive on an airport that has been flooded by a storm. We are welcomed by lovely girls in native costumes who dance for us right there in the airport. They bring garlands of flowers and put them around my neck. It is a lovely way to be received—by beautiful girls with beautiful flowers.

We stay in a hotel right out on the sea, and I spend most of my time just looking at the Indian Ocean. Ceylon is one of the major junctions between East and West, and the chef in this hotel is a Frenchman who came on a tour, was captivated by the beauty everywhere, and stayed on. The French pastry is *magnifique*. Then there is a tailor who makes anything you want—shirts, dresses, coats, pants—all out of sari material that is as light as kisses. When the band starts ordering clothes, he is busy round the clock until we leave.

Ceylon is one of the world's biggest gem producers, so naturally everybody is involved in shopping or window-shopping for rubies, emeralds, sapphires, etc. One soon learns the bargaining system, and then it becomes a sort of game. A jeweler shows me a string of ruby thumbs—rubies as big as a working man's thumb—and we begin bargaining at five thousand dollars. The ruby is my sister's birthstone, and when we are at the fifteen-hundred-dollar level I suddenly have a couple of misgivings.

"If I take them," I say, "I may lose them before I get back to New York. And, besides, I don't have any money on me, anyway."

"Well, take them," the jeweler says. "Take them with you, and I'll be in New York after the first of the year, and I'll get the money from you then."

But ultimately I don't take them. I've always goofed on profit opportunities. If I had a little business acumen, I would be a rich man just as a result of the chance I had to invest profitably in real estate in New York City, Phoenix, Palm Springs, and Las Vegas.

Despite what are described as "driving winds and monsoon rains," our two concerts on the Colombo Race Course are a great success, Sam Woodyard's five-minute drum solo on "Skin Deep" arousing a storm of applause. The three children of the Canadian High Commissioner to Ceylon, Mr. James George, whose wife was a Wellesley classmate of Mrs. Walter N. Read, come to both concerts with a note of introduction, but are unable to get through

In Ceylon, 1963

the crush to me. When their mother later speaks to me on the telephone about their disappointment, we are on the point of leaving, so all I can do is to send them an autographed album.

I must mention another kind of storm I experience in Ceylon. It happens one afternoon, and it is entirely different from all the other storms I have experienced. We can see it coming for miles across the sea, directly toward our hotel, and because of this we have plenty of time to close the windows.

But before the impact of the storm itself comes this enormous funk, a smell of decay, dirt, and germs that is just the worst. It is as though it had accumulated all the rotten vegetation in the world, and it comes as a sort of blocking force. After the storm itself hits and blows past, the rain comes, and then the whole atmosphere is as pure as pure can be.

Kandy is the cultural center of Ceylon. Sixteen hundred feet up in the mountains, it is the home of writers, artists, musicians, and dancers. The festival there includes extraordinary dancing, astonishing costumes, stupendous pageantry and processions, all of it accompanied by the throbbing Kandy drums. Strayhorn is most impressed by the elephants he sees bathing at Katugastota on the Mahaweli Ganga River. Perhaps I should say "bathed," for they are very zealously attended.

On the way to Kandy we see a python that isn't in the zoo. It has a very hospitable owner who, for a small fee, will allow you to have your picture taken with his little fifteen-foot pet around your neck. It is a funny thing, but the guys who own these friendly reptiles are always seen with them around their necks. Strayhorn even claims he saw a man with a boa constrictor around his neck! All over India we have encountered men with a cobra in a basket. If you give them some money, they take the top off and start blowing that oboe. And if the cobra is slow waking up, they don't hesitate to slap him. Once, when I looked out the hotel window in Karachi, there was a guy on the street with cobras in a basket and a mongoose on a leash. They seemed to be on amicable terms, too.

From Colombo we go to Madras, where we change planes and join up with Dr. Arthur Logan, who has arrived with a fresh supply of medicines. Our next stop is Dacca, the capital of East Pakistan. After the usual briefing, I find I am the house guest of the U.S.I.S. director in Pakistan, Mr. Donald K. Taylor. He and Mrs. Taylor are very warm and considerate. They have a delightful party in the garden of their home, and at one point I am somewhat mobbed by beautiful women, which I find very enjoyable. The Taylors, however, think that I have disappeared until I reassure them by calling attention to my whereabouts! Members of the Pakistan Arts Council garland me with flowers, and altogether I am made to feel very welcome indeed. And after the party, the wonderful Mrs. Taylor has steaks for her famished guests. The concert that night on the racecourse is a sell-out, and the reviews we are shown next day—in English and in Arabic—are extremely kind.

We go next to Lahore, which was once the capital of the Mogul emperors.

It is now the provincial capital of West Pakistan, and the center of the country's cultural and academic life. The Mall is lined by the more than forty colleges that together form Punjab University.

On the evening of our arrival on October 29, a reception is given by the Consul General, Mr. David Bane. His residence is exquisitely decorated with rich rugs and oriental vases, and his elegant wife, Patricia, is a perfect hostess. Diplomats from all countries are present, and later there is a superb dinner served with oriental splendor. The marble-topped dining table has a precious centerpiece that embodies a fruit theme with enjeweled grapes, pears, etc. I am asked not to mention this, because it has just arrived from China! After dinner, I meet Malik Firoz Khan, and we chat in a very easy and relaxed fashion. I am also very delighted to meet the gracious Begum Noon, who asks us to an intimate dinner the following night.

Hers is a sumptuous house, and dinner is served by candlelight at small tables on the terrace of an enchanting, mysterious garden. There is an atmosphere of luxury that extends from the lavishly dressed servants to the *maîtresse de maison* herself, who became a Moslem by faith and for love of her country.

Before the concert in the open-air theatre called Bagh-i-Jinnah, the Consul General makes a speech, which I have preserved:

"Distinguished guests, ladies and gentlemen: It is indeed a privilege and a pleasure for me to welcome Duke Ellington and the members of his orchestra to Lahore, and I know that the entire American community of Lahore wishes to be associated in this expression of sentiment, as do, I'm sure, Duke Ellington's many, many Pakistani friends locally. It is a privilege and a pleasure for me to welcome Duke Ellington here, because he is one of my country's most distinguished citizens, and one who is well known to music-lovers throughout the world as a truly great composer and musician. He has made a significant and lasting contribution to the world's treasury of great music. It is a personal pleasure for me as well, since I have admired and enjoyed Duke Ellington's music throughout the span of his creative years.

"Duke Ellington's orchestra is a distinguished group of artists; each is an outstanding musician in his own right. Duke Ellington and his orchestra represent one of the finest expressions of American and contemporary music —music which has established its place as one of the great music forms of all time. Duke Ellington and the members of his orchestra, however, represent something more than fine music to me—they represent my country well, and they reflect in their music something of its spirit and soul.

"I am proud to have them here and to play in this historic city of Lahore, and to have them make their contribution to the great cultural heritage and tradition of this city. I am pleased as well that they have had an opportunity to enjoy the hospitality and warm friendship traditionally extended to visitors in Lahore. We are honored to have these two concerts, co-sponsored by the Pakistan Red Cross Society, and it is with great pleasure that I introduce to you now Begum Viqar Un Nisa Noon, Chairman of the Red Cross Society, who will introduce Duke Ellington to you . . . Begum Noon."

After that kind of introduction you really have to go out there and do your best!

The third city we play in Pakistan is Karachi, where I stay in the Aga Khan's suite at the Hotel Metropole. Billy Strayhorn and Dr. Logan take off to see the Taj Mahal. Although I am not a sightseer in the normal sense of the word, I want to see it too, but I have a slight fever and colic. Paul Gonsalves calls and wants me to come over and see the belly dancers, but I miss them as well. (In fact, I miss them in every city, because somebody tells me to wait until we get to Egypt, where they have the best.)

We leave Karachi at midnight on November 4 after giving our concert. It is a beautiful flight on a very clear night, and as we approach Tehran I am fascinated by both the twinkling of many pin-pointed lights around the high mountain range and by the myriad of stars in the sky above.

It is a little chilly when we land at two o'clock in the morning, so we hurry to the Royal Tehran, which has a superb view of the Elburz Mountains. After nine weeks of careful drinking and cautious eating, here we are in a hotel where we can drink water from the faucets, and which has an all-night coffee shop with eggs, pancakes, hamburgers, and—caviar.

Caviar and Iranian vodka are waiting in my suite, and I develop a romance with caviar in the following week that I shall never forget. Caviar with everything! Here they give you caviar instead of flowers.

While shopping in the hotel store downstairs, I browse through the gem department, which by now has become a habit, and I notice a ring with a large pink stone, quite the most beautiful ring I have ever seen. When I ask the salesman the price, he says it is eighteen dollars, and I take it without any bargaining. To me, it is just the most beautiful stone I ever saw, and it has no monetary value, which is a parallel with other encounters in my life.

We have lunch with Ambassador Stone, and I am happy to find that he and I feel the same way about several things. Neither of us likes anything to garnish our caviar. Billy Strayhorn, who gets frightfully intellectual at times, speaks knowledgeably about Persepolis, Darius, and Alexander the Great.

From Tehran we go to Isfahan, a city of poetic beauty, where they give you poems instead of flowers. I seem to collect Omar Khayyám in translations of every possible language. There is much to be seen here, notably the huge *maidan* where Shah Abbas used to watch polo games. Beside it are two imposing mosques in which blue tiles have been refreshingly used.

We never really get away from the caviar thing, however. Somebody gives Harry Carney two kilos of caviar—not flowers, not poetry, just caviar. As we go from one city to another, we have to put packages of caviar in a refrigerator on the plane, and then rush them into a refrigerator at the hotel when we leave the plane. This goes on until we are about to disembark in Baghdad, when Harry Carney suddenly exclaims, "Oh, shucks!"

"What's the matter, Harry?" I ask.

"I forgot to put my caviar in the refrigerator."

"Isn't that a shame! Do you know what that means?"

"No," he says. "What?"

"We are going to have to eat it."

He was so disgusted he couldn't eat a bite, but I took full responsibility.

But before Baghdad we go to Abadan, not far from the Persian Gulf. To get to the consulate we have to take a boat across the river. It is a delightful house, nestling among green trees and with a terrace on the first floor. After dinner, we join other guests on a patio which extends out over the river. During this party, I encounter a lady who has something to do with the State Department.

"Where have you been on this trip, Mr. Ellington?" she asks.

"This is our tenth week and we've been in Syria, Jordan, Afghanistan, India, Ceylon, Pakistan . . ."

As I mention India, she begins to break in on my flow of countries.

"India—that's a terrible place!" she says.

"Why do you say that?" I ask.

"They should have birth control."

"I don't understand. What do you mean?"

"All those starving, sick people . . . They need birth control."

"I don't agree with you," I say, feeling the spur of competitivism.

A young man on the fringe of the little ring of people around us steps in here.

With Paul Gonsalves at Ctesiphon in Iraq, 1963

"You know, Mr. Ellington," he says, "I think maybe you have a point."

Then the people really begin to crowd around, waiting for this lady and me to have it out, with the fine young man in the middle as moderator. I take it easy and say, "Birth control is one thing, but the same amount of money that would make birth control work would give them twice as many healthy people."

"Oh, dear, you men . . ." the lady begins in rebuttal.

Then I think I do a little bit of a dirty trick on the nice lady by taking advantage of the fact that we are still in the land of poetry.

"Now suppose," I continue, "that the life ambition of a woman in India is to have twenty children, and you come along with your birth control and cut her off after she has had the nineteenth. Not only does she have this terrible disappointment, but the child you're cutting off is destined to be the world's greatest poet. So what happens? He flies around the universe for five thousand years and, by the time he comes back to earth, poetry is no longer in style."

We spend the next day in Kuwait, a place with a population of 365,000 people. The government takes care of everybody, pays for their education and everything, and the land enjoys the greatest security. I think they get something like 365 billion dollars a year gross from the oil in the ground. Guys out on the street sell wristwatches for five or ten dollars that would cost a hundred anywhere else.

From there we go to Baghdad, arriving in the middle of the night. We are met at the airport by the Ambassador's wife, Mrs. Hamilton, because he was sick. We are told that the concert is completely sold out. Everybody is coming. Even the Russians have bought eleven tickets.

The day before the concert, we make a trip to Ctesiphon, where there is a dramatic ruin of a gigantic palace built in the fourth century A.D. An arch, still standing, is the largest single-span, nonreinforced brick arch in the world. There is a little old blind man sitting alongside who is playing a one-string bow instrument. Our manager, Al Celley, has a tape recorder on which he records the old man's performance. We have our pictures taken beside the arch, go over and have some coffee, smoke a water pipe, and Sam Woodyard and I push the big wheel that grinds the corn. As we come back to the arch, Al Celley plays the tape of the blind musician's solo so he, the musician, can hear it, and scares him half to death. He knows that it is his playing, yet he realizes that he is not playing. We have an interpreter explain the magic to him.

On the day of the concert in Baghdad, we are told by the embassy that we should return to the hotel immediately after the concert, because there may be some trouble. We rush back, and I shall never forget how I bump my head as I scramble into the car. Late that night we hear a couple of planes flying around, approaching from different directions. We learn that they sent rockets or bombs into the front and back of some government official's house. He was lucky not to be there at the time.

Before this, Dr. Logan had been having such a good time that he decided to call his beautiful wife, Bridie-Mae, in New York and tell her to catch the next plane and meet him in Beirut. But after this night's military coup, they close the border and nobody can leave. There he is, stuck with us, and he has

327

Duke Ellington at a water wheel at Ctesiphon, near Baghdad, Iraq. Lawrence Brown in background, 1963

acquired six kilos of caviar which he has been saving to enjoy with his wife when she arrives. He waits, and finally the border is opened, and they let him go to Beirut.

We, however, are left still sitting in this ancient center of Assyrian civilization where the art of writing was reputedly invented, followed by astronomy, geometry, arithmetic, science, and the arts of peace! We hear stories of other kinds of arts, too, of how some Iraqian ladies get on the plane for Paris in all their native finery—gems, veils, and flowing robes—and, as the plane nears Paris, of how they go to the ladies' room and make adjustments in their attire, changing to high heels, cosmetics, high styling, and all the different things the

Western fashionables wear. That is a story told us, but I must confess we never see it happen.

The day before we are to leave Baghdad, Dr. Logan calls from Beirut to say that his wife has arrived, but that he forgot his six kilos of caviar in the hotel refrigerator. Will I bring it with me, he asks.

"Gladly, doctor," I reply.

When we get to Beirut airport, the place is full of reporters wanting an eyewitness report on the coup. I light a cigarette and give them a full report:

"Those cats were swinging, man!"

Next day, in the French newspapers, it looks and reads a little differently:

"Et à Bagdad, l'atmosphère?" the reporter asks.

"Ça swinguait, mon cher," I reply. "Ça swinguait."

When I arrive at the Phoenicia Hotel this time, they are ready for me with the V.I.P. treatment and the Presidential Suite on the top floor. It is an unbelievably gorgeous suite, with a view on all six sides of the main room. But before ever I go up, I give a bellboy Dr. Logan's caviar with instructions for it to be put in the refrigerator immediately. Now I can relax!

In a small nightclub where I am enjoying myself a night or so later, I hear an Italian combo that pleases me. We bring the musicians home with us to the hotel, and while we are having a few drinks up in the Presidential Suite I wonder if Dr. Logan remembered his caviar. (He and Bridie-Mae have left to climax the ball they've been having with a fling in Paris.) So I call downstairs, ask them to look in the refrigerator and bring up any caviar Dr. Logan may have left there, no matter how small the quantity. In about five minutes the man comes up on the elevator and walks into the suite with all six kilos of Dr. Logan's caviar. What can I tell you after that? I love caviar and I live with it for a week.

As we ride out at night to work at the Théâtre du Liban, we see the huge statue of Our Lady of Harissa (sometimes called Our Lady of Lebanon), which crowns a hilltop fifteen miles from Beirut. This magnificent symbol of Christianity, at the crossroads of East and West, is illuminated all night.

We leave Beirut for Ankara with a layover in Cyprus. There are several hours to wait for connections, and we go to a delightful little hotel surrounded by trees and flowers. The weather is a little cool when we arrive in Ankara, which is twenty-six hundred feet up on the Anatolian Plateau. The band continues to go crazy here, buying up meerschaum pipes, ivory, and the kind of beads the old Turks twist in their hands as they talk or take a cup of mint tea.

There is a whole new food scene to experience, too: the shish kebab; the dolmas (grape or cabbage leaves filled with beef and served with sour cream); fowl stuffed with *ic pilavi;* and what became my second love after caviar, the baklava bathed in honey.

A camera crew arrives from New York to provide television coverage of the rest of our trip in Turkey, Cyprus, Egypt, and Greece. At the Ambassador's reception, I am on the receiving line, and everyone is very gracious and wonderful. The television people shoot the reception, say they are off to a great start, and will continue next day.

Later the same night, we are about to enjoy a room-service dinner in the hotel. I have just said grace when the telephone rings. One of the State Department officers is downstairs and he says he has to speak to me right away. I tell him to come up, and when he enters the room he says, "The President has just been assassinated."

The food just sits there and gets cold. Nobody eats, nobody talks, nobody does anything for thirty minutes. When the news hits the city, it apparently has the same effect on the crowds in the street. The people all look as though they are numbed.

"Well, that's the end of the tour," I finally say, for we are in a land where they normally mourn forty days. It is, too. On the way back, we stop in Istanbul, go from there by Swissair to Zürich, and from there to New York.

Nipponese Journal, 1964-70

On our first trip to Japan in 1964, we arrive in Tokyo after stopping in Honolulu. There is the usual press conference at the airport, and then we go on to the Okura Hotel. I am awestruck at finding so modern a city. Is this really Tokyo or Scandinavian Modern? Then, on making contact with the people, I am amazed to find how thorough, precise, and, above all, how courteous they are.

The stage setting for us is just unbelievable. The backdrop, the floor of the stage, and the wings are designed in such a way that the name of every musician in the band is displayed in block letters of heroic size. It is the most fantastic and highly personalized stage setting I have ever seen.

The precision of the television people is so perfect that it seems like magic, and it means the very minimum of grief for the performer. They come to see the show at the concert hall and make a notation of the part they will telecast. In the studio next day, they are all set. They just test the lights and the audio, and then shoot. *Très formidable!*

Donald Richie, a brilliant American I met in Tokyo, takes me figuratively by the hand and leads me informatively over the cultural plateau of Nippon. We go out to his charming house, which is furnished in the traditional Japanese style. We take our shoes off on entering the front door and then have a glorious native-style dinner. He is an authority on the Kabuki Theatre, which we attend several times, and in about a week I begin to feel like an authority on Japanese culture myself.

CBS has sent over a camera crew to tape the trip for the Bell Telephone Hour, and I am sure they get some beautiful pictures in addition to what they shoot of us! We learn that it is the custom, whenever possible, to make plans to site a brand-new skyscraper hotel alongside a garden four or five hundred years old, with black and white swans in a natural pool or lake setting, and

Arrival in Japan, 1966, left to right: Harry Carney, Duke Ellington, Paul Gonsalves, Russell Procope, Stephen James, Jimmy Hamilton, Sam Woodyard (rear), Buster Cooper, Cat Anderson, Johnny Hodges, Herbie Jones, Chuck Connors

it is in such a place that the television guys want to take some shots of me listening to traditional music. The only way they can do it is by hiring some professional musicians to get some traditional instruments on which to play some traditional music! Everybody over here seems to be playing rock 'n' roll, Spanish and other nonindigenous kinds of music. Except in the Kabuki Theatre, what you hear in the nightclubs, or on radio and television, is much the same as you hear anywhere else in the world.

Kyoto is probably the one city in Japan that to a certain extent still looks

In Japan, 1966, front row, left to right: Duke Ellington, John Lamb, Paul Gonsalves, Jimmy Hamilton, Johnny Hodges, Russell Procope, Harry Carney; middle row: Lawrence Brown, Chuck Connors, Buster Cooper; top row: Sam Woodyard, Cootie Williams, Herbie Jones, Mercer Ellington, Cat Anderson

Japanese, and it is here I am eventually filmed listening to traditional music. We all gather in one of the hotel rooms for the purpose of listening and shooting. I wander past a lady playing a long, guitar-like instrument, and wind up in front of the drummers. One of them looks familiar.

"Hey," I say, "I know you. You're the drummer in that club I was in last night."

He blushes and shies away. I suppose I remember him because I had been saying there what a good swing drummer he was!

When we go back in 1966, we run into some cats playing jazz at the Tokyo Hilton who are too much. They play really well. That is why Japan sometimes frightens me, because they have the ability here to do things better than the originals. They are such baseball enthusiasts, too, that many of them go up on top of the office buildings where they work and just play catch during their lunch break.

After we play "Ad Lib on Nippon," the cheering response is followed by a backstage visit from those most sincere patrons of music, the Hot Jazz Society of Japan, led by Y. Nakajima, Jake Yamada, and Shoichi Yui. The highest compliment to me is that Duke Ellington, they say, has not resorted to the customary clichés and overtones of Chinese riki-tiki-dik-dik, but has come closest to capturing that blend of Traditional and Modern waves which parallels in music the architecture, painting, sculpture, food, and general gentility of Japan.

As one who dares to title pieces of music in direct association with countries I visit, I explain to them, I must always be on guard against condescension, for that is the vilest of offenses. And that was why Billy Strayhorn and I, after having been in the Middle East, India, Iran, and Ceylon for fifteen weeks, decided not to write any "Eastern" music until we had been away from it for three months—to avoid the re-echoing of those native sounds we had absorbed and the identical retracing of traditional melodies. The titles, nevertheless, were impressions indelibly inscribed in our minds at the moment of exposure to the splendors of the East.

I also explain to my interviewers that, when I first started to refer to "commercial" music, I meant music that was *deliberately* bland, extremely simple and elementary, so that the dullest ear could have no problem comprehending what (little) was going on. I could not imagine, I add, that anyone with whom I had ever been associated had been interested in that kind of musical nadir.

Around the time of our first trip, there had been an earthquake up north in Niigata. When we heard of it, we decided to cancel our Hawaiian date, which was set to follow immediately after the Japanese tour, and to do a benefit in Tokyo for the relief of the earthquake victims. It was a big success. The Mayor of Niigata came down and was so pleased that he made me an honorary citizen of the city. On a later tour, we played a concert there.

When we arrive in Fukuoka one afternoon, I go to my room pondering whether to lie down at once or smoke another cigarette. The carillon in the public square begins to play and what I hear is to me a little strange. The

With Japanese specialists

melody it is playing is "'Way Down Upon the Swanee River." I had a premonition that something must be wrong. "'Way Down Upon the Swanee River" in Fukuoka? Fifteen minutes later, my son, Mercer, comes to me.

"Have you been in my room?" he asks.

"No. Why?"

"Somebody has just taken seven thousand five hundred dollars off my dresser!"

Fortunately, there is a happy ending to that story, because most of the money is recovered later and the offender is forgiven.

Since our first visit, we have had the pleasure of seeing a considerable part of Japan, and it has been a thrill each time. We went to Osaka for the 1970 Expo, and also to Nagoya, one section of which looks like Saturday night on Chicago's Rush Street *every* night.

We have been much indebted to our friend and impresario Mr. Kambara, who presented us so well and received us so hospitably. Mrs. Kambara, with her lovely smiles, has always been wonderful to us too.

On the last tour, I had cocktails and dinner with Her Highness the Princess Okura and her husband.

So you will understand why I always look forward with great enthusiasm to the next trip—to the Land of the Rising Sun.

Dakar Journal, 1966

The 1966 World Festival of Negro Arts in Dakar, Senegal, is a really great accomplishment. Every field of art is represented. The Palace of Art is crammed with paintings from eighty-six countries. The Hall of Justice is packed full of sculpture. Space equal to five square blocks is devoted to literature, poetry, photography, dance, song, music, and the theatre. Never before or since has the Black Artist been so magnificently represented and displayed.

Every night in the concert hall the native theatre of a different country is presented without limitations of any kind. Every afternoon in the arena there is an outdoor show. Every café and restaurant has its own kind of art in abundance. And every night, on the balcony of the ninth floor of the Engar Hotel, I sit and listen to the sea singing her songs of the historic past on the island from which the slaves were shipped. Farther in the distance, I can hear the tribes that have gathered on another island to rehearse for their show next day. And then sometimes I wondered whether it was really a rehearsal, or was it a soul brothers' ceremonial gathering with all of its mystical authenticity. Anyway, I wish I could have seen or recorded it. Too much, baby! Full distance.

We have been invited by President Léopold Sédar Senghor of Senegal to come and participate in this the first international festival of its kind. We are met in Dakar by His Excellency the U. S. Ambassador to Senegal, Mercer Cook, the son of Maestro Will Marion Cook, the great musician who long before had given me more than the equivalent of a conservatory semester just by answering my questions. After writing African music for thirty-five years, here I am at last in Africa! I can only hope and wish that our performance of "La Plus Belle Africaine," which I have written in anticipation of the occasion, will mean something to the people gathered here.

When the time for our concert comes, it is a wonderful success. We get the usual diplomatic applause from the diplomatic corps down front, but the cats in the bleachers really dig it. You can see them rocking back there while we play. When we are finished, they shout approval and dash for backstage, where they hug and embrace us, some of them with tears in their eyes. It is acceptance at the highest level, and it gives us a once-in-a-lifetime feeling of having truly broken through to our brothers.

We usually play only three days a week on tours sponsored by the State Department, but we feel so good after this experience that when His Excellency the Ambassador has a party we insist upon playing that too.

Papa Tall is considered the best artist in Senegal, and he is also the head man at the tapestry factory. Although he studied in Paris, it is impossible to miss the feeling of Old Africa in each and every stroke of his work. I have about eight of his works, and want to buy another, but he won't let me have it. "It isn't finished," he says. He is adamant about it, no matter how much I say I love it just as it is. Later in the year, he sends it to me—and I still love it!

Papa Tall asks me how I explain jazz, or if I can give him a parallel to it. Inspired, I think, by what I had seen of his work, I come up with this:

Jazz is a tree, a most unusual tree. Can't you just see it, making its first break-through, sprouting in its environment despite the climate, completely ignorant of the nature of its own existence, but continually growing up, until it is a strong healthy child, attractive and admired? Nobody ever warned it of the hazards of adulthood.

Jazz is a tree, a most unusual tree, whose branches reach out in all directions. The heat of the tropics allows them to grow firm and strong, yet with gentle, melodic contours. The sunrise of the East awakens them as they are nursed in a soft dew that is part of a pleasant welcome to the approaching sunlight. Later, the West holds them spellbound, and makes them cast long shadows eastwards over the land while hoping that the glorious sunset will linger with her pink, orange, red, and purple, and not leave too soon. Those limbs that stretch out toward the poles tend to bundle up, as though withdrawing into their inner selves, so that sometimes their joints are gnarled and knotted. From each branch come many multidirectional twigs, no two alike, and with no two pointing the same way. All of this is like backstage preparation for the next phase.

The stems go out further to set the stage, waiting to hold just the right position—and suspense—for the arrival of the popping buds that will soon open up as blossoms. And the blossoms, if you notice, come out and present themselves in all sizes, shapes, and colors. On the tree of jazz, there are never twin blossoms, and none the same in any respect other than that they are beautiful, exotic, and healthy, all at the same time. First there is a variety of pastel colors that grow and bloom until they are fully developed blossoms. Then there are total reds, purples, yellows, just a pinch of green, and a touch of brown. Next are whites, blacks, and, of course, the blues. The designs can be heard, but not seen, for the lines of divisions between the senses are no longer observed.

Carpels bring pollen for the birds and bees, as well as questions and many decisions. Who is susceptible? Who is not infected? The inestimable beauty of this conglomerate array, with all its infectiousness, is never seen at any one time from the left, or from the right, or from front or back. But maybe top and bottom? That's it! The invisibility of treble and bass. Yet there is always the other or opposite side to the viewer's view, which can never grasp all at once.

The fruit that follows is as varied as the blossom. Some is plucked, some is out of reach, and some falls to the ground—always with a thud or a thump, and a solid beat. All of it is enjoyed: some by those who like it a little sweet and syrupy; some by those who like it a little tangy; and some by those who like it as delicate as though it still swayed on the placenta. Then again, there is always someone who enjoys all the fruits of the tree. There has been some disagreement about the aromatic properties. But all of us who are concerned with the cultivation of the tree can *feel* it according to our taste.

Ah, ha! On close examination of it, we discover that the trunk is extra sturdy, that it has a kind of translucent bark, and that unless you make a very close examination it may appear to be labeled *Made In Japan*. But as we study it more deeply, we find that its very blue-blooded roots are permanently married to, and firmly ensconced in, the rich black earth of beautiful Black Africa.

So now all I have to do is to wait for the new Papa Tall painting and tapestree!

Goutelas Journal, 1966

As I go from place to place, I always anticipate new or strange sensations. I get different kinds of inspiration, and sometimes an unexpected urge toward retaliation, dependent on the environment, or maybe the people in the environment, mostly musicians.

Sometimes they dictate my direction, and sometimes they leave me to dig into my primitive mind for a way out, or a way into their hearts, minds, and ears as I search for compatibility with their compatibility without conforming in a manner offensive to myself.

So one day, you might say, there is inspirational agreement, and the next day retaliation in the interest of sustaining my true perspective.

How I came to be involved with the restoration of a thirteenth-century French château is an improbable story.

It begins with Paul Bouchet, one of the greatest criminal lawyers in Europe, and a man with an intellectual interest in the heritage of France. In 1960, when he was visiting his family in the region, he saw Goutelas and became concerned about its pitiful, dilapidated condition. He called a friend of his, Bernard Cathelin (a great Catholic and humanist, a prominent member of the Resistance, and a famous artist whose work has been exhibited in the most celebrated galleries), who in due course went with him to Goutelas. Cathelin drove back to Paris in silence, thinking about what he had seen, and then sent a wire which read, "We must save Goutelas." When Bouchet's secretary received it, she thought it referred to a criminal who had been sentenced to death.

Work began right away on what had been, in the thirteenth century, a fortified house with ramparts. It belonged to the family of Guillemetz Beez de Goutelas until the sixteenth century, when one Judge Papon acquired it and made a Renaissance mansion of it. In the eighteenth century, an Italian architect further modified it *au gout du jour,* but it was then abandoned until 1920, when a farmer named Guillot bought and kept it.

After Bouchet and Cathelin had set the work in motion, students came from all over Europe to help the *paysans, ouvriers,* and *intellectuels* of the area in the reconstruction of Goutelas, where from 1965 onwards lithographic exhibitions by Chagall, Matisse, Villon, Braque, and Picasso were presented. It rapidly became a cultural center, different yet comparable with others in the region like Nîmes, Orange, and Avignon.

Now skip to a February morning in 1966 when I leave Madrid on the nine o'clock flight to Geneva. Bernard Cathelin and his wife Régine pick me up in their car, and we set out for Goutelas around eleven o'clock. We stop en route at Terouges in the Departement de l'Ain, a village that has maintained its tenth-century, medieval character. With its narrow, winding streets paved with large stones, and houses with red-tiled roofs, it is so fascinating that we are reluctant to leave, but we reach Goutelas at 5 P.M., where we are received at the *gentilhommière* of the Magnans. (They are cousins of two of the most famous aristocratic families in the land, the Levies-Couzan and the Levies-Mirepoix, about whom there is a funny saying in France. They are said to rank so high that they are cousins of Sainte Geneviève, the patron saint of Paris!) After refreshing ourselves, we are ready to confront a chilly, windy, but starry February night.

Bernard Cathelin, his wife, and I are joined by Paul Bouchet and his wife, Simone, who have come from Lyon. There are fifty children with torches on either side of the road leading up to the château. The wind is so gusty that some burn their hands, but they say it does not matter, and the torches stay alight until we reach the portal of the majestic building, where the Mayor, Monsieur Duclos, receives us. I walk alone, with Bernard and Paul ten steps behind me, and then all the friends who had come from Paris and Lyon. Behind them is a quiet but huge crowd of those who had worked on the château.

The left wing has been completely reconstructed, and it is ready for me to inaugurate this very night. In the *salle de musique* is the most beautiful piano I have ever seen or heard, a nine-foot Steinway concert grand, which has been specially brought there for my performance. Despite the severe cold, the doors to the hall remain open throughout, and the people, crowded inside, remain silent and attentive.

I make a short speech, which is well translated by Régine Cathelin and

Entry to Goutelas, France, 1966

Betty Roché, the wife of one of my attorney friends from Lyon. The gist of it is this:

"I have been made an honorary citizen of many cities and countries, but the honor of participating in the inauguration of Goutelas is by far the most moving. To be here to help celebrate the rebuilding of this beautiful château by men who came together from the greatest extremes of religious, political, and intellectual beliefs is an experience, and a majestic manifestation of humanism, that I shall never forget. They did not merely make a donation that others might roll up their sleeves to work; they rolled up their own sleeves and worked. To be accepted as a brother by these heroic human beings leaves me breathless. To my new-found brothers, their families and friends, I should like to dedicate one of my compositions—"New World a-Coming."

"The title refers to a future place, on earth, at sea, or in the air, where there will be no war, no greed, no categorization, and where love is unconditional, and where there is no pronoun good enough for God."

At the end of the performance, everybody stands to applaud, some crying without shame, and when I address them again as "my brothers in Goutelas," I feel it to be a rare moment of communication and joy between men of all creeds. The communist *ouvriers* had worked hand-in-hand with Father Dumas and the *paysans* who, in this almost untouched heart of France, are still deeply Catholic.

Afterwards, a banquet is served at low tables for the two hundred people who have helped rebuild Goutelas. We sit on benches and have a real French dinner, a "folkloric" dinner someone explains to me, such as few "foreigners" have ever had. The menu is:

Tarte à l'ognon (warm onion tart)
Rosette de Lyon (sausage)
Potatoes cooked *à la mode auvergnate* in the ashes with young chickens roasted over a wood fire
A fabulous *Pièce Montée* prepared with great joy by Pierre, the chief pastry

cook, a cake in three tiers based on profiterolles with nougat *dragées,* and topped with fresh cream.

The *"clou"* and literal highlight of the dinner is the *brûlot* prepared by Mayor Duclos. The *brûlot* is a kind of punch, but instead of rum a superb and perfumed brandy has been used. When he lights it, everybody screams because of the flame, which rises high and bright. All we need now is a fire after the fantastic task of giving back Goutelas its incredible beauty! But all is well and the flame is immediately under control. I must mention that besides Mayor Duclos of Goutelas-en-Forez, there are present as hosts the mayors of three other neighboring hamlets: Domonic Cheze of Lagneux, Noel Durand of Villa Marcoux, and Michele Ouzet of Sail-sous-Couzan.

When we leave, we enjoy the magnificent lighting effect accomplished by candles and lamps used to illuminate all that side of the building we can see as we make the long drive winding around down the hill. Goutelas stands beautifully silhouetted against the dark sky, undefeated because of the love of men of all kinds and beliefs. We enjoy looking back at it until it is far away, and then finally out of sight. It seems a case of pure magic, that men who cultivate the land, and men who work in factories, could thus come together not only with some of the most famous lawyers, artists, and painters in France, but also with me, Duke Ellington, their brother in heart, from another nation, from another continent far across the sea.

The following day, we go to the Château de Cousan, high up in the Massif Central at Sail-sous-Couzan. We stop on the way and leave a rose at a cross standing by the roadside. At Couzan, we overlook all the Auvergne, a relatively "closed" part of France, where "foreigners" are reputedly not easily accepted or loved. The dance of the country, I am interested to discover, is La Bourrée, and it is danced in the *sabots* (wooden shoes) that are worn in winter when the people go outdoors to work in the fields. I think it might be described as a square dance, but instead of a violin they use an instrument that dates from the Renaissance called the *vieille.* It is still made by hand, and it is a sort of mandolin that requires winding and rewinding.

It is a national holiday and officially the schools are closed, but we are happily received in those of Sail-sous-Couzan by Father Dumas and the children. They give us roses and a huge piece of beautiful red velvet made in an old tradition. Produced locally, it is as heavy as tapestry, and it is used to re-cover precious antique furniture.

Though now a little tired, we stop at the farm of M. Duclos and his son, where we go straight to the cellar to try the new, fresh wine of the last grape crop. We have lunch at 4 P.M. in Montbrizon at the Hôtel du Lyon d'Or. At this more intimate meal, as at the banquet in Goutelas, we drink the unique wine of the Massif Central, Côtes du Forez, a wine that is strong but fine, and "green," as someone says, like the forest it comes from. It goes to the head in the friendliest way! Another memorable menu consists of:

> *Cochonaille*
> *Canard aux pêches*
> *Pêches flambées*
> *Champagne Blanc de Blanc*

Numerous and versatile toasts are drunk, and we leave around eight o'clock, zigzagging a little, happy, and with all the love of the world floating around us to take the nip out of the chill night air.

We arrive in Lyon at one-thirty. Although the night is foggy and the roads slippery, everyone accepts my invitation to come up to the suite in the Grand Hotel and have some ice cream. After the ice cream has been ordered, I reach into the doctor's bag Billy Strayhorn gave me and pull out a plastic bottle full of Turkish vodka. I offer it around and some of my friends accept a drink. They sip and smile, and Régine has a funny little twist in her smile.

"What's wrong?" I ask.

"It tastes like it has something else in it."

So I have to explain that it was a little left-over aroma from what I had had in the bottle previously—scotch, or maybe cognac, or maybe bourbon, or maybe even cough medicine—because, of course, I *never* wash the bottle out! It was almost a success.

The following day, they all escort me out to the airport, these dear friends, Pascal Tishne, Marie France Berger and M. Berger, Aline Elmayan, Antoine Copel, Jean and Francine Delay, Paul and Simone Bouchet, and Bernard and Régine Cathelin. I am very much moved as we make our adieux. I fly to Paris, and then straight back to New York.

I never forget Goutelas and my experience there, but some years go by before I find the right opportunity to express my feelings musically. *The Goutelas Suite* is eventually premiered at Lincoln Center on April 16, 1971.

Halfway across the Atlantic, the captain comes back to welcome the passengers and ask how we are enjoying the trip on TWA.

"You know, Mr. Ellington," he says when he gets to me, "I flew you once before."

"Is that so, Captain? When was that?"

"Around 1940, when we were coming up from Los Angeles to San Francisco, and we could not land because of the weather."

"Oh, yes, I remember that. There was a lot of shaving soap down over the bay, and we couldn't see anything of land or sea, so you had to go over to Sacramento, and as you were coming in to make your landing a tiny little plane crossed over right in front of you, and you had to climb back up very fast!"

"Gee, you remember that!" he says.

"You're damned right, I remember. That was the day I stopped flying."

Latin American Journal, 1968

Ever since 1933, Europe has been a kind of second home to us, an essential part of our cultural plateau. We traveled there extensively, went to the Middle East, India, Africa, the Caribbean, and Japan, but never to Latin America. On the face of it, this was rather strange, because Mexico is certainly as close to the U.S. as Canada, which we visit every year. Although on several occasions we were offered contracts to play in Copacabana, we somehow always found ourselves with previous commitments that were impossible to switch. But now, finally, on September 1, 1968, we set out on a tour that will take us right round South America.

My interest has been stimulated by a series of questions a reporter asked me in New York for *Panorama,* the Argentine equivalent of *Time* or *Newsweek.* Then, too, although we were fairly close to it in Ceylon and Senegal, I have never been below the equator before. My vibrations are therefore a little strange as we take off from Kennedy Airport in an Aerolineas Argentinas jet. At first, I am puzzled, because we are flying east, but soon we swing round and head south. (This reminds me of how, when you fly from California to New York, you often find yourself flying west out over the Pacific. Until I got used to it, I would be wondering whether I had boarded the wrong plane and was on my way to Honolulu or Tokyo.)

We have an excellent dinner with red wine from Argentina and white wine from Chile, both of very good quality, and then see an amusing movie. It is about 2:40 A.M. when we cross the equator. The celebration is restrained, because regular travelers on the route and some of the more phlegmatic members of our party are asleep. Stanley Dance is traveling with me, and we toast each other—and our pretty stewardess—in champagne.

We arrive in Rio de Janeiro at 7:30 A.M. Blue Guanabara Bay with the crescent of land nestling at the foot of a wild panorama of peaks is truly a remarkable sight. Most imposing of all is Corcovado: it is over two thousand feet high, and on top of it is the world-famous statue of Christ the Redeemer. The other peaks have very fitting names like Parrot's Beak, Two Brothers, Hunchback, and Sugar Loaf, the last climbing twelve hundred feet straight out of the sea.

The view of Rio is breath-taking, and quite unlike that of any city I've ever visited. Unfortunately, we are not going to play here, but merely change planes. I would like to be able to go to the Teatro de Municipal and hear *anything* by the great Villa-Lobos, who was born here, but maybe on the next visit I'll get the whole bit, including the Carnival and all the galas, bands, floats, clubs, and beautiful girls. Or maybe I'll be here on New Year's Eve, which they tell me is also exciting, when candles are lit on Copacabana beach for mystic African rites. You can gather quite a lot of information about a country while sitting around waiting for planes, talking to people, and reading the kind of literature always handed out to visitors.

There are extraordinary cities here like the newly built capital, Brasília, in the interior of the country; or Manaus, with its opera house (imagine that!), a thousand miles up the Amazon; or Recife, "the Venice of America"; or Bahia, the sixteenth-century capital where African traditions still survive; or Petropolis, which was once known as "the Monte Carlo of South America." They arouse my curiosity, and I'd like to go to all of them. I really had no idea before how enormous and how diverse Brazil is. I knew it had the Amazon, and knew it was the biggest river on earth (ten tributaries longer than the Rhine!), but I didn't know it had a colonial past and two emperors, Dom Pedro I and Dom Pedro II. In fact, I think most people know no more about Brazil than Rio, the Amazon, coffee, the samba, and the Girl from Ipanema. The flora—a hundred thousand different species, orchids, unusual trees—is probably even more remarkable than the fauna, but man has surely made his mark.

Here we are on September 2 in São Paolo, where there are supposed to be over four million people (*paulistas*) and six thousand factories. It is the biggest industrial center in Latin America. Every one of the *paulistas* seems to own a Volkswagen, and you have to step lively on the streets. It is not a playboy's town, and they refer disparagingly here to Rio's citizens as *cariocas*. What is most striking, immediately, is the racial mix. Every color of skin and hair and every type of build and features seem to be visible on the sidewalks.

There is nothing self-conscious about this display. Whatever other problems they may have here, I get the impression they have the racial one licked.

Portuguese presents some problems to those who came equipped with a little Spanish, like two and twelve being *dois* and *doze*. The *real* jazz fans quickly recognize the significance of Paul Gonsalves' name. Here he is in a city named for Saint Paul, and he can speak Portuguese, so his ambassadorial duties begin at once. While others sleep, eat, or bargain for gems, Paul is busy explaining the mysteries, principles, and workings of Jazz. He doesn't mind at all, but seems to find this encounter with new fans exhilarating. "Beautiful cats, man," he tells me before the concert.

The tour has been organized by Alejandro Szterenfeld, the Buenos Aires impresario. We quickly learn to admire and respect him. He is as considerate of our well-being as he is efficient, and he is always available when needed. As on our 1963 tour in India, the U.S. diplomatic people have everywhere been alerted, and they extend a welcoming hand to us as soon as we arrive.

In São Paolo, Miss Caroline Millett of U.S.I.S. has organized a tremendous reception for us at the Binational Center. The members of the band are all on their best behavior, sipping up with elegance, and discussing every subject under the sun. The breadth of knowledge they display on these occasions never ceases to amaze me. The more often they encounter a loaded tray, or have their glasses refilled, the more they seem to know. Harry Carney and Stanley Dance are talking with especial dignity to an important British official—and getting themselves invited out to lunch next day. I learn from them that the British are a little envious of the success of this American occasion.

After doing some piano plunking for the people, I get back to the hotel, where the room service is marvelous. I turn on the television to see if Perry Mason, Alfred Hitchcock, or any of the faster gunmen of the West are appearing in Brazil, and who do you think is the first person I see? Paul Gonsalves.

Apparently all the cats had been invited to the Totem Club, and here most of them are, eating, drinking, sometimes blowing, and generally carrying on —live on TV. Paul Gonsalves, of course, is an irrepressible jammer, and he is not only dominating the scene musically, but visually as well. If the camera moves toward him, he moves toward the camera, so there are some gigantic confrontations. At first I am a little concerned about our image, since this is an immediate contrast with our earnest diplomatic work earlier in the evening, but everything turns out for the best, and everybody seems very happy. Beautiful cats, man!

The two concerts in São Paolo are well received. The Establishment is in position at the first, and the applause is generous but decorous. At the second, the audience largely consists of the hoi polloi, and they go wild, digging especially the more rhythmic numbers and Rufus Jones's drum solo. Willie Cook, who returned to the band just before this tour, brings his trumpet and joins me and the rhythm section at the end for the purpose of satisfying the crowd's insistent demand for encores.

After this second concert, we go to a little club whose owner has been persuaded by Peter Solmssen, the U. S. Cultural Affairs Officer, to bring in some of the native cats from the mountains. There is quite a bit of jazz being exhibited in Brazil by both local and visiting musicians, and I really don't *need* to hear that, for I hear it every day. I want to hear Brazilian music—*autêntico* or *genuino*. As it turns out, it doesn't matter too much what kind of music is played, because the chicks I am surrounded by at my table have such a luxurious aura of gorgeousness, but when I eventually get to concentrate on the sounds I realize that this is the nearest I have ever been to Africa musically—apart, that is, from our trip to Dakar last year. Yet it is not really African: it is *their* music. They use instruments found everywhere—guitar, bass guitar, piano, mandolin—and the mystique is in their very personal styling, and in the way they use the drums—bongos, conga, and cuica. The cuica is a drum with a string through the head which is used to increase and decrease tension. It is a fascinating instrument in the hands of an expert, which this guy is, and he tells a story on it that is full of hilarious innuendo. Another cat sings with an extraordinary piano accompanist. He sings in Portuguese, and although I don't understand a word, I am convinced his every syllable is the truth.

We leave on the fifth for Argentina and Buenos Aires, where we are to play a concert that night. B.A. is the biggest city south of the equator, and it is often compared to Paris, although on the long ride in from the airport the suburbs remind me of London. The *porteños,* as the citizens are called (meaning "of the port"), to distinguish them from those in the rural hinterland, are probably the most sophisticated in Latin America, but there is no racial mixture like that we had seen in Brazil. In fact, several days are to go by before we see our first soul brother, and this strikes us as strange, because I don't think we had ever been anywhere before without soon encountering soul brothers.

The venue here is the Gran Rex, a big movie house in the middle of the city, and we get a great reception—the warmest and most hospitable welcome, the longest and loudest bravos. The people who come backstage nearly all explain the enthusiasm the same way. "We have waited so long," they say. It is flattering and touching, and also surprising, because our records seem to have been very poorly distributed in Argentina. Yet, just as we did when we went to Europe the first time, we find fans of all ages who are acquainted with the most intimate details of the band's history.

I have a marvelous penthouse on the twenty-second floor of the hotel. It has an enchanting terrace, where I discover a small aquarium with angel fish. The Argentine spring has barely begun, and it gets very cold at night, so I soon acquire the habit of checking the electric device when I get back from concerts to make sure their water is warm enough. There is a splendid view from this terrace, and I can see the ships in the harbor, and hear their horns calling to each other, crying "Fog!" or "Watch out!" or "Make way!"

There is a lot of musical life in the city. The Teatro Colón has pride of place for symphony concerts, ballet, and opera. Opera seems to be very popular here, and during the season it is performed by separate Italian, French, and German companies. Music that is specifically Argentinian is discussed and demonstrated to me by new-found friends. The tango is still very big, they tell me, and it exists in three forms or phases: there's a kind of classical tango played by the Guardia Vieja (the Old Guard), a postwar tango that is popular and "sensitive," and an avant-garde tango that is claimed to have intellectual depth and modern melodic characteristics. The tendency to categorization is very familiar to me! There is also the *milonga*, which I refer to as the Argentine blues, because it always has to do with a woman whose man has abandoned her, or vice versa. Then there are the nostalgic songs of the gauchos on the pampas—"Adiós Pampas Mío!"—little different from those our guys sing in the westerns on the way up the Chisholm Trail to Abilene.

Nightlife has some new twists, too. Concerts start at 10 P.M. after everybody has had a big dinner. On Saturdays there's a before-dinner performance at six o'clock called *Vermouth*, when the taste buds are stimulated by cocktails. Steak is the thing here, and the *porteños* eat a lot of it. *Bife a caballo* (steak with fried eggs on top) is very popular. So is *dolce de leche,* which we call crème caramel, and for which I develop quite an appetite.

351

After successful excursions to Córdoba and a northern city called Tucumán, we come back to the Gran Rex for a concert at ten thirty on Sunday morning. The rest of the day, the theatre will be devoted to movies.

On the tenth, there is a big party for us at the U.S. embassy, graciously hosted by Ambassador and Mrs. Carter Burgess. Most of our musicians are present, and they are reacting with becoming modesty to the rather intense adulation. I do some more piano plunking, and both Mercer, my son, and I make speeches in English, which fortunately is widely understood here, or so it would seem to judge from the friendly response.

The next day we make the relatively short flight to Montevideo, the capital of Uruguay. The drive from the airport takes us along miles of beaches, but there are few people on them, for it is the wrong time of year. Impresario Szterenfeld, who always smokes a brand of powerful Uruguayan cigarettes wherever he is in the world, explains that Punto del Este, a hundred and fifty miles away, is the popular summer resort, and that Montevideo is a year-round café town.

The theatre is packed and jammed, and so many well-wishers come backstage that we are late getting to a reception at the embassy, where Ambassador and Mrs. Robert Sayre welcome us with warmth and friendship. I am introduced to many leaders in Uruguayan society, and enjoy several stimulating conversations despite my ill-mannered ignorance of Spanish. Occasions like this nearly always make me feel proud of our diplomatic representatives abroad, and I leave them with a renewed sense of gratitude.

After another concert at the Gran Rex, we take off on Friday the thirteenth across the Andes to Santiago in Chile. It seems an amazing coincidence that the name of the country, in the Inca language, means just what it sounds like in English. The snow on the cordillera makes a wild and unforgettable scene beneath us.

Chile has an international flavor but is somehow less noticeably Latin. There are certainly a lot of people around with Anglo-American names. I hear that the women are renowned for their beauty and elegance, and it isn't long before my eyes confirm the truth of this. As soon as we arrive at the Hotel Crillon, I find that the newspapermen of the city are already gathered for a press conference. It is about nine-thirty in the morning and none of us has had much sleep. Luckily, the questions don't tax my remaining intellectual capital too severely, and the articles that appear in the papers are approving. Señor Szterenfeld has similar conferences in each of the major

cities we visit and, while they take up a good bit of time, they seem to pay off, because the press coverage is often so extensive as to be almost unbelievable.

Before the concert in the Gran Palace tonight, there is a party at Ambassador Korry's residence. Most of the cats in the band are trying to catch up on their sleep, so only Russell Procope and Stanley Dance accompany me. The British ambassador is there, and he is very much interested in what we do, so I promise to play "The Single Petal of a Rose," the piece I dedicated to H.M. Queen Elizabeth after I was presented to her at the Leeds Festival in 1958.

Both Santiago concerts are sold out, and at the second I am given two handsome trophies by the local jazz societies. Originally we were to fly home from here, but because of our success in Buenos Aires we are to go back there for a farewell concert in the Gran Rex at ten thirty Sunday morning. I seem to be leaving a lot of unfinished business in Chile, because there is just no time to see Portillo, the huge ski resort, or Viña del Mar, the country's own Côte d'Azur, or the great statue that speaks for friendship between Chile and Argentina and is known as *Christ of the Andes*. Johnny Hodges is sick, and we have to leave him behind when we quit the Hotel Crillon at 4 A.M.

The Gran Rex is packed again, and many people in the audience have been to every one of our concerts. Knowing this, we had rehearsed *Harlem* in Santiago, and this extended work comes as a complete surprise to them. I think they will never let us off. The stage door opens right into the lobby, and there is this tremendous crowd of people who have been to the concert waiting to say goodbye, farewell, good luck, sweet kisses, and God bless you. There are tears in their eyes, and there are tears in mine as well. I am deeply moved. I hate to say goodbye to Señor Szterenfeld, too. His warmth, his unfailing courtesy, the happy experiences he has exposed us to, the high level at which he has presented us, and his constant care and attention, have made a big impression on us all. Long live the Master Impresario, Alejandro Szterenfeld!

Our trip home on Avianca, the Colombian airline, is nevertheless very enjoyable and a wonderful experience, because we stop at Santiago, Lima, Quito, and Bogotá. We have time to get off at each place and go into the airport for shopping and souvenirs. Altogether, it is a fascinating day: when not airport-shopping, we are flying and being served hors d'oeuvres and drinks, so it gets to seem like an endless sequence of food, drink, stop and shop, food, drink,

354

stop and shop . . . But we also see some fantastic scenery when we are not above cloud, and my imagination is caught by what I read of Peru, a country where Inca and Spanish civilizations met head on. There is amazing irony and paradox here. Some of the heights we can fly over so easily are formidable. Lake Titicaca is the highest navigable lake in the world, and Cuzco, the old central city of the Inca Empire, is over eleven thousand feet above sea level. And they have a standard gauge railway which operates nearly seventeen thousand feet up. Passengers on it often require oxygen! Thank goodness we don't have to blow in any of these places!

From Lima, we proceed to Quito, the capital of Ecuador, where the Andes split into two ranges and divide the country into three distinct regions. Now I think I have seen everything.

Between Quito and Bogotá, we cross the equator and are given impressive, ornamented certificates to prove it when we get home. The language they are written in makes us feel like V.I.P.'s. The message on the certificate begins like this:

"Desde la ilímite immensidad del firmamento, bajo los auspicios de Júpiter, rey de los cielos y de los infinitos cosmos, y en posesión plena de sus inconmensurables poderes certificamos que . . ." And so on.

Bogotá is often spoken of as "the Athens of South America," and it has been a cultural center since the time of the Spanish viceroys. It has so many cathedrals and churches that it was a logical place for Pope Paul to come on his tour, which was just a little ahead of ours.

From Bogotá, we take a plane direct to Miami, where Harry Carney and I enjoy the luxury of the Frank Sinatra Suite in the Fontainebleau Hotel.

After a brief interval in Nassau and the U.S., we are back at Kennedy Airport for our departure to Mexico on September 23.

Mexican Journal, 1968

Our visit coincides with the 1968 Olympic Games, and we are to contribute to what are termed the Cultural Olympics. Mexico City is *en fête*. Athletes are arriving at the same time as we are, but there seems to be considerable interest in us, too. We have just time to check into the hotel before leaving for an evening concert at Puebla, several hours away. My hotel is the María Isabel on the attractive Paseo de la Reforma, which reminds me a little of Paris. I am shown a suite which has a large crack like a cubist design on the wall facing the bed, the result of a recent earthquake. Another suite I look at is a duplex with a long and gracious staircase leading to the bedroom. I love it, but I don't need those extra steps with our tight schedule—and at such an altitude. Finally, I settle for a charming little suite with a wonderful and price-less attraction: a king-size bed.

We don't see much of Puebla, because it is dark when we get there and still dark when we get back to Mexico City, but we see enough to appreciate that is is very old and very Spanish.

The next night we play in Tequesquitengo, in an ancient building that is now a first-class hotel. It was originally established by Hernán Cortés in the sixteenth century, and it is so very picturesque that it is ideally suited to the needs of the film crew that is accompanying us throughout Mexico. The guests evidently find nothing incongruous in the contrast between our music and the architecture, and I try out sections of *The Latin-American Suite* on them. Originally, this was to have been entitled *Mexicanticipación*, because I had promised to premiere a new work in Mexico City. Our experiences in South America inevitably led to its expansion, and one of its main themes, *Latin-American Sunshine,* is applicable to all the countries we visited.

The bus is taking the band through the mountains to Acapulco, and by the time our performance is over it seems easier to go that way than to return to

Mexico City and fly to Acapulco next day, as I had intended. So I assume my navigator's seat at the front of the bus, and we have an interesting ride. It rains in the mountains and I am thankful we have such a good driver, because he also has to reckon with all kinds of animals—domestic and otherwise—who are making use of the road at night. When dawn breaks, we find ourselves in what seems to be another country, so different is the landscape. On arriving at the luxurious Hilton Hotel, the newer members of the party are excited by the sight of the sea and beach, but the others—more experienced—head for their beds first. One of the "activities" here is flying around the bay on a parachute towed by a motorboat. Sitting comfortably on my veranda, I see various wealthy and courageous members of the band go whirling past, such as Chuck Connors and Jeff Castleman, and the two vocalists, Trish Turner and Tony Watkins.

We play a concert-dance in the hotel ballroom, and it is a very happy affair. The Mayor of Acapulco honors us with his presence, and Ava Gardner brings a party. She seems as pleased to see us again as we are to see her, and she captivates everybody with her kindness and naturalness.

Early in the morning of the twenty-sixth, we leave for Guadalajara, the second largest city in the country, and there I am met by two delightful señoras who have been appointed, along with a bunch of college girls, to act as our guides and escorts. I find another incredible suite, another king-size bed, and an appetizing collection of lush fruit in a handsome native basket awaiting me at the Guadalajara Hilton. Nearby is the small town of Tequila, and by now I have had several introductions to the national liquor, so that I can take it with salt and lemon and not grimace too shamefully. We play two concerts in a splendid old theatre, and what makes them memorable is a superb, well-tuned piano. There is much enthusiasm here, and Guadalajara impresses as an alert, musical town.

We leave early in the morning for Mérida, Yucatán, with a stop en route in Mexico City, where the band is transposed—in some instances decanted—into two elderly DC-3s. It is a long flight, mostly over the sea, and by the time the instruments and baggage arrive we are already late for our concert in a ballpark. Our appearance, more or less *au naturel,* in traveling clothes, is not very impressive, and both the piano and the sound system leave much to be desired. I have the feeling that the audience has not had much experience of our idiom, but the people seemed intrigued and we get a courteous round of applause—for effort?

Afterwards, we play at an elegant country club outside the city. An original and musicianly rock group plays for dancing, and we observe a fascinating dance quite new to us. The audience is sophisticated and our sets turn into concerts, with the customers crowding all around the bandstand.

One of the tantalizing things about our tours is the frequency with which we find ourselves in interesting places with no opportunity to see or experience what makes them interesting. The mystery of the great Mayan civilization has always intrigued me, and this nonsightseer would genuinely have liked to have viewed the ruins at Chichén-Itzá and Uxmal. As it is, we recognize that Mérida has a character unlike the other Mexican cities we have seen, but early next morning (the twenty-eighth) we are back once more at the airport. A special flight is organized for us. All of us will return to Mexico City on one of the sturdy DC-3s that brought us. There is considerable delay, but this is not unfortunate, because everybody seems hungry and thirsty. I don't often enjoy filet mignon this early in the day, but I am ready for it and find it delicious with the excellent local beer. By this time we all have sombreros and rebozos, and as we sit down in the restaurant you might think a new Pancho Villa and his men had come to town. Even Johnny Hodges approves the cook and his kitchen, and spirits rapidly improve. Downstairs, after the meal, I find myself competing with Willie Cook, Harold Ashby, and Paul Gonsalves at the souvenir counter. Beautiful cats, but hard bargainers!

We get back to Mexico City in time to give two concerts at the Palacio de Bellas Artes, where *Mexicanticipación,* alias *The Latin-American Suite,* is enthusiastically received, especially the section written in honor of the two snowcapped volcanic peaks that tower over the city. Their names are Popo-catepetl and Ixtacihuatl, but I am not one to court disaster unnecessarily and don't wish to risk pronouncing those words, so my fairy-tale title is *The Sleeping Lady and the Giant Who Watches Over Her.* We are beautifully introduced by a gentleman who is reputedly a descendant of the Aztec emperor Moctezuma. After hearing his Spanish, Mercer and I determine to acquire a working knowledge of that melodious language before our next visit, but I wonder if we shall have time?

The next morning, we play a concert in association with Eastern Airlines at the Aristos Hotel, where the band is staying. Despite the early hour, this goes off very well, partly because, as they enter, the cats see the lavish preparations for their refreshment afterwards. Some of Eastern's prettiest stewardesses inspire my presentation, and Ambassador Fulton Freeman steals our thunder when he borrows Lawrence Brown's horn to play "Stardust."

There are two more concerts that night at "popular" prices in the huge Auditorio Nacional, but meanwhile I have a brief opportunity to learn more about this extraordinary city. It is amazing to think that when Cortes descended upon the Aztecs with his Spaniards, horses, and guns, it was already a bigger city than London or Paris. I don't know when I first read the story of the conquest, but it always seemed a prime example of truth being stranger than fiction.

We make a quick trip to beautiful Chapultepec Park, gape at the castle there, briefly visit the marvelous museums of natural history and modern art, view the great cathedral in the Zocalo, and have just time to reach the floating gardens at Xochimilco. There are only a few larger cities in the world, and the Olympic Games and the new subway system have apparently inspired a new drive that is quite the opposite of the old *mañana* cliché. There is great pride in the stormy past in the work of artists like Diego Rivera and David Siqueiros, and in the astonishing mosaics at the university, but this is unquestionably a *Now* city.

I love everything, and as we leave I wave my sombrero to ever-watchful Popocatepetl. *Ole, ole! Viva Méjico!*

Walls

In order to have a category, one must build a wall, or two, or more. Walls go all the way back in history. Walls may be high or low, thick or thin. The dictionary says a wall is an upright structure that divides or encloses. The Red Fort in Delhi was thought to be impregnable when it was built in 1050, because of the wall around it. Then there are the Walls of Jericho, the Great Wall of China, and the wall the Romans built to keep the Scots out of England. The best known wall is the wall around which the world of gold revolves—Wall Street. There are walls in many places where the United States of America has sent dollars, and they have signs posted on them that read, GO HOME, YANKEE!

One of the truly great walls is the sea wall that the Dutch built to protect the land from the sea. It holds hope of more land, tomorrow. The amount of land they hope to reclaim in a hundred years is tremendous. The most necessary wall is one that protects you from your enemy. Unfortunately, the Maginot Line is a very modern example, and more recently the Berlin Wall was erected to separate opinion from differences of opinion. Harem walls protect beautiful gardens, beautiful fountains, and beautiful women from prying eyes. There is the wall a man puts his back to when outnumbered by his enemies, or when he faces the firing squad. There is the wall in the Bible that man pisseth against. But of all the walls, the tallest, most invisible, and most insidious, that according to some observers mars the image of our country, is the wall of prejudice.

Did God ever build a wall?

Then there are the walls of prisons, the walls that enclose nuns, and even children build walls with blocks while playing and having fun. One must beware of the wall one talks to hoping for an affirmative answer to the question, "Mirror, mirror, on the wall, who is the fairest of them all?"

For the public, the wall may bear news that is good or bad, prohibitions or information. Walls often divide the nobility from the commoner. The fortress beyond the moat relies on walls for its ultimate defense. There is a wall around the ghetto, and, surprisingly enough, there is often a wall around the cathedral. Some walls crumble, and others, like the sound barrier, are burst asunder. There is the wall of love that Romeo climbed to Juliet, and there is the Wailing Wall in Jerusalem.

But did God ever build a wall?

Prague Journal, 1969

When we go to Czechoslovakia in 1969, we are received in Prague with much acclaim. The people are very hospitable and the audiences sensitive. Our performances are enthusiastically applauded, and there are persistent demands for encores.

After the concert and the autograph routine, I go back to the hotel, and there in the lobby is one of our principal ambassadors, Paul Gonsalves, surrounded by a group of ten or a dozen people. The enthusiasm is such that the front desk has all the appearance of a bar. As I pass by on my way up to my room, Paul calls, "Hey, there goes Duke!" The crowd then begins to disperse, and I find about eight people have attached themselves to me. They follow me upstairs and right into the sitting room.

There is silence, not a word spoken, until I say something like "Hi!" They respond with their equivalent, and then one young man hands me a beautiful porcelain deer. I think maybe he wants it autographed, and I begin looking for a place to do that. Then an interpreter, with gestures but no words, makes me understand that it is a present to me from the young man. He likes me; he approves of what we have done this evening. Then the others in turn come out with their presents, beautiful porcelain objects, all except one, a girl, who explains in mime that she doesn't have anything. But wait! She dashes out the door and up a flight of stairs, and rushes back with something for me. It is a hunting knife. I am truly overwhelmed, and I thank them as best I can. They bow graciously, but say nothing.

Finally, I make them understand that I would like to have their names and addresses so that I can at least send them a Christmas card. They dig this and start writing. All the addresses have "U.S.S.R." at the bottom.

"What country is this?" I ask.

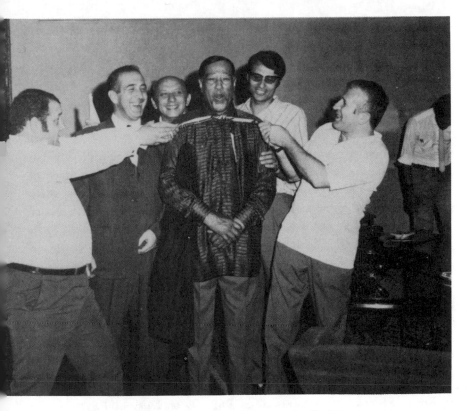

With Yugoslav jazz musicians in Belgrade, July 1970

They look at each other until I break the silence again by saying, "You mean Russia?"

"*Da, da!*" they exclaim in unison.

I feel so good, just to think that these kids from Russia know about us. I spend the next half hour talking, pantomiming compliments and good wishes. They make it known that they too are musicians, all playing in a special company. They tell me who plays what, and the girl sings and plays guitar for us. It is a pleasurable and informative encounter. They want to know why we have not been to Russia, and I explain it is only because we have not been invited. "Please fix it," I say.

Next day, when I see Paul Gonsalves on the plane, he says, "Hey, Maestro, when are we going to Russia? Beautiful cats, man!"

Russian Journal, 1971

The anticipation of our tour of Russia in 1971 is so great that there is a risk of being consumed by it. Russian music in all its endlessness is too much to contemplate, so I simply try to relax, and wait to see and hear. But all those famous names are in my mind: Tchaikovsky, Rimsky-Korsakov (the master of orchestration), Glinka, Borodin, Mussorgsky, Glazunov, Scriabin, Rachmaninoff, Prokofiev, Khachaturian and Shostakovich, not forgetting, of course, Stravinsky. On and on and on and on . . . I am going to breathe the same kind of air all those great composers breathed. And then there was Vladimir Dukelsky who, as Vernon Duke, wrote two songs that were great favorites of Billy Strayhorn's and mine: "April in Paris," which I first heard in 1933, when Mabel Mercer sang it in Bricktop's club on the Place Pigalle; and "I Can't Get Started," which Harold Ashby has played since he joined us.

Before leaving New York, Brooks Kerr teaches me how to say "Love you madly," how to count up to ten, say "Thank you" and "You are welcome" in Russian. Brooks is a twenty-year-old authority on Duke Ellington—all the way back—and his enthusiasm is such that in 1970 his mother sent him with us to make the European tour. He has not missed a single New York performance in four years.

One hour after our arrival in Moscow we are guests of the Bolshoi Ballet. It is the young troupe—it is wonderful. Next day when we eventually arrive in Leningrad, we are met by a big band that marches across the airfield toward us playing Dixieland jazz, with trombones sliding, clarinets smearing off, and all the musicians blowing in the traditional manner.

We have a very full but hospitable schedule in Leningrad. At the Friendship House, we see a film about the city's nine-hundred-day siege during World War II. Besides the heroism and the horrors, it shows Shostakovich

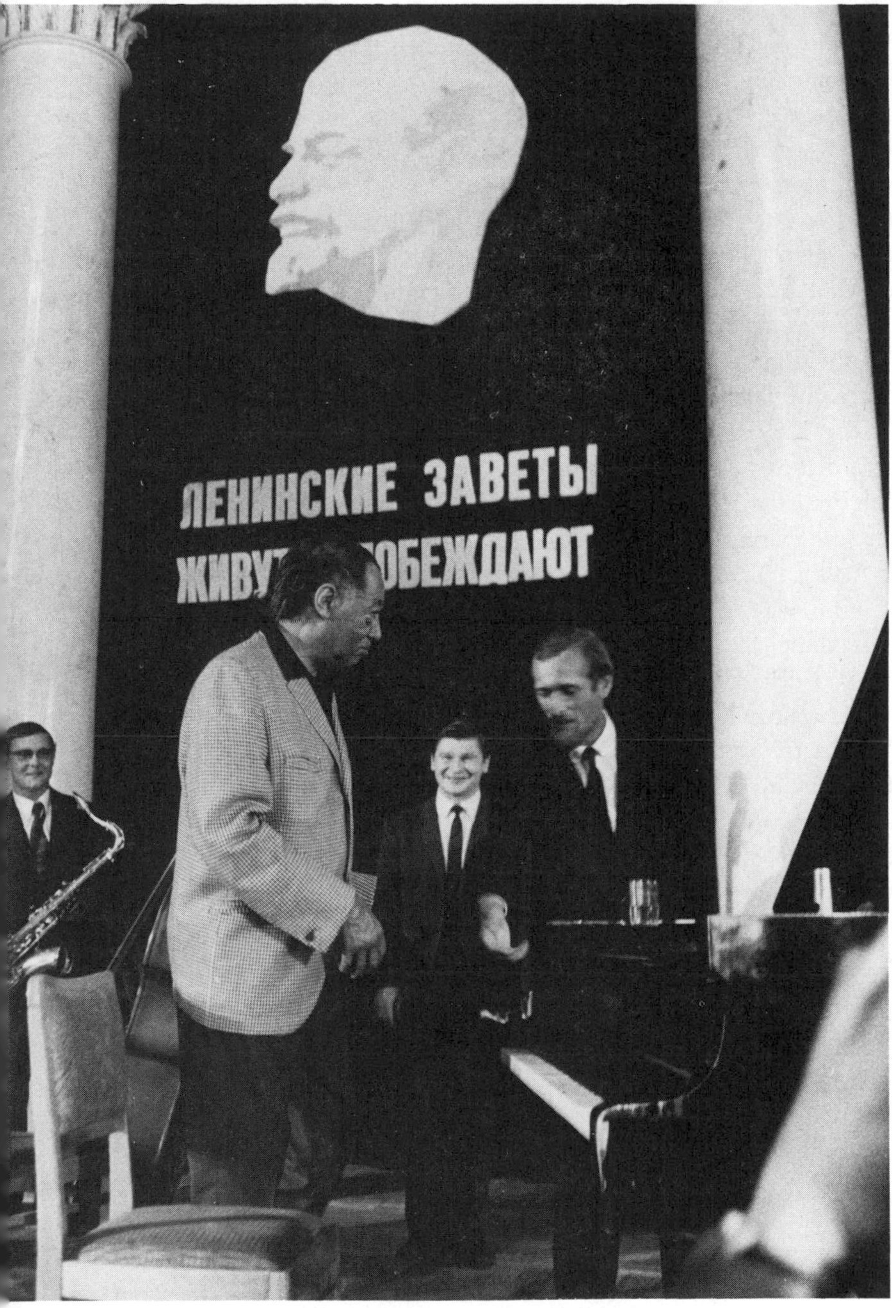
ЛЕНИНСКИЕ ЗАВЕТЫ

composing his *Leningrad* Symphony. It is all very moving, especially since we can see in the city the work of restoration that has been achieved and is still continuing.

We are invited to attend a performance in the lovely little Kirov Theatre. It seats a mere three or four hundred people—in comfortable armchairs! The stage, however, is full-size, and we see an act from an opera by Rachmaninoff based on one of Pushkin's poems. It is so skillfully and sensitively done that, although we don't understand the language, we can follow the story easily enough. After that there is a fine ballet performance of Rimsky-Korsakov's *Scheherezade*. The people who manipulate the net to depict the sea in motion do it with such artistry that it is completely believable. The theatre's director is extremely kind and personally conducts us on a tour of the building.

The U.S. consulate is in Leningrad, which, as the westernmost city, is regarded as a "window to the West." (Similarly, Russia has a consulate in San Francisco.) About fifty prominent business leaders from the San Francisco area are touring Russia at this time, and I am invited to a reception for them at Astoria House, where Consul Culver Gleysteen has his residence. The consul and his wife, Elizabeth—not forgetting their friendly dogs—could not be more hospitable. There is a superb buffet with a marvelous selection of Russian delicacies. Some of the businessmen, including Cyril Magnin, come to our concert that night, but because it is completely sold out, they have to catch it from backstage. I feel very much honored that Ambassador Jacob Beam and his wife have flown up from Moscow specially for it.

We visit the Hermitage, which is said to contain eighteen thousand paintings, many of them owned by Russian aristocrats before the Revolution. I really welcome this opportunity to see firsthand the work of Impressionists like Corot, Daubigny, Manet, Monet, Degas, Renoir, Rodin, Signac, Sisley, Cézanne, and Pissarro, as well as such post-Impressionists as Gauguin, Marquet, Matisse, Vuillard, Rousseau, Van Gogh, and Van Dongen. I am also impressed by the craftmanship and subjects of some of the eighteenth-century painters like Greuze, Restout, Detroy, and Vernet. War was evidently still regarded as a rather glorious adventure in their day. However, the biggest surprise, to me, is Picasso's pre-Cubistic "The Rendezvous" from 1902, in which the technique is so very much unlike what we now associate with him.

We are invited to visit a clandestine club called the White Nights, and after our concert—and supper—we decide to look in there. On arrival, we

At the Hermitage, Leningrad, 1971

find about five hundred people packed into a room that was probably intended to hold a hundred. Paul Gonsalves, that roving plenipotentiary, is already on the stand dispensing his special brand of good will. The enthusiasm is simply tremendous and we are literally crushed with love.

Before leaving Leningrad, I also see one of the greatest vaudeville shows I have ever seen, as well as a circus in which the bears are absolutely wonderful.

There is a visit to the Friendship House in each city we visit. In Kiev, I meet the Ukrainian composer Andriy Shtokavenko, at the Composers' Union. The Palace of Sports, where we play in that city, holds ten thousand people at each of our three concerts (September 28, 29, and 30). At one of these, I ask about the unusual number of police present, and am told they are all members of the police band!

In Minsk, we keep getting requests for "When the Saints Go Marching In," in memory of Louis Armstrong. Now "The Saints" is a legitimate hymn to play at the right time, in the right place, and for many years I have refused to rag it up. What we do instead is to have Money Johnson play and sing "Hello, Dolly!" in the Armstrong manner, and the audiences are delighted with that.

Two extra concerts are put on at the last minute in Moscow in the twelve-thousand-seat Luzhniki Sports Palace to accommodate some of the many Muscovites who have previously been unable to get tickets. In effect, the halls are sold out before ever the tickets go on sale, and there is a black market in tickets, some being sold for as much as fifty rubles each (over fifty dollars).

An article in *Pravda* by M. Davydov describes the band as "an orchestra of virtuosos." He admires what he calls its "priceless sense of ease," and likes the way the musicians make their entry on stage. "They walk on without any special ceremony, simply, one by one," he writes. "Like friends usually gather together for a jam session." He makes other perceptive comments, all of which go to show the importance of never underestimating your audience. Of course, aspects of a performance that might be taken for granted at home often take on a new significance abroad.

We attend a performance of the Bolshoi Ballet in the Kremlin at the Palace of Congress, an auditorium used for meetings of the Communist Party. The Vienna Philharmonic Orchestra was being presented in the Bolshoi's own theatre. All the auditoriums in Russia seem to be of modern design, and much

Jam Session in the U.S.S.R., 1971

attention has been paid to getting good acoustics. The stage people always know their job, and we always feel we are in the hands of professionals.

At one of Ambassador Beam's receptions, I am delighted to meet Aram Khachaturian. The conductor of the Radio Moscow Jazz Orchestra is also there, and he asks me to attend a special performance next morning at eleven. When I explain through the interpreter that this is much too early for me, his eyes seem about to fill with tears as he explains how important my presence is to him and his people. So we compromise and agree to meet at one o'clock! When I arrive at the hall in the radio station, there he is with his twenty-piece band all ready to go. They are great players, and at the end they ask me to conduct and play in "Take the 'A' Train." The hall is full of musicians and their friends who have come to witness my reaction to what they consider their best jazz orchestra. It is here, too, that I meet Dmitri Shostakovich's son. Speaking in English, he brings greetings from his father, who, unfortunately, is in the hospital and not near enough for me to visit.

Another moving occasion in Moscow is our presentation of the Sacred Concert at the request of the Reverend Doctor Sanford, the Protestant chaplain at our embassy. He makes all the arrangements for the performance in the ballroom of Spaso House, and is much responsible for getting together the choir from among members of the embassy staff and their families. Tony Watkins does a remarkable job at short notice in rehearsing the choir, selecting soloists, and taking over a lot of the roles himself. Only about two hundred guests are present—mostly diplomats from the West, Africa, and Canada, as well as our own—and momentarily the ballroom is a little oasis for the religious-minded.

Everywhere we go we are loaded down with presents. (Eventually, I send home three trunks full of them.) They give us beautiful ornaments of porcelain, pictures, paintings, sculpture, books, records, and heaps of badges and picture pins that you wear in your lapel. There are hundreds of excellent pictures of us in action in Leningrad, Minsk, Kiev, Rostov, and Moscow, the five cities where we play. I am even presented with a hockey stick on which an inscribed silver plate indicates that I am a member of the Soviet Hockey Team! But I am not permitted the opportunity to use it. I guess they feel they could not afford to put the physical condition of their favorite stars in jeopardy by actually exposing them to my play.

The audiences are incredibly responsive to everything we do, and musicians come from all the Soviet republics, from Latvia and even, we are told, from Mongolia and Siberia. I am asked many times what I think of the public in the U.S.S.R., and my answer is usually something like this:

The public in Russia or anywhere else is busy pursuing what it thinks it will enjoy, and I am doing the same thing. Whether or not we will converge in agreement is something I do not know, but when audiences, one after the other—*all* that we play to here—keep paying their admission fees and coming to hear us, I am inclined to believe they know who they want and expect to hear. Moreover, any audience that spends three or four hours listening to us— well, that audience is not to be considered the public—they are our friends. Here no one ever moves from his or her seat until the entire concert and all the encores have been played. That impresses me very much. The enthusiasm

Receiving presents at the Composers' Union in Kiev, 1971

With Paul Gonsalves (left) and Harold Ashby (right) in Moscow, 1971

is such, and the demand for encores so insistent, that some concerts run *over* four hours. Yet no one complains—not the audience, not the stagehands, and not even the cats in the band! The Russians come to hear our music, and for no other reason. Some are satisfied, and some are surprised how much they are satisfied.

They come prepared for our version of "Caravan," which has long been a favorite in Russia, but not, I think, for our extended composition *Harlem*. After we have gone through the regular program, and are into the encores, and they are thinking they have heard all the band's stars, then I feature two of its new members, Johnny Coles on flügelhorn and Harold Minerve on

Duke Ellington with his Russian interpreters, 1971

alto saxophone, who never fail to excite them. I finish every performance by playing Billy Strayhorn's "Lotus Blossom," and that also is always graciously received. It seems to leave the audience suspended in euphoria, or beyond.

Someone in Washington working for the opposition, who thinks he will irritate the Russians so that I have an unpleasant visit, prints and spreads a rumor that I am unhappy with the food and am losing weight. It is rumor that does no harm at all. In fact, I gain ten pounds while in Russia. I am very, very partial to caviar, and I discover a lot of satisfying combinations with the borscht. I also teach the chefs to make cheeseburgers. They make them successfully, too, but in their enthusiasm they make them so big that I always have to put part of them in my "doggie bag."

Room service sends me a large tureen of borscht and individual soup plates. With the borscht are dishes of rice, carrots, peas, and beets, all of which I dump into the tureen. Pushing the soup plates aside, and grasping the cheeseburger in my left hand as bread, I dip the ladle into the tureen and stuff, stuff, stuff . . .

When we eventually leave Russia, we feel we are leaving a lot of friends, and a lot of people who made the tour both possible and pleasant. On the Russian side, I should mention the Soviet Minister of Culture, Mrs. Yekaterina Furtseva; the Deputy Director of Goskontsert, Vladimir Golovin, the man probably most responsible for our going; and the representative from Goskontsert who accompanies us, Ivan Nikolaevitch Marteshevskii, along with the indispensable interpreters, Voldya, Mila, Tanya, and Natasha. On the American side there are the Cultural Counselor, Andy Falkiewiez, and his assistant, Marlin Remick. Guiding and reassuring us all the way are Joe Presel and two embassy officers, Woody Demitz and Mike Hoffman. We owe them all a huge debt of gratitude.

Our exploits have evidently not gone unnoticed at home, either, because I receive congratulatory letters from both President Richard Nixon and Senator Hubert Humphrey.

It is said that this is the first time that *Pravda* has ever acknowledged the presence of an American artist in the U.S.S.R.

Latin American Journal, 1971

After our five-week tour of Russia in 1971, we play a month of concerts in Europe, a different city every night, usually a different country, with trips across the Iron Curtain to Warsaw, Belgrade, Budapest, Sofia, and Bucharest. Although the weather in England in the middle of October is beautiful and springlike, by the time we finish we have run into ice and snow in Oslo and places like that, as well as a lot of fog.

We leave Spain on November 15 for Rio de Janeiro, and when we arrive there we are all thoroughly appreciative of the warmth and sunshine. On the 1968 tour, we had very little time in that city, but now we have three days to savor it, the music, and the people. Everything lives up to our expectations.

We are back once more with Impresario Szterenfeld, and this time the tour will be longer, because in certain cases the U. S. State Department is taking us to cities and countries where it was not economically feasible before.

After Rio, we have two days in São Paolo, where the enthusiasm is as great as before. Our visit coincides with a kind of music gala presented by the local musicians' union. All kinds of fine bands are playing there and, as guests of honor, all the cats in the band and I get silver plaques inscribed with our names. Nobody gets much sleep the last night, but we have to leave early in the morning because the State Department wants us in Montevideo.

A hard-fought presidential election is in its final week when we get there. The chief of police insists on my having a bodyguard at all times, and they never leave me till I get on the plane the next morning. The main avenue, 18 de Julio, was blocked off just the night before for a rally of about fifteen thousand people, but for our concert on November 21 they forget politics and jam the big Palacio Penarol in downtown Montevideo. The applause is thunderous, and encores—among them, at the crowd's insistence, "Stormy Weather"—prolong the concert over three hours.

375

The reception for our three concerts in Buenos Aires is just as warm as in 1968, and it is a real pleasure to meet again the friends we made then. The changes in the personnel and the program have obviously been the subject beforehand of conjecture by the critical element, but we seem to satisfy it. In fact, there is a suggestion in the press that next time we should play in the Teatro Colón, which is reputed to be the world's largest opera house.

On the twenty-fifth, we are in Mendoza, a city in western Argentina, in the foothills of the Andes, where we have not been before. The venue is the Estadio Pacífico. From there we go to Santiago in Chile, which Premier Fidel Castro is also visiting, but so far as we know he is not in our large, receptive audience.

After that, we are in Lima, Quito, Bogotá, and Caracas, where again we had not previously played. We have three days in the last city, days that are supposed to enable everyone to catch up on sleep, laundry, and other matters in arrears, but from my observations the guys seem to be busy having a good time.

Before we get to Mexico City on December 7, we play in three other hospitable cities new to us—Panamá, San José, and Managua. Between two concerts in Mexico City, we double back to perform in San Salvador's new Teatro Presidente, right behind a touring Russian ballet that had followed us in Mexico. Finally, on December 10, we make our farewells to Latin America in Guadalajara and fly out early in the morning for an engagement in Chicago.

As in 1968 the friendship and hospitality of our embassy officials help make the tour enjoyable. They seem pleased to see us, too, and I know that the musicians are always grateful for an opportunity to get some familiar food and cigarettes. Some of the embassy reports that I see later are very gratifying to me personally. These are excerpts from one concerned with the concert in Quito, Ecuador:

"Prior to the concert we had mixed feelings about the receptivity of the Quito public to Duke Ellington's music. To many under the age of forty, he was virtually unknown. We also had the competition of a Russian circus during the week prior to and up to the night of the concert.

"The theatre was almost filled to capacity, and audience reaction was extremely enthusiastic. A writer in the morning daily *El Comercio* summed it up as follows:

"'The sharp and brilliant sound which has given Ellington renown as a musical innovator was applauded from the beginning . . . Ellington achieved once again a long-awaited contact with the public, penetrating profoundly with his improvisations and mastery.' "

The excitement in Costa Rica is described in these quotations from the San José embassy's report:

"In the midst of a seeming Russian cultural offensive in Costa Rica, and during the tremendous public furor over the establishment of a Russian embassy here, the triumphal appearance of Duke Ellington in San José served as a fine counterpoint. Ellington performed before a capacity audience of five thousand persons in the National Gymnasium in a concert sponsored by the Costa Rican Ministry of Culture.

"The audience included the American Ambassador, Walter C. Ploeser, and the Costa Rican Minister of Culture, Alberto Cañas. Such favorites as 'Take the "A" Train,' 'Creole Love Call,' and 'Solitude' were greeted by prolonged applause. The Ellington composition 'Satin Doll' received thunderous applause after only the first three bars.

"The Minister of Culture . . . when interviewed on the VOA declared, 'We never believed it would be such a great success. We knew how good the artist was, but we were afraid he wouldn't be very well known by the Costa Ricans.' "

The report from the embassy in Nicaragua contained more good news:

"The Duke Ellington orchestra was a resounding success in its two Managua concerts. The 1215-seat Rubén Darío National Theatre was completely sold out December 5 and 6. The audience both nights was responsive and enthusiastic to the first appearance in Nicaragua of a U.S. jazz orchestra.

"In a reception offered by U. S. Ambassador and Mrs. Turner B. Shelton following the opening night's performance, Mr. Ellington and members of his orchestra delighted guests with their warmth and personality. Some three hundred people attended the reception including President and Mrs. Somoza, Nicaraguan intellectuals and press, businessmen and bankers, diplomats and government officials.

"The impact of Duke Ellington's performance in Nicaragua cannot be overstated. While many in Nicaragua have only a limited exposure to jazz, and feel more comfortable with classical and popular music, all were impressed by the artistry of the performance and touched by the magnetism of 'The Duke.' Nicaraguans seem to understand a little bit better what U.S. culture is all about . . . that we're something 'alive and now.' "

377

Although it is our second visit to Buenos Aires, the content of the embassy report from there is just as pleasing:

"To no one's surprise the Ellington band, and Ellington himself, took Buenos Aires by storm. At the conclusion of each concert the applause approached bedlam, to which the Duke responded with lengthy encores.

"Critical appraisal was enthusiastically favorable. Most opinion, including that of the audiences, is best summed up in the November 24, 1971, issue of *Clarin* that there was in the theater 'a current of human communication which was in the end converted into a reality almost esthetic in nature.'

"Ambassador Lodge gave a reception for Ellington to which four hundred people came, an unusually high turnout, and further indication of Ellington's drawing power. During the reception Mr. Ellington . . . played a number of tunes, and both vocalists performed with him."

The embassy parties are usually at the end of our day, but the press conferences are often early in the morning, and in Latin America they are very important, because the newspapers have not been overwhelmed by the other news media to the same extent. Sometimes, when one is tired and eager to get to bed, it is hard to avoid a little asperity in the replies, but then again one is often asked questions that have been asked hundreds of times before, which makes the task relatively easy. Nevertheless, I often look at the newspapers a little nervously next day, especially at those big headlines, to see if I have said anything I ought not to have done. I especially remember the menacing appearance of a couple one morning in Caracas:

LOS TENDENCIAS TIENEN QUE VER CON EL DINERO, NO CON LA MÚSICA.

NO ES ARTE LO QUE SE HACE SIN INTENCIÓN.

But all is well. What I have said is, "Trends have more to do with money than with music," and "There is no art when one does something without intention." I phrase the second better when the same question arises again: "There is no such thing as accidental art."

Some more of my spur-of-the-moment, early morning responses to interviewers in São Paolo and Buenos Aires as well as Caracas are:

"What do I think of Latin America? It has an endless beauty—and that would make a good song title!"

"I don't pursue anything. The only thing I always answer is my own impulse."

"I don't believe in categories of any kind, and when you speak of problems between black and white in the U.S.A. you are referring to categories again.

I don't believe there is anybody in the world who has no problem. The person who has no problem has a very dull life."

"When we give our sacred concerts, we feel we are praying—in our language."

"Anyone who knows my music and knows how to interpret it, is not ignorant of the extent I have contributed to the cause of the advancement of colored people. Much of my work is inspired by this objective. There is no contradiction between the music of my first 'period' and what I am doing now. It is all the music of Duke Ellington, so there cannot be a difference."

"To ask whether jazz is music for dancing is to introduce a category or classification I resist, but I would say that our music is intended to inspire or sustain dancing."

"The Buenos Aires audience? It gave me one of the great emotional experiences of my life. At the conclusion of the last concert in Argentina in 1968, instead of sending me off with a farewell, the public begged me to return. I can only attribute what you call the 'incredible communication' to the fact that, as my parents told me, I was blessed."

"I don't get homesick. I feel at home when I'm happy, and it doesn't make any difference whether it is here or there. In any case, I spend a great part of the time traveling outside the United States."

"It's a long time since I did any painting, although I always promise myself to return to it. I've bought brushes and painting materials, but I haven't done anything for many years. It's a pity, because this was my real talent. I should have developed it. As a designer I would at least have been considered average. And, of course, there is a direct mental relationship between design and music, for much of both is theatre. They communicate what it is not necessary to *say*. Anyone can walk on stage and say a few words, but to say these things without using words is the ultimate in theatre. When you ask if everything is theatre for me, whether my life is theatre, I can only reply that my aim in life is to obtain *balance*."

"Last year, after I composed the music for the ballet *The River,* a lady came up with a great idea: that I should use the theme of the ballet as the motif for a children's painting book. All that was needed was for me to sit down and paint. We talked a lot about it, but nothing happened."

"I originally began to compose because I wasn't able to play what other composers wrote, so I had to create something that I could play. I remain a primitive artist, extremely primitive. But paradoxically the most sophisticated

379

music in the world is primitive music, and no one is able to penetrate it easily."

" 'The multidirectional facets of simpatico'—that's an attractive phrase, but the word 'simpatico' already says everything. Everything else is superfluous. You don't need the facets to understand the *feeling* of simpatico."

"Yes, anyone can play in my band, so long as he produces sounds which I like!"

"How do I judge my music? The title of my book answers the question: *Music Is My Mistress.* I maintain very happy relations, from many points of view, with my mistress. There are times when she herself provides the sound; at others, she waits for my echo."

Pacific Journal, 1972

When we set out for the Orient once more, early in 1972, we first tour Japan for two weeks—no days off—and are everywhere received with flowers and standing ovations. I am a little apprehensive when I find Taipei on the itinerary, for Taiwan has so recently been replaced in the United Nations, but they are very civilized people there and the whole visit goes along as smoothly as our first.

Most travelers collect little souvenirs from the hotels they stay in, such as matches, shower caps, plastic laundry bags, Japanese shoehorns, stationery, and maybe even washclothes. Sometimes they may go so far as to take one of these long and most instructive books you find in Copenhagen hotels, books that have all the questions and all the answers in all the languages. Temptation nearly smothers me in Taipei, where I stay in an ultramodern, American-styled, skyscraper hotel. The stationery is in a luxurious, expensive-looking, red-and-gold cover with extra special binding. I want it desperately, and eventually I take it down to the desk and ask the clerk to sell it to me. He, of course, insists that I take it with the hotel's compliments.

The return to Manila is made in a great glow of expectancy derived from the pleasure of a seventeen-hour beauty sleep I had on our first visit. It is hot but breezy when we arrive. A tall girl dressed in sheer muslin presents me with a beautiful garland of fresh jasmine that feels delightfully cool and refreshing to the neck. During the long ride beside the sea to the hotel, a lot of small buildings are pointed out to me. They are supposed to be nightclubs, but they are really gambling joints, where dice, baccarat, girls, and anything goes. I am told they are regularly but vainly raided, because they have backdoors, sidedoors, trapdoors—every kind of door you can imagine.

The general manager welcomes me to the Bayview Hotel with the utmost graciousness and then conducts me to a truly de luxe suite. The bedroom is done in plush red velvet! I have to make up the king-size bed the way I want it, because the Philippine boy, with the best will in the world, ruins it daily. Finally, I have to tell him not to touch it. In all three rooms of the suite, too, there are huge baskets of tropical fruits. I give them all to Harold Ashby, who is currently on his fruit diet. The suite has enormous windows from which I can see gray ships silhouetted on the silky sea like huge whales. Strangely enough, there are two prints on the walls of Mexican market scenes by my brother of Goutelas, Bernard Cathelin. The very same ones, bearing his auto-graphed dedications, hang in my rooms in New York.

The room service is beyond all, and I can order hot dishes twenty-four hours a day. I begin my Asian menu here with shrimp fried rice (and steak). When a superb piano is brought into the suite, it is tuned with great care under the general manager's watchful eye. It takes at least an hour, but he is determined that everything shall be perfect. He is wearing an embroi-dered *goyabera* that I admire very much. He summons the hotel tailor to bring me samples, and I order several for delivery next morning. Later, I find all the symphony musicians are wearing their gala uniforms—wonderful white *goyaberas* and white slacks.

This time, we are to play two concerts with the National Symphony Or-chestra conducted by Redentor Romero, who is a violinist and a brilliant musician. We, of course, are soon calling him "Red" Romero! The perform-ances are given in a brand-new arts center, a concrete masterpiece of the kind one finds in all the principal cities nowadays. There are a couple of re-hearsals, and at the actual performances I conduct *Harlem*. We also play "Non-Violent Integration" and conclude with *Night Creature.* One of the great moments occurs in the second movement of the last. On our record of it, there is a violin solo by Ray Nance, and Red Romero has memorized it, absolutely perfectly. For such a virtuoso as he is to do a retake on the original solo is really a magnificent compliment to Raymond.

Everything goes off well, the President comes to the second concert, and afterwards there is an important reception organized by a group of musicians who have a compatible band. I play a couple of tunes with them, but there is a piano player present, a young boy, who is so good that I am not at all particular about following him! However, his mother—an outstanding singer and a charming lady—insists that I do.

The day after we leave, the airport buildings in Manila are burned down and no international flights are possible. We are lucky to get out, because we might have been stranded there a couple of weeks. But then, who knows, I might have had time to finish another opera. (I have written several operas, a couple of ballets, and about ten shows, but what I have written and what has been performed is something else.)

In Hong Kong for twenty-four hours, we do not see one real, old-fashioned, traditional junk. Lots of motor-powered junks, yes, but not what I, who have seen so many films, consider the real McCoy. This again confirms the views of Marshall McLuhan which inspired our *Afro-Eurasian Eclipse*. The scene, however, with soaring skyscrapers—man's phallic symbols—on nature's voluptuous mountains, is breath-taking. The expected sights, sounds, and smells are encountered, but two things stay strongly in my mind. One is the jasmine tea, the other a very modern skyway to the ferry with an interchange like the Jersey Turnpike's. It is one of the most modern, modern; modern—modern! Modernissimo. All rather like New York.

The flight to Bangkok on Thai International Airlines is very enjoyable. We are served exotic fruits that are quite new to us. One especially, that you have to peel, has a sour, astringent, yet delightfully refreshing taste. The hostesses, dressed in tight skirts of Thai silk with brief tops, are all remarkably soft and feminine.

It is terribly hot when we arrive, and who do you think is the first person we see—none other than Maurice Rocco, an old friend. Mr. Voss, the executive manager of the Oriental Hotel, is there to welcome me. He is sorry not to be able to offer the sumptuous suite that is guarded by two huge Thai lions, but it is being renovated, and he has instead a lovely suite overlooking the Chao Phraya River with a balcony facing on to a green lawn. It reminds me of Venice. The river is the main artery, a road that divides the city, of which I get a splendid view when we have lunch on the hotel roof. I soon find that watching the long, fast boats passing by can easily lull you to sleep in the heat of the day.

The highspot of our visit is when we play for H.M. the King of Thailand. We have to be at the theatre an hour before the king arrives, and we find a couple of his generals backstage. At the end of the performance, we all go forward to the lobby. His Majesty comes down from his royal box and bestows an exquisite garland of flowers on me. (Although for weeks I make ingenious attempts to preserve it with the aid of ice water in cellophane bags and refrigerators, in the end it is impossible. So I make a drawing of it, which can be a good guide to its reproduction.) Then I introduce His Majesty to the musicians, one by one. Paul Gonsalves later claims the king gave him a very knowing look, because, when Paul was playing with Sabby Lewis in Boston, the king was at Harvard and would sometimes break off from his studies to go hear the band. That's a possible explanation, too, of why the king plays such good clarinet despite his many royal duties. His Majesty asked Harry Carney how long he had been with the Duke and of course Harry Carney answered him honestly, the king complimented Harry royally, and Harry accepted it regally. His Majesty is the Art Tatum of monarchs.

One of the essential things to see in Bangkok is the Emerald Buddha, whose ceremonial attire, I learn, is changed only by the king. The Buddha has four coats, all of cloth of gold: one for the rainy season, one for the dry season, one for winter, and one for summer.

On Sunday night, at the Oriental Hotel, they have the barbecue. It takes up the whole side of the hotel along the waterfront, and they burn incense or something like it on embers under the tables to keep away the flying monsters. The barbecue is cooked by impeccably dressed chefs, and you just go along with your tray and pick out what you want, and double back whenever you wish. They have everything you can possibly think of—lamb, pork chops, beef, ribs, chicken, ham, oysters, shrimps, salads, fresh vegetables, rich pastries . . . I think it is twenty-five years since I last ate pork chops, but it seems impossible to pass up anything, and you just stuff, stuff, stuff. Of course, with my bad habit, I ask Mr. Voss if it will be all right for me to use my doggie bag, just in case I get peckish during the night. He kindly wraps up a lot of different things for me. To complete the enjoyment of this al fresco feast, native dancers perform on the lawn while it is in progress.

The second day in Bangkok, we have off, and the cats in the band spend most of it around the pool, acting like so many beachcombers. I sit on the balcony till dusk, by which time everybody has gone off to the floating market, an astonishing fleet of small boats. They are paddled along most of the time by women in funny straw hats, and they contain a tremendous selection of fruit, flowers, vegetables, and fish. On each side of the river are huge boats that are secured to trees on the banks by thick ropes. Some are used as warehouses for grain, cement, etc. Some carrying sugar cane are very heavily loaded, and they are so low in the water that it is quite scary to look at them. Others are houseboats with one or two families on them. All have the Thai eye painted on their high prow to scare away bad spirits and to see the right course.

Thai houses are built of teak, that fine, strong wood, and on all of them there is a little white pagoda with red roof and gold ornamentation. This, too, is to scare away evil spirits. When you buy a Thai house, this seems to be the first thing you acquire. The bonzes come to chant prayers that will protect the house. There are lots of temples right on the river, and the bonzes, all dressed in orange, descend steps to the river to bathe and wash their clothes.

Everybody seems to bathe in the Chao Phraya, and yet people don't hesitate to drink the river water. Around six o'clock, they are busy brushing their teeth and combing their thick, shiny hair. Pretty, naked children paddle around like little ducks. The people are remarkably clean and they hang their washed clothes on the sides of the big houseboats.

There is a lot of life on that broad, ample river. It is rippled continuously by boats taking children to school, or those that are used in the same way as buses in New York to get from one point to another. Everybody is looking forward to seeing the big, warrior elephants from the North of Thai. They will give a performance on March 20, and I am sorry I shall not be here to see it.

After arriving in Rangoon from Bangkok, we change to a charter plane for the flight to Mandalay. En route, we admire the fantastic design of a dry river bed curling along beneath us. The Road to Mandalay, our road, is a wide path lined on both sides by professors of music and musicians, who keep giving me bouquets. By the time I reach the airport building, I must have twenty of them, and the largest of all is presented by a very young and beautiful girl dressed in the traditional dance costume. She is really lovely. What a Road to Mandalay this is, with Consul General Taylor and his gorgeous wife by my side! Later that evening, His Excellency Ambassador Martin and his sparkling wife are very hospitable.

In Mandalay, too, we have an entirely new experience, because there the audience does not express approval by applauding in the conventional manner. Not, that is, in a manner we know. There are anywhere between ten and twenty thousand people at the outdoor concert and where, at the end of a number, you normally anticipate an explosion of applause, here maybe just one diplomat down front claps. I quickly realize that they must have their own way of letting you know whether they like you, and that what we are experiencing is a custom indigenous to the country.

At the end of the two-and-a-half-hour concert and a half hour of encores not a soul in the audience has moved. Everyone is still there in his or her place. We inevitably spend considerable time backstage after the closing curtain, and it is probably forty-five minutes before we are ready to leave the park and go to our hotel. As we drive by in our car, we find all those thousands of people lined up alongside the road, waiting to wave good night. They have not just disappeared into the dark. If that isn't applause, I don't know what is! I find it very moving, and heartening.

Back in Rangoon, I am met and guided around by Mary Frances Cowan, who is attached to our embassy there. She met us on our first trip, and my son, Mercer, has known her since they were at school together in Washington. A Burmese artist gives me one of his paintings, and I am so taken with it that I go to the gallery where his work is exhibited and buy more by him and other painters. I also add to my collection of elephants (teak and ebony) here and in Ceylon.

This time, we merely stop overnight in Calcutta, but in flying there from Rangoon I am finally satisfied that I have circumnavigated the globe. Previously, we had not flown west from Rangoon, nor east from Calcutta, but now I know I have been all the way around at one time or another, having closed the 560-mile gap between the two cities. Next day, we leave for Ceylon via Madras. On arrival in Colombo, we find it is a Buddhist holiday and all the shops are closed. Because wealthy members of the band—or perhaps I should say musicians with foresight—want to invest in sapphires, the shops in the hotel are opened up for two hours.

Our next stop is Kuala Lumpur, and a map is really necessary to appreciate the distances we are covering. This city has one of the most modern and attractive airports I have ever seen. There is a big convention in progress and this causes a problem about accommodation. We stay at a Chinese hotel which didn't have a suite until our embassy people took a wall out and had a doorway made between two rooms—especially for me! Evidently the news that I am a suite connoisseur has gone ahead of me. The corn soup and shrimp with rice are truly memorable here. So is a young clarinetist presented by a high government official, who wants to know if the boy should persist with his musical career.

"Go pack your bag," I say jesting, after he has played a while. "We leave at nine in the morning."

I have him meet the five clarinet players in the band. They all get together with their axes, and they endorse him as a great talent.

In Jakarta, the heat is overpowering, and I cannot help getting irritated with a photographer who insists on blasting his flashlights right in my eyes. From the time we arrive until we leave, we are escorted everywhere by two motorcycle police, which fortunately saves a lot of time in our crowded schedule. At a reception in the U. S. Embassy, I meet ambassadors from all over the world—Pakistan, Norway, U.S.S.R., the Netherlands, Belgium, etc. We visit an arts-and-culture complex where an exhibition from China attracts me. When I have stopped the car—and the escort—I have a very rewarding visit, and end up ordering some modern and traditional work, including pieces that date back to the Ming dynasty.

The concert is a smash, the people being extraordinarily sensitive to everything we play. The zenith of encores is reached, and flowers are presented by Miss Indonesia 1971. And I have a date next morning with the Governor to receive a plaque.

In Singapore, there is an airport conference where I meet a television star who is also a musician and a composer. He accuses me of conforming to some kind of neopseudoism. He goes further and blasts Stravinsky as a turncoat, because he wrote *Ebony Concerto* for Woody Herman. I challenge him on the grounds of ineligibility, insist that Stravinsky's works are monumental, and that nothing more "modern" has been written since them. Luckily, I have happier experiences in Singapore, where the wisterias are marvelous. It is just about on the equator, and it is a great place for orchids, so much so that they even have orchids pictured on the money. I like the people and enjoy some of the tales I hear, such as the one about the farmer who found a hundred of his chickens missing every morning. He thought it was a tiger, or some other cat-like thief, so he set a trap and next day found he had caught a twenty-foot python. People who have orchids on their money just have to be beautiful.

Next we fly off to Perth and the land of the kangaroo, the didjeridoo, the cricketers, and Evonne Goolagong. When we went there for the first time in 1970, we met huge, enthusiastic audiences, and, almost equally important, wonderful pianos. I was surprised then by how much people knew about us there. Little is to be seen, oddly enough, of the Australian aborigines, but I buy every available book and learn many fascinating and astonishing facts about them, and finally I am presented to a group of ladies of an aborigine tribe. They are beautiful.

In New Zealand, the Maoris come and visit. They appear at every diplomatic reception given for us, and they are particularly gracious and hospitable. In fact, they made me feel so good that for a moment I thought I, too, was a Maori. I had learned to rub noses on the first visit, when I also picked up on a new rhythm, that of a Maori *haka—E ka mate, ka mate, ka ora, ka ora!* They can swing, too.

The New Zealand promotor has advertised my appearance as a "farewell" concert. The subject keeps coming up in the course of a newspaper interview, and I keep getting more and more evil, not realizing how we have been advertised. I get so nasty with the unfortunate interviewer that he finally packs up and leaves. The promoter subsequently claims the Australian impresario had made the deal with him as part of a farewell tour, but he must have been a smart boy, because we are not advertised that way in Australia, where we play Adelaide, Melbourne, Sydney, and Brisbane as well as Perth. I am sorry to leave Brisbane, because cyclone Daisy is approaching, and Daisy was my mother's name. I want to see what this Daisy is like. She may have an idea to give me. I will always wonder, but she does not arrive until eighteen hours after we have gone.

On the way home, we stop off in Fiji for a few hours before leaving for Honolulu. (On the previous trip, we flew all the way from New Zealand to Buffalo—and into a blizzard!) We have another of those cold lunches, and another seven-hour ride. The moving picture breaks down, but we arrive in time for the most beautiful sunrise I have ever seen. In Honolulu, we do a concert with Billy Eckstine and Sarah Vaughan, and we appear with them again for concerts in Vancouver and Seattle before doing two weeks together at the Grove of the Ambassadors Hotel in Los Angeles.

I went back to Honolulu with my nephew, Stephen, on June 19. The American Federation of Musicians was having its convention there, and this is how President Hal Davis introduced me:

"Delegates, we will depart momentarily from our scheduled business to honor a most important guest. Actually, he is much more than a guest. He is one of us, and he is a symbol of all that we aspire to in the musical profession. He arrived in Honolulu last night, and must return to New York this afternoon. So we are doubly honored that he has made this long and time-consuming journey just to be with us at this morning's session of our seventy-fifth convention.

"Our colleague has been honored more than perhaps any other performer in history. That is only proper, for he is a musician, a composer, an artist, and a humanitarian whose talent reaches men and women of all ages in all countries of the world.

"It is fitting that today those of us who are privileged to represent professional musicians should honor one who has brought so much honor to the profession that we love.

"Delegates, on your behalf I now present this Gold Card Honorary Life Membership in the American Federation of Musicians. It is inscribed: 'For lasting contributions to human understanding through fine music.'

"It gives me pleasure to present our esteemed colleague and our finest ambassador, Mr. Duke Ellington."

The Taste Buds

In 1955 my doctor, Arthur Logan, told me I would have to take off twenty-two pounds. I tore up his suggested menu and made one of my own. Mine was simply steak (any amount), grapefruit, and black coffee with a slice of lemon first squeezed and then dropped into it. With the exception of a binge one day a week, I ate as much of this and as often as I pleased for three months.

When we returned to the New York area, my first date was with the symphony in New Haven. Dr. Logan came up to the concert, took one look at me, and said, "Go get yourself a banana split quick!" I had lost thirty pounds.

As I was conducting the third movement of *Night Creature* that night, I suddenly realized my pants were falling down. There I was, directing those big sweeps at the end of the piece, and holding on to my pants to keep them from falling off. The violins first, and then the whole string section, saw what was happening and broke up. They found it hilarious. The reason I couldn't pull the pants up was because I was standing on them. At the end of the number, I had to maneuver them back into position before turning to face the audience for my bow. The musicians in the symphony continued to laugh long after I had left the stage. But my doctor was happy with the overall results!

This was not entirely the end of my career as either a gourmet or a gourmand, but looking back I feel I had a pretty good run for my money.

At home in Washington, the gourmet combination whipped up from—and adding to—Sunday's leftovers was usually the specialty for Monday's dinner. The way my mother fixed it made it a sort of *pièce de résistance* of the week. It was never humdrum or drab. She had the knack, talent, imagination, and exciting skill of a pure artist. You had to taste those combinations to believe them.

Uncle George Ellington worked for Demonet's, whose top-quality, flavorsome ice cream was served to the ultra society of Washington, D.C. He used to drop a large can off at our house now and then, but my aunts and uncles all used to make their own ice cream with fresh fruit, and my cousin Sonny and I would always try to be there at the right time to test the blends.

Tuesday, at home, was the day of surprise. My mother used to change the menu every week. Sometimes it might be leg of lamb, or some kind of fish. My father sometimes brought rabbit, which my mother couldn't stand. She thought it looked too much like a cat, but I enjoyed it.

Wednesday was a very special day for me, because I loved the baked or broiled ham we usually had then with maybe kale and baked beans.

Thursday was another good day, because it often brought stew—stew such as I have never tasted since—and with it the world's greatest cornbread.

Friday was fish day, and the main course or *entrée* varied according to the season.

Saturday was the ad-lib day with something simple and easily or quickly cooked, such as hamburger steak, because Saturday night my mother had to start preparing for Sunday by mixing the dough for hot rolls at Sunday morning breakfast, and maybe soaking the mackerel, too. Sunday dinner was another long, drawn-out procedure of preparing to roast or bake chicken with macaroni and cheese, sweet potatoes and salad. After Sonny and I had spent most of the day Sunday walking from aunt to aunt, sampling the many homemade cakes (as well as the homemade ice cream), I had walked up a beautiful appetite by the time I got home to dinner. As my sister, Ruth, grew up, my father chose Sunday dinnertime to test her intellectual scope and acquirements.

When I left Washington and started to travel, I, of course, encountered many different varieties of food. I never will forget the scrumptious supper table loaded with goodies in the house of Sonny Greer's family. There was always warm hospitality at their lovely home in Long Branch, New Jersey, and Mrs. Greer always had delicious, tasty surprises.

In Boston, Harry Carney's mother always served the traditional fish cakes and baked beans for Sunday morning breakfast—beans Harry marinated overnight after they had been cooked for the Saturday night dinner.

When en route to Baltimore, Maryland, we always enjoyed the anticipation of fresh crabmeat—and terrapin if we arrived at the right time. The people of that city always say that the crab you eat in Baltimore today slept last night in Chesapeake Bay.

On our first trip across the Kentucky line, we saw people selling something beside the road that was obviously food. The bus driver knew what it was all about and stopped to see if any of us wanted to buy what they were selling, which was what they called chicken sandwiches. They consisted of a quarter of fried chicken between two slices of bread for ten cents, and it was good! But that was years ago.

Clemson College in South Carolina was established in 1896 for rich, cultured young gentlemen, but for us it was a place where we played one-nighters. On being taken for a tour of the campus, we were much impressed by the fact that there were two hundred and fifty employees in the kitchen (including waiters). But what impressed us most of all in the immense kitchen were eight impeccable devices that looked very much like deep-fat fryers. That was not what they were at all. They were specially built and only used for cooking grits, hominy grits!

If you never tasted the toast at the King Edward Hotel in Toronto when M. Boucheau was *chef de cuisine,* and for a long time afterwards, you never tasted the greatest. It was one of the most astonishing and refreshing delights to discover that a piece of toast, apparently so plain, could yet be so exquisitely tasty.

It is against the law in Canada to feed hogs and pigs on slop, and it is also illegal to bring pork into Canada that was fed anywhere else other than in Canada. I learned this the hard way on a train traveling from the U.S. to Vancouver when I went to the dining car and ordered bacon and eggs, and they brought me eggs with beef bacon. It was the worst, the shock of a lifetime. The waiter explained that trains from the States were not allowed by law to carry hog meat of any kind.

New Orleans is famous for its fish, oysters, and crayfish, but on our first trip there in 1933 we looked for and found *gumbo filé.* The day we were to leave, I stopped at a restaurant where it was great, ate some, and said I would like to take some with me. So they fixed a bucket full, and off I went to board my private pullman, only to find that two thousand people—friends, fans, etc.—were waiting to see us off. I was not about to throw away my *gumbo filé,* so I had a redcap show me a way around where I would not be seen by the crowd. We came up behind the cars, and then I had to knock on doors and windows until somebody eventually came and let me in. I hid my *gumbo filé,* and then went to the other side of the car, all smiles, to wave very grandly and pompously to the crowd. *Merci, merci! Bonne chance!*

Europe, of course, brought many surprises. In England, I soon acquired a taste for tea and scones. When we went to Glasgow in 1933, there was the thrill of haggis and wee doch-an-doris as the bagpipes serenaded us. Later, in the intimacy of a rather posh party, where they were saluting with some special vintage Old Stand Fast, they told me very confidentially that this whiskey was too good for the Sassenachs. When I returned to England and told the story, they said the only good thing that came out of Scotland was the road to England!

One of the places we used to visit in London at that time was Jig's Club, which was run by an African and a Jewish fellow. I remember ending up there with a Member of Parliament who had been showing me the Thames and the Embankment by moonlight. I was intent on showing him a bit of Wardour Street he didn't know! They served the world's best Hoppin' John in that club, but they had no two of any one thing alike—chairs, china, silver, bottles of liquor, etc. When we entered, we had been drinking scotch or cognac, but only one bottle of each was permitted, so we had to move on to vodka, and on down to gin.

When I returned to England in 1948, food of all kinds was still severely rationed. I went out to visit Helen and Stanley Dance one weekend, and quickly ate up the steak, not knowing it was a whole week's ration. What made a bigger impression on me, however, was the wonderful Devonshire cream they served with dessert. Food was a real problem in London, too, but one of the musicians in the Palladium band had a chicken farm and regularly brought me fresh eggs. I would get someone to cook them for me, but could never understand why they so often had a disappointing and rather disagreeable taste. More than twenty years later this mystery was solved when it was explained to me that cooking fat was then in such short supply that it was used over and over again until it was tired out, so that some very strange flavors were likely to survive on the freshest of eggs.

At the Dorchester in London, now, where there is all-night room service, I tend to order bacon and eggs, macaroni Mornay, and crème caramel. And at the railway stations and airports, I always pick up boxes of a candy I developed a taste for called "Poppets."

France, of course, was a whole new world of culinary delights, and here my memories tend to telescope in terms of time.

When I was at the Cordon Bleu, next door to the movie studio where we did *Paris Blues,* I would always set a tall menu between me and the person next to me who was eating *escargots.* As Skippy Williams says, "Sometimes it be's that way."

Over on the Left Bank in Paris, Billy Strayhorn and Aaron Bridgers and their In crowd used to take us to a place called Le Paysan on the Rue de Tournon, where we would have wonderful French soul food. Wine and appetizers would be served, and seated comfortably we would begin on the *Pâté de lièvre* (hare), proceed to the *Rosette de Lyon* (a small peppered sausage), the *Pâté encroûté,* Billy's favorite *andouillettes, boudin* (a blood sausage), the *Omelette Paysan* (with potatoes, onion, and a kind of smoked bacon), the *Tarte Tatin . . .* on and on until we were stuffed.

On the other bank, we would have our large holiday dinner parties at Maxim's, where we would go the full distance to the *crêpes suzettes.* But the real thing was constantly *La Tour d'Argent,* a restaurant that dates from 1582, when it was a *relai de chasse* known as *La Tour de Nestlé.* The specialty was heron *pâté.* At that time Paris was built on several islands with marshes in between, where the wild heron were hunted, their meat being very rich and nutritious. It became known as the "silver tower" because of the way the white stone it was built of sparkled in the sun. It was burned during the Revolution, but rebuilt by a certain Frédérique, who used to fish on the banks of the Seine. When customers arrived, he would rush to his kitchen. It was acquired in 1890 by M. André Terrail, since when all duck served there have been numbered. For the record, I ate No. 297,322, and drank Nuit de Saint George, 1923, with it.

Another favorite restaurant was La Sologne on the Rue de Bellechasse. I have a fond memory of composer Georges Auric there, and it was also where I first learned to say "Love you madly" in Russian—*"Yavas oujasna lublu."*

Today, we often go to Jean Houel's Rasputin restaurant, where we enjoy the Russian atmosphere and continuous—and I do mean continuous—Russian entertainment as we eat the greatest caviar and blinis. Imagine the setting there: in front of your table is a group of anywhere from eight to ten musicians and singers. No sooner is their selection finished than another number begins, and right where the original group was performing is a completely different one with different selections, different instruments, and different costumes. It is like magic.

I happen to love Beaujolais, and after concerts in Paris I would often go by my hotel and have my supper and a full bottle of it. Then I would immediately lie down across the bed and sleep five hours or so. People were always looking askance at me: "He likes Beaujolais instead of champagne! Strange fellow, Duke Ellington!"

That reminds me of when we used to play the Standish Hall Hotel in Hull, Quebec, during the '50s. The big drink for the In kids there was the Goat. We mastered it, and it doesn't taste anything like it sounds. It's gin and milk, and it's a great drink for the drinking drinker.

In 1939, in The Hague, Netherlands, we were living at the Desandes Hotel, next door to a fabulous international restaurant where they serve ninety-nine *hors d'oeuvres,* on which it was natural and easy to stuff oneself. Then the waiter brings the menu and says, "And now, sir, which soup will you have?" It's like getting knocked out before the main event.

Then there's a Polynesian restaurant called the Bali, where thirty-three waiters parade endlessly, each with a different dish. Even when they return to the kitchen, they never come back with the same dish. It is a feast for either gourmet òr glutton.

One night the same year, we were in Scheveningen, and my hotel window overlooked the North Sea. All night long there was a loud celebration out there on the beach. Crowds of people jumped and balled to the heights. Next day, I inquired what the celebration was about, and was told it took place once every year, and nobody under sixty was allowed to join the party. Oh, those beautiful, sturdy Dutch!

In Copenhagen, my kick is Danish pastry. Getting up late one day, and rushing to catch my plane, I stopped at the food counter in the airport. I looked through the glass enclosure and, out of a vast assortment of sandwiches and quickies, decided to take a few pastries with me on the plane. I munched one quickly and flipped. They were terrific. My friends, who escorted me to the airport, have been sending me Danish pastries for my birthday, Christmas, and other holidays ever since. Why are they so good and so superior? Well, the same cooks who baked them so beautifully in Denmark have on many occasions been contracted and taken over to other countries, where the pastries don't come out the same. The Danes say it is all due to something they feed the cows, but nobody will tell you what it is. When I receive my bundle of Danish pastries, I budget them one a day, and the last is just as fresh and delicious as the first.

After we came out of the U.S.S.R. in 1971, we were leaving Copenhagen one morning for Oslo. I bought my usual box of thirteen pastries, carried them aboard the S.A.S. plane, and asked the stewardess to put my "jewels" in the "vault." It was a short flight, and we had such a congenial time chatting with the plane's personnel that they and I forgot all about the pastries when the time came to get off. It was not until I was in my room in the Oslo hotel that I remembered them, and by then it was too late. The plane had already left the airport.

We did more traveling after that in Europe, toured all around South and Central America, went to Japan, Thailand, Burma, Australia, and Hawaii in a big circuit, and then came back to the U.S. All the time I was brooding about my lost pastries.

When we got to Los Angeles, I told my friend Bob Udkoff that I was going to sue S.A.S.

"Good idea," he said, and called the Public Relations Office at S.A.S.

"Duke Ellington is going to sue S.A.S.," he told them.

"For what reason?" they asked.

"Because your people forgot to give him his box of thirteen pieces of Danish pastry when he deplaned at Oslo. Do you think he should settle this out of court?"

The next day, twenty fresh pieces of pastry, flown directly from Copenhagen, were delivered to me at the Ambassador Hotel by S.A.S.

Now, normally, when an attorney wins a lawsuit for a client, he gets a 50 percent fee. In this case, Bob Udkoff got only 25 percent, or five pieces of the freshly delivered pastry.

In Brussels, Belgium, there was the Canterbury restaurant, where everything was served with a special flourish, and designed as though it were a work of art, so that fried chicken was served up to look like a statue. There was a very special parade effect that went with the serving of every dish. I never forget the show that started when I ordered some strawberries and cream. The waiter first of all brought a board, and then a bowl of sugar which was poured out and spread on the board. Next came a bowl of strawberries, and the waiter took each one separately and gently with fork and spoon rolled it in the sugar before placing it on a plate. When all the strawberries were ready, he took away the board and returned with the cream. They were doing the French thing more French than the French there. What a parade! All they needed was a can-can finale.

On our 1963 tour of Sweden, a fine young man named Hasse was given the responsibility of driving me in his Volvo for thirty-one days to the folk parks where we were engaged to play. I used to give him a laugh as we rode through the countryside by saying, "Hasse, this is so beautiful it looks just like Minnesota!" On the first day, we stopped along the road at a country cafe. I gave my regular order for steak, and he ordered something in Swedish.

"Hey, what's that?" I asked when it came.

"Oh, just a very cheap country dish," he replied.

"Well, order me some too," I said, because it looked so good. And it was delicious. I don't think I have ever had a meal in Sweden since without ordering *Räk Crêpe*. (It's a crêpe with shrimps.) I'm hooked on it, no matter what else I may have with it.

At that time, Sweden had a population of seven or eight million people, but there were three hundred and twenty-five of these folk parks. They might have tiny carnivals in the smaller towns, but in Stockholm, Göteborg, and the big cities, they had everything—outdoor bandstand, concert hall, opera house, ballroom, vaudeville and movie houses, plus all the other stuff you find at Coney Island and on Steel Pier in Atlantic City. We would play a forty-five-minute concert, and then move into the ballroom for a two-hour dance. At the end of each number, the dancers would clear the floor so that those who had not been able to get on it before could now have their turn. This is the greatest manifestation of unselfishness I have ever seen by a public audience.

In Italy, I prefer veal scallopini not with the powdered Gorgonzola cheese, but with slices of Bel Paese. And every day, as Joe Williams would say! Every day!

Some one-shot airline surprises—never before or since—stay in my memory, too. On an Air Canada flight from Los Angeles to Toronto, included in the dinner menu, and served in such a dainty little dish, was collard greens! It could have been caviar. Another time, flying from Zürich to New York on Swissair, they served venison cooked by one who really knew how to cook venison. A rare pleasure, indeed.

I knew that Pan-Am used to serve Turkish vodka out of large bottles, so when I arrived at Tokyo airport one day I bought some dainty sweets and candy. After I had boarded the plane for Los Angeles, I presented each stewardess with an assortment to choose something from that she might like. They were lovely girls, and I felt I had laid the groundwork for my big conquest.

Time came for cocktails.

"Mr. Ellington, would you like a cocktail?" a lovely stewardess asked when she got to me.

"Well," I said, "I have work to do and I'd rather not drink anything now. Maybe I can take it with me. You know, one of those miniatures."

"I'm sorry, Mr. Ellington, but we have only large bottles. Maybe you have something to put it in?"

"Oh, never mind, but thank you. I just wanted some of that Turkish vodka. You do have Turkish vodka, don't you?"

"Yes, but as I said, it's in large bottles."

"Thanks. Don't worry about it."

"Well, wait," she said, "we'll see how many passengers are drinking vodka."

"Okay, okay."

Halfway across the Pacific, there she came, as pretty as my muse, with something wrapped in a plain, brown paper bag. She slipped it into the seat beside me. I felt it, and it was a full bottle of that rare Turkish vodka. Well, you know how a hunter feels when he bags an elephant, a rhino, or a lion!

In Japan, when you order steak or whatever, they always send a side dish of snow peas (pea pods), but if you try to order them, everybody dummies up. Nobody knows what you are talking about, and I love snow peas and oyster sauce! Mr. Kambara once told me the name of the vegetable, *guyenda*, but I usually forget it, so there are no snow peas for me *à la carte*. At Tokyo airport, I enjoy *pampura*. Fried in deep fat, you never know whether you are going to get fish or vegetable next. And it was in Niigata, I must not forget, that I had the greatest crème caramel, the *primo assoluto*.

When I was in Thailand, I was invited to lunch by the U. S. Ambassador to Bangkok. As a matter of fact, he invited all the band, but luncheon is a difficult assignment for musicians who have trouble disentangling themselves from the previous night's after-gig involvements early enough to get enough sleep to be up and charming at one o'clock. There were a lot of lovely people there, however, and the luncheon was wonderful. For dessert, there was apple pie, good homemade apple pie, and a very refreshing change from the kind generally made with canned apple today. It was so good that I committed probably the most American of all Americanisms. I complimented our hostess and said, "Mrs. Unger, the apple pie was so good, could you please give me another piece in a doggie bag?" She had cooked it herself and she said this was the greatest compliment she had ever had for her food. She blushed, ran to the kitchen, and came back with a whole pie, all wrapped and ready to travel. I took it carefully to the hotel, and tucked it away safely.

By a strange and wonderful coincidence, I had a breakfast date next day at noon. I had invited Alice Babs and her husband, and they had told me they would like bacon, eggs, toast, jam, tea, etc., so I put the order into room service before I went to bed, room service usually being my wake-up call. So they arrived at noon, and the food arrived at noon. Everything was going fine until I discovered the waiter had forgotten to bring the toast and jam. Rather than gamble on the time it would take to call and get the waiter back with them, I pulled out my apple pie. It was the hit of the meal, and I was proclaimed by my guests as the Original Gourmet Host of the Century. There's nothing like an Americanism or dumb luck! But the news got around quickly. In Rangoon next day, the Ambassador's wife, Mrs. Hummel, said she didn't have any apple pie—and gave me a bag of brownies!

After fifteen weeks on the stretch between Syria and Ceylon, my appetite and desire for lamb was exhausted. Before that, I used to love lamb so much that, when we had leg of lamb for dinner, I could never get back home fast enough to get what was left out of the refrigerator and clean the bone cannibal-style.

Chris Stam, who is a great wheel man, is a natural target for cops. He loves to drive on long trips at around a hundred miles an hour. He is also a man who hates chicken, and he has a way of referring to it that makes anyone hesitate. Several times, when we have been traveling together, the subject has come up, and I have been left hog-tied, or should I say chicken-tied? Well, now I find I cannot eat chicken any more!

Years ago, when we played New England and Salem was our summer base, fresh fish was one of the big bonuses. Recently, a friend of mine, who lives down in the Bahamas, was telling about the wonder of catching fish and putting them into the frying pan so fresh they were almost alive. I had heard quite a bit about this, and one day, not so long ago, I was in a Salem restaurant that hung out over the ocean, and I ordered fish.

"I bet this fish came right out of the ocean down there," I said to the waitress as I was eating it.

"Oh, no," she said. "All fish has to clear with the union in Boston."

Ugh! There went fish!

In the West Indies, they have really fresh fish, but instead of lemons they use fresh-squeezed limes. That is how and where I got on the lime kick.

On Route 101 from Los Angeles to Tia Juana, we found a refreshment stand that sold avocado ice cream. *Crème de l'exotique!* But my greatest ice-cream experience happened when we were playing a party at a country club near Indianapolis.

In the middle of the evening, an attendant announced that there were some people to see me. I went out and was greeted by a very nice man and his wife.

"Mr. Ellington," he said, "we read in Dorothy Kilgallen's column that you liked pear ice cream but couldn't find any anywhere. We want you to know that we, the North Star Ice Cream Company of Muncie, Indiana, make fresh pear ice cream, and also fresh apple ice cream, along with several other rare flavors. We have driven over fifty miles tonight to bring you a sample of each flavor. Look!"

I looked in his station wagon, and there were ten ten-gallon cans of ice cream. I thanked him, and told the host of the party about it. Everybody at the party partook of the pear ice cream, and the other flavors, too, while that wonderfully kind donor and his family joined the party and stayed to the end. The gesture, like the ice cream, was just beautiful.

At another country club, the Doral in Miami, the chopped liver was always good for an encore, but their raisin cake—that was like the bread of life to me.

The Ambassador Hotel and its Pump Room in Chicago have for years been considered tops for great, quality food, and right up to today that is the place for prime beefsteak, the primest of the prime. And room service there—the way I usually have my meals—is just as prime.

When we were playing the Blue Note in Chicago, we would often go to Jimmy Wong's Chinese restaurant for dinner between matinees and the evening show on Sunday. On one occasion, Frank Holzfeind took me out to Fanny's in Evanston, a place so exclusive that the front door was kept locked. You had to be known to gain admission. On the way back, Frank said something I have never forgotten. "Isn't it strange," he said, "that some people can't say what they want to say without saying it?"

Then I must not forget the Mapes Hotel in Reno, where they have twenty-four-hour, Chinese-food room service, and that's for me too, baby.

Reuben's in New York is another restaurant that gives me twenty-four-hour, home-in-my-room service, so you might say I live there just as I used to at John Popkins' Hickory House. Oh, yes, they have good ice cream too. And, for me, *the* French restaurant in New York is Le Mistral.

Looking back on all this, I recall that in the '40s I had become so food-conscious I would have my dessert as the first course—something delicate like pie *à la mode*. But now I prefer to have all my courses on the table at the same time. No wonder I have lost so much weight!

Dramatis Felidae

RUFUS JONES

The first time we heard Rufus "Speedy" Jones was the night in Miami when Jackie Gleason had gathered all the big bands together for a television show. Rufus was then with Count Basie, and Sam Woodyard, who was with us, was very complimentary. Rufus had been given big solo spots, and his explosive rhythms and animation came off in very convincing, symbolic patterns. His horizontal movements—straightforward and circular—from cymbal to cymbal, along with his eyes and eyeglasses, all seemed to play a part in this mysticalizationisimist's paradiddled self-portrait tapestry.

Since Rufus Jones has been with us, his supporting role, particularly in African, jungle, and oriental pieces, has constantly led to demands from the audience for him to be featured solo. Just as constantly, his drum solos have been show-stoppers that result, half the time, in standing ovations.

Mostly a vegetarian, he is a good, clean-living guy, and a karate expert. As a man, he is easy to get along with and to respect. He is the "Cat Anderson of all Rufuses."

ELMA LEWIS

Elma Lewis is the symbol of Marcus Garvey come alive and blazing into the future of the arts. Her Cultural Center in Roxbury is an accomplishment above and beyond abnormal expectancy. She has done it all herself, with dignity, and without ever antagonizing others. The Jewish people in Boston, for example, have given her two whole buildings.

Every year we go up and play for thousands of people in Franklin Park during her annual Marcus Garvey Festival. We get a wonderful reception, and we always look forward to informal concerts of that kind—and the soul supper afterwards.

HERBIE JONES

Herbie Jones, a young veteran of Mercer Kennedy Ellington's many bands, came out and joined us in Ceylon in 1963. He broke all speed records and got his passport, shots, and papers straight in an unbelievably short time. Because of his great interest in the wisdom and culture of the East, nothing could have stopped him when we sent him the invitation, and he spent days and nights in reading and research.

He was a great asset to the band from several points of view. A good reader, he played first trumpet whenever required, and he extracted and copied scores accurately. He never demanded any special treatment or consideration. He was neat and clean, neither smoked nor drank, and always walked four miles a day.

Herbie Jones is my good friend. I love him and his beautiful family, and the only reason he is not with us today is because his duties as husband and father came, as they should, first.

HAROLD ASHBY

Harold Ashby brought his tenor saxophone and sat in with us several times. To us, these were very zesty samplings. After he had recorded with us once or twice, we could hear that Jimmy Hamilton had been strongly influenced by him. We could, in fact, hear it after his very first visit. It created a fine spirit in us all, because Ash had started out trying to play like Ben Webster, whom we all loved. But by this time he had allowed a lot of his own self to break through, to join with Ben's style, and to mature into an indescribable prime product of soul-saturated solo popping de luxe!

"How do we get this guy?" I asked. The opportunity came in 1963 when I did the show *My People*. I had to have another band for it, so I collected all the musicians I would have liked to have had myself but could not afford in addition to all those I already had. That *My People* band was marvelous, and Ash was in it, but after the show closed my urge refused to be subdued. So I hung on until we finally got him in the band on a regular basis five years later. He has been a great contributor in solos, as well as to the quality of ensemble sound on both tenor and clarinet. In the U.S.S.R., he was definitely *the* soloist, and at almost all the concerts he had to answer audience demands for an encore.

Originally, he came out of the Kansas City jazz-blues community which has produced so many outstanding swingers, and he has never lost their kind of impetus and feeling.

WILD BILL DAVIS

Wild Bill Davis is really a professor of music at heart, and sometimes I think he loves music as much as I do, or more. I think there is nothing that can take him away from music very long, not after he sees an organ, a piano, or a piece of manuscript paper.

The only thing that distinguishes him equally as much as his pure love of beautiful music is when his soul subconscious breaks through, and then I am captive. I just do my thing up and down the stage attempting to match that Kentucky Avenue wail. In the distance I seem to hear some cat at the bar saying, "Bar lady, turn 'em around again!" And then to Bill, "One more time!"

"One more time" is definitely the most outstanding colloquialism used and understood around. Demanded loudly and sincerely, without blowing one's cool, it is repeated with profound feeling, and then it has all the meaning of a drink of water in the middle of the desert.

This great man is also a great gentleman. His music wins affections, warms the heart, and makes the listener proud that he is one of the luckier ones to be there to hear firsthand, or firstear, the man with grace and taste, Wild Bill Davis. One more once!

And when we play his arrangement of "April in Paris," we always credit my good friend, Sonny Greer's cousin, the Kid from Red Bank. Count Basie and his band can settle in a groove that will unnerve the best of them. I mean it. Long live Count Basie.

BOB UDKOFF

Bob Udkoff, or rather Harold Robert Udkoff, was one of Jonesy's discoveries. He was just a kid in school when he went to Jonesy one day and asked for a job working with the band as his assistant.

"Why?" good old Jonesy asked.

Bob told him he liked our music and wanted to be where he could hear it every night. It was summer, and school would soon be out.

"Sure. Okay," Jonesy said. "Come on! You're my man!"

So Bob came, and he lasted through the summer until one day we realized that this little kid should be in school. So we gave him a little loot and a ticket, and sent him back home from San Francisco to Los Angeles. It's funny to think that this same little guy is a grown man now with grown children of his own and a wonderful wife to mother them. Every time I see her, *his* mother always thanks me for sending Bob back home to her.

Bob Udkoff still has the same enthusiasm for the music he had when he was a kid. He has flown enormous distances, such as to Russia, Mexico City, England, and the Continent, just to hear the band. He flies anywhere we go just to be with us, and fortunately he acts as though he can afford it. He owns a couple of swimming-pool companies and various subsidiaries. I think maybe Evelyn must be good luck for this cat. Oh, Evelyn is his wife—beautiful, and with brains.

JAMES LATIMER

James Latimer is a man, a big man, whom God has blessed with practically all the known virtues. His dedication to the University of Wisconsin, where he is Associate Professor of Music, is beyond appraisal. When I was honored with a degree as Doctor of Music there in 1971, he was given the responsibility of going to Saginaw to fetch me.

On arrival, he started to help and pamper me as though I was something precious. He practically carried me and my effects to the airport, where there was a specially chartered plane to take us across the lake, and then conveyed me to the hotel, leaving me nothing but the responsibility of enjoying the whole bit. His beautiful wife even prepared food to satisfy a particular yen I had that night. I sometimes get on a grits kick, and when he telephoned her in the middle of the night, she got up and cooked the most delicious gourmet grits in the history of hominy grits.

The next day, they both accompanied me to my job in Elkhart. They stayed through the concert and still wanted to know if there was anything else they could do for me. It was all so well handled that I really didn't realize how I had been floating around in the "opiate" of their grace and hospitality until they had left to drive back to Madison. Then, of course, my feet touched the ground, but even now I cannot find adequate words of appreciation. The University of Wisconsin is very fortunate to have such a man, one whose special gifts and ability are balanced by his humility.

In 1972 he set up a week-long Ellington Festival at the University of Wisconsin, Madison, and Governor Patrick Lucey proclaimed Duke Ellington Week throughout the state, one of the greatest honors ever bestowed on me. The festival was, I think, a success, and I enjoyed it very much. What was unusual about it was the series of workshop-clinics conducted by the musicians in the band. Professor Latimer had three separate auditoriums for them, and every day members of the reed, brass, and rhythm sections held forth there. After they had warmed to their task, I sensed that a certain spirit of rivalry was developing and I would have liked to have attended, but I feared my presence might inhibit the new "professors," who included Mercer Ellington, Money Johnson, Johnny Coles, Chuck Connors, Vince Prudente, Tyree Glenn, Russell Procope, Norris Turney, Paul Gonsalves, Harold Ashby, Joe Benjamin, Harry Carney, and Rufus Jones. The enthusiastic reports I received from people who were taking the "course" were very gratifying, and it seemed that Paul Gonsalves made a big impression with a piece of inspired oratory on the last day.

I was personally responsible for what were called "master" classes two days running, and it was quite an experience to stand up there and field questions for hours. Fortunately, I had a piano, and the assistance of Brooks Kerr and Two Ton Baker, to demonstrate the finer points. Paul Gonsalves also came by to help me by playing "Happy Reunion."

In the evenings, we played five different concerts, culminating with one called *Night of Suites*. We had played *Harlem* and *Togo Brava* earlier, so on this occasion we did *The Goutelas Suite*, a couple of excerpts from *The Queen's Suite*, and a new, four-part suite called *Uwis*.

I tried in this to evoke some of the happiness that Wisconsin and the inhabitants of that state had given me ever since I first went to Milwaukee by train from Chicago—ninety miles in ninety minutes. I remembered the railroad dining car at Hayward, and the circus train (which had already inspired one composition) at Baraboo. These trains went into the second movement, the first consisting of solo reflections by the piano player on the beautiful people he had met from or in Wisconsin. They included Governor and Mrs. Lucey, President and Mrs. John C. Weaver of the University of Wisconsin, Judge John Reynolds, Mr. and Mrs. Lomoe, Dr. Don Willi of West Wisconsin State, Mr. and Mrs. Lorderger, Harold Taylor (the youngest president of any university ever, and a good clarinet player), Mrs. Ethel Rich of Milton College, Paul Eduard Miller, Frank Holzfeind (whose Blue Note in Chicago was the Grand Opera House of Jazz), and Tom Detienne (at one time the able president of the Duke Ellington Society). Then there were the famous musicians from Wisconsin: Woody Herman, Bunny Berigan, Gene Schroeder, Dick Reudebusch, Freddie Slack, Les Paul, and, last but not least, Hilly Edelstein, the man who wrote the fanfare we still use at the beginning of the medley. I remembered meeting Edward Kennedy and Leonard Bernstein, both for the first time, in Wisconsin. I thought about our engagements at the Wisconsin Theatre, the Wisconsin Roof, the State Fair Park, and the Modernistic Ballroom, and the time I had my name in lights on Milwaukee City Hall (thanks to Mrs. Lomoe) when I gave my first piano recital. I couldn't forget the cheese for which the state is famous, and some of which we always sent home, and I remembered the other famous product, the beer, and our visit to one of the world's biggest breweries.

The last movement, to the audience's apparent delight and surprise, was a polka, which the cats played with great skill and dash. This reminded me of when, many years before, Yank Yankovic invited our band to participate in a polka ball, at which about eight polka bands were playing. I suppose we were regarded as a kind of intermission attraction, but I had a polka expert write some special polka arrangements for us beforehand, and when we opened up with them the polka musicians all fell out. Louis Bellson proved himself a terrific polka drummer that night.

Act Eight

Music and the Future

I am an optimist. From where I sit, music is mostly all right, or at least in a healthy state for the future, in spite of the fact that it may sound as though it is being held hostage.

Opera, for instance, has its audience (and its union problems!). Many ballet companies are obviously doing very well. The symphonies manage to keep themselves well subsidized and to do concert tours with itineraries that encircle the world. Chamber music retains its loyal following, and nobody is more enthusiastic than a chamber music aficionado. There is enough new cultural concrete and steel in the major cities of the world to build a bridge all the way to Mars and back.

This, I think you'll agree, promises well for the future.

The sound, of course, will be dependent on the good taste of everyone involved, from the symphony's Chairman of the Board down to the fourth triangle player.

As I said, I am an optimist. I do not think those in charge will ever demand that everything played in their elite edifices of culture must be Top Forty or Pseudo-Rock. Nor do I believe that the *prima ballerina assoluta* will be choreographed with ten thousand repetitions of a limp to fit the syncopation of a broken-down space tractor. Neither do I think that the contrabassoonist will become the virtuoso of the blew-fuse or the blue fugue—or is it Frug?

I am an optimist, although the big band, for example, is a hazardous gamble. Sidemen demand enormous salaries, and there are heavy overheads like transportation, orchestrations, copying, commission, and uniforms. Nevertheless, Wayne King still has his waltz audience. Benny Goodman, when he feels like working, gets more money than ever before. Count Basie is the most imitated piano player around, and his band swings like crazy. Woody Herman, Harry James, Buddy Rich, Charlie Barnet, Gerald Wilson, Ray Charles, Thad Jones, Mel Lewis, Guy Lombardo, Freddy Martin, Sammy

Kaye, Buddy De Franco, Les and Larry Elgart—they all have bands and they all sound great. They have the courage of their convictions and they are true to their own tonal personalities. George Wein's Newport Jazz Festival and Jimmy Lyon's Monterey Jazz Festival draw SRO audiences. The guys in Hollywood are writing wonderful music. Every country in Europe has great musicians, too, but they're not the kind that get the *big* play.

Maybe I have reason to be an optimist, for our band works fifty-two weeks a year, in Europe, North America, Africa, and the Orient.

*   *   *

A lot of people say the kids dictate the tone of the music today. This is not true. They are told what to listen to, from many directions. "If you want to be In," they're told by other kids who have been brainwashed musicwise, "get with the Big Beat, man!" The policy of most of the radio stations has gone Top Forty, whatever that means. Maybe it has something to do with the record you are complaining about at home, the one the kids keep playing all day.

It just isn't fashionable not to worship the Scorpions, the Ants, or the Ogres. The girl around the corner, whom the boy likes, thinks that the Scorpions, the Ants, and the Ogres are divine. She too has been told what to like. So the boy says to himself, "What difference does it make, so long as I get to hold her hand?" The disc jockey says, "Crazy, baby!" And that settles it.

Yet I have reason to be optimistic, for with all those good musicians graduating from the conservatories, the future has got to be bright. Of course, the same people who say they don't like electrically amplified guitars and basses will often add that they "just love a string section." The basic concern should not be the instrument, but the taste and skill of the person who plays it.

I know a guy who sells a trashy kind of music but wouldn't dream of missing Bernstein's winter season or Fiedler's Tanglewood season. The American listening audience is actually growing more mature every day. I believe the brainwashing will soon subside, because all the brainwashers have become wealthy. Their problem now is that their children, too, have been brainwashed.

So if you're annoyed by the music of today, watch the man who sells it. Follow him. For his kicks, he more than likely goes to listen to the music *you* like. Good music is just around the corner.

What's Happening?

A Negro musician, or a Negro who was not a professional musician, decided to do what he thought he could do on a musical instrument, just to see what he sounded like. For personal kicks, he tried banjo, guitar, violin, cornet, clarinet, trombone, saxophone, and other instruments to hand. He was strongly influenced by the type of music of his time, and the black beat was his foundation. The soul of his brothers, sisters, and neighbors broke through to reassure him of their sympathy. The music of his time—and sound devices—were always parallel to the progress of science, medicine, and labor. When you pick the jazz musician of any period, if he happens to be one of the many unique performers, you may be sure he always reflects what's happening in his time. "What's happening" is the name of the game.

Jazz became popular in one way and unpopular in another. Some people enjoy listening to jazz because somebody told them that they should. Others have more valid reasons: (1) to dance to; (2) to give one's sitting stance the dash and swank that match a ringside old-fashioned (of course, one must never tilt on the beat as one pats one's foot); (3) it's an art form, discovered by the neo-intellectuals, and some find it something to listen *down* to, like taking the ear slumming; (4) others use it for social advancement in that world of hipsters who believe everything in their lives must swing; (5) those who enjoy monetary participation; (6) professional courtesy; (7) those who genuinely get torn up emotionally when listening to an extraordinary rendition; and (8) some young people like to dig it because it is not associated with juvenile delinquency, which brings us now to those who prefer *not* to listen to jazz.

There are many romantic and colorful stories about Jazz and its upbringing in New Orleans whorehouses. Whoever started that story, of course, had to be in the whorehouse, to see and hear the musicians of the band, or else it's just hearsay, or a lie. Even if they were working in a New Orleans whore-

413

house, I like to point out, they did not learn their instruments there, and they obviously were not patrons of the joint. It's easy to visualize jazzmen in the whorehouses: sitting rather inanimately at first with or at their instruments, from which came sounds that were compatible with whatever social activity was going on. As the sound grew more attractive, the customers began to realize that the players were *people,* sitting or standing there by their instruments. Soon they realized that since they *were* people, they must have names. So they set about finding out the names of the musicians.

Later, when they were at a social gathering of more respectable climate, and engaged in conversation, one would take the floor—or spotlight—by talking about what he had heard, by this *great* and *Negro* player of jazz, as though he were speaking about an adventurous lion hunt with a master hunter in some strange and exotic land. At the end of his speech, the speaker would be accepted as more traveled and experienced, as the true sophisticate of the day. The name "Jazz," accepted as referring to a great land of adventure, accordingly spread and, as I have said before, many romantic and colorful stories about it were invented.

But one continuing story is that what's happening is happening. It was happening then and will continue in its happening until the happiest happening will be to be what's happening.

Jazz for Young People

The story of jazz is a long list of great names, rather like those lists of kings and queens and presidents in history books. Divided up by instruments instead of countries, you can easily trace how the crown was passed down—and sometimes usurped. On trumpet, for example, the order might run something like this: Buddy Bolden, Joe Oliver, Louis Armstrong, Bix Beiderbecke, Cootie Williams, Roy Eldridge, Ray Nance, Dizzy Gillespie, Clark Terry, Clifford Brown, Miles Davis . . . Similar sequences of highly influential musicians, each with popular imitators, can be made for all the other instruments.

To listen to jazz without any knowledge of its history is to miss much of its charm. The first "king" we have any knowledge of was Buddy Bolden, a powerful trumpet man who could be heard right across the Mississippi in New Orleans. When he was ready to begin playing in a dance hall or club, he would tune up, stick his trumpet out the window, and "call his children home."

There are many other colorful legends about the early days in New Orleans, where the name "jazz" was first given to a new kind of music around the turn of the century. It was an animated music with a strong African pulse beneath what often sounded like a caricature of a military band. Much of its development, in fact, came about through the playing of small Negro—or black, if you prefer—bands in street parades, especially at Mardi Gras time, the instruments commonly in use being cornet (or trumpet), trombone, clarinet, bass, and drums. These bands were accompanied by what was known as the Second Line, a group of supporters who danced attendance on them before, behind, and on the sidewalks alongside. Pomp and circumstance were not what these people wanted, and to increase their enjoyment musicians "ragged" or "jazzed up" the music, introducing humorous effects and improvising on the melodies. Sometimes, too, these bands would take part in funeral processions, and on the way to the cemetery they would play slow, solemn dirges, but coming back they would pick up the tempo and try to blow away sadness with lively versions of the same dirges and other familiar songs. Such customs still survive in New Orleans, and you can see how from the beginning there was a close relationship between jazz and dancing, or physical movement, and that is why the same musicians were soon in demand to play in dance halls.

Many fine musicians came out of New Orleans, some of the best and most famous being "King" Joe Oliver and his protégé, Louis Armstrong, both trumpet players; the clarinetists Sidney Bechet, Jimmie Noone, Johnny Dodds, Barney Bigard, and Omer Simeon; Kid Ory, the trombonist; Jelly Roll Morton, the pianist; Wellman Braud and Pops Foster, the bass players; and the drummers, Zutty Singleton, Paul Barbarin and Baby Dodds. Many of them, like Fate Marable, the bandleader and pianist, played on the Mississippi riverboats, and it was not long before they and their music started to influence other musicians in such cities as Memphis, St. Louis, Chicago, Kansas City, Los Angeles, Washington, D.C., Boston, and New York. Not all the New Orleans musicians, I must point out, were black. For example, the Original Dixieland Jazz Band, led by cornetist Nick La Rocca, was a white band and one of the first to introduce the New Orleans or Dixieland idiom to New York and Europe. But the maximum impact came when Louis Armstrong joined Joe Oliver in Chicago, a subject to which we will return.

Before ever it reached New Orleans, the original African element had made itself felt in the West Indies, and from there it branched off in two directions. In one case, it went to the Latin-American countries, where it picked up Spanish and Portuguese influences that resulted in a distinctive Afro-Latin music. The heritage of African drums survived strongly, and a more complex use of percussion instruments—conga drums, bongos, and timbales—is a striking characteristic of this music even today. African rhythms have always been considered the most sophisticated.

The African impulse was also influential on the East Coast of the United States, where a more disciplined music resulted because more of the musicians there had had the benefit of formal schooling, and even conservatory training. This was in contrast with the experience of most of the early New Orleans musicians, who played by ear. They tended to emphasize the instruments of the brass band, whereas on the East Coast the string instruments, and particularly pianos, had a more significant place. As a young man in Washington, D.C., I was impressed by many fine local pianists, as well as by men like James

P. Johnson and Luckey Roberts when they came visiting from New York. In those days, player pianos were extremely popular, and one of my major inspirations was a piano roll of "Carolina Shout" by Johnson. I also tried to copy the spectacular manner in which Luckey Roberts lifted his hands high above the keyboard as he played. Later, when I went to New York, I was enchanted by another pianist, Willie "The Lion" Smith, whose striking personality and individual style influenced me very much. My first real encounter with the New Orleans idiom came when I heard Sidney Bechet in my hometown, and I have never forgotten the power and imagination with which he played.

The different strains fused to form what was soon known throughout the world as jazz. The New Orleans men dominated the scene in Chicago during the '20s, and there they inspired such well-known white musicians as Bix Beiderbecke and Muggsy Spanier, both cornet players; the clarinetists Benny Goodman, Frank Teschemacher, and Mezz Mezzrow; Bud Freeman, the tenor saxophonist; and the drummers Dave Tough, George Wettling, and Gene Krupa. But a major development came when they and the East Coast musicians got together in New York. The westerners, as we thought of them, brought their own favorite numbers like "King Porter Stomp," "Muskrat Ramble," "Tiger Rag," and "Sugar Foot Strut," and they also interpreted the blues with a sincere, earthy kind of feeling.

Now the blues are basic to all jazz, and although they are often thought of as sad, they are in fact performed with every variety of expression. Their relative simplicity has been a great factor in their lasting popularity. In its essential form, a blues consists of twelve bars divided into three sections of four bars each. When sung, the words of the first section are usually repeated in the second, while the third offers a wry comment on the first two, or completes their meaning. The words may deal with hard times, bad luck, disastrous floods, hunger, or—most often—unhappy love affairs, but there is usually an underlying vein of humor, optimism, or defiance in them. "I may be down," they say, "but I won't be down always." For a long time the blues existed in the minds, mouths, and fingers of those who performed them, and they were seldom written down until a trumpet player named W. C. Handy collected some of the most popular and published them under titles that became world-famous, such as "St. Louis Blues," "Memphis Blues," "Beale Street Blues," and "Yellow Dog Blues."

There have been many great blues performers. In the early days, some of the most influential were Ma Rainey, Blind Lemon Jefferson, Bessie Smith, Leroy Carr, Robert Johnson, and Big Bill Broonzy. Today you can hear the same tradition maintained by Muddy Waters, Memphis Slim, John Lee Hooker, B. B. King, Joe Turner, T-Bone Walker, and Eddie Vinson. The realism and simplicity in what they sing are qualities different from those found in popular, sentimental ballads. Oddly enough, the tribute paid them, and the use made of them, by British groups like the Rolling Stones and the Beatles was much responsible for a revival of interest in this country during the '60s.

The blues were worldly songs, but the gospel songs and spirituals of the black churches were also an important element from the beginning, for the way they were sung, with soulfulness and great enthusiasm, made an unforgettable impression on most jazz musicians when they were young. If you compare records by Bessie Smith and the great gospel singer Mahalia Jackson, you will see that despite the difference in *what* they sang, there is a similarity in the *way* they sang, and that there is a joint relationship with early forms of jazz expression. The fervor and warmth of gospel music were often translated as directly as possible by jazz musicians, and for a long time the adjective "hot" was used in praise of their improvised solos and tonal qualities.

When the folky character of the blues, the fervor of the gospel songs, the rhythmic attack of the New Orleans musicians, and the more sophisticated approach of the East Coast players all came together in New York, jazz was provided with a new springboard. It was also transformed by the genius of Louis Armstrong, who influenced almost every trumpet player of his own and the following generations. He had tremendous gifts and a likable personality that won him friends everywhere. His imagination was matched by his technical ability, and he played high notes on his horn such as had not been heard before. And it was not only trumpet players who tried to imitate his phrasing, but trombonists, saxophonists, and clarinetists, too. In Chicago, he teamed up with a young man from Pittsburgh named Earl Hines, who developed an unusual style on the piano that was the counterpart of his trumpet playing. This piano style also became widely influential.

Before that, however, Armstrong had been to New York to play with Fletcher Henderson, who had one of the best dance bands of the period. It was bigger than the usual New Orleans group, and because it had more instruments written arrangements were necessary. There were three trumpets, a trombone, and three saxophones, and it was not possible for all these men to memorize or merely improvise their different parts as was done in New Orleans. So Henderson and his chief arranger, Don Redman, both schooled musicians, *wrote* the music for the band to play, leaving gaps or choruses for improvisation. The rhythmic effect created by Armstrong in his solo choruses was stirring—an extra lift above and beyond the basic beat—and this sort of thing was what became known as "swinging." Soon the whole band caught on to his way of phrasing and began to swing together. In 1932, I wrote a song which became quite famous as the expression of a sentiment which prevailed among jazz musicians at that time. It was called "It Don't Mean a Thing If It Ain't Got That Swing."

Henderson's, more than any other, was the band that introduced what became known as the Swing Era. When I first formed a big band in New York, his was the one I wanted mine to sound like. In those days, before electrical amplification, big bands were essential in big ballrooms, and singers had to use megaphones. Ballrooms were very important in the jazz story, and so was the inspiration we derived from the people who danced in them, but not all the bands who worked in them played jazz in the strictest sense of the word. Generally speaking, the black bands led the way, and besides Henderson's there were soon many others that were popular, such as McKinney's Cotton Pickers, Chick Webb's, Charlie Johnson's, Don Redman's, Earl Hines's, Luis Russell's, Bennie Moten's, Claude Hopkins', Alphonso Trent's, Zack Whyte's, Jimmie Lunceford's, and ours. Among the first white bands to get the message were Jean Goldkette's, Ben Pollack's, Paul Tremaine's, and the Casa Loma Orchestra.

As bands of this kind grew in popularity, demands for their services increased. Paul Whiteman, who was credited with having "made a lady out of jazz," hired the best musicians he could get from all over the country and played what was called "symphonic" jazz. This music was more elaborate, and designed for concert performance. In vaudeville theatres and the bigger nightclubs, bands were also required to play music that was more complex, colorful, and showy than was normally required in dance halls. This was the case at Connie's Inn in New York where Don Redman played, and at the Cotton Club where we played, and at the Grand Terrace in Chicago where Earl Hines played. During one period at the Cotton Club, much attention was paid to acts with an African setting, and to accompany these we developed what was termed "jungle style" jazz. (As a student of Negro history I had, in any case, a natural inclination in this direction.) Its most striking characteristic was the use of mutes—often the plumber's everyday rubber plunger—by Bubber Miley on trumpet and Joe "Tricky Sam" Nanton on trombone. They founded a tradition we have maintained ever since. This kind of theatrical experience, and the demands it made upon us, was both educative and enriching, and it brought about a further broadening of the music's scope. We, too, began to think in terms of concert and theatre, and when I went to Europe for the first time in 1933 I found I was expected to give a concert in one of the largest cinemas in the world, before an audience almost entirely composed of musicians!

Big bands continued to grow in public favor through the '30s, until at the height of the Swing Era theirs was the most popular form of music in the country. Besides those I mentioned earlier, Count Basie had formed a band in Kansas City that exerted a great influence with its uncompromising emphasis on swinging. There were now also white bands led by such talented instrumentalists as Tommy and Jimmy Dorsey, and the clarinetists Benny Goodman, Artie Shaw, and Woody Herman. Goodman, using Fletcher Henderson's arrangements and playing an exciting clarinet style, was the most successful of all. Out of all these bands, too, rose famous singers like Ella Fitzgerald, Billie Holiday, Sarah Vaughan, Peggy Lee, Frank Sinatra, Billy Eckstine, and Jimmy Rushing.

The foundation of jazz as we know it today had by now been thoroughly laid. What was built upon it was the work of great innovators. I must emphasize that jazz was and is a highly competitive form of music, and many of the ideas that transformed it were first heard in what were called "cutting contests" or "jam sessions," where the musicians tried to learn from and outdo one another. The rise of the big bands did not mean the end of small groups, for they were always to be heard in the smaller clubs and in those places where musicians played "after hours," very late at night. There you might find James P. Johnson, Fats Waller, and The Lion competing with one another. Or several trumpet players, or saxophonists, or clarinetists. Ideas were exchanged, and newcomers learned from those with more experience. Certain innovators, like the great virtuoso of the piano, Art Tatum, remained virtually inimitable, but they were a constant source of inspiration.

By this time, jazz had become very much identified with the saxophone, and jazz musicians found new ways to express themselves on it. Out of Fletcher Henderson's band came Coleman Hawkins, whose big tone on the tenor saxophone remained the model for the profession until Lester Young appeared with Count Basie's band during 1936. Young's approach and spare tone were quite different, and they were copied by, among many others, Stan Getz, who later did so much to popularize *bossa nova,* a Brazilian form which set "cool" jazz to samba rhythm. Years later, John Coltrane came to the fore in turn with a searching style that was all his own. On alto saxophone, similarly, there was Johnny Hodges, who played in our band and was widely imitated until Charlie Parker came along with his bop style in the '40s.

Bop was regarded by many people as a revolution against the values of the previous era. At first hearing, it sounded very difficult and complicated. Parker and Dizzy Gillespie, the trumpet player, seemed to be playing many notes very fast, and the drummer and pianist accompanying them were no longer content with providing a steady, regular beat. Because of the speed of execution, the old tonal values were sacrificed (it was no longer possible to play with the former expressive vibrato), and the new music had a shrill, cooler sound. Soon it was fashionable to play "cool" rather than "hot."

Since that time there have been new category labels for several different varieties of jazz, but each has primarily been created and dominated by the distinct tonal personality of a gifted individual. The fascination of jazz as a music lies in the performer's freedom of expression, so that the listener is always asking himself, "Where do we go from here?"

Although his background seemed to give the black musician the edge, because environment is intensely important as a shaping factor, jazz was so contagious that many white musicians were infected by it and grew close to the black soul. Names that come to mind are Bunny Berigan, Jack Teagarden, Dave Tough, Jess Stacy, Nat Pierce, and Mezz Mezzrow. On the other hand, there were black musicians who were impressed by white standards of playing, acquired comparable techniques, and retired from the competitive arena into the comparative safety of the television, movie, and recording studios.

Today, jazz is an international music that is played everywhere in the world on almost every conceivable instrument. It is a music of such extraordinary variety that it is most consistently recognizable by its rhythmic vitality. But just imagine the dilemma you could find yourself in with a creature newly arrived from outer space.

"Young man," he asks, "will you please let me hear some jazz?"

"I'll be glad to, sir," you say hospitably, turning to your record player. "Listen to these."

Now what or whose music would you play? That of Louis Armstrong, King Oliver, Dizzy Gillespie, Miles Davis, Jack Teagarden, J. J. Johnson, The

Lion, Earl Hines, Art Tatum, Dave Brubeck, Bill Evans, Johnny Hodges, Charlie Parker, Ornette Coleman, Coleman Hawkins, Lester Young, John Coltrane, Sidney Bechet, Buster Bailey, Benny Goodman, Charlie Christian, Django Reinhardt, Kenny Burrell, Fletcher Henderson, Count Basie, Stan Kenton, Buddy Rich, Woody Herman, the Modern Jazz Quartet, or . . . ? .

As I said at the beginning, the story of jazz is a long list of great names. In its different phases, different instruments have enjoyed a vogue with the public—piano, trumpet, clarinet, tenor saxophone, flute, organ, and guitar have all had their day in the sun, and drums and drum solos are *always* popular. Or if you choose to examine jazz state by state, or city by city, you will find that great musicians were born in all of them. For example, W. C. Handy, Nat Cole, Dinah Washington, Cootie Williams, Urbie Green, Dud and Paul Bascomb, Erskine Hawkins, Teddy Hill, and Avery Parrish all came from Alabama. Texas, that big state, gave us Lips Page, Tyree Glenn, Teddy Wilson, Buddy Tate, Herschel Evans, Sammy Price, Budd and Keg Johnson, Arnett Cobb, Ornette Coleman, Ray McKinley, Harold Land, Eddie Vinson, Herb Ellis, T-Bone Walker, Jack and Charlie Teagarden, and so many more.

St. Louis is a city that should be famous for more than the blues, because so many fine musicians came from there, such as Jimmy Blanton, Wendell Marshall, Clark Terry, Shorty Baker, Louis Metcalf, Milt and Ted Buckner, Gene Sedric, Pee Wee Russell, and the arrangers Oliver Nelson and Ernie Wilkins.

New Orleans, Chicago, New York, and—this may surprise you—Philadelphia would need separate pages here to list all the famous musicians they have given the world. So would countries like England and France.

The Jersey Crescent is an unusual and outstanding territory for our kind of music. For example: Willie "The Lion" Smith made his professional debut in Newark; Sarah Vaughan, the Divine One, was born in the same city; Count Basie is from Red Bank; Sonny Greer, the Sweet Singing Drummer, is from Long Branch; James P. Johnson was born in New Brunswick; Donald Lambert, The Lamb, was from Princeton; Sam Woodyard is from Elizabeth; Slam Stewart is from Englewood; Cozy Cole is from East Orange; Joya Sherrill is from Bayonne; Buddy De Franco and Butch Ballard are from Camden; Charlie Persip, Tony Scott, and Bobby Tucker are all three from Morristown; Nelson Riddle is from Oradell; Bill Evans is from Plainfield; Joe Benjamin and Chris Columbus are from Atlantic City; and in the wake of the same romantic soul wave, Newark gave us Ike Quebec, Wayne Shorter,

Babs Gonzales, Bobby Plater, Al Haig, and so many more. When Billy Stray-horn joined us, it was at the Adams Theatre in Newark!

Our concert with Henry Lewis, the great conductor of symphony and opera, and the New Jersey State Symphony, was one of my truly enchanting musical adventures. I remember, too, that New Jersey has big supporters like Bill Cook and Bill Franklin, patrons like Rose Stewart and the Fourteen Pals and Patrons, and that Mayor Kenneth Gibson of Newark acclaims both the music and us, the purveyors.

And I remember further back, to the old days in Harlem, and how, just when you were getting acclimatized and feeling yourself more or less accepta-ble and equal to exposure before the low, hip circle, one of the older Big Boys on the corner would explode your illusions. "Gather round, kids," he would say, lowering the hipper boom, "and let me tell you what time it is!" Then he would relate a spicy little inside episode on how it used to be across the Hud-son River, in Newark.

Newark remains today a sort of peripheral spread for the Jersey Crescent, which contains the homes and springboards of so many great musicians. And don't ever forget that Francis Albert Sinatra is from Hoboken! In fact, I wonder how the greatest metropolis in the world would manage, or what it would do, without the splendid auto roads and turnpike in New Jersey to serve as a red-carpet entrance way.

At the White House

We played the Inaugural Ball in Washington in January 1969, and when President Nixon entered everything came to a stop in the ballroom. The first thing he said was, "As Duke Ellington would say, it don't mean a thing if it ain't got that swing!"

During a rather intimate session upstairs in the presidential living room on the night of April 29, 1969, when the President and Mrs. Nixon, Mr. and Mrs. Spiro Agnew, my sister and I were there, I felt the time was opportune to ask about that statement.

"Mr. President, when you said that," I ventured, "did it imply that you were one of those graceful jitterbugs who used to inspire all the jazz bands down at the Rendezvous Ballroom at Balboa Beach in California, Stan Kenton's old home base?"

"No, Duke," he answered. "I have never really been a dancer. I'm a watcher."

But from there our new president went on to show us that he did have a genuine interest in music of the American idiom. While taking us around various rooms on the family's floor, he led us into one where there was an expensive stereo machine with many records and tapes. He proceeded to demonstrate all the audio possibilities—increasing the bass and the treble, one after the other, and showing how well the range was maintained at full and low volume. He was just like a kid with a new toy. I don't know what kind of stereo he thought I expected the President of the U.S.A. to have, but I do know that I found him tracking wonderfully that evening.

The president then very graciously threw a gala seventieth-birthday ball in my honor, appointed Willis Conover to bring in an all-star band (Clark Terry, Bill Berry, J. J. Johnson, Urbie Green, Paul Desmond, Gerry Mulligan, Hank Jones, Jim Hall, Milt Hinton, and Louis Bellson, with Earl Hines, Dave Brubeck, and Billy Taylor as special soloists, and Mary Mayo and Joe Williams

President and Mrs. Richard M. Nixon, Ruth and Duke Ellington at the White House, 1969

At the White House, April 29, 1969, left to right: Dave Brubeck, Hank Jones, Jim Hall, Tom Whaley, Paul Desmond, Earl Hines, Gerry Mulligan, Billy Taylor, Mary Mayo, Milt Hinton, Willis Conover, Louis Bellson, President Nixon, Duke Ellington, Joe Williams, Urbie Green, J. J. Johnson, Bill Berry

as vocalists. The guests invited—without any political partiality—included priests, canons, pastors, rabbis, university presidents, writers, doctors, lawyers, executives, artists, many of my friends and relatives, and, of course, high government officials.

I was in the receiving line next to the President and Mrs. Nixon, and he noticed that I gave all these great men and their wives four kisses each. In between greeting the guests, he turned to me.

"Four kisses?" he asked. "Why four?"

"One for each cheek, Mr. President," I explained.

"Oh!" he said.

After the line had passed, to my amazement he turned to me, and I turned to him, and without a word being said we exchanged four kisses. He seemed pleased.

"Now I'm a member?" he asked.

"Yes, Mr. President, you are a member."

At dinner, I was honored and delighted to be sitting on the right hand of the beautiful First Lady, Mrs. Pat Nixon. She told me her daughter had seen me in Woodward and Lothrop's while shopping earlier that day.

"Oh, yes," I said, "and you have a beautiful daughter!"

After a pause, I ventured further.

"Mrs. Nixon, have you heard of the White House Ordinance?"

"White House Ordinance?" she said, turning and looking a little askance.

"Yes, Mrs. Nixon, there is a law that says that no first lady should be prettier than a certain degree, and you are exceeding the legal limit. Why, you can get a ticket for it!"

To my great astonishment, the First Lady gave me a direct, accusing look and said, "I heard about *you!*"

Some of the men who had worked at the White House for twenty or thirty years said there had never been a night like that before, and I believe them. The party went on until after two o'clock. Can you imagine Billy Eckstine, Lou Rawls, and Joe Williams, all at the mike at the same time, each singing the other's blues? Can you imagine me dancing with Carmen De Lavallade? Can you imagine Vice President Agnew playing "Sophisticated Lady," or the lovely First Lady's handsome husband playing "Happy Birthday" in the key of G? Many great pianists played on that piano that night, including Earl Hines, who broke it up with "Perdido," but the big moment for me was when I saw my man, The Lion, playing the President's concert grand, still with his derby on his head!

I always say that Joe Morgen, my p.r. man, contrived a scheme to persuade the President to give me a birthday party by putting my age up thirty-one years. The truth is that I was forty the following year and now I am *fortezando.*

* * *

When President Johnson was in the White House, I had the pleasure of being invited seven times, twice to entertain, and as a guest on the other occasions. The First Lady, Mrs. Lady Bird Johnson, and her daughter were always extremely gracious. The First Lady's staff, headed by Mrs. Bess Abell and Mrs. Barbara Keehn, backed our host in such a way that I could never feel that I was anywhere but home.

My first visit was when representative members of A.S.C.A.P. (the American Society of Composers, Authors and Publishers) were received and honored by the National Council of the Arts, to which I was to be elected. Later on, our band played for the Festival of the Arts on June 14, 1965, in the White House grounds. I was very happy to see how interested the President was in all the arts. The festival itself was presented on a very high plane, and so many great artists were represented there that it gave me a real bang to be among them.

The following year, I was there again for a dinner of the Arts Council, and in 1967 I was there twice. The first time was when President Johnson had a celebration for Their Majesties, the King and Queen of Thailand.

A couple of months later, I was back again when my doctor's son-in-law, Clifford Alexander, was sworn in as chairman of the Equal Employment Opportunities Commission. Since he was a well-educated and fine young man, I felt confident he would be a valuable addition to the President's group of experts.

On March 27, 1968, there was a State Dinner honoring President and Mrs. William V. S. Tubman of the Republic of Liberia. I have always felt that I was related to Liberia, because in 1947, on the occasion of that country's centenary, we celebrated it by premiering a new work at Carnegie Hall entitled *The Liberian Suite*. I did not want to miss the evening at the White House, although we had an engagement in Las Vegas at that time. Luckily, we were able to switch our off-day. It turned out to be a wonderful party, another one of those I think Paul Gonsalves enjoyed more than the honored guests. He—or rather, we—jammed with the Marine Band's dance group, and I only wish I had a picture of Paul Gonsalves coming out the front door of the White House, weaving slightly, his horn in his hand, and just a little bombed.

I was back once more on November 21, 1968, for an Arts Council reception, and at dinner I sat next to Mrs. Hubert Humphrey. What a wonderful and charming dinner companion she was! She made so much sense in everything she talked about, and was very informative, too.

A few days later, I accompanied the First Lady on part of what was referred to in the press as her "farewell" tour across the country. With Marian Anderson and other members of the Arts Council, we went to New Orleans, where we visited Xavier University and an experimental school for training "problem" children.

At the White House, March 27, 1968, playing for President William V. S. Tubman of Liberia

The next time I saw Lyndon Baines Johnson was at the Texas-Arkansas football game in Austin. He was just a few seats away, so I went over and we embraced, and then I kissed his hand. Later, someone who saw it on television asked why I did that, and I explained that it was LBJ who had made me a member of the Arts Council, which automatically puts an "Hon." in front of your name. To me, that was the equivalent of being knighted by a monarch, and I am sure it is quite right and proper to kiss the hand of·any king or queen who dubs you "Sir Knight."

I never met President Kennedy, but I understood that he was happy about the friends and good impression we made on our State Department tour in 1963.

When I went to see and play for President Eisenhower at the White House Correspondents Dinner, I was given a sumptuous suite of rooms in the Mayflower Hotel. As I got off the elevator in the lobby, the President was just

431

With President and Mrs. Lyndon B. Johnson, White House reception for the National Council for the Arts, November 20, 1968

entering it. He gave me a big hello, and then, as I was walking away, he called out loudly, "Say, Duke, don't forget to play 'Mood Indigo'!"

I thought that was pretty good coming from the victorious general of World War II, and I got a lift from it. During our performance that night we played "Mood Indigo" four times!

Each of the presidents I met received me with warm, friendly hospitality, and all formality was abandoned. For example, when I went to see President Truman, he dismissed his bodyguard, closed the door of his private study, and invited me to sit down and talk as one piano player to another! He said he was honored to be presented with the original score of *Harlem*. After that, you might have thought we were a couple of cats in a billiard parlor, so informal was our conversation. He sort of confessed he was not the real piano player I was, but we acted as though he were Doc Perry or Louis Brown. I was very happy.

When I got outside and encountered the press, they wanted to know what I thought of the President. I told them I was thoroughly reassured, and felt as though I had just spoken to my doctor, which meant I was convinced the country was in good health and that everything was cool.

Public Relations

Selected by Irving Mills to represent Duke Ellington, Ned Williams was a man born with the natural sensitivities for public relations in any environment, social or industrial. A natural wit and a *bon vivant,* he knew all the most important figures of the press—as well as the most unimportant in the whirl of hip and all that gas. His partner in business, K. Hansen, made our first trip to Europe with us. I never knew why. But Ned E. Williams was my man—prime Iowa hip. As a matter of fact, the hippest people I've ever met were originally from Iowa: Lee Phillips, and Pat Sampson, the daughter of the president of an Iowa university, and many more whose names I cannot now recall. The Ferguson family were always superb hosts and kept open house for us at the university. And Allyn and Helen Lemme, a very handsome brownskin couple, kept open house in Iowa City year after year for the entire student body—a giant step in race relations before it became popular.

Iowa is generally known as the Corn State, but those kids at that university were 'way ahead of their time in their appreciation of philosophical, intellectual, artistic, and poetic subjects. Today, I hear the *nouvelle vague* and the *avante garde* using many of the phrases those kids used thirty years ago. I woke up on them in 1948, when we were doing *The Tattooed Bride* as our "long work" or *pièce de résistance.* We were giving a concert at the university in Iowa City, and the audience could not have been more musically aware. I gave my usual explanation of what *The Tattooed Bride* was intended to portray, and when we played it—a new number fifteen minutes long—I could feel the exchange of sensitivity, the most extraordinary sensitivity. I have never thought of Iowa as corn country since.

It is a state where forever friends drive a hundred miles in the snow to hear us. They are only matched or outdone by a sign-painter friend of ours, Ray Crowel, who always puts his family—his wife and two sons—in their station

434

wagon, and drives as much as two hundred miles over and through the snow and mountains of Idaho. You have to drive over more mountains to get anywhere in Idaho than any state in the Union.

After Ned Williams became editor of *Down Beat,* my brother-in-law, Dan James, was handling us, and he suggested and arranged for George Evans to take my account. George was doing public relations work for Frank Sinatra at the time, and I must say that it was a brilliant move. He was most fitting for me and my image when we were so social-significance prone, and he did a great job so long as I was able to have his services.

I met Pat Willard in Los Angeles when she was doing some work for the Empire Ballroom, where we were working. It was then owned by Gene Norman. She is the imaginative, creative, and authoritative type of p.r., who always dreams of adding an extra glitter to the glamour of her client.

Joe Morgen, who has been with me the longest—over twenty years—is the kind of p.r. who thinks only in terms of cover stories, full-page pictures, and big, important articles in magazines. Maybe I exaggerate a little, for he will stand still for a good word in a column. He was the one who engineered the *Time* cover story in 1956 after our success at the Newport Jazz Festival.

Joe may not appear to be too aggressive, but I think he does a great job. He is an extraordinary individual, and I always say he is a man who doesn't have the tiniest facet of the devious in his makeup. We always take advantage of the fact that he is so extremely loyal, and we kid him if we learn that he has been to hear Count Basie or any other band leader. One day, when Harry Carney and I were driving down the New Jersey Turnpike, we happened to look left as we passed another car. Whom do you think we saw? Joe Morgen in the back seat of a car with Dizzy Gillespie at the wheel. We had a good deal to say about that!

One thing Joe Morgen and I have in common is that we are both Sinatra fans.

Music and the Primeval

The human being has patterned his every move, sound, and image after God's other creatures and natural wonders. Birds whistle like birds, leopards walk like leopards, horses run like horses, gulls fly like gulls, lions roar like lions, and fish swim like fish. All animals, except people, act like their species.

Music, for instance, began with man, primitive man, trying to duplicate Nature's sounds—winds, birds, animals, water, the crescendo of fire—after which great systems of learning were set up, only to discover that music is limitless. The more you learn, the more you want to learn. And the more you hear it, the more you want to hear it.

Jazz is many things to many people. To me, it has been a banner under which I have written and played most of life, almost all the way around the world. I have enjoyed entree to many fine homes; I have enjoyed the friends I have met and talked with; and I have listened to some of the greatest music and musicians in the world. I have been received by presidents, first ladies, kings, queens, maharajahs, maharanees, champions, chief justices, *chefs de cuisine,* painters, sculptors, screen stars, butchers, bakers, doctors, lawyers, dishwashers, and streetcleaners. It would be very difficult to say whom I enjoyed more, or whose food was the more appetizing, but all brought the warm enthusiasm of the listener whose ears have had a joyous encounter with our music.

To some people around the world, jazz is the music of the people who are privileged to live in a land with mountains of gold, rivers of oil, billions of bushels of surplus food, and freedom of expression. It's not unlawful to sing or play *any* kind of music in the United States of America, no matter how good or bad it sounds. Jazz is based on the sound of our native heritage. It is an American idiom with African roots—a trunk of soul with limbs reaching in every direction, to the frigid North, the exotic East, the miserable, swampy South, and the swinging Wild West.

Ball in Munich

Retire to What?

I've never had a vacation since I started my career as a musician. I can look back on a kaleidoscope of Washington house hops, society parties, Virginia horse shows, and barn dances; on the soda jerk and piano plunker at the Poodle Dog in Washington, at Mrs. Dyer's, and in Room 5 and Room 10. In New York, it changes to Barron's, the Kentucky Club, the Cotton Club; doubling at the Palace; Ziegfeld's *Show Girl;* Maurice Chevalier's first New York personal appearance; recording, radio, television, doubling, tripling, and sometimes more. Even when I went to the hospital, the band kept on. The nearest I ever had to a vacation was when I was working on a picture, but I was still active with music, as in the case of *Anatomy of a Murder.* I was on location then at Ishpeming, Michigan, with Otto Preminger and the former attorney general of Michigan, John Volker. I was eight weeks in Paris working on *Paris Blues* with producer Sam Shaw and a fabulous art collector, Ian Woodner. *Assault on a Queen* with Frank Sinatra and producer Doug Bridges took me to Hollywood, but I did *Change of Mind* with Raymond St. Jacques right here in New York.

In spite of this constant activity, people often ask me when I'm going to retire. I answer by asking, "Retire to what?" Nobody seems to be able to think of anything for me to retire to, other than golf or traveling and seeing the world. Golf is a very good sport, I'm sure. My only experience of it was in Dayton, Ohio, when friends—a man and his wife—invited me to come with them to the golf course one day. I know the fundamentals of golf and most sports, of course, so I went along with them to the course and actually played nine holes. I shot the nine holes in thirty-six. They were surprised, and said I had accomplished the impossible with such a surprising average in one round of golf.

I have not been back to the golf course since. Why should I spoil such a

good average? And on the other hand, in order to play golf one must go outdoors, and I don't want to get fresh air poisoning. Since then, the only thing I do outdoors is concerts.

Retirement is a category. People do not retire. They are retired by others—set aside, tucked away in some category so that the retirer knows where to find them at any given moment.

The retirer enters and addresses the retiree:

"John, I want to tell you, in the name of the company, that you are our favorite man. You have done one hell of a job . . . you have given the company thirty-five years of the greatest years any company has had . . . and, John, we want you to know that we love you and we know that you would like to relax so we are going to relieve you of some of this responsibility. The Board Members want you to accept this watch, with their gratitude etc., etc. I envy your position and I can see you now, stretched out there on one of those tropical islands with all those pretty broads . . . Man! etc., etc."

The truth is that the company don't give a damn about John and that there's a new guy around who is reputed to be real sharp and with it and the company wants to get him before the opposition does.

"So John, you write your own letter of resignation anytime, *soon!*"

Pedestrian Minstrel

I am a minstrel, a pedestrian minstrel, a primitive pedestrian minstrel. Sometimes I imagine I paint, with water colors or oils, a crystal-clear lake in the sky reflecting the shadows of invisible trees upside-down beneath sun-kissed, cotton-candy snow. On the fringe, clouds so foamy white—tranquil on top, a raging storm inside . . . "I'll write it," I think, before returning to that half sleep as the plane roars on to Atlanta . . . or is it Atlantis? Plans, plans, the most impossible of enormous plans, pastel or opaque. Sometimes I'll write a play or plot, drama or comedy, revue or re-do. And sometimes I mold a figure, graceful or grotesque, out of whatever material happens to pop into my mind. If it's a chunk of rock or steel, or a trunk of a tree, or maybe just the single petal of a rose, it must be fashioned to the raw, or the ore, according to its dimensions and shape, large or small.

Steel on steel, thousands of miles of steel or tracks, with thousands of round, steel wheels—what a happy marriage! The rhythm of the motion, thirty-nine hours from Chicago to Los Angeles—what a marvel of masculinity, thirty-nine hours, power-stroking all the way. He gave her the high ball in the Loop, stopped in Englewood, and that's all she wrote, grinding up to ninety miles per hour, so hot the steam was bursting out everywhere. She had fine lubrication. You could hear her for miles, whistle-screaming, "Yes, daddy, I'm coming, daddy!" Don't pull that throttle out until you pull into Glendale . . . driving shaft pumping a steady beat . . . long and round, heavin' and strokin' . . . puffin' and smokin' . . . and shovelin' and stokin'. He stopped, let off a little steam. She, out of breath, panted, "Wash up, ready for that red-carpet reception." He got off, glanced over his shoulder at her as she backed out of Union station, out into the yard, with unraised eyelashes, like the dignified lady she was, she who, between departure and arrival, had given her all to a union laborer, opened her throttle wide, and allowed him his every wish. Truly, a tremendous romance.

441

Should I write this music with the passion they pumped over the track, or should I maybe start with the wheel, the molten steel, or with those burly black arms behind the thrust that drove the spikes into the railroad ties? There's a grunt with every thrust from the owner of those arms, as though he were rehearsing for the cool of the evening, when he and his woman would be together, when he would drag her out of that hot kitchen. Wringing wet with perspiration, she blushes, but she's been wishing for him all day, to come home and pull her out of that hot place. Now she's hotter than the kitchen

1972: Duke Ellington, piano; Joe Benjamin, bass; Rufus Jones, drums; Paul Gonsalves, Harold Minerve, Harold Ashby, Harry Carney, Norris Turney, Russell Procope, reeds

stove, sexually clobbering this cat, until he thinks she's putting everything on him but . . . do I have to say, "the kitchen stove"?

Raw or ore, gold or gook, or indigo, filigree, or feathers, carve a breach as deep as desire demands, but don't destroy the maidenhead. Blow Cootie up to the ceiling, make Cat go tooting through the roof, jam Sam into a Charleston beat, let Paul go-go, running through the lattice work of brass cacophony, while Jimmy weaves delicate lacework around the edges. Give Harry that "molto profondo," so that Lawrence will cry and wail in the wake of the

Early publicity shot

après-coup. Stomp down, those symmetrical after-beats, baby, so that Rab can smelt the melody to smoldering, and over the hush let's hear the broads in the back row whisper, "Tell the story, daddy." Russell's got the kind of wood that Barney had, when Whetsol was playing the unduplicatably dulcet. You can't use Charley Plug or Tricky—one just doesn't, any more. Bubber said it, and he was right! *It don't mean a thing if it ain't got that swing.* Mr. Braud's not going to back away from that mike. Like the great Greer used to tell Freddie Guy—"Take it down from the top, pop, and don't stop for the bop . . .

"Ole Duke used to have a pretty good left hand after he hear James P., The Lion, and Fats," Greer continues, "but then he heard Fletcher, Redman, Whiteman, and Goldkette, and got horn fever . . . *horns, horns, and more*

444

horns . . . Coppin' out and talkin' 'bout 'the band is my instrument.' What would Doc Perry and Lester Dishman say to that? From six pieces to eleven, twelve, fourteen, and fifteen. Then he got up and conducted a symphony of a hundred and ten pieces. After that there was that record album, *The Symphonic Ellington,* with five hundred of the greatest musicians in Europe.

"Will Marion Cook and Henry Grant—they would be pleased. They used to tell Duke to go to the conservatory. Black Bowie used to call him the *phoney duke,* back in Frank Holliday's poolroom. I remember when he was just a yearling, the jive relief piano-plunker. Bill Jones used to be drummin', and he'd catch him out there in those three-four, five-four switches, and scare him stiff. But he'd hang on, and as I said he had a pretty good left hand, and he'd hold the solid deuce till Bill let him off the hook. They raised him with discipline and encouragement music-wise. Those East Coast cats were like that. They had the greatest respect for the book. 'If the man didn't want it played that way,' they said, 'he wouldn't have written it that way.' And so Duke listened, and they laid down the laws, and he listened some more, and I guess that's why he calls himself the world's greatest listener today."

Yes, I am the world's greatest listener. Here I am, fifty years later, still getting cats out of bed to come to work, so that I can listen to them and so that they can make a living for their own families. This, however, does not alter the perspective of the pedestrian peddler, who sometimes imagines that he takes a pair of scissors, and some paper or cardboard, and cuts out shapes of paper dolls. He takes them out on the corner and displays them, bending them and plucking them so that they will make a noise. And, of course, the noise is the main thing, because the people hear the noise, and when they like it they say, "Ah, I'll take it . . ." So I let them have it—the noise, that is. And I collect my dolls and go out the next day, to see if I can make other people like the noise. Practically every day I go to a different corner, and sometimes for a change I take my scissors and cut out paper flowers. I wrap them neatly, put them in my pushcart, and take them to the corner. I stand there, plucking them with my third finger to make a noise, hoping it carries an attractive vibration to a passer-by's ear. When he shows interest, I'll do an encore, and when he asks, "How much?", I say: "If you like this little noise, just something in the cup. Don't hurt yourself. Whatever you can stand, and the sound is yours. I can't let you have the flowers. I need them to make more noise. I like to listen myself, you know. I think maybe there's nothing quite like planning and designing at night, and coming out and listening to it next day. I'm impetuous, you know."

There is hardly any money interest in the realm of art, and music will be here when money is gone. After people have destroyed all people everywhere, I see heaping mounds of money strewn over the earth, floating on and sinking into the sea. The animals and fish, who have no use for money, are kicking it out of the way and splattering it with dung. Money and stink, the stink of dung, the stink of money, so foul that in order for the flowers to get a breath of fresh air, the winds will come together and whip the sea into a rage, and blow across the land. Then the green leaves of trees, and grass, will give up their chlorophyll, so that the sea, the wind, the beasts, and the birds will play and sing Nature's old, sweet melody and rhythm. But since you are people, you will not, unfortunately, be here to hear it.

Money is becoming too important. So far as the hazards of the big band are concerned, I give the musicians the money and I get the kicks. Billy Strayhorn said we were exponents of the aural art. Ours is the responsibility of bringing to the listener and would-be listener—as to those unwilling to be listeners—some agreeable vibration that tickles the fancy of the eardrum. Of course, the connoisseur has a much better appreciation of duet and countermelody than the average would-be listener. Some people think modern means unattractive, whether it's 1905 or 1975, but consonance is in the imagination of the hearer. Maybe a sound gives him a nostalgic nudge, back to the one moment to which he has always wanted to return.

Roaming through the jungle, the jungle of "oohs" and "ahs," searching for a more agreeable noise, I live a life of primitivity with the mind of a child and an unquenchable thirst for sharps and flats. The more consonant, the more appetizing and delectable they are. Cacophony is hard to swallow. Living in a cave, I am almost a hermit, but there is a difference, for I have a mistress. Lovers have come and gone, but only my mistress stays. She is beautiful and gentle. She waits on me hand and foot. She is a swinger. She has grace. To hear her speak, you can't believe your ears. She is ten thousand years old. She is as modern as tomorrow, a brand-new woman every day, and as endless as time mathematics. Living with her is a labyrinth of ramifications. I look forward to her every gesture.

Music is my mistress, and she plays second fiddle to no one.

447

Epilogue

The Mirrored Self

Let us imagine a quiet, cozy cove where all the senses except one seem to have dispersed. There is nothing to smell, nothing to taste, nothing to hear, and nothing to feel but the reaction to what can be seen. Nearby is a still pool, so still that it resembles a limpid mirror. If we look in it, what we see is the reflection of ourselves, just as we thought we looked, wearing the identical clothes, the same countenance . . .

Ah, this is *us,* the us we know, and as we savor the wonderful selves-of-perfection we suddenly realize that just below our mirror, there is another reflection that is not quite so clear, and not quite what we expected. This translucent surface has a tendency toward the vague: the lines are not firm and the colors not quite the same, but it is us, or should we say *me,* or rather one of our other selves? We examine this uncertain portrait and just as we feel inclined to accept it we realize that, down below this, there is still another mirror reflecting another of our selves, and more. For this third mirror is transparent, and we can plainly see what is going on both before and behind it, and we refuse to credit that here is still another of our selves. But there we are with four reflections, all reflections of us who look at them. We accept the first three, even with the vague and misty overtones, but the fourth, on the other side of the transparent mirror, leaves us baffled and on the verge of defeat. It is hard to believe that we would do this to *me,* but we saw it with our own eyes. Which is the one we love most? We know that *I* am one of our favorite people, but which one? It does not have anything to do with what we are doing to anybody else, but what we are doing to *me,* the thinker-writer, the okayer, the nixer, the player, the listener, the critic, the corrector. What are they all saying? We can't hear them. We can only see them. A ripple in the pool and they all disappear.

Now we can hear, feel, smell, and taste.

Q. What are your major interests?

A. Well, I live in the realm of art and have no monetary interests.

Q. What do you think of people who have monetary interests?

A. I doubt whether art could survive if business and such people did not subsidize it in some form. I do not concern myself with other people's business, because I have enough problems of my own.

Q. Like what, for instance?

A. I have to answer to my other selves.

Q. Which other selves?

A. My better selves, of course.

Q. What are your better selves like? What demands do they make on you?

A. I have to answer to my better self in music, and that becomes a matter of how it sounds when I write or play it, of its consonance, its dissonance . . .

Q. What about your best self?

A. My best self writes and plays sacred music and keeps me honest to myself. My best self also prays for the health and survival of others—and for the forgiveness of still others.

Q. Do you consider yourself as a forerunner in the advanced musical trends derived from jazz?

A. There were many wonderful musicians who established themselves and the word "jazz" many years before my time. "Jazz" is only a word and really has no meaning. We stopped using it in 1943. To keep the whole thing clear, once and for all, I don't believe in categories of any kind.

Q. In the music you compose now, is there some survival of what was once characterized as "jungle style" in your performances?

A. We write from the same perspective as before. We write to fit the tonal personalities of the individual instrumentalists who have the responsibility of interpreting our works.

Q. How do you regard the phenomenon of the black race's contribution to U.S. and world culture?

A. Regarding the Negro influence on culture generally, I imagine other people too found it agreeable to their senses.

Q. Do you enjoy composing music, or do you prefer performing? And have you a magic formula for attracting audiences?

A. I like any and all of my associations with music—writing, playing, and listening. We write and play from our perspective, and the audience listens from its perspective. If and when we agree, I am lucky.

Q. Do you think your performances in the jazz field can be connected with those of other writers and artists in the U.S.?

A. I try not to conform to vogues.

Q. Do you think jazz is having a kind of revival now?

A. The word "jazz" is still being used with great success, but I don't know how such great extremes as now exist can be contained under the one heading.

Q. Why do so many people, above all abroad, consider jazz intellectual music?

A. We enjoy freedom of expression in presenting our music, and some people prefer to accept it in their own fashion.

Q. When you work with symphony orchestras, what is the greatest hurdle in conducting their musicians and yours? Do the symphony men dig your way easily?

A. There is no hurdle at all in the case of our musicians. The music is mostly all in tempo and the responsibility for togetherness rests in the main with the symphony orchestra. It's more or less a matter of establishing an understandable beat, whether it's in two-four, four-four, or five-four. They can play anything they can see, and the conductor's responsibility is to *know* thoroughly the piece he is conducting.

Q. Can you sense when something special is beginning to happen at a concert or on a record session?

A. When one is fortunate enough to have an extremely sensitive audience, and when every performer within the team on stage feels it, too, and reacts positively in co-ordination toward the pinnacle, and when both audience and performers are determined not to be outdone by the other, and when both have appreciation and taste to match—then it is indeed a very special moment, never to be forgotten.

Q. What sound, to you, is the most cacophonous?

A. I could offer numerous examples and cop-outs, but the cacophony in Damascus would take some beating. One minute there you hear the priest calling the people to prayer, and the next minute, in great contrast to the serene silence he secured, there is the tremendous uproar of traffic. At 6 A.M. every day it seemed that every automobile that had ever been converged at this intersection just outside my window. I am accustomed to sleeping in the daytime all over the world, but this racing of motors and blowing of horns made sleep impossible.

Q. Do you work better under pressure?

A. I scarcely do anything without a tight deadline. I work to the last minute.

Q. You are known to work under extraordinary conditions, with the television going, people talking, lights blazing, and telephones ringing. Do you need that kind of semiconfusion, or are you so accustomed to it that you are oblivious to it? Or can you just tune out at will?

A. In the early music publishing houses, there might be as many as ten pianos going at once, and you had to learn to write a lead sheet under those circumstances. If I were making a lead sheet to get an advance, I couldn't afford to let all those noises interfere with the noise I was trying to put down on one sheet of paper. Of course, I don't make the blueprint for coincidences of the kind mentioned, but if and when they happen, I seldom have the urge or fortitude to be a disciplinarian. Nor do I have the impudence to be rude, or the gall or brass to demand *order*.

Q. Do you hear your music mentally first? Does it work out in a pattern from a beginning? And do you hear it in single notes, chords, phrases, or larger, whole parts?

A. Each and all the ways. Acceptance is unconditional.

Q. Do you think a composor will ever be able to figure out mathematically what he wants, feed it to a computer, and let *it* compose?

A. They had the player piano years ago.

Q. An artist is now expected to do many things to "promote" himself and his work. Is there danger in overexposure on television, in radio interviews, etc., etc.?

A. Everybody is different. There is no general rule.

Q. How does the artist keep control and avoid manipulation by agents, managers, and business people?

A. The artist is either a better businessman or a better artist.

Q. You function in triplicate as performer, composer, and conductor. In what order would you put these roles, or does it change according to the situation?

A. Each is different and each must be approached with a different perspective. None is as important as—or more important than—the one being enjoyed at the moment.

Q. How do you approach an assignment to score a movie or a play? Is it dominated by your feeling or the director's interpretation of the story?

A. The composer usually has his own idea about it, but this may be altered at the discretion of the director. Scoring is primarily for background purposes and it should never overpower the action or dialogue on the stage or screen.

Q. What do you think of the new music?

A. I think that music is neither new nor old.

Q. I mean the young people's music.

A. I don't think the age of the performer should be considered one way or the other. If it sounds good, it's good music, and if it doesn't, then it is the other kind. The question of new and old music, young and old musicians, always seems to be designed to defeat me. It is usually asked by someone who is not aware of what is going on today, who, I imagine, has in mind the kids in the Top 40 who get the most publicity, like the kids who are rebellious, smoke pot, or indulge themselves in various unlawful ways. The naughty kids, in other words, always get their picture on television, in newspapers and magazines. The constructive youngsters, who are doing something normal and behaving like clean, progressive individuals in preparation for responsible positions in the society of tomorrow—they are never mentioned.

Q. Does this apply to music?

A. Of course it does. There is a whole world of college and school bands where youngsters are very diligently preparing for careers in music, and a lot of extremely talented musicians are devoting themselves to their tuition. I could never list them all, but some I know or have heard of are Herb Pomeroy at Berklee School of Music in Boston; Bill Russo at Columbia College in Chicago; Dave Baker at Indiana University in Bloomington; Leon Breeden at North Texas State University in Denton; John Garvey at the University of Illinois in Urbana; Roger Schueler at Millikin University in Decatur, Illinois; Jim Coffin at the University of Northern Iowa in Cedar Falls; Raoul Jerome at the University of Southern Mississippi in Hattiesburg; Jerry Coker at the University of Miami in Coral Gables; Derryl Goes at the University of Northern Colorado in Greeley; Evan Solot at Philadelphia Music Academy; Jim Hebert at Loyola University in New Orleans; Ron Modell at the University of Northern Illinois in De Kalb; Ladd McIntosh at the University of Utah in Salt Lake City; Alvin Batiste at Southern University in Baton Rouge, Louisiana; Tom Ferguson at Memphis State University in Tennessee; Bill Dobins at Kent State University, Ohio; Hank Levy at Towson State College in Maryland; and Dick Carlson at Los Angeles Valley College. Besides these, there are more encouraging noises coming again from black schools like Howard and Grambling.

Q. Don't these people and the bands they put together get publicity?

A. Yes, some, but it is generally at a local level, or in specialist magazines like *Down Beat* and *Music Journal.* Charles Suber, the publisher of *Down Beat,* told me that they estimated there would be nearly sixty school jazz festivals in 1971, with an involvement of around 35,000 school musicians at all levels within 1,750 big bands and two hundred combos. They also estimated that the total for all school and college jazz ensembles in the country is approximately 16,500 big bands and 2,500 combos. Now that's incredible when you translate it into a total of musically educated youngsters, and you have to consider it not merely from the viewpoint of educated performers, but also from that of educated listeners and educated ears. If this process compounds itself, as it seems to be doing, we could end up with a remarkably literate nation, musically speaking. Meanwhile, how interested are the media in, say, a twenty-year-old girl who plays first trumpet in the Cincinnati Symphony Orchestra, or the 138 kids of all ages between eleven and eighteen who compose the California Youth Symphony in Palo Alto? Not very much. Not, that is, as compared with their interest in pot-smoking, abortion, and pollution.

Q. Yet the current trend in music is surely anything but conservative?

A. Conservative is a word and a category, and when a good musician compromises on his aim in music and descends to what the brainwashed masses expect, then he is not being honest with himself. An artist must be true to himself. If money is more important to him than his music, then he is indulging in prostitution. Now I don't say that everybody who listens to music, or uses it as an atmospheric background, really knows or cares about what is being played, but a real musician cannot be swayed from his natural groove by those who believe the listings of the Top Forty indicate what sounds good or best. In any case, if the listener is to make the decision, we are all in a pretty bad situation. With the exception of movie-scoring and theatre and television backgrounds, consonance is considered desirable as agreeable to the normal ear, but there are, of course, artists who resort to shock in desperation. There are those, too, who truly dig distortion of everything. A clinker in a symphony is no less bad than a clinker in jazz or rock, so once again—why the category?

Q. How do you rate composition, arrangement, and performance in importance?

A. All are interdependent on each other. Composition depends a great deal on the subsequent arrangement, but neither should burden the performers, for if the performance fails all is lost.

Q. Was there any special reason why you set out to develop a particularly strong left hand at the piano?

A. When I started out, the left hand was considered the first step toward acknowledgment.

Q. When you began composing as a very young man, did you draw from your environment, real experiences, or what you experienced through reading and listening? Where did the initial inspiration come from?

A. The driving power was a matter of wanting to be—and to be heard—on the same level as the best.

Q. Am I wrong in assuming your aural sense is more acute than your other senses? And how strong a part do the other senses play?

A. Composers try to parallel observations made through all the senses.

Q. How does a performer "tune in" to a particular audience, to its receptiveness, reaction, or mood? People in one section of the country may want to hear something completely different to those in another.

A. There is no geographical scale for appraising audiences. When the artist encounters a sensitive audience—jackpot! If he plays to the audience according to geography, nationality, race, or creed, he is condescending, and this is the world's worst social offense.

Q. How does the composer-performer feel when a new work is premiered and there is only a mild audience reaction, perhaps because it is not understood or because the people cannot identify with it?

A. Only the artist really knows whether his performance is good or otherwise. He is the only one who knows what the work or performance was supposed to say or represent.

Q. Who is the artist accountable to?

A. If artist he be, to himself. It is prostitution to sway or bend to money, or to the many other forms of advancement.

457

Q. What artistic sacrifice would be excusable to obtain monetary success? And do you think this happens frequently, occasionally, or seldom?

A. All kinds of such "sacrifices" have been and are still being overdone.

Q. You travel the world over and all around our country. How bad a shape do you really think we are in, and what seem to be our major problems?

A. Brainwashing of children and adults in America is the worst in the world, and it's always done by those with complexes.

Q. Have audiences changed as a consequence?

A. Highly commercial, brainwashed audiences expect vulgarity, but there is still an audience for the waltz, the opera, and ballet.

Q. Can you keep from writing music? Do you write in spite of yourself?

A. I don't know how strong the chains, cells, and bars are. I've never tried to escape.

Q. Every singer does a song like "Solitude" differently. What does that do to the song, and do you care? It has been said that after Picasso finishes a painting, he dismisses it.

A. Writing a song is one phase. A major orchestration is another. Performing is the final product as heard by the listening ear.

Q. Do you write for certain people—that is, with someone special in mind?

A. We keep the musicians in the band on a steady basis, fifty-two weeks a year. We always know who we are writing for.

Q. Do you compose in your head or at the piano? Do you see the piece? Does it have shape?

A. There is no format for the activity of the brain. If it doesn't happen in the mind first, it doesn't happen.

Q. If you were stuck in a mountain cabin for a month without a piano, what would happen? Could you continue to compose?

A. Naturally.

Q. It is sometimes said that young people are the ones with money to spend on concerts and records. Is it possible that our musician-stars have priced themselves out of the range of the average citizen? If so, what can be done about it?

A. I don't understand how or why young people have or get more money more often than older people. There are a lot of things like that being said today without reason.

Q. If the work week of the foreseeable future is appreciably shortened, how do you think the cultural arts will fit into this kind of life style?

A. People who make a living doing something they don't enjoy wouldn't even be happy with a one-day work week.

Q. Is honest apprenticeship a missing factor in performances today, or is a lot of noise made to camouflage the fact that young players don't really know what they are doing?

A. Talent and ability are neither young nor old. Agedness is only vaguely related to chronology. Without know-how, nobody is anything.

Q. Is there satisfaction in knowing that what you have created gives you a chance to live and be known beyond your time? Does gratification offset the rough road you must have had to travel at times?

A. I have no interest in posterity. I have been very lucky and have not had the discomfort of treading the rough road.

Q. At this point in your career, what do you think is expected of you?

A. I don't know, and couldn't care less.

Q. When you travel to other countries as a representative of your own, what do you consciously take to other peoples, and what, in turn, do you take from them?

A. I am neither a tourist nor a sightseer, so what is observed is easily digestible—when I look. I always love to hear the music of my hosts, and hope we shall be in mutual (and total) agreement, so that we can *both* say, "Encore!"

Q. You must get extraordinarily exhausted on your travels. How do you recharge or revitalize?

A. One must always conserve the agreeable or positive. It is not expedient to try to like or enjoy the negative.

Q. When you don't feel like performing, as must sometimes happen, how do you psyche yourself into doing a first-class job?

A. I have no preferred conditions for doing what I do for a living. I love it all, all of the time.

Q. Can any artist ever honestly imagine himself not listening to his muse? Could you accept a blow that would stop your work? Does faith enter at that point?

A. Time entered first, but faith entered next, long ago. One must be aware of possible ups and downs, and try to be in position for one more turn of the wheel.

Q. Is the creative artist like an iceberg? Is a large part of him submerged and only a small part shown?

A. Everyone is that way. Art is a skill.

Q. What do you consider your most important contribution to the music world, to your people, and to your country?

A. There are quite enough professional appraisers around to enjoy that headache. I have no ambition to be a critic or a judge.

Q. Does inspiration come from sorrow, frustration, and disappointment? It has been said that great love songs have followed a broken heart or the end of an affair. Do emotions such as love, anger, loneliness, or happiness affect composition?

A. I think the artist's true position is that of an observer. Personal emotion could spoil his *pièce de résistance.*

Q. Do you think there is a strong hereditary element in great talent? Or is it, rather, an inherited potential that must be developed? How would you explain child geniuses?

A. The Bible speaks of the first, second, third, and fourth generations being affected by the acts of the fathers.

Q. If you ever questioned your path in life, how did you answer yourself?

A. I like to believe that I do my best to stay in my place on the wheel. I don't think I would want myself in anyone else's spot.

Q. Is there any achievement, outside the realm of music, that you are proud of and happy about?

A. The first social significance show, *Jump for Joy,* in 1941, and its various successors continually since.

Q. The public is always fascinated by details of the private lives of artistic people. Is there danger in the effect of this information on the public's evaluation of the artist's performance?

A. I think these highly publicized private lives are deliberately overdone for the purpose of building "box office." This is a business matter completely unrelated to art.

Q. Have there been special factors that have had an effect on your career and been a cause for concern?

A. Concern, yes. Concern for solving whatever problem faced me, or for curing an illness.

Q. Wouldn't it be marvelous to develop a study center similar to those Frank Lloyd Wright set up in Arizona and Wisconsin for young people to study architecture, so that what you began and accomplished in music may be continued?

A. I am not a teacher.

Q. There can be few musicians so well traveled as you, but do you never tire of traveling?

A. No, it's a constant pursuit, and we just keep going. There is always some place we have never been, and while we are waiting for the opportunity to go there, we just keep circling like airplanes do, until the fog clears. We get in the pattern until we can move to a new level and, eventually, to a new place—by invitation, of course.

Q. Do you live anywhere permanently?

A. Yes, in New York, but a few weeks ago I slept in my own bed for the first time in six months. After playing there five weeks, we went to Las Vegas for a month; then we went to Europe for six weeks; coming back, we overshot New York and went to Las Vegas and San Francisco. From there, we went to Tokyo, Bangkok, Taipei, Australia, and New Zealand. We even played in Vientiane in Laos.

Q. You're so seldom in one place, wouldn't it pay you to sublet?

A. Well, then you lose your grip on your security blanket.

Q. How do you keep in such good health traveling as you do, eating all kinds of food in different places?

A. No, I eat nothing much but steak. I have a friend who goes down to the Virgin Islands on a yacht and lives there all winter. On returning, it's nothing but fish, fish, fish, and stories about fish, about catching them and putting them in the pan, and cooking them fresh. They're almost alive when they put them in the pan, and that's supposed to be wonderful! Not long ago, I was in a restaurant right on the ocean in Salem, Massachusetts, and I ordered fish. "Gee, I know this fish came right out of the ocean," I said to the waitress. "No," she answered, "our fish has to clear the union in Boston, you know." So that was the end of fish! Then I had a brother-in-law who would stop you from eating chicken just by the way he *refused* chicken. Fifteen weeks in the Far East will take you off lamb, too. So the secret is to say no to all the foods offered you, and just eat steak!

Q. Well, do you ever get tired of playing those old perennials night after night?

A. No, this is a responsibility we owe people. Say, for instance, someone comes along who says, "We were married to 'Caravan,'" or "I met my girl at the Blue Note when you were playing 'Mood Indigo.'" It's important to them. We were playing one night some place down in Georgia when three people came up. "I met my wife," the man said, "for the first time when you were playing 'Sophisticated Lady,' and we danced together. It's a strange thing that you should be playing in our hometown on our daughter's twenty-first birthday!" Then they introduced their daughter. You have to respect such memories. Of course, when we get requests for numbers that are not in the book from people like that, we just say, "Fake it!"

Q. Would the sound of the Ellington orchestra change perceptibly if you changed personnel?

A. Well, it alters of itself with new music coming in all the time, and we do different interpretations of older numbers, although I suppose you might call that a cop-out. I have had the good fortune to employ several guys who became legends, and other musicians loved them so much that they imitated them. When Paul Gonsalves came in the band, he didn't even have to have a rehearsal. He loved Ben Webster so much, and he knew everything in the book. It was the same with Russell Procope and Barney Bigard's clarinet playing.

Q. How important is discipline?

A. I'm the world's worst disciplinarian. There's too much responsibility in being a *leader!* You have to have the dignity and authority of a leader, and that's all so heavy!

Q. Do you think it is easier or harder for a young musician starting out today than it was when you began?

A. The caliber of musicians is higher today. They have to be better musicians than they were then. In those days, the chief requisite was good personality of tone, identification. If you accomplished that, you didn't even have to read. Nowadays, the same guys play in symphonies, dance bands, and radio and television studios. There's no real problem for those properly qualified, and it can be very lucrative for the guy who gets in the swim of recording, television and movie studio work. Of course, you can isolate yourself to the point of nonavailability, or your timing might be off so that you are not available at the right time, when the juicy one goes by. That's a personal thing with some people, no matter what the conditions. I know when I left Washington that there were half a dozen there who knew ten times more music than I did, but they couldn't leave for one reason or another. I was just in pursuit of the melody, and it carried me to New York where, about a month later, I had a song published. I was twenty-three.

Q. Is there a point where it all becomes mechanical, even with great musicians?

462

A. It depends on how you relate their mechanical with skill. Skill is needed to operate the mechanical, and then we have to consider the degrees of taste and imagination supplied, but the skill and the mechanical are certainly two different things. The theatre, for instance, is a place for skill. Some people say, "I don't see how he can play that part every night without going out of his mind!" It may be a wild, dramatic part, but the actor doesn't necessarily have to throw his emotions into it, because he has studied how to make the people *believe* that he is doing all that suffering. It is one of the arts, and all the arts have similar qualities. Imagine a man sculpting a statue of a crying woman, or a dying man, from a huge piece of marble. He becomes emotionally involved in what he is doing, loses control of his chisel, and louses up the statue. Then our real artist comes along, sees him in his despair, takes him as *his* subject, and paints his picture. Horrible, isn't it?

Q. But isn't there a point ever where the music is coming out of your fingers, and not out of your heart?

A. I don't think it is that easy to define or analyze. If you stop to analyze it, you're going to louse it up real good! Suppose you go out in your garden and cut a flower. "It's a gorgeous flower," you decide, when you come back in the house. So you put it in some water, trim the stem, and give it proper care. Maybe you like it so much that next day you put an aspirin in the water. But if you start to pull it to pieces, and take the petals off, and examine the veins that run through it . . . then you may know everything about it, but you don't have any more flower! Which brings us to another point: I don't think people have to *know* anything about music to appreciate it or enjoy it.

Q. There's probably not a second of the day when one of your compositions is not being played somewhere in the world. Do you ever think about that?

A. No, I never do, and I've never heard it put that way before.

Q. How many are there?

A. Gee, I don't know . . . thousands . . . We write 'em every day.

Q. Where do you get your titles from?

A. You play the tune first, and then turn around and see what the girl's name is, the girl standing down by the bass end of the piano. There's always a girl in the standard original whirl!

Q. Which of all your tunes is your favorite?

A. The next one. The one I'm writing tonight or tomorrow, the new baby is always the favorite.

Q. What does America mean to you?

A. It's where I was born. It's *home*. Its music world has been an extremely competitive scene, and that in itself incites drive. Without competition you wouldn't have it. Then I've been very lucky in America. I've been allowed to live well, and in many instances I've been spoiled. My friends and relatives live well, too. I've learned a lot there, where there are so many great musicians to learn from. Opportunity and luck are so important. You have to be in the right place at the right time. A gambler in a lucky streak can't get lucky unless he's shooting dice or doing what he does best.

Q. Don't you get tired of doing what you're doing year in and year out?

A. You're talking from the perspective either of someone who doesn't love music, or who doesn't do what he enjoys most for a living. To be frank, that question annoys me very much, and not merely because it recurs so often. Millions and millions of dollars are spent building big vacation places for people to escape to from their daily chores, but they are the people who don't enjoy what they are doing for a living. Nobody else does what we do for fifty-two weeks of the year, every day of the week. It's our unique thing. Nobody does anything every day like we do, and nobody does it in so many places as we do. Doctors, surgeons, football players, bankers—you name it— they all take vacations. We go to many countries and we fly more than pilots do! We live in an entirely different climate. Three days ago we crossed the equator. Yesterday we went through a blizzard. Everybody else takes a day off, but not us. We're not captive, but we're built in.

Q. Do you have time for painting now?

A. No, although painting was my recognized talent. When I won a scholarship in fine art to Pratt Institute, I didn't take advantage of it, because I was already involved in what was just beginning to be called jazz. I told myself that that kind of music couldn't last, that I'd give it another year, and then maybe next year go and pick up my scholarship. Sometimes now I buy the materials—paint, canvas, and cardboard—but they only sit in the corner and collect dust. You can't *paint* in planes, trains, cars, or buses.

Q. But you can write music under such conditions?

A. Oh, yes, because when you get an idea, you've got to put it down while you've got it. Otherwise it changes. The notes change places, and the next time you go back in your mind to look for it, you find the third note has become the sixth note, and its value has been altered, and there is actually no resemblance to the original idea.

464

Q. What is God for you?

A. God? There's one God, and that's all.

Q. Do you believe in God?

A. Oh, yes, and that is why I do so many sacred concerts every year.

Q. What is love for you?

A. Love is indescribable and unconditional. I could tell you a thousand things that it is not, but not one that it *is.* Either you have it or you haven't; there's no proof of it.

Q. What is music to you?

A. My mistress. I live with music.

Q. What is the audience?

A. The audience is the other side of the realm that serves the same muse I do.

Q. While performing, what do you insist on from the audience?

A. I don't insist on anything. I play for the audience, and if I'm lucky they have the same taste I have. It's rather like that word "swing": when two people are together, and my pulse and your pulse are together, then we're swinging.

Q. What do you think of the narcotics problem?

A. Why ask me? You are not a doctor, a detective, or a junkie, are you?

Q. How important is improvisation in jazz?

A. The word "improvisation" has great limitations, because when musicians are given solo responsibility they already have a suggestion of a melody written for them, and so before they begin they already know more or less what they are going to play. Anyone who plays anything worth hearing knows what he's going to play, no matter whether he prepares a day ahead or a beat ahead. It has to be with intent.

Q. How is it that you have not flirted with commercial music?

A. This is where the categorization of jazz gets washed away. We may play something of our own creation like *The Latin-American Suite* or *The New Orleans Suite,* but a great artist like Sidney Bechet will play "Love for Sale," or Coleman Hawkins will play "Body and Soul," so where does it end? We've all worked and fought under the banner of jazz for many years, but the word really has no meaning. What is the relationship between Guy Lombardo, Stan Kenton, Count Basie, and Louis Armstrong—all of whom people regard as playing jazz? Music is limitless.

Q. Maybe a computer could calculate that?

A. What would you get? A lot of figures, but they wouldn't go in the ear. The only thing that's important is what goes in the ear. It's an aural art.

Q. Can you give an idea of the shape or story of the opera you are reputed to have in mind?

A. Oh, I have about four, some of them comic, some of them violent.

Q. What about the future of jazz?

A. You've got to call it music whether you want to or not. A class graduates from a conservatory—say Juilliard, Eastman, or Berklee—and they've been through the whole history, every great composer, and every great orchestrator. They've mastered all the techniques, and they can't be put into a little category called jazz. Out of such a class, a fourth may go into movies, a fourth into radio and television, a fourth to teach music or lead a church choir, and the other fourth to play what some people want to call jazz.

Q. You don't see a need for divisions of taste, but only of necessity?

A. Billy Strayhorn and I did the arrangements on the *Peer Gynt Suite*. We liked what we did, and we had fun doing it, but we did not try to do better than the symphony people. There was a certain amount of humor in it, and unfortunately the Grieg Society in Norway barred it. I don't think Grieg would have barred it.

Q. Once born, do you leave a number alone?

A. The original framework remains the same. Sometimes people come in the band who see it from a different perspective, and they do something that is a little zesty in accordance with their own personality. You're never satisfied, of course. You say to yourself, "I should have done this here, and that there." You know greater development is possible, but then we went through the conditioning of a period when we were limited to three minutes.

Q. When jam sessions could not be recorded?

A. No. A jam session is like a polite encounter, or an exchange of compliments, but in the old days they had cutting contests where you defended your honor with your instrument. I remember a great night at the Comedy Club. We arrived late one Sunday morning, but Sidney Bechet and Coleman Hawkins had hooked up, and they went at it all night long. They just happened to have their horns with them! Without them, they would have been like knights walking around without swords or armor. Chick Webb used to cut *everybody* who went to the Savoy Ballroom, because he knew what to play and when to play it for the jitterbugs. It was very much like the Olympic

Games there every night. Mal Hallet's band cut everybody who played opposite his band at Nottings on the Charles River.

Q. Your house is on fire. What would you grab first to save?

A. I would grab the old Sonny Greer adage: "Feet save ass, ass do feet a good turn someday."

Q. Do you have a favorite season of the year and, if so, what do you specially like about it?

A. Being a chronic indoorsman, it's unimaginable that I should be any sort of authority on this.

Q. What is man's greatest discovery?

A. Electricity. And the telephone is a necessity.

Q. What is your best habit?

A. Prayer.

Q. What is your worst habit?

A. Talking too much.

Q. Apart from your usual meal of grapefruit, steak, and vegetables, what would your next favorite meal be?

A. Room service Chinese food—Cantonese.

Q. What do you think is the most serious breach of trust?

A. Telling.

Q. Is "love" or "like" more important?

A. Love is supreme and unconditional; like is nice but limited.

Q. Do you throw up defense with argument or logic?

A. Sometimes it is necessary to use one to drive the other home—depending on who's home.

Q. Even with the speed of jets, don't you question whether those rigorous itineraries are worth while?

A. Or wouldn't it be better, eh, to just sit or lie in one place till you got green first on one side and then on the other as you approached stagnation; till all the slithery slok and slithery slime rolled itself into a tink tank?

Q. Do you think people change as they proceed through life, or do they remain basically the same except for shifts in tempo and purpose?

A. It depends upon who they are. There are no two people alike. If two claim to be, one is a comformist, or most likely both. All are born with different susceptibilities, which are gradually modified by environment, teaching, learning, necessity, desire, etc.

Q. What would be a perfect day?

A. Any day I wake up and look at.

Q. Where do you remember the most beautiful sunrise and sunset?

A. Seconds before dawn from Berkeley Heights, looking west over San Francisco Bay. And then in Bombay at sunset, the whole sky over the Arabian Sea was cerise from the horizon all the way up.

Q. Do you have an actual fear of anything, like heights, storms, or reptiles?

A. The snake catches the insect that would have injected you with a deadly poison. (That makes the snake a jabber-grabber.) Either one could save your life, and either one could kill you.

Q. If you were confined somewhere, all alone, what books would you want?

A. Only the Bible, because all the other books are in it.

Q. Do you think men have a tendency toward polygamy and women toward monogamy?

A. Definitely. It depends upon their minds, not their sex.

Q. What human shortcoming irritates you most?

A. Underestimation.

Q. Did you ever imagine yourself a reincarnated royal genius?

A. When I was a child, my mother told me I was blessed, and I have always taken her word for it. Being born of—or reincarnated from—royalty is nothing like being blessed. Royalty is inherited from another human being, blessedness from God.

Q. Do you think you have a more highly developed degree of anticipation than most people?

A. Some people have sensitivities in directions they never have an opportunity to use, because they have been drawn away from them for monetary reasons. They would be surprised to discover how rewarding it is to pursue the natural tendencies and become a Number One yourself rather than a Number Two somebody else. Heaven is a place where you get an opportunity to use all the millions of sensitivities you never knew you had before.

Q. Who is the most sensitive and gentle person you have known?

A. Daisy, my mother.

Q. If you could make one sure bet, what would it be?

A. Gray skies are just clouds passing over.

Q. Do you have any idiosyncrasies or beliefs that might be considered superstitious, such as not walking under ladders?

A. When you arrive here on earth, you find many superstitions already established, and as you go through different phases of life you encounter many more. From childhood on, each phase has its own, and offhand it's easy to think of many that belong to athletics, for example, or the theatre. The most difficult part is trying to decide which of them are based on someone's religion and which have just been carried down through the ages. As Geoffrey Holder says, "I don't think it's a good idea to play with or kid about another man's religion." People, of course, can be made to believe anything, true or false. I'm a people.

Q. How do you live now as compared with earlier stages of your life?

A. Since I have been out on my own, I have always lived rather expensively, but I shall never live as well as I did in my mother's arms.

Q. What has been the most valuable thing in life for you?

A. Time.

Q. How many hours do you sleep a day?

A. I try for eight, and some days I'm luckier than others.

Q. What has been the reason for your continued success?

A. The grace of God.

Q. Why do you fly first class and have the rest of your company on the same plane in coach?

A. On most flights, there is not enough room in first class for a company of twenty, so where and with whom would you make the division? On the grounds of seniority or skill? Or would you segregate according to race, religion, color, or creed?

Q. What about your son, your own son?

A. He is a member of the band and also its manager. It has always been my policy never to let the manager outclass the musicians. The coda to this is that Cootie Williams wouldn't work for a leader who didn't ride first class!

Q. Is the blues a song of sorrow?

A. No, it is a song of romantic failure.

Q. What is the spiritual?

A. A song of prayer and worship.

Q. Who are you?

A. I am a musician who is a member of the American Federation of Labor, and who hopes one day to amount to something artistically.

Q. Are you not being too modest?

A. Oh, no, you should see my dreams!

Q. How do you feel when you sit down at the piano on stage?

A. Scared! You have to enjoy a little stage fright to get that extra punch.

Q. You have been quoted as saying that the band is your instrument and that you write for your musicians individually. If that is true, how do you approach writing for symphony orchestras?

A. I must confess that I find a problem or a limitation a great opportunity. I will try to explain. When you write for a musician whose method allows him only seven good tones on his instrument, you have an opportunity to devise a design that is agreeable to the ear. With a musician who plays the full compass of his instrument as fast or as slow as possible, there seems, paradoxically, less opportunity to create. In the case where you have the luxury of a symphony to write for, it sometimes seems that the millions of possibilities have devoured the opportunities, and there you are left with nothing but your own brain to dig into!

Q. What prompted you to write for symphony orchestras then?

A. Invitations.

Q. What people or individuals outside music, unknown or celebrated, have inspired you?

A. Artist friends.

Q. Why are you not writing more popular songs as you did in the past?

A. I write more today than ever before in my life.

Q. How do you feel about the new young composers who are said to be causing a revolutionary turn in music?

A. When I hear something new, I will give you an honest answer.

Q. You are said to have been influenced by the English composer Delius. Have you ever listened to his music?

A. In 1933, in England. When I got there people were saying some of our music sounded like Delius, and when I told them I had never heard Delius, they brought me presents of Delius records by the London Philharmonic, Sir Thomas Beecham conducting. I was hooked on listening, but could not copy a bit of it.

Q. What do you think the future holds in store for the big bands?

A. Transportation costs and high salaries make them impossible from the business point of view.

Q. Is there such a thing as Black Culture in American music?

A. There was when I was a child in school. I agree, incidentally, with something that William Grant Still said in a letter to *Music Journal* in February 1971. I quote:

"In actual fact, American Negro music (which is indeed a fusion of African and various European elements) encompasses a great deal more than jazz, and any teacher who claims to teach the subject should be aware of all its forms, from the Negro folk product to the advances now being made in serious music.

"The only reason there has been such great emphasis on jazz is that it has been pushed by commerical interests, and this doesn't mean that it is the *only*—or even the most important—form in existence."

Q. It has been said that you and your orchestra have been chosen as one of five cultural attractions to represent this country in the U.S.S.R. in 1971. How do you feel about a tour there?

A. The vibrations were very good when we were in Czechoslovakia. Russia is the same place from which the Fabulous Five came: Tchaikovsky, Rimsky-Korsakov, Borodin, Prokofiev, and Shostakovich. So you know I want to breathe some of that air!

Q. Who are your favorite singers?

A. It is always a matter of the one I am enjoying at the moment.

Q. Do you think jazz should be subsidized?

A. I don't think so. The minute you start subsidizing it, you are going to get yourself a bastard product. It started as a competitive thing, and if you take away the competition, where a guy must fight to eat, it's going to become something else. Of course, if people *want* to take care of people— crazy!

Q. How did you get the scar on your face?

A. I have four stories about it, and it depends on which *you* like the best. One is a taxicab accident; another is that I slipped and fell on a broken bottle; then there is a jealous woman; and last is Old Heidelberg, where they used to stand toe to toe with a saber in each hand, and slash away. The first man to step back lost the contest, no matter how many times he'd sliced the other. Take your pick.

Q. Since your mother had such faith and confidence in you, what are your thoughts on predestination?

A. None. You are generously given ability, brain, and freedom to think.

Q. From your observations, what do you think could ultimately destroy man?

A. A combination of complacency and underestimation.

Q. When did you get on your "blue" kick? Are there colors you dislike?

A. My mother always saw to it that my Sunday clothes were blue. When she died, I was wearing a brown suit.

Q. If you could be someone else, who would you be?

A. The son of my father and mother.

Q. Besides God, what sustains you?

A. Not besides. How does one manage without God?

(The only reason an interviewer sometimes asks the interviewee stupid questions is because the interviewer thinks the interviewee is stupid.)

Appendices

THE SINGERS

We have been extremely lucky with our singers. Each seemed to join us at the time when what they were doing with songs was just right for the places we were playing. They are virtually a story on their own, beginning with Sonny Greer and Ivie Anderson, and continuing with Jean Eldridge, Herb Jeffries, Al Hibbler, Joya Sherrill, Kay Davis, Lou Elliott, Marie Ellington, Wini Brown, Marion Cox, Dolores Parker, Chubby Kemp, Sarah Ford, Yvonne Lanauze, Norma Oldham, Jimmy Grissom, Ozzie Bailey, Jimmy Britton, Lloyd Oldham, Lil Greenwood, Milt Grayson, Trish Turner, Shirley Witherspoon, Darlene Huff, Kathy Myers, Jimmy McPhail, Lena Junoff, Nell Brookshire, and on up to Anita Moore and Tony Watkins today. I must not overlook the vocal contributions of our trumpet players, Cootie Williams, Ray Nance, and Money Johnson, nor those great artists who joined us for recording or special occasions, like Adelaide Hall, Baby Cox, May Alix, Joe Turner, Marion Bruce, Margaret Tynes, Brock Peters, Ella Fitzgerald, Mahalia Jackson, Louis Armstrong, Alice Babs, Yvonne Gardner, Nanice Lund, Patricia Hoy, Roscoe Gill, and other fine singers who have participated in our sacred concerts.

ARRANGERS AND LYRICISTS

Besides Billy Strayhorn and my son, Mercer, a number of arrangers have contributed to the band's book and helped me on urgent projects. Among those to whom I owe a debt of gratitude are Jimmy Jones, Wild Bill Davis, Dick Vance, Ron Collier, Luther Henderson, Calvin Jackson, Hilly Edelstein, Raymond Fol, Gerald Wilson and Ernie Burkhardt.

Lyricists to whom I am similarly indebted include Billy Strayhorn, of course, and Don George, Bob Russell, John La Touche, Marshall Barer, Bob Schafer, Dave Ringle, Joe Trent, Ted Koehler, Paul Francis Webster, Sid Kuller, Johnny Mercer, Irving Mills, and Mitchell Parish.

THE SYMPHONY ORCHESTRAS

Since our first performance with a symphony orchestra in 1949—the Philadelphia Symphony Orchestra at Robin Hood Dell—we have had the pleasure of playing with many others around the world. A partial list includes the following:

474

The New York Philharmonic; the Boston Pops Orchestra; the Symphony of the Air; the National Symphony in Washington, D.C. (2); the London Philharmonic; La Scala Orchestra; the Paris Opera Orchestra; the N.B.C. Symphony; and the symphony orchestras of these cities: Cincinnati (2); Detroit (2); Buffalo (3); Rochester; Dallas; Houston; Miami Beach; Orlando, Florida; Savannah; Greenville, South Carolina; Memphis (2); Nashville; Stockholm, Sweden; Hamburg, Germany; Manila; Los Angeles (2); San Francisco; Pittsburgh; Baltimore; Chatauqua, New York; Aspen, Colorado; Waterbury, Connecticut; Wichita Falls; Toronto; London, Ontario; Newark, New Jersey; New Haven, Connecticut; Jacksonville, Florida; Springfield, Massachusetts.

Some of them liked us well enough to invite us more than once, as the figures in parentheses indicate.

BAND BOYS AND BARBERS

Besides musicians, a band like ours needs a "band boy." He has many duties, not the least of which is setting up the stand and dismantling it. He is also very largely responsible for handling the baggage. Among those who have labored under this distinctly inadequate title, and have helped to make our paths much smoother are:

Jonesy, Willie Manning, Tommy LaVigne (now a preacher), Timme (from Memphis), Speedy Brooks, Carl Carruthers, Henry Snodgrass, Bobby Boyd, Frank Racette, Tony Watkins, Jim Lowe, and, in England, Fred Towers and Bouga.

Because they are usually around backstage before, during, and after our performance, they also fulfill valuable liaison duties with members of the audience and the theatre staff, an area in which a lot of diplomacy is often required. In the course of time, some of them became expert in stage lighting and were able to advise the technicians on what was required to match the different musical moods we were trying to establish.

Barbers, too, have been an important part of our traveling caravan, and among those whose skill, care, and resourcefulness I remember are: Hernandez (European tour, 1948), Billy Black (Paris), Roger Simone (European and Latin-American tours, 1971, and Far East tour, 1963), Ron Smith (Europe and the Orient), Jack Anderson (Europe), Charlie Haywood (of Lake Tahoe), Larry (Europe), and Wheeler (the Fisherman). A personal barber is not the extravagance it may seem, because our work schedules and travel itineraries frequently make it impossible to get to any barbershop during normal working hours.

HONORS AND AWARDS

(1) MEDALS

The President's Medal
    Award for Special Merit—presented by the Art Director's Club   1958
The Spingarn Medal
    Achievement Award—presented by the National Association for the
    Advancement of Colored People   1959
Gold Medal
    "Musician of Every Year"—presented by the Mayor of the City of
    New York   1965
Gold Medal
    Presented by the City of Chicago, Illinois
Medal
    Special cast with bust of Ellington—presented by the City of Paris,
    France   1965
President's Gold Medal
    Presented in the name of President Lyndon B. Johnson by the
    American Ambassador, Madrid, Spain   1966
Medal
    Distinguished New Yorker Award—presented by the City Club of
    New York   1966
Presidential Medal of Freedom
    The highest civilian award of the United States—presented by
    President Richard M. Nixon   1969

(2) HONORARY DEGREES

Wilberforce College—Doctor of Music	1949
Milton College—Doctor of Humanities	1964
California College of Arts and Crafts—Doctor of Fine Arts	1966
Morgan State College—Doctor of Music	1967
Yale University—Doctor of Music	1967
Washington University, St. Louis, Missouri—Doctor of Music	1967
Columbia College, Chicago, Illinois—Doctor of Music	1968
Brown University—Doctor of Music	1969
Christian Theological Seminary—Doctor of Humane Letters	1970
Assumption College, Worcester, Massachusetts—Doctor of Music	1970
Berklee College of Music, Boston, Massachusetts—Doctor of Music	1971

My name in lights on City Hall for the first time, Milwaukee, January 18, ▶

Howard University—Doctor of Music	1971
St. John's University, Jamaica, New York—Doctor of Music	1971
University of Wisconsin—Doctor of Music	1971
Rider College, Trenton, New Jersey—Doctor of Arts	1972

(3) PROFESSIONAL SOCIETIES, COUNCILS, ASSOCIATIONS, AND INSTITUTES

George Washington Carver Memoriam Institute	
Supreme Award of Merit	1943
American Newspaper Guild	
Page One Award	1943
Page One Award	1945
National Association for the Advancement of Colored People	
Freedom Fund Drive	1958
America's Foremost Musician	1970
Image Award	1970
American Academy of Motion Picture Arts and Sciences	
nominated for Oscar award for score of motion picture *Paris Blues*	1961
National Academy of Recording Arts and Sciences	
Best Jazz Performance (Large Group)—Instrumental—Awarded to	
Duke Ellington and Count Basie for *First Time* Album	1962
Best Original Jazz Composition *Night Creature*	1964
Best Original Jazz Composition *Virgin Island Suite*	1965
Best Original Jazz Composition *In the Beginning God*	1966
Bing Crosby Award	1966
Grammy Award *Far East Suite*	1968
Grammy Award *And His Mother Called Him Bill*	1969
Grammy Award *Togo Brava Suite*	1973
New Jersey Association of Retarded Children	
Trophy	1963
National Association of Negro Musicians	
Award	1964
American Federation of Musicians, Dallas, Texas	
A Tribute to the Artistry of Duke Ellington	1964
Grace Cathedral, San Francisco, California	
Scroll—The Bishop and Trustees of Grace Cathedral	1965
Jazz Interactions, Inc.	
Master Musician of the Twentieth Century	1967
Fellow Musicians of Toronto, Canada	
Award	1967

At Washington University, St. Louis, Missouri. Commencement exercises, 1967.

With President Evert Wallenfeldt and Ethel Rich at Milton College, Wisconsin, after receiving honorary degree, 1964

Musicians Everywhere
    Award—presented by Charlie Barnet   1967
National Council on the Arts
    Appointed to membership by President Lyndon B. Johnson   1968
American Society of Composers, Authors and Publishers
    Pied Piper Award   1968
Comite de Jazz de Instituto Chileno Norteamericano de Cultura
    Commemorative Silver Platter   1968
American Parkinson's Disease Association
    Ed Wynn Humanitarian Award   1968
Ordem dos Músicos do Brasil, São Paulo, Brasil
    Trophy   1968
The Atlanta University Institutes
    Plaque for Outstanding Contributions to Humanity   1969

With Consul General of Sweden and Mrs. Gunnar Lonaeus after election to the Swedish Royal Academy of Music, March 12, 1971

Hampton Institute, Hampton, Virginia	
The Centennial Medallion Citation	1969
Improved Benevolent Protective Order of Elks of the World	
The Elijah P. Lovejoy Award	1969
American Institute of Arts and Letters	
elected to membership	1970
Black Scholarship Foundation	
Appointed Honorary President	1970
Thomas A. Dooley Foundation	
Splendid American Award	1970
Jewish Institute for Geriatrics	
Golden Chai Award	1970
American Academy of Arts and Sciences	
elected a fellow	1971

With the Shriners. Willis Conover behind at Ellington's left

Royal Swedish Academy of Music
 elected to membership   1971
Songwriters' Hall of Fame
 elected to membership   1971
Guild for Religious Architecture
 voted to honorary membership   1971
National Association of Negro Musicians, Inc.
 Highest Award for Distinguished Service in Music 1972
American Federation of Musicians
 Honorary Gold Card Life Membership   1972

(4) FRATERNITIES

Delta Sigma Theta, Detroit
 Award—Outstanding Achievements in Music and Entertainment 1952

Alpha Phi Alpha
    Distinguished Service Award   1956
    Plaque—Sigma Lamba Chapter, New Orleans   1958
    Distinguished Service Award—Gamma Mu Chapter   1963
    Silver Platter—Beta Delta—Delta Alpha, Orangeburg, South Carolina   1968
    Achievement Award—Delta Kappa Chapter   1968
    Alpha Man of the Year—Mississippi State College   1970
Kappa Alpha Psi, Los Angeles
    Civilian Achievement Award
Phi Mu Alpha Sinfonia Fraternity of America
    Trophy
    Elected to Life Membership   1969
Alpha Phi Alpha Brothers in Europe
    Plaque—Symbolizing Alpha's Spirit on Three Continents as a Musician,
    Composer, Lyricist, Arranger-Bandleader

(5) STATES

State of New York
    Proclamation—Duke Ellington Day, May 26   1969
State of New Jersey
    Plaque—A Tribute to Duke Ellington   1969
State of Kentucky
    Commissioned Kentucky Colonel   1970
State of Nebraska
    Commissioned an Admiral—Great Navy of Nebraska   1970
State of Tennessee
    Commissioned Colonel—Aide de Camp, Governor's Staff   1970
State of New Mexico
    Proclamation—Duke Ellington Day, November 24   1970
State of Wisconsin
    Proclamation—Duke Ellington Week—July 17   1972

(6) MUNICIPALITIES

a. *Keys to Cities*
    Amsterdam, Holland
    Birmingham, Alabama
    Cincinnati, Ohio
    Elizabeth, New Jersey
    Jacksonville, Florida
    Kingston, Jamaica

483

With His Worship, the Mayor of Kingston, Mr. Eric Bell, and the key to the city, Jamaica, 1970

Madison, Wisconsin
Metropolitan Dade County, Florida
Miami, Florida
Niigata, Japan
Ocean City, Maryland
Perth Amboy, New Jersey
Phoenix, Arizona
Plainfield, New Jersey
St. Andrews, Jamaica
Savannah, Georgia
Washington, D.C.
Worcester, Massachusetts

b. *Honorary Citizenship*

Bardstown, Kentucky
Chicago, Illinois
Cleveland, Ohio
Niigata, Japan
San Francisco, California

c. *Other*

Dodge City	
Appointed Marshal	1955
City of Philadelphia, Pennsylvania	
Plaque—"Composer Par Excellence"	
Citizens' Selection Committee	1956
City of Oakland, California	
Proclamation—Duke Ellington Day, September 17	1966
City of Worcester, Massachusetts	
Silver Bowl	1966
City of Boston, Massachusetts	
Paul Revere Plaque	1966
City of Los Angeles, California	
Proclamation—Duke Ellington Day, June 29	1967
Township of Dover, Toms River, New Jersey	
Frances Hopkinson Memorial Award	1968
Washington, D.C.	
Plaque—The Citizens of Washington, D.C.	1969
Lackawana County, Pennsylvania	
Appointed Deputy Sheriff	1970
City of Burlington, Iowa	
Proclamation—Commending Sacred Concerts	1971

(7) MAGAZINES

a. *Down Beat*

Second Place, Swing Band	1945
First Place, Swing Band	1946
First Place, Sweet Band	1946
Second Place, Favorite Band	1947
First Place, Favorite Soloist	1948
First Place, Favorite Band	1948

Second Place, Favorite Band	1949
First Place, Arranger-Composer	1950
Third Place, Favorite Band	1951
Third Place, Jazz Band	1953
World's Greatest Intermission Pianist	1955
Fifth Member of the Music Hall of Fame	1956
First Place, Composer	1957
Personality of the Year	1957
First Place, Jazz Critics' Poll, Big Band	1958
First Place, Readers' Poll, Composer	1958
First Place, Jazz Critics' Poll, Big Band	1959
First Place, Jazz Critics' Poll, Arranger	1960
First Place, Jazz Critics' Poll, Big Band	1960
First Place, Jazz Critics' Poll, Arranger	1961
First Place, Jazz Critics' Poll, Big Band	1962
First Place, Jazz Critics' Poll, Arranger	1962
First Place, Readers' Poll, Big Band	1962
First Place, Jazz Critics' Poll, Arranger-Composer	1963
First Place, Jazz Critics' Poll, Big Band	1963
First Place, Jazz Critics' Poll, Big Band	1964
First Place, Jazz Critics' Poll, Arranger-Composer	1964
First Place, Jazz Critics' Poll, Composer	1965
First Place, Jazz Critics' Poll, Big Band	1965
First Place, Jazz Critics' Poll, Composer	1966
First Place, Jazz Critics' Poll, Big Band	1966
Record of the Year, *The Popular Duke Ellington*	1967
First Place, Jazz Critics' Poll, Composer-Arranger	1967
First Place, Readers' Poll, Composer-Arranger	1967
First Place, Jazz Critics' Poll, Big Band	1967
First Place, Readers' Poll, Big Band	1967
Record of the Year, *Far East Suite*	1968
First Place, Critics' Poll, Composer-Arranger	1968
First Place, Readers' Poll, Composer	1968
First Place, Critics' Poll, Big Band	1968
First Place, Critics' Poll, Composer-Arranger	1969
First Place, Critics' Poll, Big Band	1969
First Place, Readers' Poll, Composer	1969
First Place, Readers' Poll, Big Band	1969
First Place, Readers' Poll, Arranger	1969

First Place, Critics' Poll, Composer-Arranger	1970
First Place, Readers' Poll, Composer-Arranger	1970
First Place, Critics' Poll, Big Band	1970
First Place, Readers' Poll, Big Band	1970
First Place, International Jazz Critics' Poll, Big Band	1971
Record of the Year, *New Orleans Suite*	1971
First Place, International Jazz Critics' Poll, Composer-Arranger	1971
First Place, Critics' Poll, Composer	1972
First Place, Critics' Poll, Arranger	1972
First Place, Critics' Poll, Big Band	1972
First Place, Readers' Poll, Composer	1972

b. *Jazz Magazine*

Jay Award—Best Big Band Album, *Afro Bossa*	1963
Jay Award—Best Reissue Album, *The Ellington Era*	1963
Jay Award—Best Jazz Album of Year, *Afro Bossa*	1963
Jay Award—Best Combo Album, *Duke Ellington Meets Coleman Hawkins*	1963

c. *Esquire Magazine*

Gold Award, Arranger, *Esquire's* All-American Band	1945
Gold Award, Band, *Esquire's* All-American Band	1945
Gold Award, Band, *Esquire's* All-American Band	1946
Gold Award, Arranger, *Esquire's* All-American Band	1946
Gold Award, Band, *Esquire's* All-American Band	1947
Gold Award, Arranger, *Esquire's* All-American Band	1947

d. *Playboy Magazine*

All Star Winner: Special Award All Stars' All Stars	1962
All Star Jazz Poll—Leader	1964
All Star Jazz Poll—Leader	1965
Record of the Year—*Ellington '66*	1966
All Star Jazz Poll: All Stars' All Stars—Leader	1966
Elected to *Playboy* Jazz Hall of Fame	1967
All Star Jazz Poll—Leader	1967
Jazz and Pop Poll—All Stars' Poll—Winner	1968
All Star Jazz Poll—Leader	1969
All Star Jazz Poll—Leader	1970

e. *Record World*

  Jazzman Hall of Fame 1968

(8) CLUB AWARDS

The Chicago Rhythm Club
  Leader's Baton 1936
Club International, Inc., Washington, D.C.
  Universal Brotherhood Award 1961
  Awarded Honorary Membership 1961
Duke Ellington Jazz Society, Chapter 80
  Plaque commemorating Duke Ellington Week 1962
Jazz at Home Club, Philadelphia, Pennsylvania
  Jazz Culture Award 1964
Duke Ellington Jazz Society, New York, New York
  Plaque 1964
Poultry and Egg National Board
  Elected Member, National Good Egg Club
Society for the Appreciation of the Big Bands, Atlanta, Georgia
  Elected to Honorary Membership 1970

(9) OTHER HONORS AND AWARDS

Pittsburgh Courier
  Trophy—Willer, Band Contest 1947–48
London Palladium
  Variety Season Trophy 1948
Bay Area Journal
  Plaque 1953
International Rescue Committee
  Citation 1956
Panorama of Progress
  Distinguished Service Award (Arts Division) 1956
Lord Mayor of Leeds
  Presentation to Queen Elizabeth of England 1958
B. B. Students League
  Musician of the Century 1962
Columbia Records
  Award of Merit—Musician of the Century 1962
Carnegie Hall—WLIB Festival
  Award 1964

The Dino Award	1965
Experiment in Anti-Poverty	
for service beyond the call of duty	1967
Neighborhood House, Plainfield, New Jersey	
Testimonial	1968
Intercollegiate Music Festival	
Hall of Fame	1968
Metropolitan A.M.E. Church, New York, New York	
Plaque	1968
République Togolaise	
Subject of Commemorative Postage Stamp—Composers Series	1968
Northside Center for Child Development, Inc.	
With thanks for the joy you give through your music to all God's	
children.	1968
Pope Paul VI	
Personal Parchment—Special Papal Blessing	1969
California Youth Symphony	
Plaque—Benefit Guest Artist	1969
Island of Jamaica, B.W.I.	
Scroll of Friendship	1969
Ching Chuen Kang, Republic of China Air Base, Taiwan	
Plaque—"World Renowned Band Leader-Arranger, Composer and	
Pianist"	1970
Third International Festival, Palermo, Sicily	
Gold Award	1970
Hubbard Regional Hospital Guild, Webster, Massachusetts	
Plaque—In gratitude	1971
Duke Ellington Fellowship Program at Yale University, instituted August 17	1972
Eleanor Roosevelt International Workshop in Human Relations:	
International Humanist Award ("for global public service")	1972

Besides the honarary college degress conferred upon me, I have also been granted honorary positions in societies and organizations. Thus I am a thirty-second-degree Mason, a Shriner, a Grand Bandmaster of the Elks, a member of Alpha, Orpheus, and the Duke Ellington Society International.

The last is a unique organization that exists primarily to propagate our music and to unite friends with a common interest in such centers as New York, Washington, D.C., Los Angeles, Toronto, and Tokyo. Bill Ross (Los Angeles), Mrs. Anger and her son, Ron (Toronto), Dr. Ted Shell and Maurice Lawrence (D.C.), Tom

Detienne, Tom Harris, Dr. and Mrs. Doug Bray, Anita Porter, Jim Springer, Jack McDonough, Katy Kotschedoff, Helen Ennico, Carrie Miller, Emil Schell (New York City), Coots Bussard and Nick (Veedersburg), Nokayuma (Tokyo), Don Swenson and Ray McClure (Minneapolis), Ethel Rich (Milton College).

A man of many parts: With the circus calliope, Baraboo, Wisconsin, 1966

Afro-Bossa	Reprise 96069
And His Mother Called Him Bill	RCA LSP-3906
At Duke's Place (with Ella Fitzgerald)	Verve 64070
At His Very Best	RCA LPM-1715
Barney Bigard & Albert Nicholas	RCA LPV-566
Beginning, The (1926–28)	Decca DL-79224
Best of Duke Ellington, The	Capitol DT-1602
Black, Brown and Beige (with Mahalia Jackson)	Columbia JCS-8015
Concert of Sacred Music	RCA LSP-3582
Daybreak Express	RCA LPV-506
Drum Is a Woman, A	Columbia JCL-951
Duke Ellington Meets Coleman Hawkins	Impulse S-26
Duke Ellington Meets John Coltrane	Impulse S-30
Duke Ellington Presents Ivie Anderson	Columbia KG-32064 (2 discs)
Duke's Big Four	Pablo 2310703
Early Ellington	Everest Archives 221
Early Years, The	Everest Archives 249
Echoes of An Era (with Louis Armstrong)	Roulette 108 (2 discs)
Ellington at Newport	Columbia CS-8648
Ellington Era, The, Volume I	Columbia C3L-27 (3 discs)
Ellington Era, The, Volume II	Columbia C3L-39 (3 discs)
Ellington Indigos	Columbia CS-8053
Ellingtonia, Volume I	Impulse 9256-2 (2 discs)
Ellingtonia, Volume II	Impulse 9285-2 (2 discs)
Ellington '66	Reprise S-6154
Fantasies	Harmony 11236
Far East Suite, The	RCA LSP-3782
First Time (with Count Basie)	Columbia CS-8515
Flaming Youth	RCA LPV-568
Francis A. & Edward K. (with Frank Sinatra)	Reprise FS-1024
Golden Duke, The	Prestige 24029 (2 discs)
Great Paris Concert, The	Atlantic SD2-304 (2 discs)
Greatest Hits	Columbia CS-9629
Greatest Hits	Harmony 30566
Greatest Hits	Reprise 6234
Greatest Jazz Concert in the World, The	Pablo 2625704 (4 discs)
Hi-Fi Ellington Uptown	Columbia CCL-830
Hits of the 60s	Reprise S-86122

Hot in Harlem (1928–29)	Decca DL-79241
Indispensable Duke Ellington, The	RCA LPM-6009 (2 discs)
In My Solitude	Harmony 11323
It Don't Mean a Thing (with Teresa Brewer)	Flying Dutchman 10166
Jazz at the Plaza	Columbia C-32471
Johnny Come Lately	RCA LPV-541
Jumpin' Punkins	RCA LPV-517
Latin-American Suite, The	Fantasy 8419
Masterpieces by Ellington	Columbia JCL-825
Money Jungle	Solid State 18022
Mood Indigo	Camden ADL2-0152E (2 discs)
Music of Duke Ellington	Columbia CCL-558
My People (Original Cast Recording)	Flying Dutchman 10112
New Orleans Suite, The	Atlantic S-1580
New World A-Coming: Harlem:	
The Golden Broom and the Green Apple	
(with the Cincinnati Symphony Orchestra)	Decca DL-710176
North of the Border (in Canada)	Decca DL-75069
Nutcracker and Peer Gynt Suites, The	Odyssey (CBS) 321-60252
On the Côte D'Azur (with Ella Fitzgerald)	Verve 64072 (2 discs)
Pianist, The	Fantasy 9462
Piano Reflections	Capitol M-11058
Popular Duke Ellington, The	RCA LSP-3576
Pretty Woman	RCA LPV-553
Recollections of the Big Band Era	Atlantic 1665
Rockin' in Rhythm (1929–31)	Decca DL-79247
Second Sacred Concert	Fantasy 8407/8 (2 discs)
Seventieth Birthday Concert	Solid State SS-19000 (2 discs)
Such Sweet Thunder	Columbia JCL-1033
Symphonic Ellington, The	Reprise RS-6097
Things Ain't What They Used To Be	
(with Johnny Hodges and Rex Stewart)	RCA LPV-533
Third Sacred Concert, The	RCA APL1-0785
This Is Duke Ellington	RCA VPM-6042 (2 discs)
This One's For Blanton (with Ray Brown)	Pablo 2310721
Togo Brava Suite, The	United Artists UXS-92 (2 discs)
We Love You Madly	Pickwick 3390
Will Big Bands Ever Come Back?	Reprise 6168
World of Duke Ellington, The, Volume I	Columbia G-32564 (2 discs)
World of Duke Ellington, The, Volume II	Columbia KG-33341 (2 discs)
Yale Concert, The	Fantasy 9433

COMPOSITIONS

Duke Ellington's compositions are listed here in their order of copyright. This does not necessarily accord with the order in which they were written, as is evident from the position of such titles as "Soda Fountain Rag," "Rainy Nights," "Oklahoma Stomp," "Tough Truckin'," "Sweet Dreams of Love," etc.

TITLE OF COMPOSITION	YEAR	COMPOSER	AUTHOR
Blind Man's Buff	1923	Duke Ellington	H. Trent
Choo Choo (I Gotta Hurry Home)	1924	Duke Ellington, Dave Ringle, and Bob Schaefer	
Pretty Soft for You	1924	Duke Ellington	Joseph Trent
Chocolate Kiddies:			
Jig Walk	1925	Duke Ellington	Jo Trent
Jim Dandy	1925	Duke Ellington	Jo Trent
With You	1925	Duke Ellington	Jo Trent
Yam Brown	1926	Duke Ellington	Jo Trent
The Blues I Love to Sing	1927	Duke Ellington and Bub Miley	
Black and Tan Fantasy	1927	Duke Ellington and Bub Miley	
East St. Louis Toodle-O	1927	Duke Ellington and Bub Miley	
Birmingham Breakdown (Backdown)	1927	Duke Ellington	
Black Cat Blues	1927	Duke Ellington	
Hop Head	1927	Duke Ellington	
Immigration Blues	1927	Duke Ellington	
The Creeper	1927	Duke Ellington	
Washington Wabble	1927	Duke Ellington	
Down in Our Alley Blues	1927	Duke Ellington and Otto Hardwick	
Bouncing Buoyancy	1927	Duke Ellington	
Gold Digger	1927	Duke Ellington and Will Donaldson	
Hot and Bothered	1928	Duke Ellington	
Blue Bubbles	1928	Duke Ellington	
Creole Love Call	1928	Duke Ellington	
Black Beauty	1928	Duke Ellington	
Jubilee Stomp	1928	Duke Ellington	
New Orleans Low Down	1928	Duke Ellington	
Take It Easy	1928	Duke Ellington	
Swampy River	1928	Duke Ellington	

Move Over	1929	Duke Ellington	
Big House Blues	1929	Duke Ellington	
The Mooch	1929	Duke Ellington and Irving Mills	
Stevedore Stomp	1929	Duke Ellington and Irving Mills	
Harlem Flat Blues	1929	Duke Ellington	
Doin' the Voom Voom	1929	Duke Ellington and Bub Miley	
Goin' to Town	1929	Duke Ellington and Bub Miley	
Flaming Youth	1929	Duke Ellington	
High Life	1929	Duke Ellington	
Memphis Wail	1929	Duke Ellington	
Mississippi Moan	1929	Duke Ellington	
Misty Mornin'	1929	Duke Ellington and Arthur Whetsol	
Rub-a-Tub-Lues	1929	Duke Ellington	
What a Life	1929	Duke Ellington	
Awful Sad	1929	Duke Ellington	
The Blues with a Feeling	1929	Duke Ellington	
Dicty Glide	1929	Duke Ellington	
The Duke Steps Out	1929	Duke Ellington	
Haunted Nights	1929	Duke Ellington	
Sloppy Joe	1929	Duke Ellington and Barney Bigard	
Rent Party Blues	1929	Duke Ellington and Johnny Hodges	
Saturday Night Function	1929	Duke Ellington and Albany Bigard	
Check and Double Check:			
Old Man Blues	1930	Duke Ellington and Irving Mills	Duke Ellington and Irving Mills
Ring Dem Bells	1930	Duke Ellington and Irving Mills	Duke Ellington and Irving Mills
The Breakfast Dance	1930	Duke Ellington	
Blues of the Vagabond	1930	Duke Ellington	
Cincinnati Daddy	1930	Duke Ellington	
Jazz Lips	1930	Duke Ellington	
The Lazy Duke	1930	Duke Ellington	
Syncopated Shuffle	1930	Duke Ellington	
Wall Street Wail	1930	Duke Ellington	
Sweet Mama	1930	Duke Ellington	
Zonky Blues	1930	Duke Ellington	
Blackberries of 1930:			
Bumpty Bump	1930	Duke Ellington	Irving Mills

Doin' the Crazy Walk	1930	Duke Ellington	Irving Mills
Swanee River Rhapsody	1930	Duke Ellington, Irving Mills, and Clarence Gaskill	
I'm So in Love with You	1931	Duke Ellington and Irving Mills	
Rockin' Rhythm	1931	Duke Ellington, Irving Mills, and Harry Carney	
Mood Indigo	1931	Duke Ellington, Irving Mills, and Albany Bigard	
Rocky Mountain Blues	1932	Duke Ellington and Irving Mills	
Best Wishes	1932	Duke Ellington	Ted Koehler
Moon Over Dixie	1932	Duke Ellington	Ted Koehler
It Don't Mean a Thing If It Ain't Got That Swing	1932	Duke Ellington	Irving Mills
The Mystery Song	1932	Duke Ellington and Irving Mills	
Sweet Chariot	1932	Duke Ellington and Irving Mills	
Sophisticated Lady	1933	Duke Ellington	Mitchell Parish and Irving Mills
Drop Me Off in Harlem	1933	Duke Ellington	Nick Kenny
Slippery Horn	1933	Duke Ellington	
Jungle Nights in Harlem	1934	Duke Ellington and Irving Mills	
Dallas Doin's	1934	Duke Ellington	
Solitude	1934	Duke Ellington	Eddie De Lange and Irving Mills
Stompy Jones	1934	Duke Ellington	
Blue Feeling	1934	Duke Ellington	
Daybreak Express	1934	Duke Ellington	
Rude Interlude	1934	Duke Ellington	
Bird of Paradise	1935	Duke Ellington	
Harlem Speaks	1935	Duke Ellington	
Delta Serenade	1935	Duke Ellington	Manny Kurtz and Irving Mills
In a Sentimental Mood	1935	Duke Ellington	Manny Kurtz and Irving Mills
Sump'n' 'Bout Rhythm	1935	Duke Ellington	Manny Kurtz and Irving Mills
Ducky Wucky	1935	Duke Ellington and Albany Bigard	
Hyde Park	1935	Duke Ellington	

Merry Go Round	1935	Duke Ellington	
Reminiscing in Tempo	1935	Duke Ellington	
Showboat Shuffle	1935	Duke Ellington	
Saddest Tale	1935	Duke Ellington and Irving Mills	
Rhapsody Jr.	1935	Duke Ellington	
In a Jam	1936	Duke Ellington	
Clarinet Lament	1936	Duke Ellington and Barney Bigard	
Echoes of Harlem	1936	Duke Ellington	
Uptown Downbeat	1936	Duke Ellington	
Trumpet in Spades	1936	Duke Ellington	
Yearning for Love	1936	Duke Ellington	Mitchell Parish and Irving Mills
Oh Babe, Maybe Someday	1936	Duke Ellington	Duke Ellington
Alabamy Home	1937	Duke Ellington and Dave Ringle	Duke Ellington and Dave Ringle
Caravan	1937	Duke Ellington and Juan Tizol	Irving Mills
Scattin' at the Kit Kat	1937	Duke Ellington	Irving Mills
Azure	1937	Duke Ellington	Irving Mills
Clouds in My Heart	1937	Duke Ellington and Barney Bigard	Irving Mills
Lament for Lost Love	1937	Duke Ellington and Barney Bigard	Irving Mills
Jazz à la Carte	1937	Duke Ellington and Barney Bigard	Irving Mills
Sauce for the Goose	1937	Duke Ellington and Barney Bigard	
Blue Reverie	1937	Duke Ellington and Harry Carney	
Demi-Tasse	1937	Duke Ellington and Harry Carney	
Ev'ah Day	1937	Duke Ellington and Harry Carney	
I've Got to Be a Rug Cutter	1937	Duke Ellington	Duke Ellington
Four and a Half Street	1937	Duke Ellington and Rex Stewart	
Black Butterfly	1937	Duke Ellington	Irving Mills and Ben Carruthers
Downtown Uproar	1937	Duke Ellington and Cootie Williams	
Ridin' on a Blue Note	1938	Duke Ellington	Irving Mills and Irving Gordon
Jubilesta	1938	Duke Ellington and Juan Tizol	Irving Mills

Pyramid	1938	Duke Ellington and Juan Tizol	Irving Mills and Irving Gordon
Gypsy without a Song	1938	Duke Ellington and Lou Singer	Irving Gordon
Lost in Meditation	1938	Duke Ellington and Lou Singer	Irving Mills
Dusk on the Desert	1938	Duke Ellington	Irving Mills
Chasin' Chippies	1938	Duke Ellington and Cootie Williams	
Empty Ballroom Blues	1938	Duke Ellington and Cootie Williams	
Swing Pan Alley	1938	Duke Ellington and Cootie Williams	
Dinah's in a Jam	1938	Duke Ellington	
Swinging in the Dell	1938	Duke Ellington and Johnny Hodges	
Jeep's Blues	1938	Duke Ellington and Johnny Hodges	
Harmony in Harlem	1938	Duke Ellington and Johnny Hodges	Irving Mills
Jitterbug's Holiday	1938	Duke Ellington and Johnny Hodges	Irving Mills
Jeep Is Jumpin'	1938	Duke Ellington and Johnny Hodges	
Krum Elbow Blues	1938	Duke Ellington and Johnny Hodges	
Rhythmoods	1938	Duke Ellington	
Chatterbox	1938	Duke Ellington and Rex Stewart	Irving Mills
Steppin' Into Swing Society	1938	Duke Ellington	Irving Mills and Henry Nemo
I Let a Song Go Out of My Heart	1938	Duke Ellington	Irving Mills and John Redmond
Prelude to a Kiss	1938	Duke Ellington	Irving Mills and Irving Gordon
Drummer's Delight	1938	Duke Ellington and Barney Bigard	
Pigeons and Peppers	1938	Duke Ellington and Mercer Ellington	
La De Doody Doo	1938	Duke Ellington, Edward J. Lambert, and Stephen Richards	

Cotton Club Parade (4th ed.):

I'm Slappin' Seventh Avenue with the Sole of My Shoe	1938	Duke Ellington	Irving Mills and Henry Nemo
Skrontch	1938	Duke Ellington	Irving Mills and Henry Nemo

Swingtime in Honolulu	1938	Duke Ellington	Irving Mills and Henry Nemo
A Lesson in C	1938	Duke Ellington	Irving Mills and Henry Nemo
Braggin' in Brass	1938	Duke Ellington	Irving Mills and Henry Nemo
Carnival in Caroline	1938	Duke Ellington	Irving Mills and Henry Nemo
If You Were in My Place What Would You Do?	1938	Duke Ellington	Irving Mills and Henry Nemo
Battle of Swing	1939	Duke Ellington	
Blue Light	1939	Duke Ellington	
Boys from Harlem	1939	Duke Ellington	
The Buffet Flat	1939	Duke Ellington	
Delta Mood	1939	Duke Ellington	
Dooji Wooji	1939	Duke Ellington	
Exposition Swing	1939	Duke Ellington	
Gal from Joe's	1939	Duke Ellington	Irving Mills
I'm in Another World	1939	Duke Ellington and Johnny Hodges	Irving Mills and Irving Gordon
I'm Riding on the Moon and Dancing on the Stars	1939	Duke Ellington and Johnny Hodges	
Hodge Podge	1939	Duke Ellington and Johnny Hodges	
Wanderlust	1939	Duke Ellington and Johnny Hodges	
Subtle Lament	1939	Duke Ellington	
Hip Chic	1939	Duke Ellington	
Beautiful Romance	1939	Duke Ellington and Cootie Williams	Lupin Fein
Boudoir Benny	1939	Duke Ellington and Cootie Williams	
Gal-Avantin'	1939	Duke Ellington and Cootie Williams	
Mobile Blues	1939	Duke Ellington and Cootie Williams	
Jazz Potpourri	1939	Duke Ellington	
Boy Meets Horn	1939	Duke Ellington and Rex Stewart	Irving Mills
Smörgåsbord and Schnapps	1939	Duke Ellington, Rex Stewart, and B. Fleagle	
Something to Live for	1939	Duke Ellington and Billy Strayhorn	Duke Ellington and Billy Strayhorn
Grievin'	1939	Duke Ellington and Billy Strayhorn	Duke Ellington and Billy Strayhorn

Title	Year		
I'm Checking Out—Goom Bye	1939	Duke Ellington and Billy Strayhorn	Duke Ellington and Billy Strayhorn
Your Love Has Faded	1939	Duke Ellington and Billy Strayhorn	Duke Ellington and Billy Strayhorn
Lonely Co-ed	1939	Duke Ellington, B. Strayhorn, and Edgar Leslie	Duke Ellington, B. Strayhorn, and Edgar Leslie
Stevedore's Serenade	1939	Duke Ellington	Hilly Edelstein and Irving Gordon
You Gave Me the Gate and I'm Swinging	1939	Duke Ellington	I. Gordon, J. Farmer and J. B. McNeely
Watermelon Man	1939	Duke Ellington	Duke Ellington
Old King Dooji	1939	Duke Ellington	
Pussy Willow	1939	Duke Ellington	
Slap Happy	1939	Duke Ellington	
Solid Old Man	1939	Duke Ellington	
Way Low	1939	Duke Ellington	
Grateful to You	1939	Duke Ellington	
Lady in Doubt	1939	Duke Ellington	
Lady Macbeth	1939	Duke Ellington	
Lullaby	1939	Duke Ellington	
Country Gal	1939	Duke Ellington	
The Sergeant Was Shy	1939	Duke Ellington	
Tootin' Through the Roof	1939	Duke Ellington	
Weely	1939	Duke Ellington	
The Blues	1939	Duke Ellington	
Lady in Blue	1940	Duke Ellington	Irving Mills
Love's in My Heart	1940	Duke Ellington and Hayes Alvis	Irving Mills
Portrait of a Lion	1940	Duke Ellington	
Rumpus in Richmond	1940	Duke Ellington	
Sepia Panorama	1940	Duke Ellington	
Jack the Bear	1940	Duke Ellington	
Junior Hop	1940	Duke Ellington	
Pitter, Panther, Patter	1940	Duke Ellington	
Me and You	1940	Duke Ellington	Duke Ellington
Charlie the Chulo	1940	Duke Ellington	
Flaming Sword	1940	Duke Ellington	
My Sunday Gal	1940	Duke Ellington	
Diamond Jubilee Song	1940	Duke Ellington and Billy Strayhorn	Duke Ellington and Billy Strayhorn
Honchi Chonch	1940	Duke Ellington and Billy Strayhorn	Duke Ellington and Billy Strayhorn
Lick Chorus	1940	Duke Ellington	
Tonk	1940	Duke Ellington and Billy Strayhorn	

Day Dream	1940	Duke Ellington and Billy Strayhorn	John La Touche
A Lull at Dawn	1940	Duke Ellington	
Harlem Air Shaft	1940	Duke Ellington	
Conga Brava	1940	Duke Ellington and Juan Tizol	
A Portrait of Bert Williams	1940	Duke Ellington	
Bojangles	1940	Duke Ellington	
In a Mellow Tone (AKA: Baby, You and Me)	1940	Duke Ellington	Milt Gabler
I Never Felt This Way Before	1940	Duke Ellington	Al Dubin
All too Soon	1940	Duke Ellington	Carl Sigman
Concerto for Cootie (AKA: Cootie's Concerto)	1939	Duke Ellington	
Serenade to Sweden	1939	Duke Ellington	
Ko-Ko	1939	Duke Ellington	
Morning Glory	1939	Duke Ellington	
Blue Goose	1939	Duke Ellington	
Blue Bells of Harlem	1939	Duke Ellington	
Lovely Isle of Porto Rico (AKA: Porto Rican Gal)	1939	Duke Ellington and Juan Tizol	
Cotton Tail	1940	Duke Ellington	
Sapph	1940	Duke Ellington	
Slow Tune	1940	Duke Ellington	
Never No Lament	1940	Duke Ellington	
Flame Indigo	1941	Duke Ellington	Paul Webster
Doghouse Blues	1941	Duke Ellington	
Just A-Sittin' and A-Rockin'	1941	Duke Ellington and B. Strayhorn	Lee Gaines
Baby, When You Ain't There	1941	Duke Ellington	Mitchell Parish
I'm Satisfied	1941	Duke Ellington	Mitchell Parish
Swing Low	1941	Duke Ellington	
Lightnin'	1941	Duke Ellington	
Plucked Again	1941	Duke Ellington	
Swee' Pea	1941	Duke Ellington and B. Strayhorn	
Warm Valley	1941	Duke Ellington	Bob Russell
Rocks in My Bed	1941	Duke Ellington	Duke Ellington
Luna de Cuba (Spanish version of "Lovely Isle of Porto Rico")	1941	Duke Ellington and Juan Tizol	Sp.: George Negrette
Jump for Joy:			
I Got It Bad and That Ain't Good	1941	Duke Ellington	Paul Webster
Brown-Skin Gal in the Calico Gown	1941	Duke Ellington	Paul Webster

Chocolate Shake	1941	Duke Ellington	Paul Webster
Bessie—Whoa Babe	1941	Duke Ellington	Paul Webster
Nostalgia	1941	Duke Ellington	Paul Webster
Flame Indigo	1941	Duke Ellington	Paul Webster
Jump for Joy	1941	Duke Ellington	Paul Webster and Sid Kuller
Give Me an Old-Fashioned Waltz	1941	Duke Ellington	Sid Kuller
Sh, He's on the Beat	1941	Duke Ellington	Sid Kuller
Sharp Easter	1941	Duke Ellington	Sid Kuller
Bli-Blip	1941	Duke Ellington	Sid Kuller and Duke Ellington
The Giddy-Bug Galop	1941	Duke Ellington	
I Don't Know What Kind of Blues I've Got	1942	Duke Ellington	Duke Ellington
Romance Wasn't Built in a Day	1942	Duke Ellington	
Fatstuff Serenade	1942	Duke Ellington and Rex Stewart	
Back Room Romp	1942	Duke Ellington and Rex Stewart	
San Juan Hill	1942	Duke Ellington, Rex Stewart, and B. Fleagle	
So, I'll Come Back for More	1942	Duke Ellington, Rex Stewart, and B. Fleagle	
Good Gal Blues	1942	Duke Ellington	
Bundle of Blues	1942	Duke Ellington	
Crescendo in Blue	1942	Duke Ellington	
Diminuendo in Blue	1942	Duke Ellington	
What Am I Here For?	1942	Duke Ellington	Frankie Laine
Azalea	1942	Duke Ellington	Duke Ellington
Going Up	1942	Duke Ellington	
I Don't Mind	1942	Duke Ellington	Billy Strayhorn
Someone	1942	Duke Ellington	
Little Posey	1942	Duke Ellington	
Don't Get Around Much Any More (vocal version of "Never No Lament")	1942	Duke Ellington	Bob Russell
Five O'Clock Drag	1942	Duke Ellington	Harold Adamson
Dusk	1942	Duke Ellington	
Oh, Miss Jaxson	1942	Duke Ellington	Duke Ellington
Sherman Shuffle	1942	Duke Ellington	
Are You Sticking?	1942	Duke Ellington	
Tea and Trumpets	1942	Duke Ellington	
C-Jam Blues (AKA: "C Blues")	1942	Duke Ellington	

Song	Year	Music	Lyrics
American Lullaby (AKA: "Lullaby")	1942	Duke Ellington	
Home	1942	Duke Ellington	
Carnaval	1942	Duke Ellington and Juan Tizol	
Baby, Please Stop and Think About Me	1943	Duke Ellington	Irving Gordon
Tonight I Shall Sleep (with a Smile on My Face)	1943	Duke Ellington	Irving Gordon and Mercer Ellington
Mr. J. B. Blues	1943	Duke Ellington	
Mood to Be Wooed	1943	Duke Ellington and Johnny Hodges	
Killin' Myself	1943	Duke Ellington	
Grace Note Blues	1943	Duke Ellington	
Do Nothin' Till You Hear From Me (vocal version of "Concerto for Cootie")	1943	Duke Ellington	Bob Russell
Ring Around the Moon	1943	Duke Ellington	Bob Russell
Chicken Feed	1943	Duke Ellington	Bob Russell
Savoy Strut	1943	Duke Ellington and Johnny Hodges	
Rockabye River	1943	Duke Ellington	
Barzallai-Lou	1943	Duke Ellington	
Three Cent Stomp	1943	Duke Ellington	
Fickle Fling (AKA: "Camp Grant Chant")	1943	Duke Ellington	
Graceful Awareness	1943	Duke Ellington	
Mobile Bay	1943	Duke Ellington and Rex Stewart	
Across the Track Blues	1943	Duke Ellington	
Blue Ramble	1943	Duke Ellington	Duke Ellington
Cotton Club Stomp	1943	Duke Ellington, Johnny Hodges, and Harry Carney	Duke Ellington, Johnny Hodges, and Harry Carney
Shout 'Em, Aunt Tillie	1943	Duke Ellington and I. Mills	Duke Ellington and I. Mills
Main Stem (AKA: Altitude, Swing Shifters; Swing; On Becoming a Square)	1944	Duke Ellington	
Hit Me with a Hote Note and Watch Me Bounce	1944	Duke Ellington	Don George
I Didn't Know About You (vocal version of "Home")	1944	Duke Ellington	
I Ain't Got Nothin' but the Blues	1944	Duke Ellington	Don George

I'm Beginning to See the Light	1944	Duke Ellington, Don George, Johnny Hodges, and Harry James	Duke Ellington, Don George, Johnny Hodges, and Harry James
Don't You Know I Care	1944	Duke Ellington	Mack David
No Smoking	1944	Duke Ellington	Duke Ellington
My Lovin' Baby and Me	1944	Duke Ellington, Don George, and Cab Calloway	Duke Ellington, Don George, and Cab Calloway
You Left Me Everything but You	1944	Duke Ellington and Don George	Duke Ellington and Don George
Jumping Frog Jump	1944	Duke Ellington	
Stomp, Look and Listen	1944	Duke Ellington	
Suddenly It Jumped	1944	Duke Ellington	
Jazz Convulsions	1944	Duke Ellington	
Creole Rhapsody	1944	Duke Ellington	Duke Ellington
I Can't Put My Arms Around a Memory	1944	Duke Ellington	Don George
Blutopia	1944	Duke Ellington	
You've Got My Heart (AKA: "Someone")	1944	Duke Ellington	
I Love My Lovin' Lover	1945	Duke Ellington	
Let the Zoomers Drool	1945	Duke Ellington and Johnny Hodges	
Esquire Swank	1945	Duke Ellington and Johnny Hodges	
The Wonder of You	1945	Duke Ellington and Johnny Hodges	Don George
Which Is Which Stomp	1945	Duke Ellington	
Heart of Harlem	1945	Duke Ellington	Langston Hughes
Fancy Dan	1945	Duke Ellington	
Riff'n Drill	1945	Duke Ellington	
Love, Strong and Consecutive	1945	Duke Ellington	Mack David
Subtle Slough	1945	Duke Ellington	
Zan	1945	Duke Ellington	
Unbooted Character	1945	Duke Ellington	
Bugle Breaks	1945	Duke Ellington, Billy Strayhorn, and Mercer Ellington	
Zanzibar	1945	Duke Ellington	
It's Only Account of You	1945	Duke Ellington	
Blue Cellophane	1945	Duke Ellington	
Air Conditioned Jungle	1945	Duke Ellington and Jimmy Hamilton	
Frustration	1945	Duke Ellington	

Strange Feeling	1945	Duke Ellington and Billy Strayhorn	
Coloratura	1945	Duke Ellington	
Dancers in Love (AKA: "Stomp for Beginners")	1945	Duke Ellington	
Prairie Fantasy	1945	Duke Ellington	
Downbeat Shuffle	1945	Duke Ellington	
Frantic Fantasy	1945	Duke Ellington and Rex Stewart	
Carnegie Blues	1945	Duke Ellington	
Teardrops in Rain	1945	Duke Ellington and William Anderson	
Ev'ry Hour on the Hour I Fall in Love with You	1945	Duke Ellington	Don George
Time's A-Wastin'	1945	Duke Ellington, Don George, and Mercer Ellington	
Everything but You	1945	Duke Ellington, Don George, and Harry James	
I'm Just a Lucky So and So	1945	Duke Ellington	Mack David
New World A-Comin'	1945	Duke Ellington	
Translucency	1945	Duke Ellington and Lawrence Brown	

Black, Brown and Beige:

Emancipation Celebration	1945	Duke Ellington	
West Indian Dance	1945	Duke Ellington	
Sugar Hill Penthouse	1945	Duke Ellington	
Worksong	1945	Duke Ellington	
The Blues	1945	Duke Ellington	
Come Sunday	1945	Duke Ellington	
Metronome All Out	1945	Duke Ellington and Billy Strayhorn	
Suburbanite	1946	Duke Ellington	
Magenta Haze	1946	Duke Ellington	
Circe	1946	Duke Ellington	
Sono	1946	Duke Ellington	
Rugged Romeo	1946	Duke Ellington	
A Gatherin' in a Clearin'	1946	Duke Ellington and William Anderson	
Blue Abandon	1946	Duke Ellington	
Eighth Veil	1946	Duke Ellington and Billy Strayhorn	
Fugue	1946	Duke Ellington	
Tip Toe Topic	1946	Duke Ellington and Oscar Pettiford	

Mellow Ditty	1946	Duke Ellington	
Hey, Baby	1946	Duke Ellington	
You Don't Love Me No More	1946	Duke Ellington	Duke Ellington
Pretty Woman	1946	Duke Ellington	Duke Ellington
Tonal Group:			
Rhapsoditti	1946	Duke Ellington	
Fugueaditti	1946	Duke Ellington	
Jam-a-ditty	1946	Duke Ellington	
Just Squeeze Me	1946	Duke Ellington	Lee Gaines
Tell Me, Tell Me, Dream Face	1946	Duke Ellington	Don George
It Shouldn't Happen to a Dream	1946	Duke Ellington and Johnny Hodges	Don George
You Gotta Crawl Before You Walk	1946	Duke Ellington, Larry Fotin, Mel Tormé, and Robert Wells	Duke Ellington, Larry Fotin, Mel Tormé, and Robert Wells
Deep South Suite:			
Happy Go Lucky Local	1947	Duke Ellington	
Sultry Sunset	1947	Duke Ellington	
Hearsay	1947	Duke Ellington and Billy Strayhorn	
There Was Nobody Looking	1947	Duke Ellington and Billy Strayhorn	
Magnolias Dripping with Honey	1947	Duke Ellington and Billy Strayhorn	
Golden Feather	1947	Duke Ellington and Al Sears	
He Makes Me Believe He's Mine	1947	Duke Ellington	John La Touche
It's Kind of Lonesome Out Tonight	1947	Duke Ellington	Don George
Indigo Echoes	1947	Duke Ellington and Irving Mills	Duke Ellington and Irving Mills
Tough Truckin'	1947	Duke Ellington and Irving Mills	Duke Ellington and Irving Mills
I Don't Know Why I Love You So	1947	Duke Ellington and Irving Mills	Duke Ellington and Irving Mills
T. T. on Toast	1947	Duke Ellington and Irving Mills	Duke Ellington and Irving Mills
You're Just an Old Antidisestab-lishmentarianismist	1947	Duke Ellington and Don George	Duke Ellington and Don George
Oh, Gee	1947	Duke Ellington	Duke Ellington
Boogie Bop Blue	1947	Duke Ellington	
Who Struck John? (AKA: "Blues")	1947	Duke Ellington and Johnny Hodges	

Frisky	1947	Duke Ellington and Johnny Hodges	
Far Away Blues	1947	Duke Ellington and Johnny Hodges	
Long Horn Blues	1947	Duke Ellington and Johnny Hodges	
Golden Cress	1947	Duke Ellington and Lawrence Brown	
Sultry Serenade	1947	Duke Ellington and Tyree Glenn	
The Beautiful Indians (Minnehaha)	1947	Duke Ellington	
The Beautiful Indians (Hiawatha)	1947	Duke Ellington and Al Sears	
Blues at Sundown	1952	Duke Ellington	Duke Ellington
A Tone Parallel to Harlem	1952	Duke Ellington	
Searsy's Blues	1952	Duke Ellington	
Personality	1952	Duke Ellington	
Blues for Blanton	1952	Duke Ellington	
Rock Skippin'	1952	Duke Ellington and Billy Strayhorn	
Smada	1952	Duke Ellington and Billy Strayhorn	
Come on Home	1952	Duke Ellington	Duke Ellington
Primping at the Prom	1953	Duke Ellington	
Merrie Mending	1953	Duke Ellington	Duke Ellington
Ballin' the Blues	1953	Duke Ellington	Duke Ellington
Satin Doll	1953	Duke Ellington	Bill Strayhorn and Johnny Mercer
Silver Cobwebs	1953	Duke Ellington	Don George
Nothin', Nothin', Baby (Without You)	1953	Duke Ellington	Duke Ellington
Kind of Moody (vocal version of "Serenade to Sweden"; AKA: "Moody")	1953	Duke Ellington	Carl Sigman
Chili Bowl	1954	Duke Ellington	
Who Knows	1954	Duke Ellington	
Janet	1954	Duke Ellington	
Reflections in D	1954	Duke Ellington	
One-Sided Love Affair	1954	Duke Ellington	
Serious Serenade in B-Flat Minor	1954	Duke Ellington	
Band Call	1954	Duke Ellington	
Alternate	1954	Duke Ellington	
Night Time	1954	Duke Ellington and Billy Strayhorn	Doris Julian

Tan Your Hide	1954	Duke Ellington and Billy Strayhorn	
Blossom	1954	Duke Ellington and Billy Strayhorn	John H. Mercer
What More Can I Say	1954	Duke Ellington	Duke Ellington
Melancholia	1954	Duke Ellington	
Retrospection	1954	Duke Ellington	
B-Sharp Blues	1954	Duke Ellington	
My Reward	1955	Duke Ellington	
Night Creature (Parts 1–3)	1955	Duke Ellington	
Kinda Dukish	1955	Duke Ellington	
Reddy Eddy	1955	Duke Ellington	
It's Rumor	1955	Duke Ellington	Duke Ellington
Like a Train	1955	Duke Ellington	Duke Ellington
She	1955	Duke Ellington	Duke Ellington
Twilight Time	1955	Duke Ellington	Duke Ellington
Weatherman	1955	Duke Ellington	Duke Ellington
Hand Me Down Love	1955	Duke Ellington	Carl Sigman
Orson	1955	Duke Ellington and Billy Strayhorn	
Oo	1955	Duke Ellington and Billy Strayhorn	Duke Ellington and Billy Strayhorn
Suburban Beauty	1956	Duke Ellington	
Frivolous Banta	1956	Duke Ellington and Rick Henderson	
Cop-Out	1956	Duke Ellington	
Just Scratchin' the Surface	1956	Duke Ellington	
Rock 'n' Roll Rhapsody	1956	Duke Ellington	
Feetbone	1956	Duke Ellington	
Happy One	1956	Duke Ellington	
Killian's Lick	1956	Duke Ellington	
Coolin'	1956	Duke Ellington and Clark Terry	
Blue Rose	1956	Duke Ellington	
Lonesome Lullaby	1956	Duke Ellington	
Newport Jazz Festival Suite:			
Festival Junction	1956	Duke Ellington and Billy Strayhorn	
Newport Up	1956	Duke Ellington and Billy Strayhorn	
Blues to Be There	1956	Duke Ellington and Billy Strayhorn	
Big Drag	1956	Duke Ellington	
Falling Like a Raindrop	1956	Duke Ellington	
Clusterphobia	1956	Duke Ellington and Clark Terry	
The Sky Fell Down	1956	Duke Ellington	Joanne Towne

610 Suite	1956	Duke Ellington
Scenic	1956	Duke Ellington
A Drum Is a Woman:		
Ballet of the Flying Saucers	1956	Duke Ellington and Billy Strayhorn
Congo Square	1956	Duke Ellington and Billy Strayhorn
Carribee Joe	1956	Duke Ellington and Billy Strayhorn
A Drum Is a Woman	1956	Duke Ellington and Billy Strayhorn
Hey, Buddy Bolden	1956	Duke Ellington and Billy Strayhorn
Madame Zajj	1956	Duke Ellington and Billy Strayhorn
Rhumbob	1956	Duke Ellington and Billy Strayhorn
New Orleans	1956	Duke Ellington and Billy Strayhorn
Rhythm Pum Te Dum	1956	Duke Ellington and Billy Strayhorn
Zajj's Dream	1956	Duke Ellington and Billy Strayhorn
What Else Can You Do with a Drum?	1956	Duke Ellington and Billy Strayhorn
Matumbe	1956	Duke Ellington and Billy Strayhorn
Finale	1956	Duke Ellington and Billy Strayhorn
Royal Ancestry (Portrait of Ella Fitzgerald):		
Beyond Category	1957	Duke Ellington and Billy Strayhorn
All Heart	1957	Duke Ellington and Billy Strayhorn
Total Jazz	1957	Duke Ellington and Billy Strayhorn
Shakespearean Suite:		
Half the Fun	1957	Duke Ellington and Billy Strayhorn
Madness in Great Ones	1957	Duke Ellington and Billy Strayhorn
Circle of Fourths	1957	Duke Ellington and Billy Strayhorn
Sonnet in Search of a Moor	1957	Duke Ellington and Billy Strayhorn

Lady Mac	1957	Duke Ellington and Billy Strayhorn	
Sonnet to Hank Cinq	1957	Duke Ellington and Billy Strayhorn	
Such Sweet Thunder	1957	Duke Ellington and Billy Strayhorn	
Sonnet for Caesar	1957	Duke Ellington and Billy Strayhorn	
The Telecasters	1957	Duke Ellington and Billy Strayhorn	
Up and Down, Up and Down	1957	Duke Ellington and Billy Strayhorn	
Star-Crossed Lovers	1957	Duke Ellington and Billy Strayhorn	
Sonnet for Sister Kate	1957	Duke Ellington and Billy Strayhorn	
Café Au Lait	1957	Duke Ellington	
Jumpy	1957	Duke Ellington and Rex Stewart	
Shades of Harlem	1957	Duke Ellington	
Wailing Interval	1957	Duke Ellington	
You Better Know It	1957	Duke Ellington	
Pomegranate	1957	Duke Ellington	Billy Strayhorn
Rock City Rock	1957	Duke Ellington	Duke Ellington
Love (My Everything)	1957	Duke Ellington	Duke Ellington
Duke's Place (vocal version of "C-Jam Blues")	1957	Duke Ellington	Ruth Roberts, Bill Katz, and R. Thiele
Toot Suite:			
Red Shoes	1958	Duke Ellington and Billy Strayhorn	
Red Carpet	1958	Duke Ellington and Billy Strayhorn	
Red Garter	1958	Duke Ellington and Billy Strayhorn	
Ready-Go	1958	Duke Ellington and Billy Strayhorn	
Prima Bara Dubla	1958	Duke Ellington and Billy Strayhorn	
Jazz Festival Jazz	1958	Duke Ellington and Billy Strayhorn	
Blues in Orbit	1958	Duke Ellington and Billy Strayhorn	
Satin Doll	1958	Duke Ellington	Billy Strayhorn and Johnny Mercer
Princess Blue	1958	Duke Ellington	

Controversial Suite:

Before My Time	1958	Duke Ellington	
Later	1958	Duke Ellington	
Jones	1958	Duke Ellington and Pauline Reddon	
Pauline's Blues	1958	Duke Ellington and Pauline Reddon	
Pauline's Jump	1958	Duke Ellington and Pauline Reddon	
Blues in the Round	1958	Duke Ellington	
Hi Fi Fo Fum	1958	Duke Ellington	
Bassment (AKA: "Trombone Trio")	1958	Duke Ellington	
Track 360 (AKA: "Trains That Pass in the Night")	1958	Duke Ellington	
Don't Ever Say Goodbye	1958	Duke Ellington, Bill Putnam, and Belinda Putnam	Duke Ellington, Bill Putnam, and Belinda Putnam
My Heart, My Mind, My Everything	1958	Duke Ellington	Duke Ellington
A Hundred Dreams from Now (AKA: "Champagne Oasis")	1958	Duke Ellington	Johnny Burke
E and D Blues	1958	Duke Ellington and John Sanders	
Pleadin'	1958	Duke Ellington	
Tune Poem	1958	Duke Ellington	
Soda Fountain Rag	1958	Duke Ellington	
Juniflip	1958	Duke Ellington	
Mr. Gentle and Mr. Cool	1958	Duke Ellington and Laura Rembert	

Jump for Joy:

The Natives Are Restless Tonight	1959	Duke Ellington	Sid Kuller
Nerves, Nerves, Nerves	1959	Duke Ellington	Sid Kuller
Resigned to Living	1959	Duke Ellington	Sid Kuller
Strictly for Tourists	1959	Duke Ellington	Sid Kuller
Within Me I Know	1959	Duke Ellington	Sid Kuller
Three Shows Nightly	1959	Duke Ellington	Sid Kuller
Concerto for Clinkers	1959	Duke Ellington	Sid Kuller
Don't Believe Everything You Hear	1959	Duke Ellington	Sid Kuller
So the Good Book Says	1959	Duke Ellington and Billy Strayhorn	Sid Kuller
Walk It Off	1959	Duke Ellington and Billy Strayhorn	Sid Kuller

If We Were Anymore British (We Couldn't Talk at all)	1959	Duke Ellington	Sid Kuller
Anatomy of a Murder (film score)	1959	Duke Ellington	
I'm Gonna Go Fishin' (theme from *Anatomy of a Murder*)	1959	Duke Ellington	Peggy Lee
Anatomy of a Murder:			
Flirtibird	1959	Duke Ellington	
Way Early Subtone	1959	Duke Ellington	
Hero to Zero	1959	Duke Ellington	
Low Key Lightly	1959	Duke Ellington	
Happy Anatomy	1959	Duke Ellington	
Midnight Indigo	1959	Duke Ellington	
Almost Cried	1959	Duke Ellington	
Sunswept Sunday	1959	Duke Ellington	
Grace Valse	1959	Duke Ellington	
Haupe	1959	Duke Ellington	
Upper and Outest	1959	Duke Ellington	
Do Not Disturb	1959	Duke Ellington	
Original	1959	Duke Ellington	
Bugs	1959	Duke Ellington	
Nymph	1959	Duke Ellington	
Tymperturbably Blue	1959	Duke Ellington and Billy Strayhorn	
Malletoba Spank	1959	Duke Ellington and Billy Strayhorn	
But	1959	Duke Ellington	Sid Kuller
When I Trilly with my Filly	1959	Duke Ellington	Sid Kuller
Show 'Em You Got Class	1959	Duke Ellington	Sid Kuller
Le Sucrier Velour	1959	Duke Ellington	
Lightning Bugs and Frogs	1959	Duke Ellington	
Walkin' and Singin' the Blues	1959	Duke Ellington	Lil Greenwood
Dual Fuel	1959	Duke Ellington and Clark Terry	
Launching Pad	1959	Duke Ellington and Clark Terry	
Idiom '59	1959	Duke Ellington	
Like Love (based on a theme from *Anatomy of a Murder*)	1960	Duke Ellington	Bob Russell
Cop-Out Extension	1959	Duke Ellington	
The Line-Up	1960	Duke Ellington and Paul Gonsalves	
Blues in Blueprint	1960	Duke Ellington	
The Swinger's Jump	1959	Duke Ellington	

Villes Ville Is the Place, Man	1960	Duke Ellington	
The Swingers Get the Blues Too	1960	Duke Ellington and Matthew Gee	
Idiom No. 2	1960	Duke Ellington	
Idiom No. 3	1960	Duke Ellington	
One More Once	1961	Duke Ellington	
The Beautiful Americans	1961	Duke Ellington	
I Want to Love You (theme from *The Asphalt Jungle*)	1961	Duke Ellington	Marshall Barer

Nutcracker Suite:

Arabesque Cookie (Arabian Dance)	1960	Tchaikovsky, arr. Duke Ellington and Billy Strayhorn
Dance of the Floreadores (Waltz of the Flowers)	1960	Tchaikovsky, arr. Duke Ellington and Billy Strayhorn
Chinoiserie (Chinese Dance)	1960	Tchaikovsky, arr. Duke Ellington and Billy Strayhorn
Sugar Rum Cherry (Dance of the Sugar Plum Fairy)	1960	Tchaikovsky, arr. Duke Ellington and Billy Strayhorn
Peanut Brittle Brigade (March)	1960	Tchaikovsky, arr. Duke Ellington and Billy Strayhorn
Toot Toot Tootie Toot (Dance of the Reed Pipes)	1960	Tchaikovsky, arr. Duke Ellington and Billy Strayhorn
Overture	1960	Tchaikovsky, arr. Duke Ellington and Billy Strayhorn
Entr'acte	1960	Tchaikovsky, arr. Duke Ellington and Billy Strayhorn
The Volga Vouty (Russian Dance)	1960	Tchaikovsky, arr. Duke Ellington and Billy Strayhorn

Paris Blues:

Battle Royal	1961	Duke Ellington
Birdie Jungle	1961	Duke Ellington
Autumnal Suite	1961	Duke Ellington
Nite	1961	Duke Ellington
Wild Man Moore	1961	Duke Ellington
Paris Stairs	1961	Duke Ellington
Guitar Amour	1961	Duke Ellington
Paris Blues	1961	Duke Ellington

Without a Word of Complaint	1961	Duke Ellington Johnny Hodges, and George Weiss	Duke Ellington, Johnny Hodges, and George Weiss
Starting with You (I'm Through)	1961	Duke Ellington, Johnny Hodges, and Pat Stewart	Duke Ellington, Johnny Hodges, and Pat Stewart
Sugar City (AKA: Pousse Café):			
Sugar City	1962	Duke Ellington	Marshall Barer
Spacious and Gracious	1962	Duke Ellington	Marshall Barer
Spider and Fly	1962	Duke Ellington	Marshall Barer
Settle for Less	1962	Duke Ellington	Marshall Barer
Swivel	1962	Duke Ellington	Marshall Barer
Forever	1962	Duke Ellington	Marshall Barer
Someone to Care For	1962	Duke Ellington	Marshall Barer
Je N'Ai Rien	1962	Duke Ellington	Marshall Barer
Here You Are	1962	Duke Ellington	Marshall Barer
Follow Me Up the Stairs	1962	Duke Ellington	Marshall Barer
Do Me a Favor	1962	Duke Ellington	Marshall Barer
These Are the Good Old Days	1962	Duke Ellington	Marshall Barer
Let's	1963	Duke Ellington	Marshall Barer
Amazing	1963	Duke Ellington	Marshall Barer
The Colonel's Lady	1963	Duke Ellington	Marshall Barer
Natchez Trace	1964	Duke Ellington	Marshall Barer
Goodbye, Charlie	1964	Duke Ellington	Marshall Barer
Thank You, Sam	1964	Duke Ellington	Marshall Barer
C'est Comme Ça	1964	Duke Ellington	Marshall Barer
And Then Some	1962	Duke Ellington	Johnny Hodges
Suite Thursday:			
Lay Be	1962	Duke Ellington	
Misfit Blues	1962	Duke Ellington	
Zweet Zurzday	1962	Duke Ellington	
Schwiphti	1962	Duke Ellington	
Peer Gynt Suite	1962	Grieg, arr. Duke Ellington and Billy Strayhorn	
Tell Me	1962	Duke Ellington and Matthew Gee, Jr.	
Lazy Rhapsody	1962	Duke Ellington	Mitchell Parish
Argentine	1962	Duke Ellington	Mitchell Parish and Irving Mills
Blue Mood	1962	Duke Ellington and Johnny Hodges	Duke Ellington and Johnny Hodges
Dear	1962	Duke Ellington and Donald Heywood	
Framed	1962	Duke Ellington and Donald Heywood	Andy Razaf

Down Home Stomp	1962	Duke Ellington	Jo Trent
Fast and Furious	1962	Duke Ellington and Harold Pottio	
Glamorous	1962	Duke Ellington	Jo Trent and Irving Mills
Jollywog	1962	Duke Ellington	
Keep on Treating Me Sweet	1962	Duke Ellington	Jo Trent
Lot O' Fingers	1962	Duke Ellington	
A Night in Harlem	1962	Duke Ellington	
Oklahoma Stomp	1962	Duke Ellington	
Savage Rhythm	1962	Duke Ellington	
Slow Motion	1962	Duke Ellington	
Sponge Cake and Spinach	1962	Duke Ellington	
Swanee Lullaby	1962	Duke Ellington, Mitchell Parish, and Irving Mills	Duke Ellington, Mitchell Parish, and Irving Mills
Sweet Dreams of Love	1962	Duke Ellington and Irving Mills	
What Would It Mean Without You?	1962	Duke Ellington, Irving Mills, and George Brown	
Who Is She?	1962	Duke Ellington, Rousseau Simmons, Irving Mills, and Bob Schafer	Duke Ellington, Rousseau Simmons, Irving Mills, and Bob Schafer
Who Said It's Tight Like This?	1962	Duke Ellington	
Wring Your Washin' Out	1962	Duke Ellington and Jo Trent	
Introspection	1962	Duke Ellington	
Reconversion	1962	Duke Ellington	
The Feeling of Jazz	1962	Duke Ellington	Bobby Troup and George T. Simon
Twistin' Time	1962	Duke Ellington	Aaron Bell
Jump Over	1962	Duke Ellington	
Single Petal of a Rose	1962	Duke Ellington	
B.D.B	1962	Duke Ellington and Billy Strayhorn	
Self-Portrait of the Bean	1962	Duke Ellington and Billy Strayhorn	
Stand By Blues	1962	Duke Ellington	Johnny Hodges
You've Got the Love I Love	1962	Duke Ellington and Della Reese	Duke Ellington and Della Reese
Limbo Jazz	1962	Duke Ellington	
Java Pachacha	1962	Arr. Duke Ellington	
Caliné	1963	Duke Ellington	
Volupté	1963	Duke Ellington	

Purple Gazelle (Angelica)	1963	Duke Ellington	
Angu	1963	Duke Ellington	
Bonga	1963	Duke Ellington	
Moon Bow	1963	Duke Ellington	
Afro-Bossa	1963	Duke Ellington	
Fleurette Africaine	1963	Duke Ellington	
Wig Wise	1963	Duke Ellington	
Very Special	1963	Duke Ellington	
The Ricitic	1963	Duke Ellington	
Take the Coltrane	1963	Duke Ellington	
Money Jungle	1963	Duke Ellington	
You Dirty Dog	1963	Duke Ellington	
Ain't But the One	1963	Duke Ellington	
Will You Be There?	1963	Duke Ellington	
Heritage	1963	Duke Ellington	
Ninety-Nine Per Cent	1963	Duke Ellington	
King Fit the Battle of Alabam	1963	Duke Ellington	Duke Ellington
Blow by Blow	1963	Duke Ellington	
The Good Years of Jazz	1963	Duke Ellington	
Silk Lace	1963	Duke Ellington	
Sempre Amore	1963	Duke Ellington	
Blue Piano	1963	Duke Ellington	Ruth Roberts, Bill Katz, and Bob Thiele
Action in Alexandria	1963	Duke Ellington	
Ray Charles' Place	1963	Duke Ellington	
Perfume Suite:	1963	Duke Ellington	
Strange Feeling	1963	Duke Ellington	
Balcony Serenade	1963	Duke Ellington	
Coloratura	1963	Duke Ellington	
Dancers in Love	1963	Duke Ellington	
Ever-Lovin' Lover	1963	Duke Ellington	Duke Ellington
What Color Is Virtue?	1963	Duke Ellington	Duke Ellington
After Bird Jungle	1963	Duke Ellington	
Jail Blues	1963	Duke Ellington	Duke Ellington
Jungle Triangle	1963	Duke Ellington	
Blues for Jerry (AKA: "Blues to Jerry")	1963	Duke Ellington	
A Hundred Dreams Ago	1963	Duke Ellington	
Fountainbleau Forest	1963	Duke Ellington	
So	1963	Duke Ellington	
It's Bad to Be Forgotten	1963	Duke Ellington	
Congo	1963	Duke Ellington	
Springtime in Africa	1964	Duke Ellington and Aaron Bell	
M.G.	1964	Duke Ellington	

La Scala, She Too Pretty to Be True	1964	Duke Ellington		
Non-Violent Integration	1964	Duke Ellington		
Timon of Athens Suite:				
Impulsive Giving	1964	Duke Ellington		
Ocean	1964	Duke Ellington		
Angry	1964	Duke Ellington		
Gold	1964	Duke Ellington		
Regal Formal	1964	Duke Ellington		
Regal	1964	Duke Ellington		
Skilipop	1964	Duke Ellington		
Smoldering	1964	Duke Ellington		
Gossippippi	1964	Duke Ellington		
Counter Theme	1964	Duke Ellington		
Alcibiades	1964	Duke Ellington		
Gossip	1964	Duke Ellington		
Banquet	1964	Duke Ellington		
Revolutionary	1964	Duke Ellington		
The Far East Suite:				
Blue Bird of Delhi	1964	Duke Ellington and Billy Strayhorn		
Vict	1964	Duke Ellington and Billy Strayhorn		
Depk	1964	Duke Ellington and Billy Strayhorn		
Elf (Isfahan)	1964	Duke Ellington and Billy Strayhorn		
Circle	1964	Duke Ellington and Billy Strayhorn		
Agra	1964	Duke Ellington and Billy Strayhorn		
Paki	1964	Duke Ellington and Billy Strayhorn		
Amad	1964	Duke Ellington and Billy Strayhorn		
Put-Tin	1964	Duke Ellington and Billy Strayhorn		
Blue Pepper	1964	Duke Ellington and Billy Strayhorn		
Tourist Point of View	1964	Duke Ellington and Billy Strayhorn		
Sex, Money and Marriage	1964	Duke Ellington		
Tutti for Cootie	1964	Duke Ellington	Jimmy Hamilton	
Searchin'	1964	Duke Ellington	Steve Allen	
Workin' Blues	1964	Duke Ellington		
My Man Sends Me	1964	Duke Ellington	Duke Ellington	

My Mother, My Father and Love	1964	Duke Ellington	Duke Ellington
Metromedia	1964	Duke Ellington	
Stoona	1964	Duke Ellington	
New Tootie for Cootie	1964	Duke Ellington	
Rude Interlude	1964	Duke Ellington	
It's Glory	1964	Duke Ellington	
Warm Fire	1965	Duke Ellington	
Making That Scene	1965	Duke Ellington	Duke Ellington
58th Street Suite	1965	Duke Ellington and Billy Strayhorn	
Ellington '66	1965	Duke Ellington	
The Far East Suite:			
Fugi	1965	Duke Ellington	
Ad Lib on Nippon	1965	Duke Ellington	
Nagoya	1965	Duke Ellington	
Love Came	1965	Billy Strayhorn	Duke Ellington
The Truth	1965	Duke Ellington	Duke Ellington
On Account of You	1965	Duke Ellington	
Concerto for Oscar	1965	Duke Ellington	
Be a Man	1965	Duke Ellington	Marshall Barer
Flugel Street Rag	1965	Duke Ellington	Marshall Barer
My Heart Is a Stranger	1965	Duke Ellington	Marshall Barer
Rules and Regulations	1965	Duke Ellington	Marshall Barer
Salvation	1965	Duke Ellington	Marshall Barer
Up Your Ante	1965	Duke Ellington	Marshall Barer
A Girl's Best Friend	1965	Duke Ellington	Marshall Barer
The Golden Broom and the Green Apple	1965	Duke Ellington	Marshall Barer
Virgin Islands Suite:			
Fiddle on the Diddler	1965	Duke Ellington and Billy Strayhorn	
Island Virgin	1965	Duke Ellington and Billy Strayhorn	
Virgin Jungle	1965	Duke Ellington and Billy Strayhorn	
Jungle Kitty	1965	Duke Ellington and Billy Strayhorn	
Big Fat Alice's Blues	1965	Duke Ellington and Billy Strayhorn	
Mysterious Chick	1965	Duke Ellington and Billy Strayhorn	
Fade Up	1965	Duke Ellington and Billy Strayhorn	
Barefoot Stomper	1965	Duke Ellington and Billy Strayhorn	

Tokyo	1965	Duke Ellington and Jim Hamilton	
In the Beginning God (Pacabe) (Olds)	1965	Duke Ellington	
The Lord's Prayer	1965	Duke Ellington	
Christmas Surprise	1965	Duke Ellington and Billy Strayhorn	Rev. D. J. Bartlett
Thank You Ma'am (from "Pousse Café")	1966	Duke Ellington	Marshall Bave
Spanking Brand New Doll	1966	Duke Ellington	Duke Ellington
Imagine My Frustration	1966	Duke Ellington, Billy Strayhorn, and Gerald Wilson	Duke Ellington, Billy Strayhorn, and Gerald Wilson
Imbo (Limbo Jazz)	1966	Duke Ellington	
Tell Me It's the Truth	1966	Duke Ellington	Duke Ellington
House of Lords (l'Earl, le Duke)	1966	Earl Hines and Duke Ellington	Earl Hines and Duke Ellington
The Second Portrait of the Lion	1966	Duke Ellington	Duke Ellington
Jive Stomp	1966	Duke Ellington	Duke Ellington
Mount Harissa	1966	Duke Ellington	Duke Ellington
The Twitch	1966	Duke Ellington	
A Song for Christmas	1966	Dean Bartlett, Duke Ellington, and Billy Strayhorn	Dean Bartlett, Duke Ellington, and Billy Strayhorn
You Walk in My Dreams	1966	Duke Ellington	
You Are Beautiful	1966	Duke Ellington	
West Indian Pancake	1966	Duke Ellington	
Veldt-Amor	1966	Duke Ellington	
The Twitch	1966	Duke Ellington	
Three	1967	Duke Ellington	
This Man	1967	Duke Ellington	
Plaything	1967	Duke Ellington	
New Shoes	1967	Duke Ellington	
Nob Hill	1967	Duke Ellington	
My Home Lies Quiet	1967	Duke Ellington	
To the Better	1967	Duke Ellington	
Tin Soldier	1967	Duke Ellington	
They Say	1967	Duke Ellington	
Man Sees Nothing	1967	Duke Ellington	
The Man Beneath	1967	Duke Ellington	
Malay Camp	1967	Duke Ellington	
La Plus Belle Africaine:	1967	Duke Ellington	
Laying on Mellow	1967	Duke Ellington	
Kisse	1967	Duke Ellington	
J. P. Williamson	1967	Duke Ellington	
I Like Singing	1967	Duke Ellington	

Full of Shadows	1967	Duke Ellington	
Eliza	1967	Duke Ellington	
Crispy	1967	Duke Ellington	
Come Easter	1967	Duke Ellington	
Circus	1967	Duke Ellington	
Cham	1967	Duke Ellington	
Canon	1967	Duke Ellington	
Fatness	1967	Duke Ellington	
Baby, You're Too Much	1967	Duke Ellington and Don George	Duke Ellington and Don George
The Matador (El Viti)	1967	Duke Ellington	
Poco Mucho	1967	Duke Ellington	
Workin' Blues	1967	Duke Ellington	
Salute to Morgan State	1967	Duke Ellington	
Rock the Clock	1967	Duke Ellington	
Ocht O'Clock Rock	1967	Duke Ellington	
Where in the World?	1967	Duke Ellington	
Rue Bleue	1967	Duke Ellington	
Up Jump	1967	Duke Ellington	
Swamp Goo	1967	Duke Ellington	
Rondelet	1967	Duke Ellington	
Mara-Gold	1967	Duke Ellington	
Lele	1967	Duke Ellington	
Lady	1967	Duke Ellington	
Bolling	1967	Duke Ellington	
Chromatic Love Affair	1967	Duke Ellington	
Drag	1967	Duke Ellington	
Eggo	1967	Duke Ellington	
Girdle Hurdle	1967	Duke Ellington	
Traffic Jam	1967	Duke Ellington	
Murder in the Cathedral:			
Becket	1967	Duke Ellington	
Gold	1967	Duke Ellington	
Land	1967	Duke Ellington	
Martyr	1967	Duke Ellington	
Women's	1967	Duke Ellington	
Exotique Bongos	1967	Duke Ellington	
The Second Sacred Concert:			
The Biggest and Busiest Intersection	1968	Duke Ellington	
The Shepherd	1968	Duke Ellington	..
Meditation	1968	Duke Ellington	
Father Forgive	1968	Duke Ellington	Duke Ellington
Don't Get Down on Your Knees to Pray Until You Have Forgiven Everyone	1968	Duke Ellington	Duke Ellington

God Has Those Angels	1968	Duke Ellington	Duke Ellington
Heaven	1968	Duke Ellington	Duke Ellington
T.G.T.T.	1968	Duke Ellington	Duke Ellington
Something 'Bout Believing	1968	Duke Ellington	Duke Ellington
Freedom (parts 1–7)	1968	Duke Ellington	Duke Ellington
Freedom (Word You Heard)	1968	Duke Ellington	Duke Ellington
Freedom (Sweet Fat and That)	1968	Duke Ellington and Willie Smith	Duke Ellington and Willie Smith
Praise God and Dance	1968	Duke Ellington	
Finesse	1968	Duke Ellington and Johnny Hodges	Duke Ellington and Johnny Hodges
Night Train to Memphis	1968	Duke Ellington and Cat Anderson	Duke Ellington and Cat Anderson
Tokyo (from "Ad Lib on Nippon")	1968	Duke Ellington and Jimmy Hamilton	Duke Ellington and Jimmy Hamilton
Be Cool and Groovy for Me	1968	Duke Ellington, Cootie Williams, and Tony Bennett	Duke Ellington, Cootie Williams, and Tony Bennett
Keor	1968	Duke Ellington	
Kiki	1968	Duke Ellington	
Ritz	1968	Duke Ellington	
I Fell and Broke My Heart	1968	Duke Ellington	Don George
You're a Little Black Sheep	1968	Duke Ellington	Don George
You Make That Hat Look Pretty	1968	Duke Ellington	Duke Ellington
Woman	1968	Duke Ellington	Duke Ellington
I Have Given My Love	1968	Duke Ellington	Patricia Petremont
When You've Had It All	1968	Duke Ellington	Patricia Petremont
My Lonely Love	1968	Duke Ellington	Patricia Petremont
Knuf	1969	Duke Ellington	
Reva	1969	Duke Ellington	
Elos	1969	Duke Ellington	
Gigl	1969	Duke Ellington	
Moon Maiden	1969	Duke Ellington	Duke Ellington
The Moon Suite	1969	Duke Ellington	Duke Ellington
Anticipation and Hesitation	1969	Duke Ellington	Duke Ellington
Just a Gentle Word from You Will Do	1969	Duke Ellington and Onzy Matthews	Duke Ellington and Onzy Matthews
Mexicali Brass	1969	Duke Ellington and Onzy Matthews	Duke Ellington and Onzy Matthews
Fifi	1970	Duke Ellington	
Pamp	1970	Duke Ellington	
Rapid	1970	Duke Ellington	
The Spring	1970	Duke Ellington	
Opus 69	1971	Duke Ellington	
Cafe	1971	Duke Ellington	Duke Ellington

The Blues Ain't	1971	Duke Ellington	Duke Ellington
99 Percent	1971	Duke Ellington	Duke Ellington
Lovin' Lover	1971	Duke Ellington	Duke Ellington
Perdido Cha Cha Cha Cha	1971	Duke Ellington	Duke Ellington
New Orleans Suite:			
Bourbon Street Jingling Jollies	1971	Duke Ellington	
Aristocracy à la Jean Lafitte	1971	Duke Ellington	
Thanks for the Beautiful Land on the Delta	1971	Duke Ellington	
Blues for New Orleans	1971	Duke Ellington	
Second Line	1971	Duke Ellington	
Portrait of Wellman Braud	1971	Duke Ellington	
Portrait of Louis Armstrong	1971	Duke Ellington	
Portrait of Mahalia Jackson	1971	Duke Ellington	
Portrait of Sidney Bechet	1971	Duke Ellington	
Brot	1971	Duke Ellington	
Snek	1971	Duke Ellington	
Roth	1971	Duke Ellington	
Math	1971	Duke Ellington	
Loud	1971	Duke Ellington	
The Hard Way	1971	Duke Ellington	
Black Swan	1970	Duke Ellington	
Fife	1970	Duke Ellington	
4:30 Blues	1970	Duke Ellington	
Hard	1970	Duke Ellington	
In Triplicate	1970	Duke Ellington	
Mixt	1970	Duke Ellington	
What Time Is It?	1970	Duke Ellington	
Soft	1970	Duke Ellington	
Afrique	1970	Duke Ellington	
Rext	1970	Duke Ellington	
Stud	1970	Duke Ellington	
The River (ballet):			
Well	1970	Duke Ellington	
The Run	1970	Duke Ellington	
The Giggling Rapids	1970	Duke Ellington	
Meander	1970	Duke Ellington	
The Lake	1970	Duke Ellington	
The Falls	1970	Duke Ellington	
The Whirlpool	1970	Duke Ellington	
The River	1970	Duke Ellington	
The Village of the Virgins	1970	Duke Ellington	
The Mother, Her Majesty the Sea	1970	Duke Ellington	
Hick	1971	Duke Ellington	

Dick	1971	Duke Ellington	
Road of the Phoebe Snow	1971	Duke Ellington and Billy Strayhorn	Duke Ellington and Billy Strayhorn
Everybody Wants to Know Why I Sing the Blues	1971	Duke Ellington	
Afro-Eurasian Eclipse:			
Dash	1971	Duke Ellington	
Buss	1971	Duke Ellington	
Acac	1971	Duke Ellington	
Yoyo	1971	Duke Ellington	
True	1971	Duke Ellington	
Tenz	1971	Duke Ellington	
Tego	1971	Duke Ellington	
Soso	1971	Duke Ellington	
Nbdy	1971	Duke Ellington	
Gong	1971	Duke Ellington	
Dijb	1971	Duke Ellington	
Sche	1971	Duke Ellington	
The Goutelas Suite:			
Goof	1971	Duke Ellington	
Gogo II	1971	Duke Ellington	
Gogo I	1971	Duke Ellington	
Gigi	1971	Duke Ellington	
Ray Charles' Place	1971	Duke Ellington	
Tina	1972	Duke Ellington	Duke Ellington
Everyone	1972	Duke Ellington	Duke Ellington
Almighty God	1972	Duke Ellington	Duke Ellington
Mich	1972	Duke Ellington	
New York, New York	1972	Duke Ellington	Duke Ellington
Rainy Nights	1973	Duke Ellington	Duke Ellington
Jumping Room Only	1973	Duke Ellington	Duke Ellington
Celebration	1973	Duke Ellington	Duke Ellington
Soul Flute (Flute Ame)	1973	Duke Ellington	
Addi	1973	Duke Ellington	
Togo Brava Suite:	1973	Duke Ellington	
Right On Togo	1973	Duke Ellington	
Soul Soothing Beach	1973	Duke Ellington	
Naturelement	1973	Duke Ellington	
Amour, Amour	1973	Duke Ellington	

BIBLIOGRAPHY

Duke Ellington by Barry Ulanov (Creative Age Press, New York, 1946)

Duke Ellington: His Life and Music, an anthology edited by Peter Gammond and containing Richard O. Boyer's 1944 profile from *The New Yorker* (Phoenix House, London, 1958)

Duke Ellington by G. E. Lambert (Cassell & Company, London, 1959)

The World of Duke Ellington by Stanley Dance (Charles Scribner's Sons, New York, 1970)

Duke Ellington, King of Jazz by Elizabeth Rider Montgomery (for young readers) (Garrard Publishing Co., Champaign, Ill., 1972)

Chapters and essays devoted to Duke Ellington may be found in:

Music Ho! by Constant Lambert (Faber & Faber, London, 1934)

Hot Jazz by Hugues Panassié (M. Witmark & Sons, New York, 1936)

Frontiers of Jazz, edited by Ralph de Toledano and containing Wilder Hobson's 1933 *Fortune* article (Frederick Ungar Publishing Co., New York, 1947)

Hear Me Talkin' to Ya, edited by Nat Shapiro and Nat Hentoff (Rinehart & Co., New York, 1955)

Jazz: Its Evolution and Essence by André Hodeir (Grove Press, New York, 1956)

The Jazz Makers, edited by Nat Shapiro and Nat Hentoff (Rinehart & Co., New York, 1957)

The Decca Book of Jazz, edited by Peter Gammond (Frederick Muller, London, 1958)

Music in a New Found Land by Wilfred Mellers (Knopf, New York, 1965)

Early Jazz by Gunther Schuller (Oxford University Press, New York, 1968)

The Jazz Tradition by Martin Williams (Oxford University Press, New York, 1970)

Ecstasy at the Onion by Whitney Balliett (The Bobbs-Merrill Co., Indianapolis, Ind., 1971)

From Satchmo to Miles by Leonard Feather (Stein & Day, New York, 1972)

Jazz Masters of the '30s by Rex Stewart (The Macmillan Co., New York, 1972)

Celebrating the Duke by Ralph J. Gleason (Atlantic Monthly Press, New York, 1975)

(*Black Beauty* by R. D. Darrell, perhaps the earliest attempt at assessing Duke Ellington published in America, appeared in the magazine *Disques,* Philadelphia, 1932)

Other titles of interest

SIDNEY BECHET
The Wizard of Jazz
John Chilton
380 pp., 48 illus.
80678-9 $14.95

BEYOND CATEGORY
The Life and Genius of
Duke Ellington
John Edward Hasse
Foreword by Wynton Marsalis
480 pp., 119 illus.
80614-2 $15.95

BILLIE'S BLUES: The Billie
Holiday Story 1933-1959
John Chilton
272 pp., 20 photos
80363-1 $13.95

CELEBRATING THE DUKE
and Louis, Bessie, Billie,
Bird, Carmen, Miles, Dizzy
& Other Heroes
Ralph J. Gleason
Foreword by Studs Terkel
New introd. by Ira Gitler
302 pp., 9 photos
80645-2 $13.95

ELLA FITZGERALD
A Biography of the
First Lady of Jazz
Stuart Nicholson
368 pp., 29 illus.
80642-8 $14.95

GOOD MORNING BLUES
The Autobiography of Count Basie
As told to Albert Murray
432 pp., 56 photos
80609-6 $15.95

JAZZ PEOPLE
Photographs by Ole Brask
Text by Dan Morgenstern
Foreword by Dizzy Gillespie
Introduction by James Jones
300 pp., 180 photos
80527-8 $24.50

BLACK BEAUTY, WHITE HEAT
A Pictorial History of Classic Jazz,
1920-1950
Frank Driggs and Harris Lewine
360 pp., 1,516 illus.
80672-X $29.95

SATCHMO
My Life in New Orleans
Louis Armstrong
220 pp., 20 photos
80276-7 $11.95

SWING THAT MUSIC
Louis Armstrong
New foreword by Dan Morgenstern
200 pp.
80544-8 $12.95

TREAT IT GENTLE
An Autobiography
Sidney Bechet
256 pp., 16 photos
80086-1 $12.95